UNDERSTANDING THE FAMILY

EDITED BY
JOHN MUNCIE, MARGARET WETHERELL,
RUDI DALLOS AND ALLAN COCHRANE

SAGE Publications
LONDON • THOUSAND OAKS • NEW DELHI

SAGE Publications Ltd
6 Bonhill Street
London EC2A 4PU

SAGE Publications Inc.
2455 Teller Road
Thousand Oaks, California 91320

SAGE Publications India Pvt Ltd
32, M-Block Market
Greater Kailash – I
New Delhi 110 048

British Library Cataloguing in Publication data

A catalogue record for this book is available from the British Library

ISBN 0 8039 7954 1
ISBN 0 8039 7955 X   (pbk)

Designed and typeset by The Open University

Printed and bound in Great Britain by
Butler & Tanner Ltd, Frome and London

CONTENTS

ACKNOWLEDGEMENTS

Grateful acknowledgement is made to the following sources for permission to reproduce material in this book:

TEXT

Boxed extract pp. 107–8: Craig, G. and Glendinning, C., *The Impact of Social Security Changes: the view of young people*, 1990, © Barkingside: Barnado's.

FIGURES

Chapter 1: *Figure 1*: OPCS *Social Trends*, no. 24, 1994, HMSO/CSO [OPCS], © Crown Copyright 1994; *Figure 2*: Law Report, 'A love whose name the judge should dare to speak', *The Guardian*, 17 October 1990, © The Guardian; *Figure 3*: Copyright © 1987 SCPR; **Chapter 3**: *Figure 1*: Dyer, C. and Carvel, J. 'Euro-court punches hole in migrant laws', *The Guardian*, 8 July 1992, © The Guardian; *Figure 2*: Dyer, C. 'Mother takes benefits battle to European court', *The Guardian*, 13 March 1992, © The Guardian; **Chapter 4**: *Figures 1 and 2*: OPCS *Population Trends*, no. 57, 1989, HMSO/CSO [OPCS], © Crown Copyright 1987; **Chapter 5**; *Figures 1,3,4,7,8 and 9*: adapted from Dallos, R. (1991) *Family Belief Systems, Therapy and Change*, Open University Press, © Rudi Dallos.

TABLES

Chapter 1: *Tables 1 and 3*: OPCS *Social Trends*, no. 24, 1994, HMSO/CSO [OPCS], © Crown Copyright 1994; *Table 2*: Haskey, J. 'Estimated numbers and demographic characteristics of one-parent families in Great Britain', *Population Trends*, no. 65, 1991, HMSO/CSO [OPCS], © Crown Copyright 1991; *Table 4*: OPCS *Social Trends*, no. 22, 1992, HMSO/CSO [OPCS], © Crown Copyright 1992; **Chapter 4**: *Table 1*: OPCS *Social Trends*, no. 22, 1992, HMSO/CSO [OPCS], © Crown Copyright 1992; *Table 4*: OPCS *Social Trends*, no. 19, 1989, HMSO/CSO [OPCS], © Crown Copyright 1989.

PHOTOGRAPHS AND CARTOONS

p. 43: Topham; *pp. 45, 51, 54, 64*: from *Be a Bloody Train Driver* by Jacky Fleming, 1991, copyright © Jacky Fleming 1991, by permission of Penguin Books; *p. 46 (both)*: Hulton-Deutsch Collection; *p. 57: (top)* Anthony J. Coulson, *(bottom)* Counter Information Services; *p. 62*: © The Guardian; *p. 66*: The Advertising Archives; *pp. 97, 101*, 239: © Posy Simmonds 1986, 1987, 1979 reproduced by kind permission of Peters, Fraser and Dunlop Ltd; *p. 130*: Judy Harrison/Format; *p. 134*: Brenda Prince/Format; *p. 145*: Mike Abrahams/Network; *p. 151*: © Eugene Richards/Magnum Photos; *p. 160*: Tom Learmonth; *p. 162*: Sally and Richard Greenhill; *p. 222: (left top and bottom)* Sally and Richard Greenhill, *(right)* Judy Harrison/Format; *pp. 223, 247*: Universal Press Syndicate © 1986, 1985 G.B. Trudeau; *p. 233*: Barry Lewis/Network; *p. 258*: Mary Evans Picture Library/ Sigmund Freud Copyrights; *pp. 260, 262, 273, 279, 281, 287*: © Estate of Mel Calman; *p. 265*: Kobal Collection; *p. 274: (left)* Mansell Collection; *pp. 283, 284*: Annie Lawson.

INTRODUCTION: PUBLIC DEFINITIONS AND PRIVATE LIVES

The emphasis in the title of this edited collection on 'the family' is intentionally ironic. Whilst we are aware of the ideological power that notions of *'the family'* wield, this book also reveals a remarkable diversity of 'family forms' in contemporary society. Whilst acknowledging the pervasiveness of such binary opposites as the public and the private in formulations of the family's relationship to the state, this book questions the utility of continuing to view the political and domestic spheres through such frames. It is precisely the explanatory power of the terms – the family, the public, the private – that this book brings into question.

Understanding the Family brings together the insights that sociology, social policy, psychology and social psychology have brought to bear on the study of 'family life'. Its underlying approach is one which stresses the importance of different *levels of analysis*. We argue that the diversity of contemporary society demands interdisciplinary forms of analysis if we are to capture its true complexity.

Part 1, *Politics, Policy and the Law*, has two main aims. The first is to show that 'the family' is not a simple concept whose meaning can be taken for granted. There are families, and certainly most of us experience or have experienced some form of family life, but it is impossible to find a model of 'the family' which is universally accepted. Many people have living arrangements which simply do not fit with dominant models. The second aim is to show how notions of the family have been shaped (or constructed) by wider social processes, in particular by the operations of political discourse, policy formulation and implementation and the law, and to consider the tensions that exist between the dominant assumptions of state and society and the lived realities and everyday experiences of family life.

Chapter 1 provides a broad introduction to the sociology of the family. It outlines key debates concerning 'what is the family?', 'what is the family for?', 'how has it changed?' and 'with what consequences for society overall?' In particular it identifies and discusses some changing interpretations of 'the family' over time and according to class, gender and ethnic position.

Chapter 2 explores how particular notions of 'the family' have been, and continue to be, constructed through political discourse and prioritized in various social policies. Whilst there may be a clear mismatch between the assumptions of politicians, policy formulations and the reality of people's lives, the chapter establishes how dominant ideas about the family become material forces in their own right. In other words, ideas about the family generated in the political sphere may be partial or rhetorical, but also powerfully influence the ways in which we experience family life.

In Chapter 3 Hilary Land looks more closely at the legal aspects and at the way in which the rights and responsibilities of family members have been regulated and constrained through systems of private and public law. Although 'family values' have never been defined in legislation, and the United Kingdom has never formally adopted a set of policies termed *family policies*, it is clear that much of British social policy and family law is predicated on a set of underlying assumptions about how families are (or should be) constituted. For example, the law, both in principle and in practice, discourages mothers from achieving independence from men, either via the labour market or via the benefit system, despite significant recent growths in single parenting and in married women going out to work. Such anomalies are reflected in inconsistencies between different areas of law. The objectives of some areas of law (for example, the Matrimonial and Family Proceedings Act 1984) may well undermine the objectives of others (for example, the Child Support Act 1991). Chapter 3 stresses the importance of the ways in which the detail of legislation impinges on people's everyday lives by reinforcing particular ideas and in materially limiting what it is possible for them to do.

Chapter 4 then explores the gaps between the dominant images of (nuclear) family life encapsulated in ideology, policy and law and the existence of a variety of forms of 'family' living arrangements. The chapter looks at alternatives to the family and at different forms of family life, but also acknowledges the continuing 'pull' of what appear to be the more traditional models of the family. In particular it argues that the term 'the family' is of limited analytic purchase, rather a more dynamic definition of *family life as a process* is suggested. Such a definition not only acknowledges diversity – nuclear, lone-parent, step-family, extended family, communes – in family forms, but also suggests that any such social grouping will share some fundamental tasks, such as regulation of sexuality, childcare, identity formation, obligations and patterns of intimacy. It is the 'internal' negotiation and completion of these tasks which will come to define the parameters of family life.

Collectively, these four chapters show that it is not possible to view families as if they are simply private arenas separate from the public sphere. On the contrary it is clear that families – in whatever form – are shaped by and are a part of wider social and political systems. Such systems set agendas and to no small degree establish what is materially possible. However, even within these boundaries, the ways in which individuals experience and gain meaning from family life can reveal some sharp contrasts and differences.

The second part of this book – *Interactions and Identities* – focuses on lived experiences: how individuals perceive family life and the way in which their continual internal negotiations crucially affect how families are made and re-made. It examines some of the many processes which are involved in making the family work: such as how relationships are created and changed, how individuals establish identities and how they negotiate inequalities of position and access to resources. Chapters 5, 6 and 7 present three different theoretical positions derived from family systems research, feminist social psychology and psychoanalysis respectively, which attempt to describe and explain the processes involved in 'making a family'.

Chapter 5 examines insights from family therapy and stresses the characteristic patterns of interaction which develop within a family as it progresses through its developmental cycle. These are accounted for by analyses of the interplay between family members' beliefs, choices and actions. Out of this nexus are seen to emerge changing patterns of coalitions and alliances which are continually formed and reformed in response to changing life tasks to make up a family's dynamics. Within such dynamics, relations of power and authority may not be as clear-cut and as unidimensional as some sociological and social structural arguments suggest. Rather than family life being simply constructed from 'the outside', a belief systems approach argues that people construct their own families with reference to internal beliefs and negotiations and informed by their own sense of internal family history.

In Chapter 6 Margaret Wetherell moves from an interpersonal analysis of family interactions to one which considers the influence of social roles and 'external' power relations on the formation of identities within families. A detailed study of parenting is used to illustrate how the wider social context impacts on the 'private' experience of childcare. This feminist social-psychological approach alerts us to the ways in which individuals frequently have to reconcile their experiences of family life with the sometimes contradictory social expectations about 'good mothers', 'well-behaved children', 'reliable husbands' and 'happy families'. Negotiations are not simply freely made and unique to each family, but are characterized by a degree of regularity and predictability across all families. Chapter 6 thus shows further how the belief systems of families are also connected to broader ideologies and social expectations.

By contrast, Chapter 7 discusses various psychoanalytical accounts of identity development, shifting the focus of analysis away from systems or social roles and towards individual needs and desires, unconscious motivations, problems of sexual and gender identity and the emotional interior of the family itself. Here a true complexity is revealed. Early forms of psychoanalysis see a kind of fixity, depth and history to the private self which can only be accounted for by consideration of unconscious motivations and instincts, whilst more modern forms − such as Chodorow's object relations theory − acknowledge that whilst the *content* of subjectivity may always be diverse in relation to the social context, the *forms* in which it is realized may have a more general applicability.

Chapter 8 then provides a broader picture of the ways in which feminist scholarship has responded to, and developed, such theoretical debates. Tracing how feminist writing has veered between critique and celebration of women's domestic and maternal roles, Lynne Segal notes how it has become increasingly difficult to demarcate, from all the increasingly possible permutations of parenting and family life, exactly what is either 'normal' or politically progressive. Indeed a post-structuralist feminism of the 1980s has begun to reject any theory which attempts to impose an unwarranted order and regularity out of the instability, uncertainty and complexity of 'family life'.

Finally Roger Sapsford's Endnote brings us back to one of the key themes running through the book: that is, the relationship between the public and the private. Once more he points out how these assumed separate spheres are also indelibly intertwined, to the extent that it makes no sense to talk of *the* private or *the* public. Nevertheless the distinction remains prevalent: not only in underpinning certain ideologies of 'the family' but also in helping to reinforce the idea that sets of structured inequalities are natural and inevitable. Not least, the concepts of 'the family', 'the private' and 'the public' allow the state to demarcate where its responsibilities to individuals begin and end.

The purpose of this book is to examine how 'the family' is constituted both 'internally' and 'externally', and to introduce a variety of theoretical perspectives and empirical evidence to shed light on the complexity of the individual–family–social–state nexus. Each of the chapters was originally prepared as part of the Open University course *Family Life and Social Policy* which shares these general concerns and which sought to review these debates for students. As a result, this book is not simply an edited collection, but an integrated set of teaching materials. You will find that the chapters are in dialogue with each other and that the text addresses the reader directly in order to encourage comprehension and critical reflection. Unlike other edited collections, these chapters are designed to be read sequentially, with each building upon and developing the knowledge base established in preceding sections. The rationale and relevance of each chapter can only be properly grasped, if the book is used in this way. The book also introduces key concepts such as gender, power, representation, ideology and discourse and provides important guidance for the reader on the ways in which 'evidence' is gathered and can be evaluated within the social sciences.

The influences on this book stretch far beyond its editors and the authors of individual chapters. It reflects the commitment and perseverance of an entire Open University Course Team – consultants, tutor-testers, assessors, managers, editors, designers and secretaries. Without them this book would never have managed to achieve its present form.

John Muncie

Margaret Wetherell

Rudi Dallos

Allan Cochrane

PART I
POLITICS, POLICY AND THE LAW

CHAPTER 1
ISSUES IN THE STUDY OF 'THE FAMILY'

JOHN MUNCIE AND ROGER SAPSFORD

CONTENTS

INTRODUCTION

This chapter raises two key questions: (a) 'What is the family?' and (b) 'What is its relationship to social policy?' The problem, as we shall see, is that what seems a simple concept turns out to be a complex one. What *exactly* do we mean when we talk of 'the family'? Why do so many *different* ways of organizing domestic relations all appear to belong under the same descriptive heading? Why does the concept of 'the family' bulk so large in political rhetoric and in social policy? Can we make any distinction between 'the family', 'families' and 'family households'? What is implied by these different formulations?

Such questions are particularly important in exploring the connections between what we perceive as family-based and state-based systems of welfare. Clearly, the family can be viewed as a welfare system in its own right – providing financial, material and emotional support for its members. However, these 'private' functions can, in some circumstances, come to be questioned. For example, when notions of the 'unrespectable', 'dangerous', 'impoverished', 'criminal' or 'needy' family come into play, it appears legitimate for 'public' and state intervention to enter into what has been traditionally upheld as the most 'private' of institutions in our culture. In what circumstances, then, are private troubles turned into public issues? How, when and why does the family become the object of state intervention? What forms does such intervention take? Are these designed to support the institution of the family or are they aimed at controlling the family's more negative aspects?

Part of this problem lies in the concept itself. What exactly is 'the family'? Should a definition be restricted to the traditional notion of parents and their children in one household? Do two unmarried people living together constitute a family? Do these two people have to be of different sexes? Are 'lone-parent' families considered as a normal family pattern or are they represented as something unusual, even deviant – and by whom? Does the term 'the family' suggest a common way of living which has little bearing on actual lived realities? Would we be better served by talking of 'households', 'kinship structures' and 'domestic living arrangements' if we are to grasp the diversity of ways in which people live their lives in contemporary society?

As a result of such uncertainties, the study of the family is faced with two related dilemmas. First, what is its most appropriate subject matter? (What exactly are we studying when we talk of *the* family?) By phrasing questions in terms of '*the* family', do we sometimes admit as truths what are only assumptions, or even prescriptions – and, particularly, prescriptions about the 'proper' balance of power between men and women and between the old and the young? Secondly, even if we can agree on a sense for the term 'family', what is 'the family' *for*? Is it just a 'place', a part of life different from other parts, or is it a set of processes in which individuals influence other individuals and/or by which societal forms of order are imposed on individuals? In what senses can it be said to have a *function*, something at which it can be seen as succeeding or failing? And what should follow from its failures?

In this chapter we shall be examining five areas of controversy within the study of the family:

1   *The concept of 'the family'* How has the family been defined? What relation does such definition have to existing diverse ways of living?

2   *The family and social change* Is the family a natural and universal feature of all societies? Is it grounded in biological imperatives or a more transient form consistently changing in response to wider economic concerns?

3   *The functions of the family* Does the family produce stability in society or is it a primary cause of conflict and disharmony? Does it fulfil its members' needs? Is it a cause of, or solution to, personal/social problems?

4   *Power and family life* Is the family a prison or a haven for its members? How and by whom is power exercised?

5   *The family and welfare* What is the relationship between the family and the state? Is the family breaking up? Do we need more or less intervention? Should the family in the main be a provider or receiver of welfare?

It is our intention to use these key questions as a means of beginning to help you to think critically about the concept of 'the family' and its relation to other agencies and institutions in society.

I   THE CONCEPT OF 'THE FAMILY'

One of the first and most intractable issues to be faced in the study of the family is its definition. You should begin your work on this chapter by addressing the questions and issues set out in the exercise below.

ACTIVITY I

Using no more than a few sentences, write down what immediately comes to mind when considering the essential components and structure of the family. The questions below should help you to work towards a definition of 'what a family is'.

What are its main purposes?

How many people make up this family?

What percentage of all households represent 'the family'?

Is your definition grounded in contemporary British society or is it capable of including families from different cultures and different historical periods?

Does your definition correspond to your own present position and/or your past experience? If neither, do you consider yourself to be without a family?

From where do you think that your ideas about 'the family' have come?

Definitions of 'the family' can be extremely broad – say, anyone who stays in contact with a member of their own kin. So now ask yourself the question in reverse: what is *not* a family?

What a family is may at first seem obvious to you. In our society 'people expect' – it is part of the stereotype – that companionship, sexual activity, mutual care, child-bearing and the rearing and support of children will all be primarily focused on the *nuclear family*. This concept defines the family as a small unit derived from the relationship between a man and a woman legally bound together through marriage as husband and wife. The nuclear family is created when a child is born to this couple. The unit shares a common residence and is united by ties of affection, common identity and support. This taken-for-granted and 'commonsense' conception of how the family is constituted may, however, be more a reflection of traditional beliefs as to how sexual, emotional and parental relationships *ought* to be structured. It may not be at all helpful in unravelling how different individuals actually do organize their lives. However, the *idea* of the nuclear family clearly retains a potency such that all other forms tend to be defined with reference to it. It is widely assumed that the nuclear form is the most dominant in contemporary society. As a result, the tendency is increased to define other forms as 'unusual', 'deviant', even 'pathological'. The 'discourse of the family' wields a power to declare what is normal and what is unacceptable.

But the existence of alternative forms is clear enough. For example, we may find *extended families* where more than one generation of parents cohabit with their children. Families which are technically nuclear – that is, live in a 'parents-plus-children' unit – but interact extensively with a locally resident *kin group* are probably even more common. Also common in contemporary society is the *lone-parent family* where a man or, more usually, a woman carries out the tasks of parenthood on his or her own. This task again may be carried out in isolation, or in the home of other relatives (frequently the parents), or in technical isolation but calling on the resources of a kin network. Every conceivable way of drawing the boundaries between 'parent(s) plus child(ren)' and the families and kin groups of origin, to *include* some as part of daily life and exercising or being subject to authority and to *exclude* others, is currently exemplified in at least one 'family unit' somewhere in the United Kingdom. A taken-for-granted acceptance of the centrality of the nuclear form in the structure of contemporary society is also complicated by instances of cohabitation, same-sex pairings, adoption, fostering, separation and divorce, remarriage and step-parenthood. Indeed the so-called typical family of a married couple with father in employment and mother at home with 2 dependent children represents only 1 in 20 of all *households* at any time (FPSC, 1985), though a substantial number will *pass through* this stage at some point.

Here we have introduced two more concepts which reveal why a universally agreed definition is hard to reach.

Firstly, we need to distinguish between 'the household' and 'the family' (see Table 1). Ball (1974) defines the household as a spatial category where a group of people (or one person) is bound to a particular place. Families, on the other hand, are generally seen as groups of people bound together by blood and marriage ties. The two are not coterminous. Families may form households but do not always do so. Parents may separate; children may be sent to boarding-school. Conversely, an extended kin group may live under the same roof but may not in all circumstances regard themselves as one family. Older relatives living with a nuclear family may not entirely regard themselves as part of that family – and may or may not be so regarded by the nuclear family. If they do regard themselves as part of the family, is the family then nuclear or extended?

Secondly, a similar problem with asserting the dominance of the nuclear family arises when we place this form in the context of a family life-cycle. The Family Policy Studies Centre (1985) notes that at any one time the population is made up of:

- 1 household in 3 containing a dependent child
- 1 household in 5 consisting of a single person
- 1 household in 4 being a childless married couple
- 3 households in 10 being married couples with dependent children
- 1 household in 10 containing one or more people over retirement age.

Which of these constitutes a family and which do not? Some are nuclear families; some are other but broadly similar forms of domestic arrangements; some are lesbian/gay partnerships; some are people who have emerged from a nuclear family and not yet formed another; some are relics of a nuclear family in the past. The concept of 'the family', however, also implies a *cycle*: we grow up in a family, leave it, form another, in which children grow up to leave it and form another.

The notion of a family cycle assumes a certain continuity. Although it is acknowledged that at any one time we may not all be living in situations which correspond to a nuclear model, the argument is that it is the form to which we always return, and which has a formative influence on our lives. Thus despite the existence of variations some analysts have preferred to suggest that, whatever the particular forms of cohabitations and kinship, *all* societies' child-producing and child-rearing arrangements will *resemble* nuclear family units. In such accounts certain biological imperatives are often cited as evidence not only that the nuclear family is universal, but also that it is a natural form. In all societies, it is claimed, the basic functions of reproduction, satisfying sexuality and the rearing and caring of children are necessary to ensure its survival. The most efficient

Table 1   People in households: by type of household and family in which they live, Great Britain (percentages)[1]

Type of household	1961	1971	1981	1991	1992
Living alone	3.9	6.3	8.0	10.7	11.1
Married couple, no children	17.8	19.3	19.5	23.0	23.4
Married couple with dependent children[2]	52.2	51.7	47.4	41.1	39.9
Married couple with non-dependent children only	11.6	10.0	10.3	10.8	10.9
Lone parent with dependent children[2]	2.5	3.5	5.8	10.0	10.1
Other households	12.0	9.2	9.0	4.3	4.6
All people in private households (=100%) (thousands)	49,545	52,347	52,760	54,056	–

Notes: 1 1961, 1971, 1981 and 1991 census data. 1992 General Household Survey.

2 These family types may also include non-dependent children.

Source: Office of Population Censuses and Surveys data; table taken from *Social Trends*, no. 24, 1994, 2.6, p. 35

way of achieving these ends is the nuclear family. Thus the argument is made that whatever (superficial) variations may be made to the structure of a kin group the requirements of child production and child protection mean that the nuclear family will always form the basis of any society. Murdock (1968) claims, on the basis of a cross-cultural study of 250 societies, that the nuclear family is a 'universal human grouping'. Despite the existence of polygamous forms of bonding, Murdock argues that each is reducible to a nuclear form largely because it is functional for each society's survival. Whilst his evidence undermined the Western Christian ideal of love–marriage–family in that he found that 65 of the 250 societies permitted complete freedom in sexual matters and only 54 explicitly disapproved of premarital sexual liaison, the question of survival remained paramount. Sexual relationships, reproduction and child support are best performed if fused within a single institution, he argued.

In opposition to such argument, anthropologists have been able to cite instances of societies where either the conjugal ties are absent or (more usually) the father is absent and plays little part in child-rearing. The discovery of such forms has led some to argue that the nuclear family is a *social* arrangement and not a universal and biologically determined form. The most commonly cited instance is that of the Nayar, a warrior caste of south-west India. Fox (1967, p. 100) contends that here the roles of sexual partner, biological parent and social parent were not held by two people. Because Nayar men were engaged as full-time soldiers, they were frequently absent from home. As a result, sex was not related to marriage and neither of these had necessarily anything to do with a family domestic unit. Nayar men, then, did not have any particular rights of attachment to their wives or children and as a result the nuclear family was not institutionalized as a legal, productive, residential, socializing or consumption unit. Cross-cultural research thus does not unambiguously support the notion of 'the family' as a universal norm.

However, we do not have to search out such 'exotic' examples to find variations from the biologically-based nuclear family. An increasing pattern in Western industrial societies is that of serial mating replacing monogamy and the lone-parent family in which a conjugal bond has either been severed or has never been initiated. In the United Kingdom the number of families with dependent children headed by a lone parent increased from 6 per cent in 1961 to 19 per cent in 1991. In nine out of ten of these families the mother was the lone parent (see Figure 1).

An increase in lone divorced mothers constituted some of this rise but there has also been a significant increase during the 1980s in the proportion of families headed by never-married mothers. National averages, however, mask regional and cultural variations. For example, whilst the national average of births outside marriage in England and Wales is some 27 per cent , this ranges from 54 per cent in North Manchester to 13 per cent in Northallerton, Yorkshire (OPCS, 1990). Similarly, in 1981 the percentage of lone-parent families in Birmingham was 18.8 per cent, in Liverpool 19.9 per cent, in Glasgow 20.4 per cent and in Lambeth 32 per cent (Kiernan and Wicks, 1990, p. 14). Haskey (1991) has also estimated

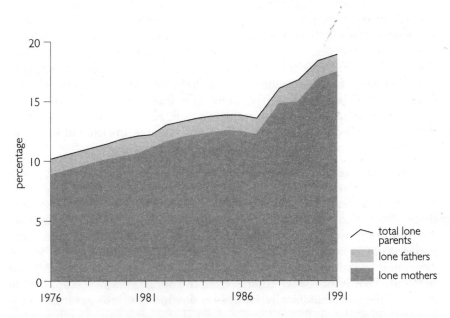

Figure I   Families headed by lone mothers and lone fathers, as a percentage of all families with dependent children, Great Britain

Note: Three-year moving averages used (apart from 1991)

Source: Office of Population Censuses and Surveys data; taken from *Social Trends*, no. 24, 1994, 2.8, p. 36

that 15 per cent of all white families were headed by a lone parent in 1987-9, compared to 49 per cent of all Afro-Caribbean families. In Table 2 the data also suggest that there are more one-parent families in mixed and African ethnic groups; their prevalence decreases significantly in Indian, Pakistani and Bangladeshi families. (Note: These categories are based on self-definitions of those interviewed; for Afro-Caribbean Haskey uses the term West Indian.)

Household composition also varies between different European countries. Here, for example, we find that the percentage of lone-parent families in the population varies from 5 per cent in Ireland to over 12 per cent in Luxembourg and Denmark (FPCS, 1985).

Another means by which the universality of the nuclear family has been questioned is with reference to historical evidence. Until recently the conventional wisdom on this matter has been that only from the mid eighteenth century has the modern sense of the nuclear family appeared. Even then this form did not become dominant until the early nineteenth century. A common distinction is made that prior to the Industrial Revolution the dominant form of family life was the extended family. The nuclear form came into being because it correlated with the functional necessities of an industrial economy.

Within sociology, this argument has been most forcefully put in the work of Talcott Parsons (1959). He contended that the economic division of labour characteristic of industrial societies is incompatible with the maintenance of extended families, but ideally served by the nuclear family. When the family is restricted to a small group with a single breadwinner, who is also head of the family, conflicts between family members working in different occupations are avoided. The nuclear system prevents the competitive elements of industrial wage labour from undermining family solidarity. Similarly, there is a functional 'fit' between the nuclear form and the needs of industrialism. Small units are both geographically and economically mobile and thus able to respond better to the changing demands of an industrial economy.

Parsons characterized the pre-industrial family as a large-scale kinship unit which performed religious, political, educational and economic functions. Obligations to this kin group were paramount and superseded those afforded to the mother–father–child relationship, largely because this kin group was also a unit of production. Kin obligations and occupational obligations overlapped. Such an arrangement, though, is not functional to industrialism, which requires that the nuclear family be segregated both from other kin and from the public sphere (except for the breadwinner), so that family values do not intrude into external occupational roles. People do not have to choose between loyalty to kin and the more impersonal standards demanded by their occupation. Parsons concluded that the nuclear family is an adaptive response to industrial economies and is thus typical in all modern societies.

Table 2   Estimated numbers of lone-parent families by ethnic group, 1987-89, Great Britain (numbers and percentages)

Ethnic group of head of family	Type of family with dependent children				
	Lone mothers	Lone fathers	Lone parents	Married couples[1]	All families
Estimated numbers (thousands) of families					
West Indian	39	4	43		
African	7	(1)	9		
Indian	8	(1)	10		
Pakistani	5	(2)	9		
Bangladeshi	(1)	(1)	(2)		
Chinese	(0)	(0)	(0)		
Arab	(1)	(0)	(1)		
Mixed	9	(1)	10		
Other	(2)	(0)	(2)		
All ethnic minority groups	71	9	85		
White	863	139	997		
Not stated	7	(1)	8		
All ethnic groups	941	149	1,090		
Percentage of all families					
West Indian	44	5	49	51	100
African	27	(2)	30	70	100
Indian	6	(1)	6	94	100
Pakistani	6	(2)	8	92	100
Bangladeshi	(5)	(3)	(8)	92	100
Chinese	(1)	(0)	(2)	98	100
Arab	(4)	(1)	(5)	95	100
Mixed	33	(3)	36	64	100
Other	(16)	(0)	(16)	84	100
All ethnic minority groups	16	2	18	82	100
White	13	2	15	85	100
Not stated	19	(3)	22	78	100
All ethnic groups	13	2	15	85	100

Notes:
Dependent children are defined as under 16 or 16 to 18 and in full-time education.
Components may not sum exactly to totals, because of rounding.
1   Includes cohabiting couples.
( )   Bracketed estimates are based on sample sizes of 30 or fewer.
Source: Haskey, 1991, p. 38

Accounts such as Parsons' have, however, attracted considerable criticism on counts of both empirical accuracy and theoretical sophistication. For example, the work of Laslett and the Cambridge Group for the History of Population has questioned the notion that industrialization brought about a decrease in average family size. In a quantitative study using listings of inhabitants of 150 English communities from the sixteenth to the nineteenth centuries, Laslett and Wall (1972) found that average *household size* stayed fairly constant at approximately 4.75 persons. From the late Middle Ages the predominant form of household appears to have been a nuclear family plus servants, with even modest rural families having one female servant living in. Their evidence also suggests that geographical mobility was commonplace, with children being sent away from home to go into domestic service or apprenticeships. Furthermore, because of high mortality rates, few children were likely to have parents still alive when they themselves married. Laslett thus suggests that in pre-industrial society the nuclear family predominated and was able to adapt relatively easily to industrialization.

Parsons' insistence on the primacy of the isolated nuclear family within industrialism has also been questioned by studies of post-industrial revolution kinship structures. Anderson's (1971) study of the family and household structure in Preston in the 1850s found that as the town developed as a cotton manufacturing centre, there was an increase in co-residence and family size because income could be increased if both parents were available for work. Childcare was performed by grandparents living within the same household. Rather than the family becoming more nuclear, this evidence suggests a move towards the extended family structure. Similarly Young and Willmott's research in the 1950s argued that working-class urban communities, such as that found in Bethnal Green, continued to depend on extensive kinship networks and constituted an important basis for community solidarity (Young and Willmott, 1962).

Through considering such historical and contemporary evidence, it is clear that there exists no simple pattern of a shift from extended to nuclear families with the onslaught of industrialism. Rather it is safer to conclude that continuity of the nuclear unit as a key domestic grouping is just as prominent as change and fracture. However, Elliot (1986, p. 60) rightly warns against accepting the ubiquity of the nuclear family form, because doing so obscures the presence of alternative domestic arrangements both past and present. Moreover the 'ubiquitous argument' glosses over fundamental changes in the relation of the family to wider economic and social conditions which have undoubtedly altered its position in society. These include: a shift in its role from one based on agrarian and domestic production to one supporting factory production and increasingly becoming a unit of consumption; the emergence of state-organized institutions of education and social welfare which have absolved it of sole responsibility for childcare and yet with which it must co-exist; and the development of effective methods of birth control.

ACTIVITY 2

Return to the definition you arrived at in Activity 1. Would you now revise it in any way? Even if you are happy with your original formulation, ask yourself 'Why is it difficult to define the family'?

The problem with the concept of 'the family' is that we commonly assume its pre-eminence and seem to understand its meaning, but yet even the most superficial probing reveals a diversity of family forms. Reaching an acceptable definition becomes more difficult the more we acknowledge historical and cultural variations as well as the contemporary reality of alternative 'family forms' or 'domestic living arrangements'. Some argue that this impasse can only be overcome by referring to 'families' rather than 'the family' (Berger and Berger, 1983). In this way an acceptance of diversity and a reluctance to ascribe moral superiority to any one form would be promoted. This line of reasoning thus allows for 'foster families', 'adoptive families', 'lone-parent families', 'lesbian families', 'cohabiting families' and so on. However, this does not resolve all the issues. The use of the term 'the family' in all of these different contexts continues to imply a sameness which may be unwarranted and indeed unwanted by those people involved. It begs the question 'what is the opposite of "the family"?' For example, some gay and lesbian partners may actively reject the 'family' connotation because of a conscious decision to live outside its traditionally perceived confines. In other words, the way in which some people choose to live their lives is in direct resistance to 'the family' and all that implies for mother, father and child relations and roles. Indeed, even the use of the term 'families' may inadvertently continue to under-line the moral and ideological primacy of 'the family' because all divergent and different forms remain defined in terms of their relation to a presumed norm. The incessant use of the term 'the family' effectively denies any reality or validity to other forms of lived relations.

Our purpose here is not to promote the use of alternative terms such as 'domestic units' or 'living arrangements', but to alert you to the inherent connotations and constraints that the term 'the family' evokes. Always ask yourself: what types of family are under discussion? Would its members recognize themselves as being part of a family? What sort of household structure is being implied? Are wider kinship ties being recognized or denied? Are the facts of diversity and difference being attended to?

One useful distinction is that made by Gittins (1985). She notes that there are many different ways in which people order their domestic arrangements, many of which would be seen as 'families' by those who live according to them. 'The Family', however, she sees as an ideological object – a stereotype produced and maintained *for the purpose of* exerting certain kinds of social control. Institutions, laws and welfare policies are constructed around this stereotypic form not *because* it is the norm but *in order that* it shall be the norm. We might, indeed, go further and identify

Law Report

A love whose name the judge should dare to speak

Court of Appeal
In re C (a minor)
Before Lord Justice
Glidewell and Lord Justice
Balcombe
August 24 1990

The fact that a mother lives in a lesbian relationship does not of itself make her unfit to have the care and control of her child. But it is an important factor in deciding which of the two alternative homes that the parents can offer is most likely to advance the child's welfare.

The facts

C's parents, who are divorced, first separated in 1984 when C was one. C lived with her mother but saw her father regularly. In 1988 the mother, a prison officer, started a lesbian relationship with M, a woman serving 12 months for wounding and theft. The mother left the Prison Service and got another job and a flat. M, who was released from prison, lived with the mother and C.

The father remarried and in November 1989 he applied for care and control of C. The judge awarded care and control to the mother. The father appealed.

The decision

Lord Justice Glidewell said that it was clear from the House of Lords' decision in G v G [1985] 1 WLR 647 that an appellate court may only interfere with a judge's discretion in relation to child custody if it is satisfied that the judge was "plainly wrong". In his Lordship's view the judge's conclusion about the effect on C of her mother's lesbian relationship was plainly wrong.

Despite vast changes in society's attitudes to marriage, sexual morality and homosexual relationships, it was axiomatic that the ideal environment for a child's upbringing was the home of loving, caring and sensible parents, her father and her mother. That ideal could not be achieved when the parents'

marriage ended. The court's task in deciding which of two possible alternatives was preferable for the child's welfare, was to choose the alternative closest to that ideal.

Despite society's changed attitudes, a lesbian relationship between two adults is an unusual background in which to bring up a child. The judge accepted it was undesirable that C should learn or understand at an early age the nature of her mother's relationship, but thought that C was just as likely to acquire that understanding if living with her father and staying periodically with her mother, as she was if living permanently with her mother. In that respect the judge was plainly wrong.

The judge also disregarded the effect on C of her school friends learning of her mother's relationship. If they did, she was bound to be asked questions which could distress or embarrass her. If she were living with her father in a heterosexual household she would be much less likely to be exposed to that. The disregarding of those factors was a plain error. His Lordship was not saying that the fact that a mother was living in a lesbian relationship was conclusive or that it disqualified her from ever having care and control of her child. A court might decide that a sensitive loving lesbian relationship was a more satisfactory environment for a child than a less sensitive or loving alternative. But the nature of the relationship was an important factor to be put in the balance. The judge had also failed to refer to another relevant factor – M's conviction for violence which must be a matter of some concern.

Lord Justice Balcombe, agreeing, said that in this case the law was clear. When the court was considering the legal custody or upbringing of a child, the paramount consideration was the child's welfare.

Although views would frequently differ as to what the child's welfare required, the judge should not be influenced by subjective considerations.

What standards, then, should a judge apply if he was not allowed to apply his own subjective views? he should start on the basis that the moral standards which are generally accepted in the society in which the child lives are more likely than not to promote her welfare. In our society it is still the norm that children are brought up in a home with a father, mother and siblings, if any, and, other things being equal, such an upbringing is more likely to be conducive to their welfare. A very material factor in considering where a child's welfare lies is which of two competing parents can offer the nearest approach to that norm. In the present case it was clearly the father.

If the judge had adopted that approach and concluded that the advantages of C being with her mother outweighed all other relevant factors, their Lordships would not have interfered. But it was clear that the judge was not bringing into the balance even the existence of the lesbian relationship because of his view that in any event C was going to have at least visiting rights to her mother. That was an error.

The judge also gave no weight to M's conviction for a crime of violence. That would have been just as relevant even if the mother had remarried a man with a similar record.

The appeal was allowed but it did not automatically follow that the father was awarded care and control. A rehearing was ordered. Pending that interim care and control was given to the father with reasonable access to the mother. The Official Solicitor was to be invited to act as C's guardian ad litem.

Shiranikha Herbert
barrister

Figure 2
Source: *The Guardian,* 17 October 1990

'the family' as part of a *discourse* of control – part of a way of speaking about social relations which helps to define the roles people shall play and the power structures within which they shall play them. To define people as 'mother', 'father' and 'child' rather than 'female adult', 'male adult' and 'young male or female' strongly implies duties for them and asymmetrical relations between them which might not otherwise be taken for granted.

ACTIVITY 3

The issue of definition is not just a matter of semantics or of clarifying concepts. It has important repercussions for what are considered appropriate gender and social roles and thus for social policy in maintaining or supporting them. For an example of how assumptions about the 'normal' family can affect legal decisions regarding the guardianship of children, read the article reprinted as Figure 2.

Use this article to make notes on how the ideological prominence of the nuclear family has material effects in establishing ways in which our lives are ordered.

---

2   HOW IS THE FAMILY CHANGING?

Despite the apparent fixity of the stereotype, in fact the population structure changes and with it the structure of families. The most obvious way in which change in family structures can be illustrated is with reference to birth rates. As Smith (1986) indicates, in 1860 the average marriage produced seven children; in 1980 the average was two. In 1900 the birth rate per 1000 population was 28.7; in 1976 it was 12. There has thus been a marked tendency for family and household size to decrease in all West European countries (except Ireland) as they become more industrialized. Children appear to be less of an essential element in the family's economic survival, probably because of the development of state social security systems. Reductions in the level of child mortality have also contributed to lower birth rates. As Table 3 shows, the trend towards smaller household size is continuing.

Another change in population structure is brought about by increased life expectancy. As people live longer, a larger proportion of a couple's life together may occur *after* children have grown up and left home. Thus a larger proportion of couples without children will be relics of nuclear families rather than nuclear families in process of formation. (The kin structure also alters. At the turn of the century it would have been rare for a young child of a large family to reach adulthood with a grandparent still surviving; now, great-grandparents are not uncommon.) Successive waves of immigration also change the population structure, because they are more likely to consist of young adults and children than of older people. This has little effect nationally since immigration accounts for

Table 3   Households by size, Great Britain (percentages and numbers)

Household size	1961	1971	1981	1991
1 person	14	18	22	27
2 people	30	32	32	34
3 people	23	19	17	16
4 people	18	17	18	16
5 people	9	8	7	5
6 or more people	7	6	4	2
Number of households (=100%) (millions)	16.2	18.2	19.5	21.9
Average household size (number of people)	3.1	2.9	2.7	2.5

Source: Office of Population Censuses and Surveys data; table taken from *Social Trends*, no. 24, 1994, 2.2, p. 34

only a tiny proportion of population growth, but effects may be visible in particular locations because of the racial structuring of the labour and housing markets.

Another notable factor affecting family change has been the numbers of marriages and divorces. The United Kingdom currently has the second highest divorce rate in Europe – 12.3 per 1000 marriages, after 13.1 in Denmark. All other countries are below 9 per 1000 (see Table 4). A trend towards more numerous divorces was most notable after the 1969 Divorce Law Reform Act. This legislation created a single ground for divorce – that marriage had irretrievably broken down. This replaced the old grounds of adultery, cruelty and so on where one party tended to be labelled as 'guilty'. The Act enabled divorce by mutual consent provided that the parties had not cohabited for three years (reduced to one year by the 1984 Matrimonial and Family Proceedings Act). Since then the number of divorces has more than trebled. Correspondingly it has been estimated that the majority of lone-parent families come from separated and divorced families. As we have seen, the proportions of families with dependent children headed by a lone parent increased from 8 per cent in 1971 to 19 per cent in 1991. However, such evidence has to be put alongside an increasing number of remarriages which suggests that lone parenthood is often only a transient status. Marriage remains a popular institution: 85 per cent of the population get married at some time, although there is some evidence to suggest that for younger age groups the marriage rate has declined. Whether this is due to a preference for cohabitation or simply postponement is open to debate (Smith, 1986, p.12).

Looking at the increase in divorce rates, in cohabitation without marriage and in 'lone parenthood', politicians and moralists of the new right (and

Table 4   Marriage and divorce: EC comparison, 1981 and 1989 (rates)

	Marriages per 1000 eligible population		Divorces per 1000 existing marriages	
	1981	1989	1981	1989
United Kingdom	7.1	6.8	11.9	12.6[1]
Belgium	6.5	6.4	6.1	8.6
Denmark	5.0	6.0	12.1	13.6
France	5.8	5.0	6.8	8.4
Germany (FDR)	5.8	6.4	7.2	8.7[2]
Greece	7.3	6.1	2.5	–
Irish Republic	6.0	5.0	0	0
Italy	5.6	5.4	0.9	2.1
Luxembourg	5.5	5.8	5.9	10.0
The Netherlands	6.0	6.1	8.3	8.1
Portugal	7.7	7.1	2.8	–
Spain	5.4	5.6	1.1	–

Notes: 1 1987; 2 1988.

Source: Statistical Office of the European Communities data; table taken from *Social Trends*, no. 22, 1992, 2.12, p. 43

others) have identified a series of threats to what is considered the 'normal' family: a threat believed to have been brought about in part by state interference over the past decades.

> The case for the normal family needs to be powerfully argued because the normal family is threatened from three directions. First there are brands of feminism which are deeply hostile to the family, most especially to the role of fathers. Secondly, the expansion of the modern state has led to the responsibility of the family for children and young people being subverted by the state itself and by professional bodies of doctors and teachers, whose autonomy from, that is irresponsibility to, the family, the state endorses. Further the web of incentives and penalties set by the tax and benefit system is now firmly loaded against the normal family. Thirdly, modern technological developments such as new techniques of embryo fertilization threaten, unless controlled, to dislocate traditional relations in the family.
>
> (Anderson and Dawson, 1986, p.11)

As Abbott and Wallace (1992) summarize, such developments are viewed as particularly disturbing by such writers because:

> According to the moral New Right, not only does the family discipline men and women in economic and sexual terms, but it also socializes children ... The properly functioning family instils in the children the 'correct' moral values, the core values of society.
>
> ... The family provides the moral basis for the moral society. The breakdown of the family is the cause of moral decay in society ... The breakdown of the family ... is also blamed for increased crime rates, high unemployment, drug-taking ... [It] not only stifles initiative by taking money out of the economy ... it penalizes the 'conventional' family ... by higher taxation which supports those who lead immoral life-styles.
>
> (Abbott and Wallace, 1992)

ACTIVITY 4

Do you think that the available evidence on divorce, cohabitation and so on indicates the breakdown of the family? Part of the problem in reaching a satisfactory answer is that the statistics of population and family are complex, reflecting complex and changing underlying realities. Consider, for example, the following statements:

1 The divorce rate in England and Wales has increased sixfold in the last twenty years.
2 One child in every eight currently lives in a lone parent family.
3 One child in five could see their parents divorce before they reach 16.
4 Nine out of ten people will marry at some time in their lives.
5 Nine out of ten married couples will have children.
6 Eight out of ten people live in households headed by a married couple.

(Family Policy Studies Centre, 1985)

Which of these suggest a breakdown, and which a continuity, with the past?

Clearly the first three statements suggest change in family forms but the final three stress that continuity is also evident. Certainly there is more divorce, more cohabitation without marriage, more single parents and therefore proportionately fewer 'conventional families'. Easier divorce legislation and the treatment of cohabiting couples as married has almost certainly contributed to this situation. (Until recently, for example, there were tax advantages to cohabitation without marriage if both partners were in well-paid employment.) However, there is no clear evidence to suggest that marriage and child-rearing is being avoided or that the ideal of a happily married couple with children is no longer sought after. For example, witness the regularity with which divorce is followed by re-marriage and the number of stable, cohabiting couples who would regard their relationships as having the force of a marriage. No evidence has been presented here that any decay in 'the family' is responsible for the ills which new right thinkers attribute to it, and such evidence is hard to find; the case rests by and large on assertion. Those who take a different view might regard this as just another ideological use of the family, to distract attention from underlying economic processes and the failure of government policies.

3   THE FUNCTIONS OF FAMILIES

The picture of 'the family' as a crucial institution within modern society, discussed in the last section in the context of the new right, was by no means invented by them. It is in fact the basic position of writers such as Parsons, stemming from the 'functionalist' school which dominated soci-ology in Britain and the United States in the 1940s, 1950s and well into the 1960s (and is still very influential in the USA). This view sees society as upheld by social institutions, each of which has well-defined functions to perform. The functions of 'the family' are the rearing and socialization of children and the physical and emotional support of the male workforce. The isolated nuclear family is seen by Parsons as particularly well suited to the needs of industrial society, being mobile and adaptable to the needs of the labour market. Concern about the decline of the family is also not new, having been raised in the 1960s and 1970s in the context of (a) the increasing numbers of mothers taking paid employment, leading to an increase in 'latch-key children', and (b) the weakening of paternal auth-ority by increased state provision of, and control over, basic elements such as health and education. The effect of these two trends, it has been suggested, would be to undermine the socialization of the next gener-ation.

There were opponents of this pessimistic view, however. Both Fletcher (1966) and Shorter (1977) are concerned to demonstrate that in the twen-tieth century the family is not in decline, but rather is a rewarding institution meeting the needs both of the economy and of individual self-realization and autonomy. Both authors describe the pre-industrial and Victorian family in wholly negative terms. For Fletcher, unceasing work, lack of recreational or educational facilities and poor housing conditions made pre-industrial family life a barely tolerable state of affairs. Simi-larly, Shorter asserts that industrialism freed the family from its custom-ridden form in which its needs were secondary to those of the community. Industrialization thus allowed 'natural' emotions and individual freedom to flourish. For Shorter,

> The nuclear family was a nest. Warm and sheltering, it kept the children secure from the pressure of the outside adult world and gave the men an evening refuge from the icy blast of competition ... [W]omen liked it too, because it let them pull back from the grinding exactions of work and devote themselves to childcare. So everyone huddled happily within those secure walls, serene about the dinner table, united in the Sunday outing.
>
> (Shorter, 1977, p. 272)

The twentieth-century family, then, is if anything a strengthened version of its predecessors. Addressing the question of whether the development of state institutions has stripped the family of a key role in education, health, government, economics, religion and recreation, Fletcher argues that, 'Both in the sense of being concerned with a more detailed and refined satisfaction of the needs of its members, and in the sense of being more intricately bound up with the wider institutions of society, the functions of the family have increased in detail and in importance' (Fletcher, 1966, p. 197). Lying at the root of both of their arguments is the view that the modern family offers opportunities for greater closeness and intimacy than was possible in pre-industrial societies. A key function of the family, then, according to this approach, is its ability to provide a locus for emotional support and fulfilling relationships.

Not surprisingly such rosy images of family harmony have themselves been subjected to extensive criticism. One of the earliest of these was Engels' (1884) account of the development of the modern family. Working from Marxist premises, he argued that the development of private ownership of property was pivotal in the origins of the monogamous marriage and the nuclear family. Through this form men could ensure that they were in fact the fathers of their prospective heirs. At the same time, the bourgeois family was, in Engels' view, a form of prostitution which rested on the husband materially providing for a wife in return for her fidelity and the reproduction of his children. Engels' work is now generally viewed as pioneering – in that it raised the issue of the nuclear family as a vehicle by which men control women's sexuality – but also seriously flawed. Contemporary readings of Marxism stress that the chief function of the nuclear family is its utility in reproducing the capitalist system. In particular they suggest that the nuclear family provides a supportive retreat for the alienated worker, impedes working-class solidarity by privatizing the household and reproduces labour power by providing daily sustenance and the capacity to work. Other arguments along these lines (as summarized by Elliot, 1986, pp. 64-5) stress that the unpaid domestic labour of the housewife 'lowers the minimum cost of labour to the advantage of capital since workers would have to buy in domestic and childcare services if the family did not exist, thus adding to their living costs and raising wage levels'. Beechey (1977) develops this argument by suggesting that the housewife is functional to capitalism as a source of unskilled, flexible and cheap labour which can be brought into the labour market as a reserve army when needed and discarded back into the family when not, without affecting levels of unemployment.

Orthodox Marxist accounts share some ground with the otherwise diametrically opposed functionalist arguments (such as those of Parsons, Shorter and Fletcher discussed above), in that both agree that the family offers opportunities for personal freedom and emotional support which are denied elsewhere. Of course, whilst functionalists tend to view the family in positive terms as supportive of wider economic processes, Marxists locate the family as an instrument of capitalist oppression: as a major means by which the relations of capitalist production are able to reproduce themselves.

This latter argument has been most forcibly put by Zaretsky (1976). He argues that, as capitalism advanced, individual identity became increasingly lost. A sense of the 'personal' could not be found in either factory labour or indeed in the ownership of property. As work and family became separated, a new form of family was created in order to provide an avenue for the expression of subjectivity, emotion and personal relationships. The family came to be seen as a protected enclave against the impersonal, rational and anonymous world of capitalism. This split between the personal and the economic is thus a social construction, a direct result of capitalist forms of production. Despite the destructive consequences of this process, particularly for women in separating them further from the productive process, Zaretsky maintains the value of the family as establishing a 'real sphere of personal freedom and independence which previous labouring classes did not have' (p. 138). This in turn, though, places a heavy burden on family members.

> Under capitalism, almost all of our personal needs are restricted to the family. This is what gives the family its resilience, in spite of the constant predictions of its demise and this also explains its inner torment; it simply cannot meet the pressure of being the only refuge in a brutal society ... the dilemma of the housewife is a classic expression of this contradiction: her family's income may rise, technology may lessen the burden of work, but she remains oppressed because she remains isolated.
>
> The prerequisite to realising the promise of personal life is to abolish its forced separation and isolation.
>
> (Zaretsky, 1976, p. 141)

As Zaretsky suggests in the above passage, the price paid for greater personal freedom is frequently the greater oppression of women. Elliot

(1986, pp. 126-31) notes how feminist authors have elaborated on this theme by describing how:

1   the family regulates women's labour through the housewife role;
2   the family gives men more power and control over women's sexuality and fertility;
3   the family structures and reinforces separate and inequitable gender identities.

Such arguments have been sustained in a number of ways. For example, Oakley (1974) maintains that because women's work in the home is not only unpaid and thus regarded as low status, but also monotonous and isolating, the experience of daily domestic labour is more alienating than that of industrial workers. Moreover, if the housewife–mother is able to find outside work, it is most likely to be in the part-time sector. The working mother in effect takes on two jobs – both under-valued and of low status. Similarly, the family can be seen as an active agent in suppressing female sexuality to a far greater extent than male. For Campbell (1983), women's sexuality has been conventionally tied to a marriage in which chastity and fidelity predominate. Similarly, the prolonged failure from 1736 to 1991 of the English courts to legally recognize rape by a husband, has long been seen as denying women any rights of control even over their own bodies. It was not until October 1991 that the Law Lords brought England into line with France, Sweden, USSR, Norway, Denmark, Poland and various US and Australian states by overturning the 255-year-old legal ruling which had given husbands immunity from marital rape.

In addition, the family supports and promulgates an ideology which locates women in the private sphere and men in the public, thus maintaining structures of inequality and dependence. Ideas of domesticity, maternity and dependence for women, and breadwinning, responsibility and autonomy for men are articulated and reproduced by the family.

In these ways the family actively denies women the same opportunities as men and, as a result, has been viewed as a key agent in women's oppression.

ACTIVITY 5

By coupling Marxist and feminist analyses, a picture emerges of how the family may be functional to, and supportive of, capitalist, *and* patriarchal, social relations. Whatever freedom it provides for men, it is argued, is paid for in the greater oppression of women.

Is this statement true for all women? How do class and gender *interact* to restrict the lives of women? How are these relations altered by the dimension of race?

The statement would certainly appear to hold good for the structural position of some white *working-class* women. Here comparative household poverty and the poor wages available in 'women's jobs' (increasingly becoming 'part-time') may combine to make marriage and dependency appear the only viable route for bearing and rearing children. One might argue that it is less true for middle-class women who are able to obtain reasonably paid jobs on something of the same terms as men. We should note, however, that there is a tradition in some middle-class male areas of employment – the law, the church, some parts of the civil service, medicine, some sectors of industry – for wives *not* to hold paid employment outside the home, and indeed for their (unpaid) labour to be necessary for the proper performance of the husband's job. In these cases a deserted or deserting wife might find it very difficult to obtain sufficiently well-paid employment to support herself and her children, after a long period away from the labour market.

The picture is also made more complex when we consider the position of black women. For example, Thorogood (1987, pp. 25–30) has argued that Afro-Caribbean family structures have developed as a systematic response to their own particular historical and political experiences. She suggests that the separation of economically active men from their dependants (and thus the prevalence of female-headed lone-parent households) has been historically engendered by West African kinship systems and the experience of slavery, colonialism and migration. As a result, she argues, the economic and emotional independence of Afro-Caribbean women has evolved as a cultural norm. They are more likely to work full-time than white (or Asian) women and their average weekly earnings are likely to be higher (although not necessarily higher per hour). This relative 'freedom', however, does not deny that black women's employment is clustered around particular industries (clothing manufacture, catering, cleaning, nursing and hospital ancillary work) in which pay is low and hours long and anti-social. What it does bring into question is whether the concept of patriarchal domination is sufficient to 'cope with the question of race as a cross-cutting division to the social divisions of gender' or is able to recognize different constructions of femininity, masculinity and family life in different ethnic groups (Barrett and McIntosh, 1985, pp. 38-40). In essence a recognition of some black family structures, which are less likely to include a male breadwinner, leads us to question whether the family *per se* is *the* major site of black women's oppression or whether such oppression more directly flows from their colonial and labour history. If the latter is the case, then the black family becomes not a primary site of oppression but rather a vital source of refuge and resistance to external racism and labour exploitation. As Carby (1982, p. 231) concludes, 'It is important not to romanticize the existence of [black] female support networks, but they do provide a startling contrast to the isolated position of women in the Euro-American nuclear family structure'.

4 POWER, AUTHORITY AND FAMILY LIFE

Whilst it is clear that the family is not simply a site of oppression but can provide a haven of warmth, security and solidarity, any adequate conceptualization of the modern family must also raise such issues as the inherent tensions in the child–parent relationship, the sexual division of labour and domestic violence.

Throughout the 1950s and 1960s and again in the late 1980s increases in married women's involvement in paid work (albeit largely part-time) led to the assumption that women had achieved near equality with men. Such 'equality' was presumed to aid female economic independence and thus enhance the potential for greater freedom and self-autonomy. The Equal Pay Act 1970 and the Sex Discrimination Act 1975 are frequently cited as the main legislative measures which have reinforced this move to 'equality'. Such authors as Willmott and Young (1973) were indeed led to a talk of a 'symmetrical family' in which men and women also increasingly took an equal share of responsibility for domestic life. They reported, for example, that 72 per cent of married men 'helped their wife' in the home in some way other than washing up at least once a week. Oakley (1974), however, maintains that equal sharing of domestic tasks is a myth and astutely points out that the phrase 'helps their wife' reveals where the true responsibility for domestic chores lies. Where the husband goes out to work and the wife stays home, this imbalance is not remarkable; he is not in the home long enough, or regularly enough, to shoulder an equal half of the daily maintenance. However, a study of dual-career families – in which both husbands and wives had professional occupations – concluded that the responsibilities of childcare and housework still fell firmly on the wife's shoulders; husbands remained tolerant of their wives' careers as long as they did not interfere with their own needs (Rapoport and Rapoport, 1976). In short, female roles still remained firmly attached to the domestic sphere (see Figure 3). Brannen's and Moss's (1987) research on dual earners found that, whilst a woman's income contributed very significantly to household income, a gendered division of responsibility remained prevalent, with men's earnings geared to housing costs and regular bills and women's earnings used more for shopping and for children and childcare. Similarly, Edgell (1980) found that in middle-class couples routine housekeeping decisions were made by the wife, whilst career-related decisions were made by the husband. The husband thus determines where the couple live and the family income is determined by the husband's career decisions. Considerable power to order the life of family members, then, lies with the husband. The lives of wives from every social class tend to be structured around their husbands' jobs to an extent that is rarely reciprocated (Finch, 1983).

Moreover, women's position in the labour market is characteristically in the low-paid and part-time sectors. Thus women remain economically dependent on men, and consequently men's power in marriage is deemed legitimate. As this is continually reinforced through religion, the state, the divorce courts and the social security system, a large proportion of

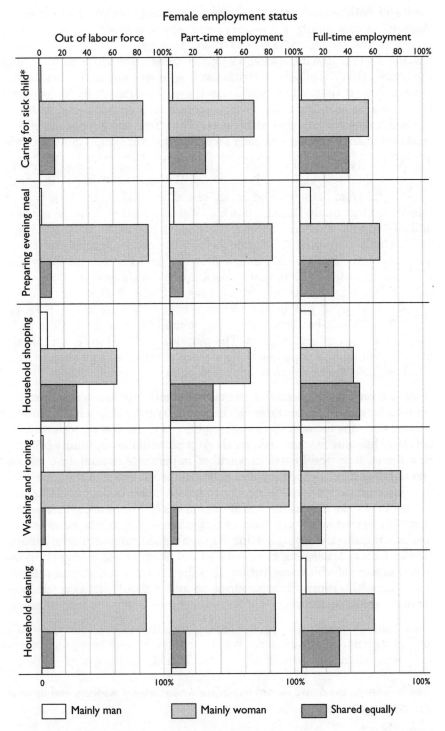

Figure 3   Domestic division of labour: household tasks and female employment status

Note:* Respondents married, or living as married, with children aged under 16

Source: data from SCPR's British Social Attitudes Survey, 1987; taken from Kiernan and Wicks, 1990, p. 29

adults of both sexes continue to treat husbands' power as legitimate. Women's responsibility for children and the home both restricts their access to the labour market and tends to mean – because *employers* assume a world in which women's first responsibility is for children and the home – that the opportunities for well-paid jobs and for promotion are not available to them when they do get there. (Restricted pay for 'women's jobs' is more a working-class phenomenon, but restricted access to training and promotion holds for all classes.) Thus 'free and equal individuals' tend to be men; women are neither structurally equal nor, if mothers, free.

The centrality of male authority in marriage has also been underlined by studies of domestic violence. Dobash and Dobash (1980) argue that wife assault, far from being viewed as abnormal or deviant, has largely been considered legitimate through much of Western history. In an analysis of official statistics of violent offences in two Scottish cities, they found that wife assault accounted for a quarter of all serious assaults and three-quarters of all family violence. The first national survey on rape within marriage reported in 1991 that women are seven times more likely to be raped by their husbands than by a stranger. One in four women, out of a thousand surveyed, had been a victim of rape (*The Guardian*, 16 February 1991). Woman-battering is not an isolated phenomenon but is widespread and has cultural support. The paradoxes of the family include the fact that whilst it is supposed to be a place of intimacy and support, it is also the place where violence against women is most tolerated.

What we have said about the structural position of women in families holds in far more extreme form for children. Structurally, being 'a child' in 'a family' means being subject to discipline, both for the smooth running of family life and 'for your own good'. At a personal level, family life may be a haven from the heartless world of impersonal, demanding schools and domineering, all too personal peer groups. As parents we mostly try to make sure that it is so. Some psychiatrists (such as Cooper (1972) and Laing (1971); see also Laing and Esterson (1970)) have argued, however, that all such attempts are doomed to failure – that the 'atmosphere' of families is quite the wrong setting for turning children into sane capable adults. Other sociologists have pointed out that for the young child the family is more of a total institution than the prison or the mental hospital is for the adult: control is near absolute and if family life becomes hell, there is no escape from it.

The duality of 'haven' and 'prison' is used by Elliot (1986) to explore such ambiguities and contradictions. Whilst the family may be a place of control, oppression and potentially unstable relationships, such negative readings tend to fail to recognize the diverse ways in which family life may be experienced and do not explain its continuing widespread appeal. She concludes:

> Images of the conjugal family as both haven and prison lead to ambivalence and neutrality and are not well developed in the litera-

ture. Yet attention to the nurturant and supportive as well as the oppressive sides of families is not just an ambivalence. It is, in part, a recognition of the fact that family life may be experienced in different ways by different people and, in part, a recognition of the tragic paradox that security in personal relationships implies commitment and loss of freedom. It recognises that not only love and altruism but the whole range of human feelings find expression in family life.

(Elliot, 1986, p. 133)

ACTIVITY 6

What has this section told you about the structural position of women and children in the family?

---

5   THE FAMILY AS A 'PROBLEM'

It is a commonplace to say that the family has become a problem. As we have already seen, the family has been described as a place of male dominance, oppression of women and denial of children's freedom and individuality. It has also been viewed as an active agency in reproducing social inequalities, isolating individuals from each other and eroding a broader sense of community. Traditionalists, meanwhile, have lamented the growing divorce and crime rates and the increasing number of lone-parent families as evidence of moral degeneration and an apparent lack of parental responsibility towards their children. Such conceptions of the family as a problematic institution have been directly influential in the development of social work and welfare institutions during this century. These have largely been concerned to protect and support the family and encourage its development, but usually within officially approved guidelines. Thus social policy not only has a caring welfare objective but also carries with it notions of 'normality' to which families are directed to conform. However, whilst it may be considered appropriate to intervene in families which have been (or can be) classified in some way as special or deviant, widespread regulation of family life is likely to be condemned as trespassing on essential areas of privacy. Perhaps for this reason the United Kingdom has never adopted a clear and unambiguous *family* policy. Certainly many social policies (in health, housing, education, social security and taxation) have a direct effect on family life but, as Parker (1982, p. 359) argues, 'It is politically much less hazardous for a government to adopt family policies which are implicit, fragmented or disguised as the incidental effects of other initiatives'. The family is not immune to political and professional interventions, but as such interventions are not ubiquitous and uniform we can expect wide variation in when and how they are deemed appropriate.

We may fruitfully think of state intervention in families as being of four kinds:

1   Family as a *location*: a useful 'place' for locating particular categories of people (e.g. for the payment of Child Benefit).

2   Family as a *process*: as, for example, the way children are socialized into 'adult values' – which the state may wish to support.

3   Family as a *target*: when a process 'goes wrong' or is seen as at risk of going wrong (e.g. social workers' intervention to protect particular children, or health visitors' routine monitoring of all children).

4   Family as a *norm:* as the proper way for adult sexuality to be conducted and/or children to be socialized.

Families are most likely to be seen as 'social problems' when they appear not be conforming to a norm and are thus viewed as requiring some form of moral rehabilitation. Government concern in the early 1990s over the number of lone parents and the subsequent establishment of the Child Support Agency to enforce absent partners to contribute child maintenance would be a case in point (see Chapter 3).

A simple view of family problems would be to regard them as stemming from instances when the needs of particular groups such as children, young people, isolated housewives and older people are not being met. But, of course, belonging to such categories may not be *personally* experienced as particularly damaging and, even when they are, they may not be considered worthy of a wider *social* cause for concern. Similarly it may be recognized that the family creates problems for particular individuals at particular times, but not that the family itself is the problem.

The idea that the family, in itself, constitutes a social problem originates only from the late eighteenth and early nineteenth centuries. Such a conception was indelibly tied up with the emerging class relations of the time, in particular the growing political and economic dominance of a bourgeoisie. At this time an ideal of family life was being constructed in which the importance of new categories of 'childhood' and 'adolescence' was central. As the middle classes began to devote more time to the public education of their children, these stages in the life-cycle came to assume a greater importance. 'Proper and adequate' upbringing of children was increasingly defined in middle-class terms. However, as social constructs, 'childhood' simply did not exist for a majority of the labouring poor until late in the nineteenth century, and 'adolescence' is an even more recent creation; so it was predominantly to patterns of working-class family socialization that the label of 'social problem' was readily applied. In response, voluntary bodies and later the state thought it necessary to intervene in working-class family life, by setting up industrial schools for children considered neglected and reformatories for those considered to be delinquent. Decisions of when to intervene on these grounds were, and remain, keenly debated. For example, social workers are still not immune from criticism for taking working-class and black children into care, not because they are being abused or neglected but because their upbringing

differs from the social worker's own – primarily middle-class – perceptions of good and bad child-rearing practices (Smith, 1986, p. 4).

Such problem definition became more generalized as the nineteenth century progressed. In particular the notion that it was unsafe to trust the
task of education to urban, industrial working-class parents was influential in the establishment of compulsory education in the 1870s. The
debate was not only one of what should be taught and how, but also of how
children should be socialized and regulated. This widely perceived failure
of the working-class family throughout the nineteenth century has indeed
laid the foundation and legitimacy for many contemporary education,
health and childcare policies. They remain, however, sources of considerable debate and controversy. Does state intervention strengthen the family or erode its autonomy? Does the state provide too much support or too
little? Does it pressurize and constrain us to conform to an idealized but
non-existent norm? Does it increase the tendency to define some families
as deviant and pathological and promote forms of intervention which may
be more oppressive than supportive?

In response to such issues, supporters of the traditional nuclear family
have argued that, whatever the successes of the education and welfare
reforms in the past, the state is in danger of becoming too involved. In this
view intervention has encouraged families to depend upon state benefits
rather than upon each other. In the process parental responsibility for the
upbringing and behaviour of their children has been eroded. Such reasoning indeed has a popular currency. The idea that parents are to blame for
their children's misdemeanours is widespread. Accordingly, the Criminal
Justice Act 1991 advocated that the courts be empowered to bind over the
parents of juvenile offenders to exercise control of their children. Of
course, whether such responsibility can be enforced by legal sanction or
whether it would only act to increase family break-up (and thus instances
of youth homelessness) is hotly disputed. Similarly, the outcome of the
Child Support Agency initiative in the early 1990s to enforce absent
fathers to pay maintenance for their families remains controversial. Will
it help 'failed' marriages to stay together or increase the likelihood of
resentment and violent reaction on the part of such fathers? Such measures clearly contain a coercive element, yet they are promoted as means
by which family members can be protected and encouraged to develop a
greater responsibility for each other.

The argument that the state should be less involved in the financial
support of families also has wide support in traditional views. During the
1980s state provision for the poorest families has indeed been eroded.
Within the first two years of the first Thatcher administration, the total
value of state support to an unemployed couple with two children fell by
40 per cent (Novak, 1988). The number of families headed by someone
earning a wage below the 'poverty line' increased by nearly a fifth (DHSS,
1988). The Social Security Act 1986 abolished the universal Maternity
Grant and replaced it with a means-tested payment. Tax and National
Insurance changes during the 1980s have disadvantaged poorer families

severely. During the period from 1978 to 1988 the tax paid by a man on average earnings with two children increased by one per cent, whilst it decreased by 45 per cent for men earning ten times national average earnings.

The burden falls most heavily on lone-parent families. In 1987 they formed 10 per cent of those families making up the bottom fifth of the income distribution, up from 9 per cent in 1982. The state has consistently provided less, rather than more, financial support. As a result bringing up children may be more stressful than need be. France, Belgium and Luxembourg have a far more generous child benefit system than the United Kingdom, and in countries like Sweden, Norway and Germany parents are allowed paid leave to care for a sick child (Lister, 1982, p. 144). Such measures are not even on the political agenda in the UK. Equally, the reduction of institutional care for older people and disabled people – introduced in the name of community care and reduced state involvement – has meant that the burden of such caring has fallen primarily on relatives, most commonly women, without any adequate financial remuneration.

It could therefore be argued that the state does not intervene enough and, despite the rhetoric, fails to support the family. The implications of such failure fall most heavily on large two-parent families, lone-parent families and women generally. However, arguments for increasing state support are double-edged. They may help keep families out of poverty, but if the family can be a repressive and discriminatory institution, as is sometimes argued, then social policy to support it must be regarded with suspicion and ambivalence.

ACTIVITY 7

Write a few initial notes on the following questions:

- Why is it difficult to formulate an explicit family policy?
- When and why is the family viewed as a problem?
- Is the state more concerned to support or to regulate families?

---

6   CONCLUSION

This chapter has raised a number of academic and personal issues which are pertinent to understanding the complex relationship between social policy and family life. This task is arguably made all the more difficult because, unlike such countries as Sweden, Norway, Hungary and France, the United Kingdom has never had an integrated set of social policies explicitly termed 'family policies'. However, it is clear that UK social policies have frequently been based on certain assumptions about what families are like, how families should be constituted and organized and how responsibility and dependency should be allocated between its members. To tease out these interconnections we clearly need to know more of how the law, politics and economics, as well as social policy, have helped to frame the way in which we live both within and without our families. Chapters 2 and 3 of this volume address these issues in more detail.

REFERENCES

Abbott, P. and Wallace, C. (1992) *The Family and the New Right*, London, Pluto Press.

Anderson, A. (1971) *Family Structure in Nineteenth Century Lancashire*, Cambridge, Cambridge University Press.

Anderson, D. and Dawson, E. (1986) 'Popular but unrepresented: the curious case of the normal family', in Anderson, D. and Dawson, E., *Family Portraits*, London, Social Affairs Unit.

Ball, D.W (1974) 'The family as a sociological problem', in Skolnick, A. and Skolnick, J. (eds) *Intimacy, Family and Society*, Boston, Little, Brown.

Barrett, M. and McIntosh, M. (1985) 'Ethnocentrism and socialist feminist theory', *Feminist Review*, no. 20.

Beechey, V. (1977) 'Some notes on female wage labour in capitalist production', *Capital and Class*, no. 3.

Berger, G. and Berger, P. (1983) *The War Over the Family*, London, Hutchinson.

Brannen, J. and Moss, P. (1987) 'Dual earner households', in Brannen, J. and Wilson, G. (eds) *Give and Take in Families*, London, Allen and Unwin.

Campbell, B (1983) 'Sex: a family affair', in Segal, L. (ed.) *What is to be Done About the Family?*, Harmondsworth, Penguin Books.

Central Statistical Office (1992) *Social Trends*, no. 22, London, HMSO.

Central Statistical Office (1994) *Social Trends*, no. 24, London, HMSO.

Carby, H. (1982) 'White women listen', in Centre for Cultural and Community Studies (eds) *The Empire Strikes Back*, London, Hutchinson.

Cooper, D. (1972) *The Death of the Family*, Harmondsworth, Penguin Books.

Department of Health and Social Security (1988) *Low Income Families 1985*, London, HMSO.

Dobash, R. and Dobash, R. (1980) *Violence Against Wives*, London, Open Books.

Edgell, S. (1980) *Middle Class Couples*, London, Allen and Unwin.

Elliot, F.R. (1986) *The Family: change or continuity?*, London, Macmillan.

Engels, F. (1884) *The Origin of the Family, Private Property and the State* (London, Lawrence and Wishart, 1972).

Family Policy Studies Centre (1985) *The Family Today: continuity and change*, London, FPSC.

Finch, J. (1983) *Married to the Job*, London, Allen and Unwin.

Fletcher, R. (1966) *The Family and Marriage in Britain*, Harmondsworth, Penguin Books.

Fox, R. (1967) *Kinship and Marriage*, Harmondsworth, Penguin Books.

Gittins, D. (1985) *The Family in Question: changing households and familiar ideologies*, London, Macmillan.

Haskey, J. (1991) 'Estimated numbers and demographic characteristics of one-parent families in Great Britain', *Population Trends 65*, London, OPCS.

Kiernan, K. and Wicks, M. (1990) *Family Change and Future Policy*, London, Family Policy Studies Centre.

Laing, R.D. (1971) *The Politics of the Family and Other Essays*, London, Tavistock.

Laing, R.D. and Esterson, A. (1970) *Sanity, Madness and the Family*, Harmondsworth, Penguin Books.

Laslett, P. and Wall, R. (eds) (1972) *Household and the Family in Past Time*, Cambridge, Cambridge University Press.

Lister, R. (1982) 'Income maintenance for families with children', in Rapoport, R. *et al.* (eds).

Murdock, G. (1968) 'The universality of the nuclear family', in Bell, N. and Vogel, E. (eds) *A Modern Introduction to the Family*, New York, Free Press.

Novak, T. (1988) *Poverty and the State*, Milton Keynes, Open University Press.

Oakley, A. (1974) *The Sociology of Housework*, Oxford, Martin Robertson.

OPCS (1990) *Key Population and Vital Statistics, Local and Health Authority Areas, 1989,* London, Office of Population Censuses and Surveys.

Parker, R. (1982) 'Family and social policy: an overview', in Rapoport, R. *et al.* (eds).

Parsons, T. (1959) 'The social structure of the family', in Anshen, R. (ed.) *The Family: its function and destiny*, New York, Harper and Row.

Rapoport, R.N. *et al.* (eds) (1982) *Families in Britain*, (British Family Research Committee), London, Routledge.

Rapoport, R. and Rapoport, R. (1976) *Dual Career Families Re-examined*, Oxford, Martin Robertson.

Shorter, E. (1977) *The Making of the Modern Family*, London, Fontana.

Smith, D. (1986) *The Family, Marriage and Divorce*, London, Longman.

Thorogood, N. (1987) 'Race, class and gender: the politics of housework', in Brannen, J. and Wilson, G. (eds) *Give and Take in Families*, London, Allen and Unwin.

Young, M. and Willmott, P. (1962) *Family and Kinship in East London*, Harmondsworth, Penguin Books.

Young, M. and Willmott, P. (1973) *The Symmetrical Family*, London, Routledge.

Zaretsky, E. (1976) *Capitalism, the Family and Personal Life*, London, Pluto Press.

CHAPTER 2
FAMILY POLICY AND POLITICAL DISCOURSE

JOHN MUNCIE AND MARGARET WETHERELL

CONTENTS

INTRODUCTION

Our discussion of politics and policy in this chapter develops one particular theme. We wish to examine the structuring effects of the *idea of 'the family'* in these areas. We will examine how stereotypes, norms and ideals of family life have organized political rhetoric and policy-making. And, more broadly, we will try to grasp the role and influence of ideas of 'the family'. To what extent, for instance, can we talk of an ideology of family life, and what does it mean to describe some ways of thinking about the family as examples of ideological thinking?

Two key moments in UK policy-making are reviewed: firstly, the formulation of 'the family' in the 1940s, particularly the immediate post-war period, and, secondly, its reformulation in the 1980s. We will look, too, at the themes which structure contemporary political discourse about 'the family', comparing and contrasting the discourses associated with the British Labour and Conservative parties in the 1980s which can be seen as expressions of wider social democratic and conservative traditions. By the end of the chapter, therefore, some of the connections between political ideology, welfare policy initiatives and assumptions about what counts as a normal and healthy family life should be clearer, as well as some of the dilemmas and contradictions in political and policy discourse.

At times in this chapter we will be analysing the formal, deliberate and sometimes Utopian statements of political leaders, at other points we will be considering much more implicit and less consistently articulated statements, statements which nonetheless contain sets of assumptions about what the family is – or should be – and the extent to which the state is entitled to interfere in family matters.

As Chapter 1 pointed out, the United Kingdom has never formally adopted a set of policies explicitly termed *family policies*. Although family values have never been defined in legislation, much of British social policy is nevertheless based on a set of underlying assumptions about ideal and real family forms, including assumptions about responsibilities and dependencies in marriage and the obligations parents have to their children. The effects of these assumptions can be seen in the formulation of policy in such diverse areas as taxation, divorce, Child Benefit, abortion, immigration and education and have a direct impact on how family life is experienced. In this chapter we concentrate in particular on those policies affecting social security and community care. Here we should find a clearer picture of the forms of family life and familial relationships that are being promoted in the negotiations, discussions and statements of policy-makers.

Finally, our examination of public discourse on the family will demonstrate the extent to which family life, whilst widely presumed to be a personal and private matter, is also a political issue. The politicization of the family is evident not only in the symbolic purchase it may have for particular political ideologies, but also because there are few aspects of state legislation that do not have a direct or indirect impact upon the family and very few practices of state officials that do not have some sort of family dimension.

In summary, this chapter aims to:

1   Review two crucial periods in the construction of UK 'family policy': the reconstruction of the 'normal' family in the post-war period and the reformulation of the role of the family in the 1980s.

2   Compare and contrast conservative and social democratic political philosophies of family life.

3   Investigate some of the images, themes and rhetoric structuring particular public representations of the family found in political discourse and in popular culture.

4   Inquire about the possible role and power of familial ideology.

ACTIVITY 1

This chapter will be partly descriptive, outlining policies, images, ideas and assumptions, but it will also try to develop some concepts and theories to make sense of these images and their role in social life. You may well find it useful to begin building up your own glossary of key concepts and finding definitions for unfamiliar terms both in this chapter and in following chapters.

The concept of 'ideology' is an obvious place to begin. You will find, however, that the task of definition is not always easy since some concepts, like ideology, are 'contested', meaning that they are defined in different ways in different theoretical traditions. Here is one definition you could use as a starting-point:

> Ideologies are sets of ideas, assumptions and images by which people make sense of society, which give a clear social identity, and which serve in some way to legitimize relations of power in society.
>
> (McLennan, 1991, p. 114)

---

1   CONSTRUCTING 'FAMILY POLICY'

According to Land and Parker (1978, pp. 332–3), there are three main reasons why assumptions about men, women and parental responsibilities in families are not readily articulated but remain implicit in British social policy. Firstly, they note the widely held view that family life should remain a private matter. The family provides a sanctuary from the 'external' world and thus the state should not be seen to be intervening directly in its affairs. Secondly, particular patterns of responsibilities, dependencies and the division of labour between the sexes are viewed as natural and normal. The illusion that the family is a solely private domain is preserved. Thirdly, whilst a range of social services has been developed for adults and children, they are presented as facilities for individuals, rather than as for families per se. Intervention is generally directed at those who are defined as 'abnormal' or 'deviant', usually in respect of them being 'without a family' or being in a family which is viewed as problematic in some way.

By presenting social policy in this framework, governments have consistently been able to claim that they are not interfering in family life, whilst at the same time sustaining the boundaries of those family obligations which are thought to be important.

Below, with reference to the implicit assumptions carried in social policies about the 'normal family', we examine where those boundaries are set and their implications for different family members. As we have noted, our discussion is limited to two significant moments in British post-war social policy – the 1940s and the 1980s – for, arguably, it was at these times that the parameters of family life have been most clearly defined.

1.1   THE POST-WAR RECONSTRUCTION OF THE 'NORMAL' FAMILY

Since the introduction of the 1601 Poor Law, the obligation of parents to support children, husbands to support wives and adults to support their aged parents has been a key feature of family life. Such financial responsibilities fell hardest on the poor, particularly in the legal obligation of children to maintain parents.

Although the state began to supplement the incomes of many families from the late nineteenth century through such means as free school meals, pensions, unemployment and sickness insurance, the legal responsibility of families for their dependent members was not significantly altered. The law thus assumed, and was predicated on, an image of society being made up of families of three generations. The legal change from the extended to the nuclear family came only in 1948 when financial responsibilities were reduced to those of husband and wife and of parents for their children aged under 16 (Crowther, 1982, p. 133).

The welfare legislation of the 1940s built on the piecemeal reforms of the late nineteenth century and the earlier part of the twentieth century to produce the welfare state in its recognizably modern form. The major legislative reforms were:

- the 1944 Education Act, providing compulsory secondary education;
- the 1946 National Health Service Act, reorganizing health provision to provide a free and universal service;
- the 1945 Family Allowances Act, providing universal benefits for families with two or more children;

- the 1946 National Insurance Act extending the scope of unemployment and sickness benefits; and
- the 1948 Children Act, empowering local authority Children Departments to coordinate services for children in need.

Here we focus on the reforms of social insurance and family allowances following the Beveridge Report of 1942, for it was this report that came to symbolize a post-war welfare society through which the 'evils' of squalor, disease, ignorance, idleness and want would be overcome. In particular, Beveridge envisaged that the extension of social insurance schemes would redistribute wealth and guarantee a minimum living standard for all. It was presumed that state action would abolish unemployment, the health service would make health care universally available and a system of family allowances would prevent families, particularly those with a high number of dependants, from falling into destitution. This blueprint caught the popular imagination as an image of a fairer society for which the Second World War was fought, although it was opposed by some Conservatives as a programme of costly ideals and false hopes.

The main attack on poverty (want) was to be through the National Insurance scheme in which the payment of an insurance stamp would ensure entitlement to benefits in times of sickness, industrial injury, unemployment or in old age. This, however, was no blueprint for total equality or a bottomless well of state support for poor families. Benefits

William Beveridge (1879–1963)

were to be universal – for men – and paid at subsistence level and to last as long as the need; on implementation of the scheme, however, benefit levels were kept below subsistence and benefits for the unemployed lasted only twelve months. The Beveridge Report was at pains to point out that 'the state in organizing security should not stifle incentive, opportunity, responsibility ... it should leave room and encouragement for voluntary action by each individual to provide more than a minimum for *himself and his family*' (Beveridge, 1942, p. 6; emphasis added). The underlying assumption was that people's needs would be met through income from work or from dependency in the family. It was around the question of family dependency, and who was responsible for whom in families, that Beveridge was most explicit. In particular the proposals for National Insurance specifically assumed that married women would be dependent on their husbands for financial support, and that man and wife should be treated as a couple requiring less resources than two single people. As a result, married women's entitlement to benefits was restricted:

> During marriage most women will not be gainfully employed. The small minority of women who undertake paid employment require special treatment differing from that of a single woman. Since such paid work will in many cases be intermittent it should be open to any married woman to undertake it as an exempt person, paying no contributions of her own and acquiring no claim to benefit in employment or sickness. If she prefers to contribute ... she may do so but will receive benefits at a reduced rate.
>
> (Beveridge, 1942, p. 50)

In giving married women a separate insurance class, Beveridge assumed that marriage would be their 'sole occupation' and that on marriage a woman 'gains a legal right to maintenance by her husband' (p. 44) whilst as child bearer and rearer she can devote herself to vital unpaid service in 'ensuring the adequate continuance of the British race and of British ideals in the world' (p. 53). The model of social security established after the war was firmly predicated on *male* patterns of employment; married women's employment was treated as unimportant because women were presumed to be dependent on a man. The Beveridge settlement helped to define welfare citizenship around notions of the British (*white*) family within a declining empire. The welfare state was expected to play a significant role in re-establishing a strong British 'nation'. Pascall (1986, p. 198) identifies three main features of the family ideology expressed in the Beveridge Report:

1   Women are available to do housework and care for children and elderly relatives, without pay.
2   Couples consist of one full-time worker (usually a male breadwinner) and one 'housewife' whose work outside the home is insignificant, being merely for 'pin money'.
3   Women can look to men for financial support.

every woman needs a man
to look after her

Even in the 1940s there was something of an anomaly in this vision of family roles and obligations. During the drafting of the Report women were involved in a wide range of occupations – as members of the armed forces, working in munitions factories and so on – as they had been during the First World War. By 1943 two out of five married women were in employment, compared with one in ten in 1931. In 1946, the year the National Insurance Act was passed, there were 875,000 more women in paid employment than at the beginning of the war. Between 1951 and 1971, 2,500,000 *more* married women joined the labour market and much of this was on a full-time basis. By 1987, 68 per cent of married women were in employment – though virtually all of the more recent increase in the 1970s and particularly in the 1980s was in part-time employment (Kiernan and Wicks, 1990, p. 26). Interestingly, part of this increased participation can be accounted for by the creation of part-time and full-time jobs in the welfare state itself.

The 1946 National Insurance scheme effectively debarred most married women from entitlement to National Insurance benefits. Those without husbands or without paid work because of full-time caring responsibilities had to rely on the 'safety-net' of National Assistance (renamed Supplementary Benefit in 1966 and Income Support in 1986). Beveridge wanted to pay an 'end of marriage' allowance to those women whose marriages ended through no fault of their own, but the government rejected this proposal. As a result, lone mothers have always had to rely on means-tested benefits. Whilst in the 1940s it was assumed that the numbers of lone mothers would be insignificant, by 1991 this had risen to over one million. A growing majority of lone parents, particularly lone

Women at work in the 1940s and '50s

mothers, rely on means-tested benefits rather than on earnings and, as a result, there is a gross over-representation of female-headed, single-parent families among the very poor.

The principle of dependency is also brought to bear on single women if they are suspected of cohabiting with a man. In such cases the woman is presumed to be reliant on male earnings and thus to be ineligible to claim income support:

Women on supplementary benefits lead precarious lives, always at risk of being pushed by the 'safety-net' into dependence on men, and always at risk that men may decline support. This is the sharp end of a social security practice which is founded on the assumption that women do not need an independent source of income.

(Pascall, 1986, p. 218)

In the immediate post-war period, pressure on women to dedicate their lives to a male-dependent and domestic role was also forthcoming from the popularization of the theories of the psychoanalyst, John Bowlby. Bowlby's 'maternal deprivation' thesis proposed that numerous social problems – including some forms of criminal behaviour, juvenile delinquency and certain kinds of depression and mental disorder – were caused by a lack of adequate and continuous mothering of young children. Bowlby's work (1951, 1953) established that poor institutional care was detrimental to young children. Institutions which did not allow for personal expression and personal relationships with familiar adults were shown to have a damaging effect on a young child's personality. This realization had a positive effect since it provided the impetus within the welfare state to improve institutional conditions, but gathered a wider import in Bowlby's insistence that 'what is believed to be essential for mental health is that an infant and young child should experience a warm, intimate and continuous relationship with his mother (or permanent mother-substitute – one person who steadily "mothers" him)' (Bowlby, 1953, p. 13). Bowlby implied that without continuous maternal care within the home, children would grow up disturbed and affectionless and go on to damage their own children in the same way. Bowlby's arguments were popularly received at least by health and welfare workers and used to criticize nurseries for children, to argue that they were harmful to a child's development and to reinforce the view that a woman's natural and proper place was in the home. A ready equation was also made between juvenile delinquency and latch-key children or the 'abandonment' of children in crèches.

Bowlby's thesis was disseminated by government Ministries of Health and Education and childcare manuals in the 1950s as it appeared to offer a way forward in dealing with the problems of homeless and deprived children. It suggested some concrete changes that could be made in the design and staffing of orphanages and similar institutions. But its impact proved to be much broader, being part of a re-emergent ideology that the post-war reconstruction and the nation's future depended on the reassertion of motherhood in the nuclear family. The 'evidence' of 'maternal deprivation' added authority, and sometimes hysteria, to the assumptions held by the 1945 Ministry of Health that 'mothers of children under 2 should be positively discouraged from going out to work' (cited in Pascall, 1986, p. 79). Such 'commonsense' reasoning continues to underpin policy for nursery-school provision. State-provided nursery places, particularly since the late 1970s, have largely been restricted to those children with special needs; nurseries are not for children of 'ordinary' mothers or for women who prefer full-time employment to full-time childcare. Ideology is thus reinforced by policy and practice: through the absence of nursery places, it is assumed that childcare can – and it should – be provided from within the family.

As a result, those women who cannot afford to pay for alternative child-care support or who find it difficult to obtain suitable alternative provision for their children have been (and continue to be) restricted to part-time low-paid employment. Working-class women in particular have often found it necessary to find patterns of paid work that allow them to fulfil family responsibilities at the same time. Women, such as those black women recruited to the lowest-paid jobs in the health service, who have had to work full-time from economic necessity have frequently found that not only do they suffer from the difficulty of finding appropriate childcare, but they are more likely to be accused of being 'bad' or 'pathological' mothers.

SUMMARY

In conclusion, the foundation of the welfare state was firmly rooted in a particular conception of the family. A traditional division of labour between white men and women was assumed and the structure of women's dependence on men in the family was reinforced. The assumptions of the post-war reconstruction regarding the structure of families and their relation to the state can be summarized as follows:

1 Marriages are for life: the legal obligation to maintain persists until death or remarriage.

2 Married men are responsible for their partners and children.

3 Men's place is in the world of an external labour market.

4 Women's place is in the home as provider and child-rearer.

5 The role of the family is to produce national unity by reproducing the values of a British, white (and by implication Christian) culture.

6 The state has some obligation to intervene to prevent family poverty. Further intervention should only be made in the 'exceptional' circumstances of family breakdown or of a perceived family inadequacy.

1.2   'HELPING THE FAMILY' IN THE 1980s

Beveridge's assumptions about family structure have continued to inform the formulation of social policies. Thus in the half-century since his report there has been an underlying continuity in practice, even if this has not always been matched by a consensus in political rhetoric (see section 2).

The deficiencies and inequalities embedded in the Beveridge proposals have, however, been exacerbated by economic circumstances and changes in family forms. For example, the relative value of National Insurance benefits has declined and the numbers resorting to means-tested income support (formerly National Assistance) has more than trebled. In 1987 over two-thirds of lone-parent families relied on income support – a six-fold increase since 1961 (Kiernan and Wicks, 1990, p. 33). Nevertheless the popular image of the breadwinner/housewife couple continues to underpin many aspects of social security, taxation, unemployment and insurance benefits, even though assumptions about family life may be less explicit in contemporary legislation than those expressed in the Beveridge Report.

Beveridge's principles were substantially modified in the 1960s and 1970s (see Chapter 3) and with the election of successive Conservative governments after 1979 it became clear that what remained of Beveridge's notion of a universal welfare state was to be replaced by a more residual 'state welfare' (Digby, 1989, p. 65). Basic benefits were to remain for those most in need, while others were to rely on the informal sector in which public provision was replaced by voluntary self-help, charity and the family. The 1979 Conservative manifesto claimed that 'the balance of our society has been increasingly tilted in favour of the state'. Now was the time to reverse that process and return more auton-omy and responsibility to the family. Cutting expenditure on welfare services, encouraging demand for private welfare, promoting market (rather than state-managed) systems and cracking down on benefit fraud and abuse were heralded as ways of 'helping the family'. The conserva-tism of the 1980s thus viewed the family as an alternative to the welfare state. As Smart put it,

> One universal theme is that the family or its members, have become far too dependent upon the state. Hence even 'normal' families are at risk of being undermined in their efforts to retain traditional values, whilst 'less desirable' families are able to waste scarce resources and become trapped into a spiral of unemployment and declining moral values.
>
> (Smart, 1987, p. 100)

Two of the main means by which the family has been 'helped' to be more independent and self-reliant have been through changes to the social security system and in the expansion of programmes of community care.

As Lister (1989) recalls, the 1980 budget represented a watershed in post-war social security policy. Child Benefit (a universal benefit payable to mothers and introduced by Labour in 1978) was cut in real value by 9 per cent, the National Insurance earnings-related supplement payable for the first six months of sickness, unemployment, maternity or widowhood was abolished, and benefits were also restricted for occupational pen-sioners and those in trade disputes.

Smart's (1987) analysis of the social security reviews of the mid-1980s finds that the underlying aim of reducing state expenditure was dependent on constructing 'responsible families' in which the male breadwinner would be motivated to work and the dependency of women and children would be reinforced. The chief concern of the Social Security Act 1986 was to prevent people falling into poverty. However, rather than supporting older people, lone-parent or large families, the Act was directed mainly at the two-parent family with children whose earnings were lower than their entitlement to benefits. The fear was that benefit levels were too high, thus providing no incentive to find employment. The legislation, according to Smart, mainly focused on the issue of how to keep *men* economically active, the assumption being that a male income would be sufficient to take care of women and children privately and protect the family from poverty. This assumption, however, may have proved to be unfounded. On implementation, the social security reforms appear to have acted more as mechanisms for pushing both men *and* women into the labour market and into the lower paid, least secure and least regulated sectors (see Chapter 3). For example, by 1991 almost 50 per cent of women who left their jobs to have children were back in full-time or part-time work within nine months of giving birth. The numbers of women returning to full-time jobs had increased from 7 per cent in 1979 to over 20 per cent by the beginning of the 1990s (McRae, 1991). Reforms of Income Support, Family Credit and maternity benefits were also designed to make individuals less dependent on the state and more dependent on other family members. For example, claimants for means-tested benefits aged under 25 years were assumed to need less benefit than individuals over 25 because they were more likely to be living at home. The abolition of the right to benefit for most 16- to 17-year-olds under the Social Security Act 1986 prolongs the economic dependency of the young unemployed on their families. Family Credit, introduced under the 1986 Act in 1988, is a means-tested benefit which was designed as an alternative to an overall increase in the universally available Child Benefit. Child Benefit rates were frozen for four years from April 1987. Similarly, the 1986 Act abolished the universal maternity grant and replaced it with a means-tested payment. Here again the government was intent on reducing the state's responsibility for the health of children and emphasizing that children were first and foremost a private concern. Through these measures the family 'is becoming the main welfare agency of the 1980s' (Smart, 1987, p. 113).

The same trend is evident in the formulation of community care policy in the 1980s. As Wicks (1987, pp. 119–20) argues, the rate at which publicly financed institutional care for mentally ill, disabled and elderly people is being run down far outstrips the rate at which community-based services – such as half-way houses – are becoming available. The result is that the reality of community care is largely care by families, either in the form of help to pay for institutional care in the expanding private market or in the form of providing actual care. Family care almost invariably means care by women (Lewis, 1989). Moreover this burden on families is likely to increase as state-financed resources decrease, the private market expands and the numbers of elderly in the population increase. The notion of 'community' (in reality, 'family') care also assumes a particular family structure – that in which a nuclear family is stable and contains an able-bodied person at home, usually a woman financially supported by her husband. For women, the promotion of community care and the lack of pre-school and day-nursery provision makes dependency more difficult to escape. Attempts to encourage women to take on the role of unpaid domestic carer was an explicit element of 1980s social policy. Yet this aim stands uneasily against the increasing number of working mothers in the labour market. Between 1985 and 1988 the proportion of working mothers with children under 5 rose from 29 per cent to 37 per cent (Pilkington, 1991, p. 21). The majority of these though were in part-time employment. In this respect the United Kingdom compares unfavourably with most other European countries mainly because of a dearth of publicly funded childcare (see Clarke and Cochrane, 1993). It is difficult for mothers to participate full-time in the labour market unless either they have relatives or friends willing and able to provide childcare or they can afford private childcare. During the 1980s more and more mothers purchased childcare in the private market and relatives (other than fathers) provided less childcare.

Examination of the impact of economic and social policy during the decade, characterized by tax cuts and reductions in benefit, reveals that 57 per cent of families in Britain lost while only 40 per cent gained from these policies. Families with children have been most seriously affected. 74 per cent of lone-parent families and 81 per cent of couples with children found themselves entitled to reduced rates of benefit as a result of the switch from Supplementary Benefit to Income Support in 1988 (Becker and Golding, 1991, p. 15). The introduction of the Community Charge (or poll tax) in Scotland in 1989 and England and Wales in 1990, whilst revised in 1991 and abandoned in 1993, disproportionately affected large families with several eligible adults. These measures, coupled with increases on VAT for goods and services, the dismantling of the school meals service

and the freezing of Child Benefit meant that by the end of the 1980s a quarter of the population relied on means-tested benefits – the highest proportion ever.

> Such policies have deliberately reduced the incomes of poorer families in an attempt to reconstitute the ideology of the family: all families – especially those on low incomes – are to take on greater responsibilities (for support, income maintenance, care in the community), shifting the focus of concern from the state to informal and formal networks of individual, family and collective responsibility.
>
> (Becker and Golding, 1991, p.17)

The 1980s, then, were characterized by attempts to consolidate the nuclear family by, somewhat contradictorily, increasing its responsibilities whilst reducing levels of financial support. Relatively well-off families have – through reductions in income tax – undoubtedly gained from this strategy, whilst the poorer – through growing dependency on means-tested benefits – have seen their level of income decline. The promotion of a new private market in welfare is only likely to increase such inequalities. Alcock (1989, p. 109), for example, argues that divisions of race and gender will be particularly accentuated. Because of their weaker position in the labour market and their greater responsibility for child and adult care, women are generally less likely to be able to take up private insurance schemes and thus are forced to rely on minimal state provision – exacerbating the historical process of the 'feminization of poverty'.

Similar marginalization is also likely to affect Britain's black population, generally because of their experience of lower wage and higher unemployment rates than those of the white population, more specifically because black people's 'recourse to public funds' is also mediated by the fact of their 'race'. Gordon and Newnham (1985), for example, showed that in the early 1980s black people were experiencing greater harassment in the receipt of state benefits because of suspicions about their immigration status. The checking of passports by the Department of Social Security is now a common practice and misinterpretation of status not unknown, thus depriving legitimate claimants of benefit (ibid., p. 25). Racist assumptions also operate with regard to the Asian community. Assuming families to be close-knit and interdependent, DSS staff have used informal transactions of money, shared property or resources abroad to invalidate claims for benefit. British immigration policy has also effectively enforced the separation of some black families by tightening up the criteria by which their partners can enter the country and gain residency status. The sanctity of the nuclear family is thus more likely to be overlooked when considering cases of Asian or Afro-Caribbean origin, particularly so for black women in Britain wishing to be joined by their foreign husbands (Cook and Watt, 1987, p. 68). (Immigration law is discussed further in Chapter 3.)

1.3 THE IDEA OF 'THE FAMILY' IN SOCIAL POLICY

Our reviews of the Beveridge reforms of the 1940s and the reforms of the 1980s demonstrate how the formulation of policy in key areas such as health and social security directly affects the experience of family life. The extent to which reforms and policy are predicated on various 'structuring ideas' about the nature of the family is also clear, however. A considerable part of the policy-makers' task seems to lie in actively formulating and arguing for different working definitions of the family (Gill, Potter and Webb, 1992). In this respect, politicians and policy-makers resemble those social scientists who are also concerned to define the family. The formulations of politicians, however, are vested in a string of other political commitments and impinge directly on people's lives.

A fundamental task for social scientists and researchers in family studies is thus to analyse the way in which ideas about 'the family' and images of family life help to organize and justify governments' responses to what are perceived as the pressing social problems of the time. For social scientists, the concept of 'the family', or the idea of 'the family', is not just a tool in our own analyses of social phenomena, its use in various public and private contexts must also be a topic of study in its own right.

In general, social policy research has been slow to take up this study. Researchers have investigated the rationality, for instance, of different social policies and the power of different interest groups to set the social policy agenda for governments. There have been fewer studies of how central terms in social policy debates, such as the notion of 'the family', or 'welfare', have been constructed and how this construction influences the course of state intervention in family life. For social scientists as well as politicians it is perhaps also the case that the family has seemed such a 'natural' and normal institution, it has proved difficult to examine the status of the concept (Oakley, 1987). Feminist scholars, for obvious reasons, have been in the forefront of this new study.

Yet the influence of structuring ideas, constructions and representations is crucial. The political scientist, Murray Edelman (1977), argues that whether or not something is seen as a 'social problem' can depend more on how it is constructed discursively, as a social phenomenon, than on any inherent features. But what does Edelman mean by this notion of 'discursive construction'? We are familiar, for example, with the way social problems move in and out of fashion, so that for a period crimes of mugging or football hooliganism have a high profile only to disappear from view in other periods. The appearance and disappearance of problems is, of course, affected by what is actually happening on the streets and on the terraces, but Edelman's argument is that the way an issue becomes identified and talked about in newspapers, on television, in parliament and in public debate has a considerable effect on the way the agenda for events becomes established and on the course of action which emerges.

Edelman points out that this discursive process – the construction of social categories and social problems – is often easier to see in retrospect.

Thus it seems obvious to us now that medieval policies against witches were based on a delusion, that the witch is an imaginary category and not a rational basis for social policy. It is more difficult to see in our own time how categories of people become created and then defined as problematic, and how the definition of the category becomes linked through chains of association to solutions which have material consequences for those defined.

There is a danger of presenting this discursive process as though it always runs smoothly with one political and policy construction displacing another progressively through history, as we move from witches, for instance, to lone-parent families as the perceived source of social ills. But, as Edelman and others (e.g. Gusfield, 1989) have pointed out, the definition of problems and solutions is usually contested, a matter of argument and dispute: 'Political and ideological debate consists very largely of efforts to win acceptance of a particular categorization of an issue in the face of competing efforts on behalf of a different one' (Edelman, 1977, cited in Gill *et al.*, 1992, p. 17).

And it is not just politicians who enter the fray. Those who are the focus of attempts to define them as a problem are capable of resisting what Gusfield (1989) calls these 'controlling definitions', substituting their own definitions. Gusfield describes, for example, how the gay rights movement has successfully upset the pervasive equation of homosexuality with illness and sinfulness, to the extent where it becomes possible to take over

the nomenclature of the 'family' in descriptions of, for example, lesbian families. In these cases, a traditional concept which seemingly excludes lesbian women and gay men has been successfully extended. The efforts of politicians, governments and policy-makers to construct the nature of social problems and remedies are thus not necessarily monolithic; they do not always succeed. And even in formal public discourse the structuring ideas informing policy and politics are frequently fragmented and cross-cut by contrasting, often contradictory, themes and ambitions.

ACTIVITY 2

Now go back over the reviews of social policy developments in sections 1.1 and 1.2, or your notes on these sections, and approach this material again in light of these comments about the discursive construction of social problems. First, using section 1.1, take the Beveridge reforms. How was the family defined in the post-war period?

Gusfield (1989) has argued that bringing one facet of a social phenomenon into prominence inevitably leads to the neglect and obscuring of other facets. What groups tended to become obscured or made invisible in the post-war consensus about the family?

Finally, new definitions of key institutions such as the family tend to lead to the discovery of new social problems. What became seen as problematic about family life in this period?

Using section 1.2, now turn to the 1980s. Here there seems to be continuity in definitions of the family but what becomes seen as the new over-riding social problem? List the measures and policies this analysis provoked.

DISCUSSION

As section 1.1 noted, the Beveridge reforms seemed to effectively consolidate the nuclear definition of the family, based on a husband, wife and dependent children, organized around a sexual division of labour and gender inequality. Within this definition, it is groups such as women workers, lone-parent families and families where the woman is the main breadwinner which become obscured, not only rendered invisible but also likely to become defined as problematic where they do become noticeable. Finally, a new social problem emerges – the unfit parent, particularly the unfit working mother. In the post-war period attention became directed towards the quality of the mother–child relationship as a cause for concern and intervention. Mothers became responsible not just for the physical and moral welfare of their children but for their psychological development.

To Beveridge and other social reformers of the period it seemed obvious that there was not enough state support or welfare. Lack of support, within certain boundaries, was the problem. In the 1980s this consensus, as section 1.2 made clear, became overturned and the problem became defined as dependency on the state and the waste of state resources. However, it also seems that this reversal did not disrupt the dominant definition of the traditional nuclear family on which policy was based, and lone parents and others deviating from this form came more sharply into focus as social problems.

ACTIVITY 3

Return now to section 1.2. How did the community become defined in the 1980s and what were the effects for women?

In the 1980s the idea of the 'community' began to become mobilized and self-consciously adopted as a way of characterizing and describing policy moves. Several studies of the effects of characterizations such as 'community care' (Potter and Collie, 1989), as opposed to other descriptions of the same policies, have demonstrated how the idea of the community acts as a powerful and persuasive rhetorical resource and perhaps even as an impediment to the development of alternative critical perspectives on those policies aiming to integrate groups previously institutionalized. Potter and Collie, for example, compared laypeople's reactions to two descriptions of policy for people with learning disabilities. The description couched in community terminology led to significantly more positive reactions to the prospect of integration.

'Community' – like 'family' and 'neighbourhood' – is part of a signification system, or chain of concepts and associations, which includes other key terms – 'natural', 'harmonious', 'organic', 'healthy', 'warm', 'evolving', 'supportive', 'personal' etc. (Williams, 1973). It is not surprising, therefore, that the term becomes endlessly repeated in the public contextualization of policy initiatives. Advocates of government policy wish to draw upon people's positive experiences of community and on their positive attitudes to communal life and link that chain of associations to new social policies. Critics of government policy want to argue that community care is a form of privatization of the health and other services which places the burden of care on women who are often unsupported in this task. The argument against community care is rendered more difficult by the reassuring humanistic imagery of neighbourliness, close ties, social support and a lifestyle more akin to a mythical image of village life than the urban housing estate.

We have talked so far about discourse, structuring ideas and the rhetorical representation of living arrangements, social groups, policies and social problems. We have noted how ideas of 'the family', representations and descriptions of family life, can have quite powerful effects. To summarize, it is clear that the way something is defined can affect what is publicly seen. If the nuclear family is defined as the normal

Tower blocks or village
fêtes: which is the real
'community'?

mode of family life, then alternative arrangements become viewed, by contrast, as problematic and as a source of difficulty. The way family life is represented can also 'hide' or obscure certain aspects of reality. Governments have tended to ignore, for instance, cases where women are 'the head of the family', since these fail to conform to the expected pattern.

How does the train of events work here? The cause and effect can work in two directions. We can see the ideas and representations of family life promoted by politicians and policy-makers as contrived and deliberate representations developed to justify the policy aims and the material consequences governments wish to generate. But it is clear, too, that politicians and policy-makers generate policy in response to prevalent ideas. Prior definitions of family life shape their perception of relevant issues and the articulation of the appropriate policy response. Finally, it is clear how the realm of ideas and images of the family needs to be viewed as a crucial part of the political battleground as the rhetoricians on competing sides slug it out on the terrain of words.

Many of the points we have been making in this section are, of course, entailed in the notion of 'ideology', defined in Activity 1. The analyst of ideology is also concerned with meaning and language, with representation, and the chain of associations, or the cluster of significations, built up around politically important concepts and terms such as the family and the community. The concept and theory of ideology also draw our attention to the clash and contestation of the ideas and the assumptions informing policy.

The concept of ideology asks us to pay attention to the way signification systems (systems of meaning) act as frames, organizing our view of reality so that some phenomena seem connected together – the family and the community, the community and care, men and paid labour – while other connections are mystified – such as women as heads of households, the community and alienation. The point is often made that ideologies work through presenting a state of affairs as normal and natural, universal and immutable. And it is clear, too, how the constant use of the concept of 'the family' represents the triumph of simplicity over complexity. Whenever the term 'family' is used, an enormous diversity of households become covered by an ideal and simplified picture of kinship.

In general, despite differences in theoretical emphases, analysts of ideology share an interest in the *power of ideas* to shape, organize, construct, define and selectively obscure material realities. Section 3 will return to this notion of the power of ideas. How can something so apparently ineffable as an idea or description be made powerful? We need to ask, too, about the functions that family ideology might serve and about the general connotations of this characterization of ideas about 'the family'. First, however, we turn to the politics underlying policy and compare and contrast conservative political discourse on the family with contemporary examples of social democratic discourse.

2 POLITICAL IDEOLOGIES AND POLITICAL RHETORIC

Despite attempts to subvert it, our laws and systems must acknowledge the family as the basic building-block of the nation. Instead of simply calling for more money as the solution to every problem, or even trying to accommodate unconventional lifestyles, the nation's spiritual leaders should unashamedly extol the virtues of normal family life.

(Gerald Howarth, Conservative MP, 1991)

Family policy needs to recognize that families come in all shapes and sizes ... to claim that one kind of family is right and others wrong can do considerable harm by stigmatizing those who live in non-traditional family settings. Public policy cannot alter private choices, but it can mitigate the painful effects of change.

(Harriet Harman, Labour MP, 1991)

If assumptions about 'normal' family life remain relatively implicit in social policy, the two quotations above suggest that in the world of political philosophy and political rhetoric such assumptions are more likely to be made explicit. For example, Howarth openly extols the virtue of a nuclear family structure as the only natural and proper bedrock of society on which social order and stability depend. Harman, on the other hand, acknowledges the existence of a diversity of family forms and is reluctant to give privileged attention to any one. Indeed divergencies from the nuclear form are both welcomed and seen as deserving of state concern and support. Whilst Howarth reflects the dominant view of welfare in the 1980s, that families should take more financial and social responsibility for their members, Harman argues that the increasing presence of people living outside of the nuclear 'ideal' necessitates more resources from the state, if those families are to survive.

The political debate over the legitimate roles of the family and the state reached something of a watershed in the early 1990s. Whilst Conservative and Labour party policies had maintained a certain consensus on family matters during the 1970s and early 1980s, changes in family structure and in the labour market during the 1980s have increasingly produced a bifurcated approach. What had traditionally only been made implicit was by the early '90s being made public in a dispute over the moral high ground of family policy. In certain respects both political parties were being forced to recognize and respond to the issue of the 'decline in the family'. The increased divorce rate, the number of lone-parent families, the increase in cohabitation, increased female employment in the labour market and the growth in the number and proportion of children born outside of marriage remain the long-term structural trends which helped to place the family question at the centre of the political arena. Whilst these trends did not mark the death of the family as such, they did challenge traditional notions of family life and call into question their relevance to actual lived realities (Wicks, 1990, p. 31).

2.1 CONSERVATIVE PARTY DISCOURSE

The Conservative party has long claimed that it is the true 'party of the family'. It has characteristically stressed the worth of the 'traditional' family in which parents marry and stay married, children are disciplined, and a clear-cut division of labour exists between men and women. The Skolnicks (1974, pp. 7–8) summarize the features which inform this model:

1 The nuclear family – a man, a woman and their children – is universally found in every human society, past, present and future.

2 The nuclear family is the foundation of society, the key institution guaranteeing the survival and stability of the whole society.

3 The nuclear family is the building-block, or elementary unit, of society. Larger units – the extended family, the clan, the society – are combinations of nuclear families.

4 The nuclear family is based on a clear-cut, biologically structured division of labour between men and women, with the man playing the 'instrumental' role of breadwinner, provider and protector, and the woman playing the 'expressive' role of housekeeper and emotional mainstay.

5 A major 'function' of the family is to socialize children, that is, to tame their impulses and instil values, skills and desires necessary to run the society. Without the nuclear family, the adequate socialization of human beings is impossible.

6 Other family structures, such as mother and children, or the experimental commune, are regarded as deviant by the participants as well as the rest of society, and are fundamentally unstable and unworkable.

(cited by Rapoport, 1989, p. 59)

In the 1980s this traditional conservative model was used to stress that there can be only one true family form; that the family should be autonomous of the state and that the family is the key site of social control, in particular *paternal* control (Coote, Harman and Hewitt, 1990, p. 10). Thus alternative family forms were more readily defined as imperfect, self-destructive or deviant. In particular, families without fathers were seen as a major cause of social problems, ranging from delinquency to truancy. In some ways this ideology mirrored the concerns of Bowlby forty years before, but was now bolstered by the work of Ferdinand Mount, a former adviser to the Thatcher administration, Charles Murray, the American theorist of the new right, and the British philosopher, Roger Scruton.

Scruton's (1980, 1986) work has been seen as an attempt to revitalize traditional teachings about monogamy and marriage in response to a perceived contemporary lack of moral values which in turn is viewed as the underlying cause of family breakdown and social disorder. Mount's (1982) contribution was to make a strong defence of the private nature of the family – that it was something natural, universal and enduring which stood outside of historical changes or state and market forces. Mount was most concerned to correct those histories of the family that view it as a continually changing and transient form. For him such histories are inherently anti-familial and act to undermine the family. Where others have stressed change, Mount is intent on establishing the nuclear family's continuity and its main role of counteracting collectivist or state tendencies. Thus he argues, 'the family is a subversive organization. Only the family has continued throughout history and still continues to undermine the State. The family is the enduring permanent enemy of all hierarchies, churches and ideologies' (Mount, 1982, p. 1).

Such positive evaluations of 'the family' rested easily with a conservative philosophy that the family should be the prime focus in all matters of care for the aged, the sick and for children. As a private haven it symbolized the last bulwark against the encroachment of a potentially totalitarian state (Morgan, 1985, p. 60). However, Mount's thesis was not without its own contradictions. His vision of a golden age of the family arouses a romantic familiaism which is empirically contestable. The state – from the Poor Law to Beveridge and the 'rolling back of welfare' reforms of the 1980s – has always 'politicized' the family by providing or withdrawing 'support' for those deemed in 'need' and in 'trouble'. Mount's conservatism was also tempered by economic liberalism. He was supportive of mothers who took paid employment and recognized the case for women's equality as long as these were gained without state intervention and without the family being undermined as a basic unit of care.

Such concerns were central to the 1979 Conservative campaign on the family. When in office the issue was subdued. It was not a major feature of the 1983, 1987 or 1992 elections. However, it did re-emerge in 1989 through the work of Charles Murray. He argued that the growth in illegitimacy and family breakdown was creating an underclass in the United Kingdom and the United States. Moreover this underclass was a primary source of moral and social degeneracy, delinquency, under-achievement and general social disintegration. The crux of Murray's argument was that the virtue of marriage lay in its capacity to civilize men by turning them into breadwinners: '...[Y]oung males are essentially barbarians for whom marriage – meaning not just the wedding vows, but the act of taking responsibility for a wife and children – is an indispensable civilizing force' (Murray, 1989, p. 37). An underclass, for Murray, could be identified by illegitimacy, lone-parenthood, violent crime and drop-out from the labour force and the danger presented by such a class was clearly associated, though not exclusively, with black populations.

For these ideologues, there is a clear intent to establish the dominance of the nuclear family with marriage as the origin of a stable and morally healthy social order. Ideas of this kind were a key reference for Conservative politicians in the 1970s and 1980s. For example, Keith Joseph in

1974 claimed that the so-called permissiveness of the 1960s had produced a moral degeneracy in which 'problem families' (in his view working-class, lone mothers) had thrived. He advocated not so much a strategy of interventionism, but preservation – that government should take measures to strengthen the institution of marriage and halt the growth in lone-parenting (Fitzgerald, 1983, p. 48). In 1977 Patrick Jenkin, then shadow spokesperson for social services, asserted not only the naturalness of the family, but the biological essentialism of gender roles: 'Quite frankly I don't think mothers have the same right to work as fathers do. If the Good Lord had intended us to have equal rights to go out to work he wouldn't have created men and women. These are biological facts' (Jenkin, 1977, cited by Fitzgerald, 1983, p. 49). Discussing the problems of the inner cities in 1985, Norman Tebbit, then Chairman of the Conservative Party, declared that stability and order could only be gained by strengthening a sense of personal responsibility most notably within families. The family as lynchpin of all social relationships (as opposed to the state) was underlined by Margaret Thatcher's now famous observation in 1987 that, 'There is no such thing as society; there are only individuals and families' (Thatcher, 1987, cited by Douglas, 1990, p. 412). At the 1990 Conservative Party Conference the theme of family responsibility was central, in the proposals to fine parents for their children's misdemeanours and to enforce absent fathers' obligations to support their children.

However, whilst all such proposals rest on images of the traditional nuclear family as the saviour of all ills, there is no consensus in conservative ideology on how the family should be supported. The fundamental dilemma was how to respond to changes in the labour market in the late

On duty at the Conservative Party Conference in Bournemouth, October 1990

1980s and the return of married women to part-time and full-time employment. Some Conservatives talked of the importance of mothers staying at home to look after young children whilst others preferred to allow market forces and individual choice determine the extent of women's contribution to the labour market. This contradiction is part and parcel of the twin conservative ideologies that individuals must be free to make their own choices, but that the state has a duty to intervene if those choices are deemed to be 'wrong'. Similarly, the insistence that there is no such thing as society, only individuals and families, sets itself against notions that fatherless families destroy the moral fabric of society (the very society which elsewhere is being denied?).

Paternalist conservatism, too, is wary of an absolute non-interventionist approach, noting that the market needs to be regulated to prevent families falling into abject poverty. But in general the Right appears split on the need to intervene to strengthen family ties or to withdraw state regulation so that the family can regain its autonomy. Much of this dispute centres on a sole interest in the economic circumstances of the family and can indeed be located in the contemporary desire to restrict public expenditure by strengthening family ties. Thus whilst debate abounds on such issues as whether mothers should have financial incentives to work, the Right is generally silent on the issues of resourcing nurseries and childcare facilities, or of providing family conciliation and counselling services.

The issue is encapsulated in the apparent paradox of promoting policies which support traditional family structures, whilst the long-term international trend is towards more divorce and more lone-parenting. To protect the traditional family in these circumstances would appear to require more, rather than less, public intervention into the private sphere of home and personal relationships.

2.2 LABOUR PARTY DISCOURSE

In many respects the position of the Labour party on the 'family question' has mirrored that of the Conservatives. In aligning itself with the post-war welfare state, it has historically appeared to promote the ideal of the patriarchal family as the norm of family life. However, whilst in conservative ideology the family is a private and natural institution, in social democratic ideology the family is viewed as a *social* institution and the state as having a positive role in equalizing opportunities for all through a mixed economy. From this it follows that individual initiative is not enough: childcare, family income and equality of opportunity are the responsibility of the state and society at large.

In the late 1970s the Labour PM, James Callaghan, argued that, 'the family is the most important unit of our community ... our aim is straightforward: it is to strengthen the stability and quality of family life in Britain'. Such forthright promotions of the family have not been a major component of Labour party policy. Whilst socialist and feminist critiques of the patriarchal family in capitalism have surfaced on the fringes of the party, however, of far more significance has been the largely unstated Methodist tradition 'which attaches great importance to family life and family loyalties and which is firmly rooted in the working class communities whence Labour has drawn so much of its support' (Coote *et al.*, 1990, p. 12). Out of office during the 1980s, the Labour Party was particularly silent on family issues. However, its position was gradually shifting – away from defensive postures on the sanctity of the family and towards a positive vision of women and men being able to combine parenthood and paid employment on an equal footing. In particular a 1990s' version of the social democratic vision of the family appears more open to acknowledging a variety of family forms and to avoiding discriminatory policies. Rather than asserting the primacy of a family unit, it has been more concerned to disaggregate its members and recognize their different needs and interests. Partly for this reason, the Labour party has rarely used the symbol of 'the family' as the cornerstone of its policies. Rather it talks of specific policy issues in the fields of female employment, childcare facilities, training, education and so on. For example, the 1990 policy document *Looking to the Future* contains no direct reference to families per se, but addresses itself to discriminatory tax allowances (to take the married couples allowance away from the husband), the training needs of women and young people (to encourage participation in the labour force), childcare (to enable both women and men to participate in the labour force whilst caring for their families), and social service support for children (to reduce child poverty and youth homelessness). The first attempt to place these policies in the context of family and employment structures

of the 1990s was made by the Institute for Public Policy Research paper *The Family Way* (Coote *et al.*, 1990). In contrast to the Right's emphasis on financial responsibility, authority and discipline, this paper stressed the role of *men* in the family as sharing responsibilities and caring for children. Rather than lamenting the decline of traditional family structures, it addresses the issue of family diversity and in particular how best to support lone-parent families.

Above all, the vision of *The Family Way* shifts the key focus away from the family per se and towards policies which would guarantee children a safe upbringing. To this end, families, it is argued, need strong self-reliant women and men who develop more emotional responsibility for their children. The starting-point of family policy for the 1990s is thus contained within the rhetoric of the child's best interests.

Approaching family policy from such a position also contains its own contradictions. If children are to be privileged in policy, will this mean less attention given to the position of women? Enhancing childcare within the family may only act to reinforce traditional notions of woman as mother. Supporting the financial position of poor and lone-parent families may be attainable, but the reforming of popularly held stereotypes about appropriate gender roles might prove more stubborn.

3 IDEOLOGY AND IDEAS ABOUT THE FAMILY

We have talked throughout this chapter of family ideology, but what is at stake if we talk of ideology in this context? What kinds of claims does this characterization entail about the statements and utterances of politicians and others? We began noting some of these claims in section 1.3. The concept of ideology, like Edelman's points concerning the discursive construction of social problems, suggests that ideas are powerful in organizing, shaping and constructing our experience of family life and our expectations about what family life should be like. To describe a claim as ideological suggests we should investigate how reality is being represented in ways which may serve the interests of some social groups over others, as part of a general struggle between competing groups to define the agenda for social change and social policy.

Ideology is frequently also defined, however, as sets of partial, false and distorted ideas, and ideology is also often associated with ruling groups within a society and seen as a tool or method by which these groups protect their economic and other interests, and thus 'dupe' or deceive other groups. There are considerable difficulties, however, if we apply this kind of conception of ideology, which stresses falsity and distortion, to ideas about 'the family'. In what sense could we say that the ideas about 'the family' in political debate are a form of 'false consciousness' which conceals the real truth about social relations and the real interests of oppressed groups?

Some theorists have argued that commonplace assumptions about the family should indeed be seen in just this way. You may remember, for example, the arguments presented in Chapter 1 from Engels (1884) and Zaretsky (1976). These theorists argue in different ways that, although people in the UK and other places seem quite attached to and motivated by the idea of family life, families, particularly nuclear families, while serving important functions for powerful groups, are not in the best interests of the mass of society . One function they might serve for these ruling groups is the reproduction of the conditions for capitalism, ensur-

Happy Families?

ing a steady supply of workers who are cared for and looked after by the unpaid labour of women within the home. As some feminists (for example, Wilson, 1977) have pointed out, families can be seen as a private haven, a sop for the male worker, a sphere where he can experience the autonomy and personal fulfilment that he might not be able to find in the workplace. The family also encourages consumption and the turnover of commodities, thereby reinforcing the ideas of private ownership (Mitchell, 1971).

It is for these reasons, the argument might go, that the political establishment is so set on strengthening the family and is so unwilling to examine alternative forms of living arrangements which might encourage a revolution in social organization and the division of labour between women and men. The threat might lie in communal forms of living and a different, less docile, attitude to the demands of the workplace as well as to the division between the external public world of work and the private world of the home.

In this section we shall explore this conceptualization of ideology further, but we shall also develop a rather different conceptualization of ideology and the role of ideas of 'the family', following the work of Stuart Hall (e.g. 1988) which in turn is based on the work of the Italian political theorist Antonio Gramsci and the French social theorists, Louis Althusser and Michel Foucault. This conceptualization of the way ideas work in social life presents a contrasting framework for thinking about the social functions of ideas about 'the family' and is critical of some aspects of the 'false consciousness' view taken by Engels and others.

Hall argues, as a first point, that we should not assume that the most prevalent ideas of family life or any other prevalent ideas in the public domain simply reflect the interests of a ruling group. We should not assume that the dominant social class, political and economic groupings, hold a unified and coordinated ideological position. There is no such unity, he suggests, in the presentation of ideas. A survey of British society and politics, for example, does not demonstrate that there is one coherent ruling philosophy which can be neatly opposed to the philosophy which might be articulated by those representatives and intellectuals of the working class who are not duped by false consciousness. It makes more sense, according to Hall, to talk of ideologies than of ideology. The study of ideas reveals not two seamless and coherent philosophies – such as capitalism and socialism – confronting each other, but a plurality of arguments, conceptions and positions engaged in a constant battle for pre-eminence.

Ideological dominance, Hall argues, cannot be guaranteed through membership of the ruling class. Ideas are not powerful in themselves, simply because they reflect the interests of certain social groups; they have to be made powerful, and made to work for those groups over and over again. Every social group has to actively organize its world-view, not just of the family, but in every arena, and make these views persuasive in the face of continual competing versions. For the social scientist, therefore, it is not sufficient to argue that ideas are dominant because they are articulated by dominant groups; social scientists need to be able to demonstrate how some ideas become seen as more persuasive than others.

This view of the ideological battlefield as constantly fragmented and divided meshes with the picture emerging from our reviews of political discourse and social policy. We have seen that politicians and policy-makers deal in combinations of ideas about the family which frequently contradict each other. Conservative discourse, for example, tries to com-bine free choice with authority. There is also much agreement across the political spectrum, from right to left, rather than competition between unambiguously differentiated blocs of thought. We saw, too, how the 1980s were distinguished by a considerable ideological upheaval as the political establishment sought to change the prevailing consensus about the family and the state. These new ideas favouring privatization and minimal state support had to be fought for and were part of a highly successful political campaign. The new orthodoxy of the family could not simply be assumed, it had to be struggled for.

Hall and other theorists of ideology also argue against the emphasis on social class groupings typically found in the 'false consciousness' concep-tion of ideology. This is a second theme in his reconceptualization of ideology. And, certainly if we ask the classic question the ideology prob-lematic suggests, namely 'who benefits from these ideas of "the family"?', it is difficult to argue that it is the bourgeoisie who benefits at the expense of the working class. As feminist theorists (such as Beechey, 1985) have pointed out, gender groupings also need to be taken into account in assessing the connections which might be operating between ideas of the family and social interests. 'Race' is also crucial: Cook and Watt (1987, p. 57), for instance, argue that since black families suffer disproportionately from economic and social marginalization, black families may frequently serve as an important refuge from, and as a major site of political and cultural resistance to, racism. In these cases it is difficult to argue that the idea of 'the family' is necessarily oppressive.

Hall similarly questions the notion of 'reproduction' which underpins some traditional views of ideology. This is the argument that ideology functions to reproduce the conditions of existence for the capitalist state so that the main function of the idea of 'the family', for instance, is to reproduce the next generation of workers. This perspective suggests an uninterrupted and inevitable movement through history, as one gener-ation placidly gives way to another generation, with one social formation and organization perfectly reproduced and reinstated through time. Hall suggests that we should see ideology instead as in a state of continual production and uneven transformation.

Denise Riley (1983) has made the same point in her studies of the pro-motherhood campaigns of the post-war period. With hindsight it looks inevitable and unsurprising that certain ideas – such as that women should be back in the home – won out in the 1940s and 1950s. But investigations of the actual connections between the ideas, policies and social changes involved suggest a more fragile, arbitrary and less coordinated set of circumstances and outcomes. From a feminist perspective and from the perspective of those who wish to change social arrangements, this view of ideology is thus more optimistic. It suggests that there is some point to the resistance and struggle against certain definitions of the family. In contrast, a strong emphasis on reproduction downplays the possibilities and opportunities for change.

These points can be summarized by noting that Hall and other recent theorists of ideology want to break the strong connections assumed in some classic theories of ideology between the forms of ideas and the forms of social relations. But if ideas of the family or other key political ideas are not directly linked to the material interests of ruling groups, what is their access and relationship to power? Hall's own position is as follows:

> The social distribution of knowledge *is* skewed ... the distribution of the available codes with which to decode or unscramble the meanings of events in the world, and the languages we use to construct interests, are bound to reflect the unequal relations of power that obtain in the area of symbolic production as in other spheres. Ruling or dominant conceptions of the world do not directly prescribe the mental content of the illusions that supposedly fill the heads of the dominated classes. But the circle of dominant ideas *does* accumulate the symbolic power to map or classify the world for others; its classifications acquire ... the inertial authority of habit and instinct. It becomes the horizon of the taken-for-granted: what the world is and how it works for all practical purposes. Ruling ideas may dominate other conceptions of the social world by setting the limit to what will appear as rational, reasonable, credible, indeed sayable or thinkable, within the given vocabularies of motive and action available to us.
>
> (Hall, 1988, p. 44)

In part, therefore, certain ideas become powerful not because they are illusions fostered by particular groups, but because they become the only medium available to us, and the only available conceptions circulated in newspapers, schools, the media and so on through which we can make sense of our lives. Other alternatives become literally unimaginable. It seems clear that conceptions of the family can be seen as working in this way. Certain images of family life come to act as powerful constraints on habits and expectations, not necessarily because we have been duped, but because, to a very large extent, it has become difficult to imagine and bring into being alternative ways of life.

There are some other elements to this argument about the potential power of ideas which are worth pursuing. One element concerns the way ideas become 'materialized', the other concerns questions of identity. In each case we will be forced to question what we mean by power.

It seems reasonable to make a distinction between ideas and material reality. The stuff of thought, language, conversation, the mental seems clearly distinct from the world of objects. But when we come to the study of policy and politics, certainty about these distinctions tends to disappear. One emerging consensus in work on ideology is that ideas must be seen as a material force in their own right, rather than as a secondary or insubstantial epiphenomenon, and thus as effective in moving and shaking social processes.

Ideas can be seen as material in several senses. First, the claim simply means that ideas such as the structuring idea of the nuclear family are forceful and have visible results. Ideals and images are – in register offices, churches, hospital delivery rooms, school classrooms, estate agencies and elsewhere – translated into practical actions. Second, this point about the material effects of ideology draws our attention to the way in which ideas become embodied in institutions, laws and policies. Thus we saw, for example, in sections 1.1 and 1.2 how a dominant and unquestioned idea of the 'normal family' becomes woven into legislation and into financial and other provisions, so the idea becomes inseparable from the material consequences.

Finally, ideas are material in another sense, and this is where identity comes in. Think back to the argument about false consciousness. As Hall points out, it seems rather implausible that people should organize their lives, in this case for generation after generation, on the basis of deception and confusion: 'It is a highly unstable theory about the world which has to assume that vast numbers of ordinary people, mentally equipped in much the same way as you or I, can simply be thoroughly and systematically duped into misrecognizing entirely where their real interests lie' (1988, p. 44). Hall's point is that ideology is a form of 'real consciousness' rather than 'false consciousness' and this is another reason why ideologies are so effective. The living arrangements implied in the dominant idea of 'the family' may not be in our best interests but they are nonetheless *real* to us. Ideology becomes 'real consciousness' because all the important aspects of our lives, our sense of identity, our sense of who we are, where we belong, where our interests lie, become organized through its lens.

This point becomes especially vivid in relation to familial ideology, since the notion of the family depends on and works through ideas about certain identity positions – mothers, fathers, adolescents, grandparents and so on. Now, of course, motherhood is not just an idea, it involves an obvious physical state, but in every culture 'interesting physical conditions' of pregnancy, mothering and infancy are shot through with ideas and expectations about behaviour, attitudes and practical conduct. And these structuring ideas come to be psychologically and behaviourally real and in this sense a material force.

Along with the clear distinction between the material and the mental, representation and reality, there also often goes a rather narrow conception of power. Power frequently becomes equated with physical force, coercion and the power to make someone or some object do something. It becomes defined in instrumental ways. Familial ideology can indeed have this type of coercive power. Even after the Second World War, for example, there were still cases where young women were institutionalized in mental hospitals, and defined as feeble-minded, because they had sex whilst legal minors. In this case a strongly held norm about the appropriate times and occasions for expressions of sexuality, linked to ideas about marriage and the family, were coercive in the literal sense of the word.

As some feminists have pointed out (for example Campbell, 1992), this instrumental view of power – as a capacity against others – is a view of power more often held by men than women. There is another side to power, sometimes described as expressive power, or the acknowledgment that power is also productive as well as negative. Child-rearing, for example, partly involves parents in exercising instrumental power, in directly controlling and prohibiting. But parents are also powerful in more creative and expressive ways – setting out the structures in which children live and thus influencing, one hopes in positive ways, the child's sense of who they are and what they can achieve.

Although family ideology can be directly prohibitive and instrumental, the power of ideas or family ideology can also work through the productive or expressive modes. In acting in terms of dominant ideas of the family, a person is subjecting themselves, as a child does to their parents, to a form of physical, social and mental discipline which may not necessarily be perceived as coercive since it creates new possibilities for identity and, most importantly, these new identities may be experienced as opportunities for new forms of pleasure and self-assertion. Hall, for example, points out how the political philosophy of Thatcherism, established as a dominant ideology in the 1980s, carefully worked through a set of positively imbued identities which people could imagine themselves into – for example, the respectable housewife, the worried parent, the careful manager of the household budget, the concerned patriot, the solid English citizen and so on.

To develop this analysis of power implies moving away from a model of action where the administrators of power are seen as agents – *someone* (or some group) who does something to somebody (Clegg, 1989). Instead ideas, ideologies or discourses become seen as social actors with their own sphere of autonomy in a social formation. We gain a different view of how ideas might work – fixing people in position, in ways which some see as harmful to their interests, not through prohibiting or through coercion, but through 'empowering' people to act out certain identities, ways of thinking, habits and actions.

In this section we have tried to review some of the theory behind the use of the term 'ideology', and we have presented two quite contrasting conceptualizations of how ideology works: the 'false consciousness' type of view and the account developed by Stuart Hall. The general argument that any analysis of the social processes surrounding the family must include an analysis of the power of ideas is difficult to dismiss. Social scientists disagree over the value of family life. Some, as we have seen, within Marxist and feminist traditions, want to debate the utility and function of the family. For these scholars, the concept of ideology retains its critical and negative edge. Their invocation of the concept is bound up with a critical analysis of social structures and the power relations underpinning policies and practices. But the concept of ideology is useful even for those who want to argue that the family is a functional, adaptive and highly advantageous method of social organization. In this case the study of family ideology comes to resemble the more general study of culture, values and norms. In either case the role and relative influence of ideas about the family need to be examined along with the mechanisms through which these ideas are transmitted and made persuasive.

ACTIVITY 4

You will find below some statements from various politicians. Try to answer the following questions as a means of summarizing section 3, and as a way of organizing your notes on ideology. You will find answers to these questions at the end of the chapter.

When is it appropriate to use the term ideology and when is it inappropriate? If you described statements like these as examples of ideology, what type of claims would you be making, and what points about these statements would you have in mind? On what grounds could you defend your description if challenged?

John Patten: ... just as it is the efforts of individuals which ultimately create a dynamic economy, so it is individuals who hold the key to a responsible and caring community, centred on the family.

Neil Kinnock: The whole community, the whole nation and any Governments over it therefore have a strong vested interest – as well as a clear moral obligation – in doing what it is possible to do to see that, whatever its structure, the nature of the family flourishes.

Margaret Thatcher: I believe that in the 1960s, far too many young people were ridiculed out of their true beliefs by the proponents of the permissive society who believed in precious little but themselves.

Harriet Harman: Public policy cannot alter private choices, but it can mitigate the painful effects of change.

4   SOME IDEOLOGICAL DILEMMAS: THE BOUNDARY BETWEEN THE STATE AND THE FAMILY

As social scientists have moved towards a more pluralistic, fluid and variable notion of ideology and its workings compared to earlier notions of unified class based positions, they have become more interested in ideological contradictions and inconsistency. Contradictions appear not just between ideology and 'reality' or between two ideological systems, but become apparent within the forms of dominant ideas themselves.

The social psychologist Michael Billig and his colleagues (Billig *et al.*, 1988) have argued that commonsense and the sets of ideas which inform policy and politics are typically 'dilemmatic' in nature. What they mean by this is that commonsense, the commonplaces and clichés we take for granted are frequently organized around sets of dilemmas and contrary arguments. There is not one coherent set of ideas which informs everyday practice but sets of conundrums. Our political views, including views of the family, are often inconsistent and made up of 'on the one hand and on the other hand' interpretations and arguments.

Commonsense and ideology, Billig *et al.* suggest, are a composite of, for example, both egalitarian and authoritarian strands, of arguments for individualism and arguments for collectivism; they emphasize both special professional expertise and shared knowledge, contain arguments for prejudice and for tolerance. Take, for instance, some of the commonplace maxims typically found in contemporary political discourse – 'nobody should be compelled', 'everybody should be treated equally', 'it is important to be practical and use resources wisely', 'injustices should be righted'. These maxims sum up the collective wisdom of a liberal democracy and yet they are deeply contradictory since, frequently, the demand for equality is seen to conflict with what is seen as the practical use of resources, and so on.

This final section of the chapter demonstrates that the ideas of the family constituting policy and political discourse are not immune from 'dilemmatic' thinking in Billig *et al.*'s terminology. In the end, public discourse about 'the family' needs to be seen as structured around a pervasive and difficult set of contradictions. Some would argue that it is precisely this contradictory aspect, its multi-faceted nature, which makes family ideology so resilient, guaranteeing its persistence in both private and public realms. Look, first, at this statement: 'The family is the natural and fundamental group unit of society and is entitled to protection by society and the State' (Universal Declaration of Human Rights, Article 16(3)).

This human rights declaration, whilst appearing comprehensive in its scope, highlights contemporary contradictions in social policy concerning the boundary between the public and the private, and personal and state responsibilities. For whilst the family (presumably the nuclear family) is lauded as a natural unit around which societies are structured, it is also seen as in need of protection. The question arises that, if traditional family structures are being undermined through individual choice or economic circumstance, then in what sense can they claim to be 'natural'? Equally, such definitions of the family–state relationship beg the question of where exactly the responsibilities of individuals end, and where those of the state begin.

As we have seen, the relationship between politics, social policy and family life has achieved a greater prominence in political discourse in the 1980s and 1990s. Political rhetoric has become more explicit and bifurcated along party political lines, whilst the impact of specific policies upon relationships within families has been subject to more critical analysis. Finch (1989a, p. 160) uses the concept of social engineering to explore these relationships in the context of 1980s social policy. She argues that in that decade Conservative governments overtly engaged in a number of attempts not only to question what we should expect from the state but what we can expect from each other. The Conservative attempt to shift the boundary between the state, the family and the market in the provision of welfare has been the catalyst which has once more brought these issues into the open.

The Conservatives' promotion of the family as an independent and self-reliant unit is indelibly tied up with the issue of reducing public expenditure in welfare, health and social security systems. To justify the rolling back of state welfare, it has become politically expedient to extol the virtues of traditional images of the family: as a stable unit, a private domain, as the bedrock of society. Whether families have ever existed in such an ideal form remains open to question, but the obvious implications for family members is that their claim on the state has been reduced and family dependency has been strengthened. This presentation of the family may indeed evoke strong sympathies, particularly in its insistence that family lives should be free from external control, but it fails to recognize how family life is inevitably regulated through existing social security and taxation measures and the implicit role that social policy has historically played in defining family obligations.

Finch (1989b, p. 7) describes the state–family relationship as one of 'reluctant but necessary intervention'. A central theme of British social policy has been that families, especially working-class families, do not always fulfil their natural obligations to each other and thus the state has had to intervene to ensure that those responsibilities are met. In this sense social policy also attempts to create a particular moral order. But this becomes all the more problematic when increasing numbers of people – single parents, lesbian families, step-families, cohabiting couples – have adopted ways of living which fall outside of the assumed norm. Should social policies be formulated which recognize, and respond to, such divergencies in actual lived realities or would such encouragement of 'deviants' herald a collapse of the social order? However one responds to such a question, it is clear that a recognition of family diversity not only entails questioning the ideological prominence of the nuclear family, but also raises fundamental questions about the 'natural' roles of men and women. Arguably, it is because the *fact* of diversity raises such difficult (and to some, uncomfortable) issues, that the aim of supporting the traditional family continues to command broad assent and crosscuts the conventional left–right divide in politics.

Left and right, however, are characteristically divided on what form such support should take. The state–family boundary is thus continually contested. In broad terms the debate falls in the ambit of whether the state should only provide residual support (after family provision and obligation have been exhausted) or whether the principle of citizenship provides individuals with the constitutional right to make claims upon the collective resources of the state. British social policy has characteristically tried to compromise these two positions with the result that it is replete with mixed messages. As Finch (1989b, p. 11) argues, 'The mixed messages are: the autonomy of the family must not be interfered with but as an institution it needs to be protected; the family is the "natural" unit of support, but the state must ensure that people fulfil their obligations in practice'. Governments clearly have to tread carefully because, even if the political will exists to support the family (in the Right's sense) or different family forms (in the Left's sense), their interventions must take cognizance of the imbedded cultural expectation that family life is an intensely personal and private matter.

However, whilst social policy is rarely explicit on this issue, it is possible (as we have seen) to unearth the dominant and enduring assumptions it holds about family structures and appropriate gender roles within families. Finch (1989b, p. 125) argues that British social policy has been predominantly informed by a model of the 'gendered, modified extended family'. This assumes that independent nuclear households, composed of male breadwinner and female and child dependants, are linked through mutual aid and a partial dependence on each other. Care of children, the sick and the elderly will in the first instance be the responsibility of the female or other close (usually female) relatives. The responsibility of the male is first and foremost to meet a financial obligation to support his dependants. The role of the state is assumed to be largely non-interventionist and reserved for those 'deviant' cases which need to be coerced, cajoled or directed into conforming to this assumed norm. Even though such a model may increasingly not accord with the reality of some people's lives, there is, as Finch (1989b, p. 126) concludes, 'little sign that the model of the family which has informed social policy for some years is about to be revised'.

As a result the broad issue of 'family policy' is likely to remain keenly contested. The notion of family privacy may be firmly embedded, but how far does this only serve to absolve the state from responsibility? The idea of the private may find a resonance in aspirations for individual autonomy, but does this only mask the reality of state policies – that they continue to play an important role in constituting the family in particular ways which privilege certain lifestyles and disadvantage others? By acknowledging the role of the state in selectively allocating resources through its welfare and economic policies, is it useful – even possible – to continue to talk of a private–public divide in family matters? The family is not simply a way of organizing our private lives but is a powerful symbol in politics and policy and one which sets the parameters of how we understand the world to be.

ACKNOWLEDGEMENT

We would like to thank the Family Discourse Group (Rosalind Gill, Jonathan Potter and Adrian Webb) in the Social Sciences Department, University of Loughborough, for giving us access to their collection of contemporary political and media discourse on the family, and to their analyses of this material.

ANSWER TO ACTIVITY 4

An activity like this reveals some of the difficulties of working with a concept such as ideology. First, it is clear from section 3 that different theoretical perspectives supply different criteria for defining ideology. Here we shall base our answer on the general criteria offered by Hall, stressing features which most theorists of ideology would broadly accept, even though they might want to disagree with some aspects of the proposed functions and role of ideology.

Secondly, there is the difficulty that to describe something as ideological is to involve *oneself* in the battleground of ideas. The assessment that a representation is ideological is always speculative and open to dispute; it involves values and a process of reasoned judgement. To describe something as ideological is to become involved in an argument. It is a very different kind of social scientific activity, therefore, from other kinds of research based on observing, surveying and measuring to determine the nature of a social process.

How, then, do you make a case that a statement is ideological? As noted in the chapter, you need to be able to argue that there is some connection between the ideas, images or statements you are interested in and the form of power relations in society. The connection might be uneven, unpredictable and worked out in unexpected ways. There may not be any direct connection between the idea and one, clearly defined, social and political group. But nonetheless, ideological beliefs, ideas and opinions are typically seen as those which are articulated by powerful interests to justify their position. They are ideas which contribute to what have been called 'wars of manoeuvre'.

This connection with power relations might be evident because the representations in question may legitimate and rationalize the interests of some powerful groups and generalize these interests so they appear to be in the interests of everybody. Secondly, the representations, if not actually false, irrational or logically incorrect may present a partial or one-sided account. This account may obscure other kinds of explanations. Finally, to count as ideological a representation must be collectively shared. This should not be just one person's view, but a commonly held perspective which may be part of what is uncritically taken-for-granted in society. These are usually ideas, too, which have a practical impact on people's lives; ideas which have material consequences.

How would we respond, then, to the particular statements in the activity? We would argue – obviously you may disagree – that, irrespective of whether we agree or disagree with the sentiments expressed, all these statements can be seen as ideological to some extent. Unlike weather reports or train timetables which can also be partial, wrong and over-generalized, these statements contribute significantly to a political climate and maintain different conglomerations of power. They are powerful statements, not just because they are articulated by powerful people, but because they legitimate certain courses of action and, crucially, set in place a particular context for policy-making.

To substantiate this claim, we would have to develop a counter-argument for each statement, to show what alternative view is obscured, whose interests are neglected, or the way in which the representation is partial. For instance, with Harman's statement we could question whether the public and the private are as divorced as she suggests and how her statement might help obscure the nature of state involvement in family life. With Kinnock's statement the question arises about whether family life is actually in the interests of every individual – feminists, for instance, might argue that in many cases family life is oppressive for women. Whereas the assessment that Patten's statement is ideological might be based on an elaboration of the claim that to stress the role of the individual ignores and hides the role of social structures and divisions.

It is rather misleading, of course, to focus on one-off statements which are part of much longer arguments. To characterize some material as ideological usually involves some judgement of the entire context of presentation, not just in the sense that we need to consider the rest of the speech but because we are also judging the place of these statements within a particular historical, social, economic and political period. However, we hope these examples make it clear that there are some criteria for distinguishing ideological material, that you can use the term in your written work, but that to do so, unlike some kinds of descriptions, you need to be prepared to argue a case, since ideology is often a matter of claim and counter-claim. There are, unfortunately, no uncontested or neutral standpoints for making these judgements.

REFERENCES

Alcock, P. (1989) 'A better partnership between state and individual provision: social security into the 1990s', in Gamble, A. and Wells, C. (eds).

Becker, S. and Golding, P. (1991) 'On the breadline', *Community Care*, 17 January.

Beechey, V. (1985) 'Familial ideology', in Beechey, V. and Donald, J. (eds) *Subjectivity and Social Relations*, Milton Keynes, Open University Press.

Beveridge, W. (1942) *Social Insurance and Allied Services*, Cmnd 6404, London, HMSO.

Billig, M., Condor, S., Edwards, D., Gane, M., Middleton, D. and Radley, A. (1988) *Ideological Dilemmas*, London, Sage.

Bowlby, J. (1951) *Maternal Care and Mental Health*, Geneva, World Health Organisation.

Bowlby, J. (1953) *Child Care and the Growth of Love*, Harmondsworth, Penguin Books.

Campbell, A. (1992) 'Social representations of instrumentality and male violence', Paper presented at British Psychological Society Annual Conference, Scarborough, 10 April.

Clarke, J. and Cochrane, A. (eds) (1993) *A Crisis in Care? Challenges to social work*, London, Sage/The Open University.

Clegg, S. (1989) *Frameworks of Power*, London, Sage.

Cook, J. and Watt, S. (1987) 'Racism, women and poverty', in Millar, J. and Glendinning, C. (eds) *Women and Poverty in Britain*, Brighton, Harvester.

Coote, A., Harman, H. and Hewitt, P. (1990) *The Family Way*, Social Policy Paper no. 1, Institute for Public Policy Research.

Crowther, M.A. (1982) 'Family responsibility and state responsibility in Britain before the welfare state', *Historical Journal*, vol. 25, no. 1.

Digby, A. (1989) *British Welfare Policy*, London, Faber and Faber.

Douglas, G. (1990) 'Family law under the Thatcher government', *Journal of Law and Society*, vol. 17, no. 4.

Edelman, M. (1977) *Political Language: words that succeed and policies that fail*, New York, Academic Press.

Engels, F. (1884) *The Origin of the Family, Private Property and the State* (London, Lawrence and Wishart, 1972).

Finch, J. (1989a) 'Social policy, social engineering and the family in the 1990s', in Bulmer, M. *et al.* (eds) *The Goals of Social Policy*, London, Unwin Hyman.

Finch, J. (1989b) *Family Obligations and Social Change*, Cambridge, Polity Press.

Fitzgerald, T. (1983) 'The New Right and the family', pp. 46–57 in Loney, M., Boswell, D. and Clarke, J. (eds) *Social Policy and Social Welfare*, Milton Keynes, Open University Press.

Gill, R., Potter, J. and Webb, A. (1992) 'Public policy and discourse analysis: a rhetorical approach', unpublished manuscript, Loughborough University.

Gordon, P. and Newnham, A. (1985) *Passport to Benefits: racism in Social Security*, London, Child Poverty Action Group/Runnymede Trust.

Gusfield, J. R. (1989) 'Constructing the ownership of social problems: fun and profit in the welfare state', *Social Problems*, vol. 36, no. 5, pp. 431–41.

Hall, S. (1988) 'The toad in the garden: Thatcherism among the theorists', in Nelson, C. and Grossberg, L. (eds) *Marxism and the Interpretation of Culture*, Urbana, ILL, University of Illinois Press.

Jenkin, P. (1977) Speech to Conservative Party Conference.

Kiernan, K. and Wicks, M. (1990) *Family Change and Future Policy*, London, Family Policy Studies Centre.

Land, H. and Parker, R. (1978) 'United Kingdom', in Kanerman, S. *et al.* (eds) *Family Policy: government and families in fourteen countries*, New York, Columbia University Press.

Lewis, J. (1989) 'It all really starts in the family ... community care in the 1980s', in Gamble, A. and Wells, C. (eds).

Lister, R. (1989) 'Social security', in McCarthy, M (ed.) *The New Politics of Welfare*, London, Macmillan.

Loney, M., Bocock, R., Clarke, J., Cochrane, A., Graham, P. and Wilson, M. (eds) (1987) *The State or the Market: politics and welfare in contemporary Britain*, London, Sage (2nd edn, 1991).

McLennan, G. (1991) 'The power of ideology', Unit 17 of D103 *Society and the Social Sciences*, Milton Keynes, The Open University.

McRae, S. (1991) *Maternity Rights: the experience of women and employers*, London, Policy Studies Institute.

Mitchell, J. (1971) *Woman's Estate*, Harmondsworth, Penguin Books.

Morgan, D. (1985) *The Family, Politics and Social Theory*, London, Routledge.

Mount, F. (1982) *The Subversive Family*, London, Cape.

Murray, C. (1989) 'Underclass: a disaster in the making', *Sunday Times*, 26 November.

Oakley, A. (1987) 'Gender and generation: the life and times of Adam and Eve', in Allatt, P., Keil, T., Bryman, A. and Bytheway, B. (eds) *Women and the Life Cycle*, London, Macmillan.

Pascall, G. (1986) *Social Policy: a feminist analysis*, London, Routledge.

Pilkington, E. (1991) 'Working it out', *Community Care*, 21 February.

Potter, J. and Collie, F. (1989) '"Community care" as persuasive rhetoric: a study of discourse', *Disability, Handicap and Society*, vol. 4, pp. 57–64.

Potter, J. and Wetherell, M. (1987) *Discourse Analysis and Social Psychology,* London, Sage.

Rapoport, R. (1989) 'Ideologies about family forms: towards diversity', pp. 53–69 in Boh, K. *et al.* (eds) *Changing Patterns of European Family Life,* London, Routledge.

Riley, D. (1983) *War in the Nursery,* London, Virago Press.

Scruton, R. (1980) *The Meaning of Conservatism,* London and Basingstoke, Macmillan (2nd rev. edn, 1984).

Scruton, R. (1986) *Sexual Desire, a Philosophical Investigation,* London, Weidenfeld and Nicolson.

Skolnick, J. and Skolnick, A. (1974) 'Intimacy, family and society', Boston, MA, Little, Brown.

Smart, C. (1987) 'Securing the family? Rhetoric and policy in the field of social security', in Loney, M. *et al.* (eds).

Wicks, M. (1987) 'Family matters and public policy', in Loney, M. *et al.* (eds).

Wicks, M. (1990) 'The battle for the family', *Marxism Today,* August.

Williams, R. (1973) *The Country and the City,* London, Paladin.

Wilson, E. (1977) *Women and the Welfare State,* London, Tavistock.

Zaretsky, E. (1976) *Capitalism, the Family and Personal Life,* London, Pluto Press.

CHAPTER 3
FAMILIES AND THE LAW

HILARY LAND

CONTENTS

INTRODUCTION

It is an important function of the law to provide a model of behaviour which is generally believed to be desirable. This gives people an indication of what is expected of them and a framework in which they can negotiate themselves. Thus even a provision which has only symbolic usefulness may be of some value.

(Law Commission[1], 1986, p. 106)

This statement was made in a review of law relating to children and parental responsibilities for their care and maintenance, but it is generally applicable to other areas of law. The United Kingdom does not have an explicit family policy in the sense that some other countries have, but in practice state policies do regulate family relationships. In property law, tax law, law relating to social security and pensions, inheritance law, immigration law and bankruptcy law as well as in family law, assumptions are made about the nature of marriage as well as about the responsibilities of parents for children and children for parents. Sometimes the duties and rights of other relatives are spelt out.

Of course, the law does not operate only at this ideological level, but it very directly affects people's circumstances and the resources which they have at their disposal; it may even determine where and with whom they live. Some resources are 'private', i.e. they belong to individual members of the family, and our system of *private* family law exercised in the courts allocates these when things go wrong, i.e. on desertion, separation, divorce or death of a spouse or parent. Some commentators on English law argue that the law *only* steps in when the family breaks down: 'The normal behaviour of husband and wife or parents and children towards each other is beyond the law – as long as the family is "healthy"' (Kahn-Freund and Wedderburn, 1971). However, as this chapter will show, the law may play a part in shaping definitions of 'normal behaviour' and what constitutes a 'healthy family' by depriving or withholding resources from those deemed to be deviant. This is sometimes more obvious in the area of *public* law which includes the social security and tax systems, for these allocate public resources – benefits, services and tax reliefs – and are therefore more closely and systematically controlled and scrutinized. There is a tendency in public law not to recognize the diversity of family life but to use a standardizing model – namely that a family comprises a breadwinning husband, a dependent wife and children. The regulations in the system of public law seldom allow those administering it as much discretion as magistrates and judges can exercise in the courts. Professionals sometimes have more discretionary powers although in practice doctors, social workers and teachers find that these may be severely curtailed when resources are scarce. In both private and public law 'the couple' is a heterosexual couple. This chapter will look at these standardizing models and comment on their appropriateness.

Assumptions about family relationships can be found in the legal frame-work of what is called *primary legislation* or *statutes* (Acts of Parliament) which at some point as Bills must have been debated and passed by the two Houses. There is, however, an extensive area of law which is not made by this route. There are regulations that are made by the Lord Chancellor or the relevant Secretary of State under the authority of these statutes or Acts; they include permissions and restrictions as to what may or may not be done as well as requirements on what *must* be done. Secretaries of State may also issue guidance documents and circulars explaining the regulations; they also issue codes of practice which are intended to be a statement of what is held to be good practice. The content of all these documents directly affects the manner in which the law is put into practice.

Very often, however, it is the *detail* of the legislation which impinges on people's everyday lives. This chapter will therefore examine some of the major pieces of legislation passed in the 1980s, and will look carefully for the assumptions being made about relationships between husband and wives, mothers and fathers, and parents and children. It will also study how concern about cutting public expenditure on welfare and about preserving work incentives has influenced this legislation. A close scru-tiny is needed since these details are not necessarily obvious from read-ing the relevant Act. One of the features of the Acts passed in the 1980s has been the extent to which they have been *lacking* in detail: they have become what Lord Mishcon has called 'legislative skeletons'. This com-ment was prompted during the debate on the Child Support Bill in which there were 94 regulations, only 12 of which were debated by Parliament.

This lack of detail makes it very difficult to predict what impact a change in law will have in practice on everyday life. This only becomes clear once an Act is implemented and there have been some individual cases tested in the courts; this builds up the case law interpreting the actual working of the Act.

In examining the assumptions about families embedded within the vari-ous legal frameworks, it will be seen that the assumptions made are not necessarily consistent in every respect between different areas of law; indeed the objectives of one area of law may undermine the objectives in another. This is hardly surprising given that their impact on families has never been the only factor determining their development. Moreover some laws have their history rooted in the needs and circumstances of wealthy families, others in the circumstances of the poor.

1   A BRIEF HISTORY OF FAMILY LAW IN THE UK

The origins of the systems of family law in the United Kingdom go back centuries – to feudal times and earlier. While this chapter is not, and cannot be, concerned with the history of family laws[2], it is important from the outset to note some aspects of our legal heritage because they still shape our laws today. In particular, it is useful to explain the continuing differences between the laws regulating family rights and obligations in England and Wales, and those in Scotland – and indeed most of the rest of Western Europe, now our partners within the EC.

This fundamental difference stems from the countries' divergent histories over a millenium. Until the eleventh century the northern half of Western Europe, including England, was governed largely by principles of Germanic law. Subsequently, with the establishment of the medieval feudal system, in England the King's courts, which administered common law, won jurisdiction over property and inheritance from the ecclesiastical courts. The ecclesiastical courts, however, retained jurisdiction over marriage (and retained it until 1857). A more important factor was that England was little affected by the re-establishment of Roman law which occurred in most of the rest of Western Europe, including Scotland, between the twelfth and sixteenth centuries. As a result, one of the key concepts embedded in English family law is that of 'private' property held by an individual whereas elsewhere that of 'community' property, in which ownership of property is vested in both spouses (and sometimes wider kin), held sway.

This has meant that under English law children have protected property rights, even against their parents: they controlled what they inherited, what they were given and what they earned. Against a background of the wide-scale use of money, the development of markets and an extensive system of wage labour which were all well established in medieval times in England, children could be *de facto* as well as *de jure* separate economic individuals. Given the widespread systems of apprenticeship and servanthood, many children left the parental home at an early age; once they had reached the age of majority they could enter into marriage contracts without their parents' permission. Men were free to determine who would inherit their property. Women's capacity to own, control and dispose of property was constrained by their fathers, guardians or husbands. It was in this context that, Alan Macfarlane argues, English individualism flourished (Macfarlane, 1986).

Children's obligations to maintain their parents and vice versa were weak compared with those in legal systems based on Roman Law in which the principle of reciprocity between ascendants and descendants was – and is – far stronger. English common law 'did not recognize any enforceable duty on a parent (unless he had made a contract to do so) to support his child or pay his debts or to educate it' (Finer and McGregor, 1974, p. 100). Maintenance of minor children was a common law duty only in so far as it derived from a husband's duty to maintain his wife. This could not be enforced directly under common law while the wife still lived with her husband: she could only 'pledge his credit' or, until 1978, use 'agency of necessity'.[3] Even if she left her husband, it was not until 1878 that a wife could sue for maintenance in a magistrate's court, and then only if he had severely assaulted her. It has only been possible to apply separately in a magistrates court for maintenance for the children since 1920. In Scotland, in contrast, under common law, a man had a duty to 'aliment' (maintain) his wife and legitimate children. Moreover, this obligation was – and still is – directly enforceable by them and does not arise only in cases of family breakdown 'but also in the normal current of family life' (Scottish Law Commission, 1974, p.106). The ecclesiastical court's jurisdiction over marriage, separation and divorce, which affected the propertied classes far more than ordinary families who followed custom, developed differently in Scotland from England and Wales, both before and after the Reformation.

The systems of poor relief also had very different histories in England and Wales and in Scotland. For the purposes of this chapter it is important to be aware of one of the consequences of the different development of poor relief. In Scotland, until the 1845 Poor Law (Scotland) Act there was no system of public relief for the able-bodied poor, beyond granting them a licence to beg. Other destitute people had to rely on charity organized locally. In England, a system which included the able-bodied as well as the impotent poor and which was administered by the Church parish had been established 250 years earlier. The famous statute of 1601, 43 Elizabeth, established a national system by which the public provided support for the destitute but required 'liable relatives' to reimburse the authorities. Parents and children and grandparents and grandchildren were liable relatives for these purposes. As Finer and McGregor wrote, 'One fundamental principle of 43 Elizabeth, namely the designation in the public assistance legislation of liable relatives, and the right of the public authority granting such assistance to seek reimbursement from the liable relatives, still retains its vitality in the social security legislation of today' (Finer and McGregor, 1974, p.149). The public and private dimensions of familial obligations have long been interwoven in our legal systems particularly in the law affecting the obligations which members of poor families have for each other. The Child Support Act 1991 (which will be discussed below) is the latest manifestation of the vitality of this principle.

Thus an important consideration in many areas of family law has always been to limit demands on the public purse whether this was controlled by the parish in Tudor times, local Boards of Guardians in Victorian times or by the Treasury in more recent times. Indeed, as will be discussed below, the desire not just to control but to *cut* public expenditure is a very important part of the background against which the 1980s' reviews of social security, family and childcare law took place.

ACTIVITY I

Note down the origins of the obligations of fathers to maintain children and relatives to maintain family members.

What are the main differences between the legal system in England and Wales and the system in Scotland?

---

2 THE BACKGROUND TO THE 1980s

The economic and social changes of the 1980s raised important issues concerning the law. Unemployment and the changing structure of the labour market had a profound effect on the job opportunities of young people, older workers and women and therefore on economic relationships within the family.

High levels of unemployment among young people in the early 1980s and again in the 1990s brought to the fore questions concerning the extent to which parents should be responsible for the maintenance of their children into their late teens and early twenties. One hundred years ago, parents were only required to send their children to school until they were ten and children would then make an economic contribution to the family, albeit a small one. By the time they were nineteen years of age, half of all boys and girls were no longer living in the parental household but were resident in someone else's. (Many working-class girls were domestic servants, for example.) Until the end of the Second World War, children could leave school at fourteen years of age (and half did so) and many more jobs provided accommodation than is the case today. Until 1958 conscription removed all young men in their late teens both from home *and* the labour market for at least two years. However, in 1971 the school-leaving age was raised from fifteen to sixteen years of age and from the 1970s various government training initiaitives were set up to provide vocational training for school-leavers; in the 1990s the intention is to greatly increase the number of teenagers in full-time further education.

There has thus been a trend towards young people entering the labour market later, while older people have been leaving it earlier. In 1961, 95 per cent of men aged 60 to 64 years of age were economically active; so too were nearly a third of those aged 65 years and over. By 1981 these proportions had fallen to 73 per cent and 10 per cent respectively, and by 1991 they had continued to decline to 55 per cent and 8 per cent. During the same thirty-year period, life expectancy for men and women increased by nine years.

As the boundaries of the formal labour market have been drawn more tightly, systems for spreading income and resources between one generation and another, as well as mechanisms for distributing income from wages and salaries earned while of working age over an individual's and his spouse's lifetime in the form of pensions, have become more important. The laws regulating these various systems of redistribution and the assumptions upon which they are based have therefore become of greater significance to a growing number of people. This is particularly so for older women because over retirement age they outnumber men by two to one.

Full-time employment has declined both proportionally and in absolute numbers (there were 2.5 million fewer full-time jobs in 1990 than in 1960) and there has been an increase in part-time employment: in 1992 more than one in five of all employees work fewer than thirty hours a week compared with one in twenty, forty years ago. As the manufacturing sector has dwindled (by 1989 there were two million fewer jobs than in 1979) and the service sector has expanded, traditional job opportunities for men have disappeared and opportunities for part-time employment for women have been created. These changes raise questions about the model of the family which assumes that economic support is, and indeed should be, provided by a single, male breadwinner. In other words the dramatic changes which have occurred in the pattern of paid work for men and for women raise very important questions about the rights and responsibilities arising from marriage and, increasingly, cohabitation.

However, the increasing incidence of divorce followed by remarriage has also raised important questions about the responsibilities a husband has towards both a current and a former wife, even after death. Three-fifths of all divorces involve dependent children and it is now estimated that before their sixteenth birthday one in four children will experience the divorce of their parents. Many of these will then experience a period of living with their mother alone, followed by a period living with one natural parent and a step-parent. This also raises the question of how the rights and responsibilities for children should be shared between natural parents and step-parents.

In particular what should be the rights and responsibilities of fathers compared with those of mothers? Until 1886 the father had exclusive rights and authority over his legitimate children for he was their 'natural' guardian and women had no independent rights during marriage. In fact it was nearly another century before the Guardianship Act 1973, under which mothers were granted the same rights to custody of their children as fathers. However, the practice of the divorce court judges in the 1970s and '80s was to award custody to the mother when the marriage ended: in 1987, 82 per cent of custody orders were for sole custody, 74 per cent being a sole order to the mother (Brophy, 1990, p. 220). To some this looked like discrimination against fathers, particularly as access rights whether given to fathers or mothers are difficult to enforce. There was pressure to re-examine the position of the non-custodial father, increased by research that showed that half of all non-custodial fathers had lost all contact with their children within two years of the divorce (see, for example, MacLean and Wadsworth, 1987).

The rights of fathers in relation to their illegitimate children also began to be scrutinized. The increase in the numbers of births taking place outside of marriage increased from 8 per cent in 1971 to 13 per cent in 1981 and accounted for 28 per cent of all live births in the United Kingdom in 1990. Historically mothers have had sole custody over their illegitimate children and until the Guardianship of Minors Act 1971, natural fathers could not even attempt to claim custody of their child(ren). They have, however, always had an obligation to maintain them and in Scotland this was – and is – shared with the mother.

ACTIVITY 2

Should there be any distinctions between the rights and responsibilities of parents who are married and those who are not legally married but may be cohabiting? If so, what should these be?

Developments in reproductive technology have separated biological and social parenthood for mothers as well as for fathers, in ways which were not possible for previous generations. These also pose fundamental questions concerning the custody, care and maintenance of children and the legal definitions of motherhood and fatherhood.

At the other end of the life-cycle, a greater number of people are surviving to very old age: the number of people over the age of 75 years increased by 40 per cent in the 1980s. Many of them live independent lives, but some require considerable support in the form of both services and income. In 1948 the National Assistance Act abolished the duty placed on adult children centuries earlier to maintain their parents should they cease to be capable of self-support and become dependent on public relief. Does the law in other ways still assume children could and should support their infirm parents?

In periods of rapid social and economic change it is not surprising that laws regulating family life are subject to revision and review. The 1980s were no exception. The law relating to social security, income tax, childcare, child custody, guardianship, illegitimacy, divorce, inheritance of family property, and reproductive technology were all subject to major reviews and changes.[4]

Moreover, in addition to the changes outlined above, at the end of the 1970s a government was elected in the UK which was committed to 'rolling back' the state. It challenged the view which had had a major influence on many social policy developments during the previous thirty years, namely that the state should provide services and benefits to people by virtue of their citizenship, rather than because people were poor. It was argued instead that the state was providing too much, thereby creating a culture of dependency and apathy among those who used state welfare services and benefits. Worse, such high levels of public expenditure required levels of taxation that stifled initiative among the enterprising and able members of society. Our economic prosperity was therefore threatened. In this new view the state should only step in when individuals, through no fault of their own, could not meet their own needs out of their own earnings or by support from their families. In other words, the model of state welfare informing social policy debates during the 1980s was what Richard Titmuss many years ago termed the 'residual model' which replaced the 'universalistic model' of previous decades (Titmuss, 1974, p. 31). Paradoxically such a view may lead to policies which, while aiming to reduce public expenditure, require more intervention by the state in the family as, for example, certain obligations to maintain are enforced. This will become very clear when we discuss the Child Support Act passed in 1991.

ACTIVITY 3

Think about the main differences between social and biological parenthood. List your reasons for and against all fathers having regular contact with their biological children. What do you think the rights and responsibilities of fathers should be?

---

3   THE FRAMEWORK OF PRIVATE FAMILY LAW

Since the early 1970s there have been major changes in the framework of private law governing the relationship between spouses both during marriage and after it has ended. There have also been major reviews within the areas of public and private law of responsibilities of parents for children, culminating in the Children Act 1989, the Criminal Justice Act 1991 and the Child Support Act 1991. In addition to the demographic and social changes outlined in the previous section, these reviews were influenced by concern to reinforce the responsibility of parents for their children, whether this be providing adequate discipline, care or financial support. At the same time growing evidence of physical and sexual abuse of children occurring *within* the family raised the question of whether the state's powers to intervene in family life were either sufficient or were being appropriately used. The debates surrounding the reviews took place against the background of a government determined to constrain public expenditure and to encourage greater interdependence between family members and heavier reliance on private or occupational provision. Not surprisingly, therefore, although the legal framework within which families live their lives has been simplified in some respects, there remain some major unresolved contradictions.

Before discussing the changed legal framework, it is important to note that the changes made in the 1980s did not have a uniform impact on all families. Young, childless couples can now divorce easily and, having made a 'clean break' with the old relationship, can move on to a new one. 36 per cent of all marriages in 1990 were remarriages for one or both parties. Men are three or four times as likely to remarry as women. In contrast couples with children, although able to end their marital relationship, cannot choose to end their responsibilities as parents. Their responsibilities to the children of their first marriage are presumed to take precedence over any stepchildren acquired in a subsequent marriage. Unless couples with property or assets can agree the division between them, they still face uncertainty in the courts. The English law still operates with the concept of individual property rights which may be modified by the judge's evaluation of each spouse's contribution in cash, kind or services to the marriage; this is modified by judgements about their conduct towards each other and, if there are any children, decisions about the division of future responsibility for childcare. Scottish law is clearer about the division of matrimonial property and assets because it is based more closely on the concept of 'community property' as will be discussed below.

Immigrants who are settled here are, of course, subject to the same laws governing marriage and divorce although a marriage made lawfully in their country of origin will be recognized. (This means a polygamous marriage contracted in a Muslim country is recognized as lawful although it could not legally be contracted in the United Kingdom.) However, recent immigrants may find it more difficult to marry and establish a family at all in the UK than was formerly the case because of changes in the immigration laws. The British Nationality Act 1981 means that children born after 1983 are no longer automatically British citizens: their citizenship depends on the citizenship or settled status of their parents.

3.1   IMMIGRATION LAWS

Immigration laws which determine an individual's citizenship and the right to transmit that citizenship to a spouse or children were reviewed and amended in the 1980s. Citizenship gives rights to hold property, to vote and to take part in public affairs. Until 1948 a British woman marrying a foreigner lost her *own* citizenship, although a foreign wife of a British man automatically acquired British citizenship. A woman was expected to follow her husband and not vice versa. The Immigration Act 1971 required a female British citizen to prove that she would suffer exceptional hardship if she were to live in his country before her husband was allowed into the UK to live with her. The law has subsequently been modified and, under the British Nationality Act 1981, British citizens who have at least one grandparent born in Britain (i.e. mainly white women) have the right to bring in a foreign husband, but they must be able to establish that the marriage is not for the primary purpose of settlement – a test aimed at 'arranged marriages': 'Women are seen by the legislators purely in relation to men, not as individual people; either as passive "dependants"… or as agents being used by (black) men in order to

Husband overturns 'primary purpose' rule on marriage

Euro-court punches hole in migrant laws

Clare Dyer and John Carvel

HOME Office rules which restrict the entry of foreign husbands of British women were declared unlawful by the European Court of Justice in Luxembourg yesterday.

It ruled that the restrictions breach European Community rules on the free movement of EC nationals between member states. The decision has far-reaching implications for Britain's immigration laws and deals a blow to the "primary purpose" rule, under which the Home Office refuses husbands the right of abode if it deems the main purpose of the marriage was to gain the right to live in Britain.

The ruling means that foreign husbands and wives of British nationals will be able to circumvent the primary purpose rule by taking up temporary residence with their spouses in another EC state before coming to Britain.

A Home Office spokeswoman acknowledged that a big loophole had been opened. Under what she described as a worst case scenario, it might be possible for a British citizen to arrange to marry a non-EC national after a very brief stay elsewhere in the EC.

The case ends a four-year battle by Surinder Singh, an Indian national, to stop his deportation from Britain after his marriage to Bradford-born Rashpai Pureval broke down in 1987.

Mr Singh claimed protection from deportation under the Treaty of Rome and a 1973 EC directive which says EC nationals moving to another member country have automatic rights of residence in that country with a spouse and any children.

The couple, who have a seven-year-old child, married in Bradford in 1982 and worked in West Germany from 1983 to 1985, when they returned to Britain to set up a business. In 1986, Mr Singh was given leave to stay in Britain as the husband of a British national, but the Home Office cut short his leave after his wife obtained a divorce decree nisi in July 1987.

Mr Singh's appeal against a deportation order was dismissed by an immigration adjudicator in 1989. But the Immigration Appeal Tribunal allowed his appeal against that decision, holding that he had a right to stay under EC law as the spouse of a British citizen.

The Home Secretary challenged the tribunal's ruling in the High Court, which referred the question to the European Court of Justice.

The European Court ruled yesterday that member states must allow rights of entry and residence to foreign spouses of their own citizens who accompany them to another EC country to work.

To rule otherwise would deter citizens of EC states from going to other member countries to work, the judges said. The rights of free movement under the Treaty of Rome could not be fully effective if EC nationals were deterred from exercising them by obstacles raised in their country of origin to the entry and residence of their spouses.

But the judges said the rules could not be used to evade national laws and member states would still be allowed to take measures to tackle fraud.

Before the judgment, the Home Office had started moves to relax the primary purpose rule. Earlier this year it sent confidential guidance to immigration officers to admit people who had been married for at least five years or who had one or more children with right of abode in the UK.

Max Madden, Labour MP for Bradford West, said this change was an attempt to avoid criticism after the Surinder Singh judgment. During the general election, the Conservatives had represented Labour's plans to get rid of the primary purpose rule as "an open door immigration policy". Yet within weeks of being returned to office the Government relaxed the rules.

A Home Office spokeswoman said the changes were in response to earlier European Court judgments and had nothing to do with the Surinder Singh case. She could not give estimates of the numbers affected. According to the latest official statistics, immigration officers at New Delhi, Bombay, Dhaka and Islamabad refused 1,280 husbands, wives, fiancés and fiancées in 1990 because they failed to pass the primary purpose test. Another 1,040 were refused partly for this reason.

Mr Madden said he feared the authorities would now switch to refusing people on grounds that they had inadequate financial support or accommodation.

● The Home Secretary, Kenneth Clarke, agreed last night to publish a draft agreement on EC immigration policy which ministers had previously insisted must remain confidential. In an interview last week with the Guardian, he was asked to justify withholding EC draft conventions until they had been signed by ministers from all 12 member states and could no longer be amended by Parliament.

He claimed ignorance of the restrictions and promised to investigate. "I am amazed that British ministers have been allowed to get away with it for so long." Mr Clarke agreed to place a copy of the draft convention on European frontier control in the Commons library.

Figure 1

Source: *The Guardian*, 8 July 1992

come to this country to work' (Joint Council for the Welfare of Immigrants Conference, quoted by Atkins and Hoggett, 1984, p. 186). Neither the tax nor the social security system any longer recognizes the responsibilities a recent immigrant may have towards any legitimate children living in their country of origin. Indeed, as will be described in a later section, their own rights to social security have been severely curtailed since 1985. At the same time people settled here have had difficulty bringing their own children into this country becuase immigration officers refused to believe they were their children. (DNA testing has eased this problem.) The European Court ruled in July 1992 that some of the Home Office rules restricting the entry of foreign husbands of British women were unlawful: see Figure 1.

3.2   MARRIAGE AND DIVORCE

The Matrimonial and Family Proceedings Act 1984 ended the lifelong obligation – placed on men centuries earlier by common law – to maintain their wives. It also enabled couples to petition for divorce after one year rather than three years of marriage. The concept of 'a clean break' was introduced to determine the divorce settlement, the aim being to enable each spouse to be self-sufficient as quickly as possible. For example, a husband may be required to maintain his ex-wife only while she acquires a qualification or retrains in order to improve her earning capacity. Since the Divorce Reform Act 1969 it has not been necessary for the 'innocent' spouse to prove that the other is guilty of a matrimonial offence, such as adultery, cruelty or desertion. Instead it is necessary to show that the marriage has broken down irretrievably. This is established with evidence of separation of two years (if both partners agree the divorce) or five years (if one partner does not), unreasonable behaviour, two years desertion or adultery. Three of these are matrimonial offences and providing evidence for them may not seem very different from establishing one spouse guilty of a matrimonial offence. Is the break with the past as complete as may appear at first sight?

Women use unreasonable behaviour as grounds for seeking divorce more frequently than men; working-class women use it more often than middle-class women. This does not necessarily reflect different tolerances between men and women towards certain kinds of behaviour but does indicate differences in access to economic resources. The use of separation as grounds for divorce requires that one spouse is able to find and pay for alternative accommodation. This became harder in the 1980s when both private and public rented sectors declined (by a total of nearly three million dwellings) and mortgages became bigger and more expensive. As the English Law Commission pointed out,

> This situation is exacerbated at present where local authorities are unable or unwilling to rehouse parties until there is a divorce decree or other injunction. Paradoxically, the advent of secure tenancies in the public sector ... has made it more difficult for local authorities to

reallocate the tenancy between them. Even if this could be changed, the general housing shortage is likely to prejudice certain categories of spouses far more than others and this has caused the sole separation ground to work in a discriminatory way.

(Law Commission, 1988, p. 178)

Their proposal to make separation the *sole* grounds for divorce (as in New Zealand or Australia, for example) would create difficulties for poorer families, and more difficulties for women than for men. This is an example of how public policies can interact with private law to the detriment of some groups although the general intention – in this instance to strengthen tenants' rights – is a socially desirable one. As we shall discuss later, in the 1980s the social security rules changed in ways which undermined attempts to improve the level of private maintenance paid to lone parents.

The Law Commission's proposals, published in 1990, which would have allowed a couple to divorce after one year's separation, provided they could agree about the key aspects of the divorce settlement, were not acceptable to the Lord Chancellor, Lord Mackay: 'There are some people who feel that some form of matrimonial fault should still be at the root of all law' (quoted by Edwards and Halpern, 1992, p. 113). The fear seems to be that without the concept of fault, wives – who already initiate three-fifths of petitions for divorce – will display an even 'greater propensity to divorce their tiresome and dull but innocent spouses' (Gibson, 1991, p. 339). If there are no children, the husband's liability to maintain his wife is very limited, but if there are children, as a result of the Child Support Act 1991 it could be significant. During the debates on the 1969 Divorce Law Reform Bill it was feared that 'innocent' *wives* would be the main losers as a result of the clause which allowed a spouse to divorce his or her unconsenting partner after five years' separation. In 1988 one and a half times as many wives as husbands used this clause. This is used by those on the new right as evidence that life outside marriage is becoming too attractive to women.

The consultation document on divorce published in December 1993, *Looking to the Future: Mediation and the Ground for Divorce*, takes a slightly different approach in its review of the processes and arrangements for divorce. As the Chancellor said in the foreword: 'I believe that a good divorce law will support the institution of marriage by seeking to lay out for parties a process by which they receive help to prevent a marriage being out-lived' (Lord Chancellor's Department, 1993, p. *iii*). It is clear that the government is considering a substantial reduction in the role of the courts and access to publicly funded legal advice (legal aid, which currently five out of six women petitioning for divorce use) and offering instead mediation services. The grounds for divorce would still be irretrievable breakdown of marriage but a minimum of twelve months would be needed in which to demonstrate this, as well as to settle practical questions about the children, home and finance. There would be a family mediation service to assist in this process, the aim being to avoid resorting to the traditional adjudication through the courts. While this may help to save some marriages and reduce ill-feelings about spouses, it may mean that women do not obtain such good advice about an appropriate property settlement. Issues concerning access to the equity in and use of the matrimonial home are bound to be contentious in the light of the Child Support Act 1991.

3.3 MATRIMONIAL PROPERTY AND ASSETS

> Family property law is one of the least precise areas of the law. On divorce, much of the eventual allocation of the assets of the marriage is left to the discretion of the courts and the law has little to say about who should own what within a marriage ... [T]he law ... has not yet caught up with the reality that women working outside the home are now the norm, that one-third of first marriages end in divorce, and that the value of assets particularly homes and accumulated pension rights, owned by ordinary people is now quite large.
>
> (Freedman *et al.*, 1988, p. 4)

This was how the Institute of Fiscal Studies introduced a recent discussion paper on property and marriage. They proposed that all property, including debts and pensions, *acquired* during the marriage would be divided equally on divorce or death, unless there are special circumstances to justify a different division. This is similar to the system incorporated into the Family Law (Scotland) Act 1985 in which 'fair sharing' of assets, responsibilities for the support of children and any economic *dis*advantages arising from the marriage is the starting-point for making any decisions about the division of matrimonial property. It is in effect a system of community of acquisitions. (The others being *universal* community, i.e. anything acquired before as well as after the marriage is shared equally, and *deferred* community of acquisitions, in which the increase during the marriage in the value of each spouse's property is shared equally when the marriage is ended.)

Before the passing of the Married Women's Property Acts during the 1880s, the English system was based on *individual* property rights. However, as women once married did not exist as legal individuals, on marriage a wife's personal property and income became her husband's, although his ability to dispose of her property was often limited in the interests of preserving the property for the children. Over the years the courts have exercised discretion and to some extent modified a husband's individual property rights. This is very clear in inheritance law, where since 1925 the balance has been shifting in favour of widows at the expense of the deceased's heirs. The Inheritance (Provision of Family and Dependants) Act 1975 strengthened the rights of the surviving spouse to make claims on the deceased's estate. It also allowed relatives and cohabitees to claim, provided they could establish they had been dependent on the deceased. As Ruth Deech has commented: 'Taken overall, the rules give effect to a concept of inheritance dominated by dependency, not by kinship, and certainly not by title or free disposition' (Deech, 1984, p. 250). This reduces demands on the public purse and, as residential care becomes more expensive, the equity in older people's houses is likely to be used to pay for this care rather than to be passed on to their children.

Divorce law is not clear-cut and the Child Support Act 1991, while reducing the uncertainty of levels of maintenance for children, may have increased uncertainty in relation to the division of matrimonial property. It will certainly make 'a clean break' more difficult to achieve because it makes it less likely that a husband will be willing to give up once and for all any claims on the matrimonial home in return for lower or no maintenance to his ex-wife who is caring for his children. During the 1980s the courts encouraged once-and-for-all property settlements. The Family Law Reform Act 1987 which strengthened the parental status of unmarried fathers also enabled them to make a once-and-for-all capital settlement on the child in cases where the father wanted no further relationship with that child. The philosophy of the Child Support Act is quite different; it was summed up by Lord MacKay thus: 'There can be no question of a clean break between parents and children' (House of Lords Debate, 25 February 1991).

One feature of the husband's common law obligation to maintain was that it was always conditional on the wife's behaviour. For example, until the Domestic Proceedings and Magistrates Courts Act 1978, a single act of adultery relieved the husband of any common law obligation to maintain his wife although his obligation towards his children remained. The absent parent's obligation to maintain contained in the Child Support Act 1991 presumes the other parent is doing the *caring* by definition, but no other aspect of her (or his) behaviour will modify his (or her) responsibilities. However, the division of matrimonial property, and in particular the allocation of the use or ownership of the matrimonial home, a power which remains with the divorce courts, has become, if anything *more* dependent on the divorce court judge's evaluation of the wife's behaviour, not so much in respect of her sexual fidelity – provided she is heterosexual – but more in respect of her past caring responsibilities and her willingness *and* suitability to continue them in the future. (For a discussion of custody rights for lesbian mothers refer back to Chapter 1, Figure 2.)

It would seem that the views of Lord Denning whose judgements in the area of family law have been influential over the past thirty years, still informs current practice, although it is justified in terms of consideration for the welfare of the child(ren) – a requirement that has been a part of divorce legislation since 1959. He said: 'Some features of family life are elemental in our society. One is that it is the husband's duty to provide his wife with a roof over her head and the children, too. *So long as the wife behaves herself*, she is entitled to remain in the matrimonial home' (Denning, 1980, quoted by Deech 1984, p. 259; emphasis added). Since Watchel vs Watchel in 1973, in which the Court of Appeal awarded the husband two-thirds of the value of the matrimonial home and an income two-thirds of the couple's joint income, in English courts the starting-point for the division of matrimonial property has been one third to the wife, not half as in Scotland.

The allocation of pension rights on divorce is a different matter altogether, although they may be as valuable as the matrimonial home. The state pension scheme only provides a widow's pension to the former wife if she was divorced over the age of 50. Currently neither the English nor the Scottish courts have access to occupational or personal pension assets held in funds, so they have no power to split pensions rights as in Denmark or Germany, for example. Edwina Currie's advice to women is: 'You want a pension? Stay married, or pay for your own' (Currie, 1990, p. 238). In the circumstances this is sound advice.

ACTIVITY 4

If a woman decides to leave her husband, what difficulties might she face over:

(a) moving into local authority housing;

(b) staying in the matrimonial property; and

(c) securing pension rights?

In what ways would she be in a better position if she lived in Scotland rather than England or Wales?

3.4   PARENTAL RESPONSIBILITY

The Children Act 1989 emphasizes the importance of promoting the welfare of children. To this end the concept of parental responsibility is of paramount importance. Parents individually and jointly must maintain, care for and protect their children from abuse or neglect and control their behaviour. Parents are not free to give up these responsibilities even if their marriage ends. Children not only have the right to know who their parents are but, as the Lord Chancellor explained, 'the right to *contact* with the parents is the right of the child. The child's interests require that in the vast majority of cases. That is the philosophy on which the Children Act is based' (House of Lords Debate, 25 February 1991, col. 302; emphasis added).

In contrast to the Child Support Act 1991 in which the female pronoun is used to denote the caring parent and the male pronoun the absent parent, the Children Act 1989 contains ungendered parents with whom children must share their time. The objective is that parents should come to their own agreement about sharing care. If they cannot agree, the courts can now order that parents share the care of a child and can grant each parent a resident order. However, the reality remains that mothers pattern their

employment around childcare, whereas fathers do not – and neither public law nor their employers expect them to do so. Substantial changes in employment practices and public provision would be necessary for parents to share the care of children less unequally than is currently the case – assuming they wished to do so.

Parental responsibility for children under 16 has been further emphasized by the Criminal Justice Act 1991. Failure to attend without a good reason a court hearing involving a child can result in the parents being fined. Section 55 of the Act requires a court to order the parents to pay the child's fine unless the parent '"has not conduced" to the commission of the offence by neglecting to exercise due care.' In addition the court must order a parent to be bound over to take proper care and exercise proper control over the child. If the parent refuses, then again he or she can be fined. Such emphasis on parental responsibility is based on the view that delinquent behaviour is more a product of bad parenting than of social or economic factors.

4   SOCIAL SECURITY

4.1   DIRECTIONS OF CHANGE

Public expenditure is at the heart of Britain's present economic difficulties.

(Treasury, 1979, para. 1)

Cutting public expenditure was one of the main objectives in reforming social policies. The social security system was a prime target because in 1979 it accounted for 26 per cent of all public expenditure. In the 1970s it had been subject to major review and the Beveridge principle of a flat-rate benefit in return for a flat-rate contribution had been replaced by an earnings-related scheme funded by earnings-related contributions levied on earnings up to one-and-a-half times male average earnings. However, in 1982 sickness and unemployment benefits lost their earnings-related supplements, together with additional allowances for dependent children. The basic insurance and assistance benefits also became taxable and were no longer automatically uprated in line with inflation. Pension rates were pegged to the *lower* of either the increase in prices or in earnings, not the greater as Barbara Castle had intended. Pensioners therefore did not necessarily share in rising standards of living enjoyed by those of working age. The use of the benefit system as a means of redistributing resources towards poorer people in society and of narrowing the gap between the generation in paid work and the generation who had retired was thus restricted.

The redistributive potential was also limited by allowing the more highly paid worker to opt out of the State Earnings Related Pension Scheme

(SERPS) and instead to pay a lower contribution for the basic pension only and contribute to an occupational or private pension scheme. In other words, the resources generated from those able to pay higher contributions is used to pay those *individuals* higher pensions and are not available to boost the pensions of those only able to pay a low contribution. Changes were also made to the means-tested Supplementary Benefit system, in particular making the rules relating to additional allowances more restrictive.

The 1986 review of social security downgraded the contributory insurance schemes still further. In particular the gains made for women while Barbara Castle was Secretary of State for Social Services in the mid-1970s were lost. Barbara Castle recognized that most women did not have the same employment patterns as men and this had to be taken into account if they were not to be disadvantaged in old age. Women – and men – had their rights to the basic pension protected while they were looking after children or a sick or infirm person. Moreover, the formula used for calculating SERPS was based on earnings over the best *twenty* years and not a forty-year working life. A spouse could inherit the whole of the SERPS entitlement of the deceased spouse, although in the case of a widower he had either to have been retired or economically dependent upon his wife at the time of her death.

In 1985 the government tried to abolish SERPS but not even the pensions industry wanted to take on large numbers of poorly paid workers, who were mainly women. Instead the government modified it so that now the earnings-related addition to the basic state pension is calculated on earnings over the whole working life instead of the best twenty years. This disadvantages those who have periods of part-time employment or reduced earnings because of their caring responsibilities. Spouses can now only inherit half instead of the whole of their partner's SERPS.

The model of the family embedded in the Beveridge Report had been modified. In the 1970s for the first time married women who contributed on the same basis as their single sisters received the same benefits (previously they had received a *lower* sickness or unemployment benefit in return for the *same* contribution). The option to rely on their husband's contributions for a retirement pension instead of contributing directly to their own began to be phased out. In other words, marriage did not automatically create a dependent wife. Contribution conditions were tightened in the 1980s so that sufficient contributions for unemployment, sickness or maternity benefits have to be paid over *two* years instead of one year as was previously the case and incomplete contributions no longer qualified for a reduced benefit. Those deemed to have left their jobs 'voluntarily' or who have been dismissed have to wait longer before being eligible to claim unemployment benefit: from the beginning of the scheme in 1911, the 'waiting period' had been *six weeks* and this remained the case until under the 1986 Social Security Act it was extended to thirteen weeks in 1988; in October 1990 it was extended to *six months*. In other words, in less than ten years from the time when women became members of the National Insurance scheme in their own right instead of as dependants of their husband, the scheme was substantially devalued. This applied to both short-term benefits and to pension entitlements. As a result married women ill, unemployed or pregnant are likely once again to be dependent on their husbands.

At the same time more and more women have fallen outside the contributory scheme altogether. As National Insurance contributions increased to make up for the reduction in the Treasury contribution to the insurance 'fund' – from 18 per cent in 1979 to 13 per cent in 1983 and 5 per cent in 1988 and *nothing* in 1989 – there was an incentive for both employers *and* employees to keep their earnings below the level at which contributions become payable. More and more part-time workers, mainly married women, have earnings too low to pay contributions to become members of the National Insurance scheme – 2.25 million in 1991 (Lister, 1992, p. 27). This has particularly severe consequences for women as access to means-tested Income Support to replace or supplement inadequate contributory benefits depends on whether or not the claimant is married or cohabiting. This means that women have no claims on the state when they are pregnant, sick or unemployed, unless they live alone. If they are married or cohabiting they cannot turn to the means-tested scheme now called Income Support. Thus, although the formal rules do not discriminate against women in the way the system prior to 1975 did, the *outcome* of these changes is highly disadvantageous to women and forces them to be dependent upon their male partners.

However, partly as a result of the 1978 European Community directive on equal treatment, which required member-states to treat men and women equally in their social security systems, the rules were changed in 1980 to allow for the possibility of a female breadwinner. Studies had shown these were rare, for the more common pattern was *shared* breadwinning. So, the traditional model was modified slightly: if women behaved like men and their husbands stayed at home they could claim Supplementary Benefit (Income Support since 1988) on behalf of themselves and their families but a family could have only *one* breadwinner. The marriage relationship recognized by the benefit system remains an unequal one.

In addition to cutting public expenditure and supporting a 'traditional' model of the family, the government also wanted to end what was called 'the benefit culture'. It was feared that the social security system gave people a choice about whether or not to accept a job, particularly if the wages were low. Thus people were pricing themselves out of the labour market because their expectations of wages were 'unreal', and so unemployment levels remained high. The government therefore wanted to use the social security system as a means of imposing discipline on working people in general, and on family men and young people in particular. This is very evident from the changes proposed to the benefit system in 1985, although in the case of benefits designed to support families with children, the government were not able to implement the new scheme quite as they wished, as we shall see below.

ACTIVITY 5

What major changes were made in the 1980s to contributory insurance schemes and how have these changes increased women's dependence on men?

4.2   FAMILY MEN WITH CHILDREN

The government in the early 1980s had placed increasing emphasis on means-tested benefits for families with the breadwinner on a low wage and had allowed the real value of Child Benefit to fall. The government would have liked to have abolished Child Benefit which is paid for all children irrespective of the marital, employment or income status of their parents. Changing a costly universal benefit into a selective one would have considerably reduced the social security bill: in 1986–87 Child Benefit cost £4.5 billion, compared with less than £1.5 billion for means-tested allowances paid to low wage earners with children (in the form of Family Income Supplement, now Family Credit) and for children in families on Supplementary Benefit (now Income Support). Targeting benefits for children on families in most need would also have been consistent with their view that children are the private responsibility of their parents, and their fathers in particular, unless they are poor or inadequate in some way. However, Child Benefit turned out to be more popular than the government had supposed. Moreover they were not able to implement Family Credit, which replaced Family Income Supplement (FIS), in the way that they had intended.

Family Credit, like FIS, pays a supplement to low wage earners based on the number of children in the family. Unlike FIS it is based on net income rather than gross income, thus reducing the marginal tax rates facing families whose earnings increase; in other words, families do not lose such a high proportion of every extra pound earned. Moreover, unlike recipients of FIS, families receiving Family Credit do not qualify for free school meals and welfare food: the 1986 Social Security Act restricted these to families on Income Support. This, it was argued, 'will prevent families in nearly all circumstances from facing a position in which there is little or no financial benefit to be gained *from continuing in lower paid jobs'* (DHSS, 1985, vol. 2, para. 4.53; emphasis added).

In the 1985 reviews the government also proposed that Family Credit would be paid by the employer into the father's wage packet. In contrast FIS had always been paid by order book, usually to the mother. This, it was argued, would 'offer significant advantages for employers in ensuring that employees perceive more clearly the total net remuneration they receive rather than earnings net of tax and national insurance alone' (DHSS, 1985, vol. 2, para. 4.50). During the health-workers' strike in the early 1980s, Ministers had learnt that Child Benefit did not diminish demands for a 'family wage' (i.e. a wage large enough to support a wife and children) because it made no difference to the man's take-home pay. Later on during the miners' strike it was clear that Child Benefit and free school meals were used to cushion the effect of the strike and its after-math on miners' families. The advantage of paying Family Credit through employers meant that it could be withheld when the father was on strike. The proposed Family Credit was therefore very clearly as much an instrument for improving labour discipline as for protecting the wel-fare of children.

In practice, many small employers did not want the trouble and expense of administering the scheme. During the final stages of the Bill their organizations, together with the women's lobbies and the poverty lobby, were successful in getting the government to agree to administer Family Credit in the same way as FIS. The take-up of Family Credit (actually introduced in April 1988) remains low – less than 50 per cent – in spite of big advertising campaigns.

Child Benefit was not uprated until 1991 when, for the first time, the Chancellor of the Exchequer committed the government to reviewing it on an annual basis. The government saved £140 million in 1988–89 by failing to uprate Child Benefit and a further £210 million in 1989–90 (House of Commons Debate, 16 March 1990, col. 808). Despite this, and although they may be far from satisfactory, benefits for children were not devalued as substantially during the 1980s as the government had intended.

4.3 YOUNG PEOPLE

Child Benefit is paid for all children until the age of 16, or until 19 years of age if they are still in full-time education. Since the 1940s those who left school and became unemployed had been entitled to claim social security benefits – either an insurance benefit if they had paid contributions for a year or a means-tested benefit. They were not expected to be completely financially dependent on their parents. However, during the 1980s benefit for young people became a public issue.

First, pressure was exerted by demographic changes. The birth rate in the United Kingdom had peaked in 1964 when there were nearly a million births, compared with around three-quarters of a million annually throughout the 1970s. This large cohort of young people were coming onto the labour market in the early 1980s at a time when unemployment was rapidly rising. By the summer of 1983 it was clear that the Treasury favoured cuts in young people's benefits. There were nearly three-quarters of a million unemployed people on benefit and living with their parents. It was estimated that £300 million could be saved if benefits for unemployed young people were 'targeted' on those whose parents were also in receipt of benefit. This meant that parents would recieve an allowance for their unemployed teenage child in addition to their own allowances (in the same way that they received additional allowances graduated by age for any dependent child). Parents not on benefit would receive nothing.

The advantage to the government was not just the immediate saving of £300 million. By removing an entire group from eligibility to claim benefits, it would be easier in future to remove other groups. As *The Times* commented in August 1983, such cuts, as well as being real ones, provided the opportunity 'more important for the long run, to establish the viobility of basic social benefit and do it for a group over which the political screams will not be too loud' (quoted by Allbeson, 1985, p. 86), i.e. to show that even benefits regarded as fundamental to the scheme could be devalued or abolished.

Moreover, the selection of young people as the thin end of the wedge, intended to be driven in further at later stages to reduce the scope of the social security system, was consistent with the government's view of the family. Sir Keith Joseph said, 'In as much as personal responsibility has been eroded by a shift of housing, education and welfare provision excessively to the state, we are going to shift that balance' (*The Guardian*, 19 February 1983). When a year later the government removed the rent contribution for teenagers on benefit, the Secretary of State commented, 'A young person without a job, on Supplementary Benefit will often be living in a household with parents who will not need to look to him for a contribution towards housing costs' (quoted by Allbeson, 1985, p. 86). At the same time, it was assumed *employed* teenagers would contribute *more* towards their parents' rent. The deductions from housing benefit for contributions from 'non-dependents' was increased; 850,000 families with a young unemployed, disabled or pensioner relative living at home had their housing benefit reduced in 1985 as a result of this change.

Those young people who left home in search of a job were equally a cause for concern and their rights to claim board and lodging allowances from the Supplementary Benefit system were reviewed. At the end of 1984, 70 per cent of the 163,000 claimants of board and lodging were claiming because they were unemployed. Half of them were aged between 16 and 25 years (Audit Commission, 1986). Thus public concern was focused on these young people who, it was claimed, were having seaside holidays at the taxpayers' expense. Ministers were reported to 'have been shocked by tales of jobless youngsters removing to cheap winter lettings at holiday resorts to enjoy a life of doubtful morality at the State's expense' (*Sunday Times*, quoted by Allbeson, 1985, p. 88).

Controls were introduced in 1985 and young people's rights to claim board and lodging allowance in a particular locality were limited to two, four or eight weeks according to area; if they could not find a job they were expected to move elsewhere or – preferably – return home. Failure to do so resulted in their benefit being substantially cut or stopped altogether. At the same time, their ability to set up an independent household was being reduced in other ways. For example, in the early 1980s furniture grants for Supplementary Benefit claimants were restricted to families: single people could claim only in 'exceptional circumstances'. Ministers justified this by saying that, without this restriction, 'The family unit would not be encouraged. It would instead encourage people to move away from the family after the slightest argument and would be costly' (Rhodes Boyson, quoted by Allbeson, 1985, p. 89).

The Social Security Act 1986 introduced further restrictions on young people's benefits. For the first time the means-tested benefits system differentiated between claimants over and under 25 years of age. Those under 25 years of age were deemed not to 'need' as much benefit as older claimants because they were more likely to be living at home. Moreover, it was believed that benefit levels were discouraging young people from accepting jobs at rates employers were willing to pay. Young people had priced themselves out of the labour market. As Professor Minford, one of Margaret Thatcher's economic advisers, said reflecting on the Youth Training Scheme (YTS) and the Social Security Act 1986: 'The whole object of these schemes from an economic point of view is to drive down wages. If they don't drive down wages there is no job creation' ('The Welfare Revolution', *File on Four*, Radio 4, 9 February 1988).

From September 1988, 16- and 17-year-olds could *only* get means-tested assistance if they took a place on an Employment Training Scheme (the successor to YTS), except when it would cause 'severe hardship'. There was no possibility of being able to claim contributory unemployment benefit because, since April 1988, contributions have had to have been paid for *two* years. The benefit received (in 1989–90 £29.50 for 16-year-olds and £35.00 for 17-year-olds) was too low to enable them to live independently except with extreme difficulty.

Meanwhile the government was attacking young people's wage levels in other ways. In 1986 the government abolished the jurisdiction of Wages Councils over workers under 21 years of age and limited their task to setting minimum basic hourly and overtime rates. This, together with the erosion of young people's benefit entitlements discussed above, the Department of Employment believed encouraged 'more realistic levels of youth pay' (Department of Employment, 1988, p. 27). Between 1979 and 1986 the gap between the earnings of young workers and adults widened: from being 60 per cent of average adult pay they fell to 54 per cent. The Employment Act 1989 repealed the restrictions on hours of work for 16- to 18-year-olds, thus opening up further possibilities for exploiting young people.

Changes in the housing market during the 1980s have also increased young people's dependence on their parents. During the 1980s the number of dwellings available for rent from local authorities and New Town Corporations fell by 1.5 million, representing a reduction of 20 per cent of the stock. Young single people were rarely eligible for housing from local authorities but, as a result of the shrinking of this sector, they now faced stiffer competition – and higher rents – in the private sector. The size of this sector has declined too and this, coupled with deregulation, resulted in increased rents. Between 1979 and 1987 the number of rented dwellings in the private sector fell by 1.3 million (Raynesford, 1990, p. 194). Not surprisingly the number of homeless people, including a significant proportion of young people, grew dramatically in the 1980s. Shelter estimated that 150,000 young people experience homelessness every year (Bradshaw, 1990). The Department of Environment explains this by stating: 'A major cause [of homelessness] has been the increase in the number of households *wanting* to live separately due to relationship breakdown and the younger age at which people *choose* to leave home' (Department of Environment, 1991, p. 83; emphasis added).

Nevertheless the government, under considerable pressure from many charities and pressure groups, had to recognize that not all homeless young people left home by choice. While in the 1970s physical abuse of children became a public issue, fuelled by a number of public enquiries into the deaths of young children at the hands of their families (usually their stepfather or father), in the 1980s evidence of sexual abuse surfaced and could not be ignored. For some children the family home is a very dangerous place from which some children need to escape. The evidence that these runaway youngsters were at risk not only of destitution but of being forced into prostitution, drug-dealing or thieving just to stay alive was too strong to be ignored completely. In July 1989 young people 'genuinely estranged' from their parents were added to the list of those school-leavers eligible to claim in their own right for a maximum of 16 weeks. At the same time young people in night shelters were 'automatically' considered for claims of 'severe hardship' and payments made by local authority social service departments were disregarded in assessing benefit entitlement.

The Children Act 1989 requires local authorities to 'advise, assist and befriend' young people leaving care. This is important for these youngsters because they are particularly at risk of becoming homeless and comprise a significant proportion (as many as a third) of those who do so (see The Children's Society, 1987, p. 2). However, if local authorities do not have sufficient resources, this provision of the Act will not improve their situation in practice. Research conducted prior to its implementation (October 1991) shows that despite the slightly relaxed eligibility rules for benefit, many young people are not receiving the income they so desperately need.

The following case-study examines the experience of Steven, a 17-year-old who had been thrown out of his home by his mother and new boyfriend and subsequently became homeless; below he describes how he feels trapped in a system which offers no escape even though he has followed the 'rules'.

ACTIVITY 6

Looking at the above evidence, trace the effects of the current legislation on a 16-year-old school-leaver seeking employment.

Now read the case of Steven and add to your notes some comments about his likely future.

Do you think cuts in benefits to young people will improve the economic prosperity of the UK in the long run?

What view do you think Steven is likely to have of policies whose stated objective is 'not to make people dependent but to enable them to stand on their own feet, independent and free in their choices' (Tony Newton, Minister for Social Security, addressing a Barnados Conference 'Perspectives on Poverty', February 1991)?

STEVEN

Steven is 17 and is currently homeless. He is doing a YTS course in printing which pays him £29.50 a week. When Steven left school at 16, he got a labouring job, earning £75 to £80 a week. He paid £20 of this to his mother towards his board and lodgings. However, when he lost his job after three months: 'They kicked me out ... I didn't get on, always fighting with me mum's boyfriend'. He went to the local social services office and was found board and lodgings accommodation. This was before the social security regulations for 16–17-year-olds changed in September 1988, so he was able to claim income support: 'I just said that they'd kicked me out and I'd no money, nowhere to live, so I just started signing on. I got a (social fund) crisis loan of £111. That were until I get me first Giro through. Then it were £136 a fortnight'. (This was after deduction of £3 for the Social Fund loan repayment.) Steven paid £90 a fortnight for his board and lodgings, which left him with less than £20 a week to buy all his 'dinners, clothes and stuff. It were hard'.

Steven did not get on with the landlady and left after three months. He stayed with friends for a few nights and then went to a nearby town where he found bed and breakfast accommodation: 'It were a dive, there were holes in the walls, stuff like that.' By this time the income support regulations had changed and Steven was no longer able to claim while unemployed: 'They wouldn't let me sign on in [town], it were too late, so I have to leave that bed and breakfast. It were nearly two weeks after I's moved in, so I had to move straight out. Then I came to [city] ... I were hoping to go to London or summat'.

Steven tried to obtain a hostel place but was refused because he was under 18. He then found a place in a furnished rented house owned by a Housing Association: 'It were like a house for two of us, fully furnished, £40 a week rent but we had to buy all our food'. Steven also found himself a place on another YTS course – general catering this time – which meant that he was also able to claim income support and housing benefit on top of his YTS allowance to cover his rent and living expenses. Unfortunately he had no help with budgeting and quickly got behind with his rent: 'If I got it fortnightly, I'd spend it all in the first few days. I wouldn't have anything then for the rest of the fortnight ... I tried to pay my rent first, then I went out and bought my food for the week, then what I had left was for myself'.

After about three months, having failed to pay off his rent arrears, Steven had to leave the house. He returned to the town near his parents' home. He started yet another YTS course and found another bed and breakfast place, again claiming income support to 'top up' his YTS allowance and cover the bed and breakfast charges:

> Then I left that and went to a board and lodgings. Then with the new [April 1989] rules in board and lodgings, it were £45 board and I had to pay £22 out of £29.50 [YTS allowance]. There were my bus fares to YTS and I ended up with £4.50 a week.

This amount had to cover Steven's lunches during the week, clothing and any personal items. He was completely unable to survive financially, had to leave the board and lodgings after six weeks and returned to the city, where he found yet another YTS place. When he was interviewed for the study, he had no spare clothes as they had all been stolen on the train back to the city; he had only 18p to last till he collected his YTS allowance the following day; and he was staying in emergency temporary accommodation until a vacancy in a hostel became available.

Steven did not feel that his experience of claiming social security had been at all positive:

> They just tell you you can't have nothing ... sometimes you just get sent away, they tell you you can't have owt ... Some of the questions [they ask] are hard – 'Where've you lived? How many rooms is there in the place you're living? All the people's names who's living there? ...' The staff just give you a hard time ...

Steven is aware of the discretionary provision for 16–17-year-olds to claim income support to avoid 'severe hardship', but thinks,

> [I]t takes too long to come through, so you're still left with nothing. It could take months ... They've got to send off to London, stuff like that. [I applied] when I was living in [town] first time, when I weren't on a YTS and I was getting no money, and I didn't hear nowt from it ... Social Services, I went down there and they told me to go for a hardship claim, told me what to say, but I still didn't hear nowt from them.

Steven also believes that the 1989 changes in regulations for board and lodgings claimants now preclude the possibility of any help from the social fund: 'They won't give you [a loan] if you're on YTS, you're earning a weekly wage. It's housing benefit now, you can't claim anything from the social'.

In the long run, Steven hopes to:

> Settle down, get a nice place. Get a proper job. A place of me own would be better [than a hostel] but I can't get one till I'm 18 because I haven't got a guarantor ... another 11 months. Council flats, they just won't give you it; and now with the new [IS] rules landlords don't like to take in people under 25.

The effects of the last year have been serious:

> You're knackered all the time. Can't be bothered to do owt. Because sometimes I won't have food for a few days, stuff like that. No money ... I've had all these YTSs and I've moved around to different ones ... four ... It leads to crime as well, no money ... attempted burglary ... just couldn't get any money from anywhere ... Everything's bad, I've just not got money for myself, to go out or anything.

Source: Craig and Glendinning, 1990, pp. 22–3

4.4   LONE MOTHERS

While benefits for families and young people attracted the government's attention in the early and mid-1980s, those for lone parents were not thoroughly reviewed until the end of the decade. By this time the large increase in the numbers of lone parents *and* the disproportionate increase of those among them dependent on state benefits were causing concern. By 1987, 14 per cent of all families with dependent children were headed by a lone parent (generally women) compared with 9 per cent ten years earlier. Even more worrying to a government committed to reducing public expenditure, a growing proportion were dependent upon state benefits. In 1979, 322,000 lone parents were receiving means-tested Supplementary Benefit on behalf of themselves and half a million children; this represented half of all lone parents. By 1989 this had doubled to 644,000 lone parents with over a million children; this represents two-thirds of all lone parents. As a result, the cost of income-related benefit payments to lone parents more than doubled during the 1980s: from £1.4 billion in 1981–2 to £3.2 billion in 1988–9 (1991 prices) (House of Lords Debate, 25 February 1991, col. 775). Conversely, the proportion in paid employment had fallen during this period so that the labour force participation rate of lone parents is now *lower* than that of married mothers. This reverses their relative positions in the 1970s. Their rate of employment is one of the lowest for lone mothers in Europe.

While there is some evidence that divorce rates are stabilizing and divorces involving children are even falling (OPCS, 1991), the numbers of lone mothers who have never married are increasing. The number of births taking place outside of marriage grew rapidly in the 1980s – from 11 per cent in 1979 to 27 per cent ten years later. Until 1960 the percentage of births outside marriage throughout the country had remained around 5 per cent (with the exception of the two World Wars). Among teenagers, over three-quarters of births took place outside marriage in 1989; overall, however, the number of children born to teenage mothers has declined, reflecting the fall in the numbers of women who marry and have children while in their teens.

The third worrying trend for the government was the decline in the proportion of lone parents receiving maintenance from the absent parent. In 1981–82 half of lone parents on benefit received some maintenance, but by 1988–89 this proportion had fallen to less than a quarter (DSS, 1990, vol. 2). Research conducted towards the end of the 1980s found that maintenance accounts for less than 10 per cent of the total net income of lone parents, compared with 45 per cent from Income Support and 22 per cent from net earnings (Bradshaw and Millar, 1991). The DSS was only recovering a small proportion of the cost of benefits from those liable to maintain lone parents – £126 million in 1988 (DSS, 1990, vol. 2).

Some interpreted this as evidence of an increase in irresponsibility among men – an irresponsibility encouraged by the benefit system itself and potentially dangerous for society. Charles Murray, whose ideas were influential among the new right in the United States in the 1980s, was listened to by Mrs Thatcher and those advising her on social policies (discussed in section 2.1 of Chapter 2). He said: 'If a young man's girlfriend doesn't need him to help support the baby, it makes sense to have some fun – which in turn makes hustling and crime more attractive, marriage less attractive' (Murray, 1990, p. 31). However, others pointed to the cuts in social security staff in general, and in 'liable relative' officers who were responsible for tracking down absent fathers, in particular. Both the National Audit Office and the Public Accounts Committee attributed the decline in maintenance payments in part at least to the reduction in the resources the DSS was spending on recovering maintenance during the 1980s (National Audit Office, 1990, p. 7 and Committee of Public Accounts, 1990, p. *vi*).

Clearly, then, whatever the cause of the problem something had to be done to reduce the dependence of lone parents – and lone mothers in particular – on state benefits.

LONE MOTHERS AND THE LABOUR MARKET

There was evidence from research studies that three-quarters of lone mothers receiving income support wanted to take up paid work at the time or at some point in the future (DSS, 1990, vol. 2). However, changes made to the social security system during the 1980s had made it harder, rather than easier, for lone parents to remain in contact with the labour market while on benefit. Prior to the 1986 Social Security Act, lone parents could earn £12 a week *net* of childcare and travel expenses before their benefit was reduced. Since the Act was implemented in 1988, the earnings take no account of work expenses and it is the level of *gross* earnings which affects the level of income support. (This was £15 a week until the Autumn 1991 upratings when it was increased to £25.) At the same time the number of hours it was possible to work while still claiming Income Support was reduced to a maximum of 24 hours, and the number of hours of employment necessary to be eligible to claim Family Credit was reduced to a minimum of 24 hours. From April 1992 these limits were changed to 16 hours for *all* claimants, not just lone parents.

It is clear that one motive behind these changes is to make it easier to combine some paid work with the care of children, without the government having to spend more on childcare provision. As the White Paper states,

> Many parents, including lone parents, work 24 hours or more a week and would wish to do so. However, there are others for whom the best or only practicable combination of work and child care is to work for less than 24 hours. For example, this would make it possible for them to take the children to school in the mornings and be free to collect them from school in the afternoons.
>
> (DSS, 1990, vol. 1, para. 6.7)

The government's view throughout the 1980s was that childcare arrangements are the responsibility of parents. As Mrs Thatcher said in an interview with a women's magazine in 1989, 'Women make their own arrangements now and they can carry on doing so' (*She*, February 1989, p. 54).

There are, however, other advantages in such a system to a government determined to keep low both wages and the associated labour costs to employers. Employees who work for fewer than sixteen hours fall outside the scope of employment protection legislation, including rights to maternity and redundancy pay. During the 1980s the proportion of part-time employees working fewer than sixteen hours a week increased: in 1979, 30 per cent of manual workers and 23 per cent of non-manual workers worked fewer than sixteen hours a week; by 1988 this had increased to 41 per cent and 32 per cent respectively.

These changes in the social security system are likely to reinforce this trend for, while lone mothers (since April 1992) can move off Income Support and on to Family Credit, once they work more than sixteen hours a week there may be considerable disadvantages to them if they do so. First, they will lose free school meals, free prescription charges etc. and those responsible for a mortgage will no longer have any of their housing costs met: Housing Benefit paid to those on Family Credit only includes those in *rented* accommodation. Second, and for the 46 per cent of lone mothers whose youngest child is under 5 years this is very important, Family Credit, like Income Support, does not take account of childcare expenses which almost certainly will be higher, the longer the hours worked. This is currently being challenged in the European Court on the grounds that this rule disproportionately affects lone mothers and is therefore discriminatory (see Figure 2).

Heather Joshi in an analysis of the obstacles which constrain lone mothers' employment opportunities, concluded: 'Making childcare expenses allowable in the calculation of means-tested benefits could be a tremendous help towards making full-time employment a viable option. One way to make part-time employment a worthwhile opportunity would be to have a larger maximum payment on Family Credit and a lower minimum hours condition' (Joshi, 1991, p. 146).

Since Joshi completed her analysis the minimum hours for Family Credit have been reduced, as discussed above; the only other positive steps taken by the government was to disregard up to £15 maintenance (from April 1992) and to announce (in November 1993) a disregard for childcare expenses limited to a maximum of £28 per week. Meanwhile the other barriers against lone mothers participating in the labour market remain high. Joshi calculated, using 1986–87 figures but taking into account the reforms of the 1986 Social Security Act, that:

> ... with the exception of some very low levels of part-time earnings on Income Support, there is no fundamental gain from employment unless the job offers more than £125 per week. This range of earn-

ings accounts for the lower half of the full-time female earnings distribution, in other words, the woman would have to be at least in the top half of the potential wage distribution to gain any cash at all from paid work.

(Joshi, 1991, idem.)

Some employers, in particular those who rely heavily on homeworkers, will benefit from having a group of workers trapped below a low earnings or hours threshold. However, the system as it stands does not offer an escape from dependence on means-tested benefits via the labour market.

Mother takes benefits battle to European court

Clare Dyer
Legal Correspondent

Benefit rules which leave single parents with child care costs worse off working than jobless will be challenged in the European Court of Justice in Luxembourg today.

Patricia Cresswell, aged 40, brought the case, which affects thousands of lone parents, after discovering she was £10 a week poorer working part-time than relying solely on state benefits.

She is accusing the Government of indirect sex discrimination in refusing to allow her to deduct child care expenses from her earnings when calculating her top-up benefit.

Mrs Cresswell, from Exeter, took a job as a graphic designer at Exeter University in 1988, claiming income support to top up her earnings. The rules allow the first £15 of earnings to be disregarded, after which benefit is reduced pound for pound. But a childminder for Mrs Cresswell's younger son, Toby, then two, cost £25 a week.

Mrs Cresswell, who is backed by the Child Poverty Action Group, took her case through the social security system. In 1990 the case reached the Court of Appeal, which referred it to the European Court of Justice.

Her lawyers will argue today that the income support rules indirectly discriminate against women and breach EC directives on equal access to employment and equal social security treatment for men and women.

Some 812,000 single parents are on income support, 96 per cent of them women. Nine out of 10 lone parents caring for children are women.

Mrs Cresswell, who has since given up work after developing cancer, said she was continuing her fight to help other single parents. Before income support replaced supplementary benefit in April 1988, child care expenses were deductible in calculating benefit.

Penny Wood, a solicitor with the Child Poverty Action Group, said the Government should change the rule in line with European legislation.

A judgment is expected in the summer.

Figure 2

Source: *The Guardian*, 13 March 1992

LONE MOTHERS AND MAINTENANCE

It could be argued that the government's intention was not in fact to encourage mothers back in to work; the main focus of the government's concern was to get the absent parent to pay more maintenance. In other words, the intention of the changes is to reduce women's dependence on the state by increasing her dependence on the father of her children. As we shall see in the discussion below, absent fathers are not only obliged under the Child Support Act 1991 to maintain their children – an obligation firmly rooted in the centuries old common law – but also their mothers, as carers of their children *irrespective* of their marital status. The government denies that this represents a major break with the past but the father of a child born outside marriage has not previously been under any direct duty to support the mother. Indeed, in Victorian times it was thought to be very undesirable for a woman to have *any* claims on a man for maintenance, even for her children, *unless* she was married to him. As one of the Poor Law Commissioners wrote in the Annual Report for 1840:

> What shall we say to the infringement of the exclusive privileges of the married state implied by the conferring on the mother of a bastard that claims for its support from a definite father, which it is one great object of matrimony to secure? Does not the principle that anything short of marriage is sufficient to fix the paternity of the child involve in itself a direct attack on that institution?
>
> (quoted in DHSS, Report of the Committee on One Parent Families (The Finer Report), Cmnd 5629, vol. I, 1974, p. 118)

It is difficult to see in practice what the difference is between paying maintenance to a mother and paying her for caring. The Lord Chancellor attempted to explain the difference to the House of Lords like this:

> I should also make it clear that, although the formula contains an element to take account of the costs of looking after a child, this in no way represents spousal maintenance. A child, particularly a young one, needs to be looked after, either by the lone parent herself or by someone else. That care costs money, either directly to the paid carer or by the caring parent. It is absolutely right that those costs should be taken into account since they are directly caused by the existence of the child. In no way can they be considered to be spousal maintenance.
>
> (House of Lords, 14 March 1991, col. 343)

If the Lord Chancellor is right, then it is difficult to justify deducting up to 20 per cent from the *personal* allowance received by the lone parent herself, because neither the rates of benefit for adults nor for children have ever been based on what it costs to *care* for children over and above feeding them and clothing them. Arguably the family premium and lone-parent premium recognize in part the caring responsibilities of parent(s) but in 1991 these totalled just £11.45, and it is not proposed to deduct an amount from *this*.

Before examining the provisions of the Child Support Act in more detail, it is worth looking at some of the changes made in the social security system and family law since the end of the 1970s. Women's claims to means-tested benefits have been gradually modified in an attempt to reduce the cost to the state of supporting lone mothers. Because those changes have been made gradually and were 'concealed beneath the turgid prose characteristic of most social security legislation' (Bryan, 1991, p. 59), they have attracted little comment and debate.

Prior to 1979, maintenance payments for children affected the level of dependency additions included in the Supplementary Benefit paid to the parent but they did not affect the parents' *own* entitlement. In other words, if maintenance for the children was sufficiently high, the parent would receive no Supplementary Benefit in respect of *their* needs but her (or his) own benefit was unaffected. However, in 1979 the rule was changed. This had the effect of reducing or even extinguishing the parents' *own* entitlement to Supplementary Benefit if the father was willing and able to pay more generous maintenance payments. This forced women to be dependent on their children and thus indirectly on the father of their children, even though the marriage was over. Thus changes in family law, such as those embodied in the Matrimonial and Family Proceedings Act 1984, which placed increased emphasis on the welfare of the children in maintenance settlements in divorce, were negated for those dependent on state benefits by the operation of the social security system. As we have seen, the proportions of lone mothers receiving maintenance while on benefit declined during the 1980s. Is that so surprising, given not only the reduction in liable relative work described above but also that the payment of maintenance could do *nothing* to improve their standard of living as every pound of maintenance paid resulted in a pound lost in benefit? It would seem that by emphasizing a father's *public* duty to reimburse the state for maintaining his children, his *private* duty to maintain his children was being undermined.

More generous maintenance payments do, of course, help the lone parent in paid employment and perhaps it is not surprising that research studies conducted throughout this period have continued to show a positive correlation between the payment of maintenance and the mother being in paid employment (Bradshaw and Millar, 1991).

The Social Security Act 1990 went further than the previous legislation by extending the relationships covered by the liable relative procedures which allow the DSS to recover Income Support paid. Prior to October 1990, the following relationships were included:
- a spouse was liable in respect of Income Support paid to his or her spouse;
- a parent was liable in respect of Income Support paid for his or her children irrespective of whether the child was born within marriage.

Ex-husbands and ex-wives were not liable except in so far as it was paid to an ex-spouse for their children.

The 1990 Act inserted a new Section 24A into the Social Security Act 1986 which meant that a former spouse could be liable not only for the Income Support paid for the children but also for the Income Support paid for the maintenance of the parent with the care of the children. It also applied to *unmarried* parents if a maintenance order was in force in favour of one or more of the children or the parent (an unlikely situation).

There are circumstances, however, in which a mother has allowed a main- tenance order to lapse because, for example, attempts to enforce it have created difficulties over the arrangements for access to the children. So although the Social Security Act 1990 did not give the Secretary of State the power to *initiate* an application for a maintenance order, it gave considerable discretion to the DSS officers to reactivate orders; this dis- cretion – if used insensitively – could engender considerable hostility.

The Child Support Act 1991 has even wider powers and the Secretary of State now has the power to initiate an application for a maintenance order, even if the claimant wishes to have no further contact with the absent parent. In the White Paper, *Children Come First* (DSS, 1990) which set out the main features of the proposed legislation, the govern- ment only envisaged allowing mothers to refuse to name the father of her child(ren) if 'the child has been conceived as the result of rape, or where there has been incest' (para. 5.36). Otherwise her refusal to co-operate in the enforcement of a maintenance order against the father would incur a penalty of a reduction of 20 per cent in her benefit. The penalty still stands (the House of Lords removed the penalty but the House of Com- mons reinserted it) but such was the opposition to the narrow range of circumstances in which it was legitimate for a mother to refuse to be forced into dependence on the father of her children, the Act does recog- nize a slightly wider range. Section 6(2) of the Act states that the Sec- retary of State will not take action to recover child support maintenance from the absent parent where there are:

> ... reasonable grounds for believing that
>
> (a) if the parent were to be required to give that authorization, or
>
> (b) if she were to give it,
>
> there would be a risk of her, or of any child living with her, suffering harm or undue distress as a result.

Similarly Section 46(3) of the Act states that the child support officer, before serving notice requiring compliance, must consider these risks when the mother has failed to comply even though the Secretary of State has required action to be taken. A great deal therefore will depend on how sensitively child support officers exercise their very considerable dis- cretion. Bradshaw and Millar's study found that one in six of divorced and one in ten of single and separated mothers on benefit gave violence as the main reason for leaving the father of their children, so the penalties incurred by the mothers – and their children – if the child support officers interpret Section (6) too narrowly, may go far beyond financial ones.

During its passage through Parliament there was concern about the possible negative impact on the welfare of lone mothers and their children, in particular the requirement that they name the fathers of their children and penalizing them with a cut in a benefit if they refused without a 'good cause'. There was also concern that payment of maintenance would leave parents and children on Income Support no better off because any increase in maintenance paid would result in an equivalent reduction in benefit. Nevertheless there seemed to be widespread public acceptance of the principle that parents should provide realistic financial support for their children whenever possible. While lawyers were concerned about splitting the determination of maintenance from the system dealing with other financial aspects of divorce into an administrative agency with an extremely limited appeals mechanism, they welcomed the reduction of uncertainty which the application of the formula would bring to their clients.

In its first year the Child Support Agency has attracted enormous media attention, often featured in front-page headlines and much of it highly critical. Hate mail and death threats have led to round-the-clock security at its regional offices. On the day of the Agency's first anniversary, wreaths were laid outside the home of the chief executive, Ros Hepplewhite, because six suicides have, unofficially at least, been attributed in part to the Agency's dealing with fathers faced with increased bills for maintenance. There is an active and vocal campaign against the Child Support Act. By the autumn of 1993 there was sufficient concern for the House of Commons' Social Security Committee, which examines the expenditure, administration and policy of the Department of Social Security and its associated public bodies, to examine its operations. Following its report in December, some aspects of the formula were modified and a further review of the Agency's work was announced the following April.

The complaints arising from the application of the formula for calculating maintenance which received most media attention came predominantly from fathers already paying some maintenance and/or still in contact with their children. There are several reasons for this. As Ros Hepplewhite told the Select Committee:

> 'I think there was a lack of awareness about the nature of the new arrangements. Certainly we had a great deal of coverage about the concerns of parents with care. We also had a great deal of coverage … about "run-away fathers". In reality, the new arrangements affect *all* fathers.'
>
> (Social Security Committee, 1993, p. 19; emphasis added)

Those fathers who did not see themselves as 'runaway' or 'absent', did not expect to attract the attention of the CSA. When they did, they were very angry at having to pay substantially increased levels of maintenance, particularly as they felt the formula was far too crude in a number of respects.

There was resentment that the legislation was being applied retrospectively and thus overturning agreements made in court. 'Clean break settlements' were ignored and fathers who had given up their share in the equity in the matrimonial home or had borrowed money in order to secure a home for their former wife and children, in return for reduced maintenance payments, were outraged to be faced with large assessments. Those who saw their children regularly were angry that expenses connected with visiting children or having children visit were ignored by the formula and some decided they could no longer afford to maintain contact with their children. Those with second families found that their standard of living was sharply reduced because the cost of maintaining stepchildren and a second wife are ignored in the formula whether or not the absent father is actually maintaining his second family. They and their new partners felt second families were being treated unfairly compared with first families. There was particular resentment at having to pay £44 to 'the parent as carer', particularly as this continues until the youngest child is 16 years – an age well beyond that which prevents a mother from taking paid employment. (In fact any earnings of the parent with care are taken into account and reduce the amount of maintenance paid.)

The anger of this group of fathers was fuelled by the belief that they were 'soft targets'. The government had set the CSA the task of saving £530 million in their first year by increasing the amount of maintenance paid to lone parents on benefit and thus reducing the benefit paid. Moreover Ros Hepplewhite was on performance-related pay and it was widely believed that CSA staff received bonuses on the basis of the amount of maintenance recovered. The anger spilled into the media on 13 September 1993 (*The Guardian*), when an internal CSA memorandum was leaked to the press: 'The name of the game is maximizing the maintenance yield. Don't waste a lot of time on non-profitable stuff.' In her evidence to the Select Committee Ros Hepplewhite admitted that a year before the CSA began its work, it was agreed 'that the absent parent who currently paid should be given priority' (Social Security Committee, 1993, p. 8). However, she went on to say that they were only a quarter of the group the CSA was dealing with in their first year because the majority of cases being dealt with were people newly claiming Income Support or Family Credit. By the end of their first year the CSA were aiming to have one million cases and in 750,000 of those maintenance would be payable although some of the assessments would not be made until 1994–95. There has been far less publicity from the 11,000 lone mothers who have stopped claiming Income Support because, say campaigners, they want to avoid contact with violent fathers or from the 1,000 women involved in difficult paternity suits. However, as the CSA goes back through long-standing cases in which no maintenance is being paid, these groups can be expected to grow. It will be interesting to see whether the media will give them as loud and sympathetic a voice as they have given middle-class fathers.

The Child Support Act 1991 is attempting to achieve a major cultural change and, as Ros Hepplewhite has said,

> '[This] does mean that many people will be affected by these changes and that a fair proportion of them will perceive that they are affected by these changes adversely because it will actually cost them more to maintain their children than in the past.'
>
> (Social Security Committee, 1993, p. 21)

Here she is referring mainly to the impact on fathers. However, the changes reflect much more than a government's wish to reduce public expenditure and to make men pay more. They have raised central issues concerning women's and children's claims on the state as citizens in their own right; the balance between a man's private duty to maintain his children and his public duty to reimburse the state for doing so; the dichotomy imposed by the legislation between maintenance (used to define fatherhood) and care (which defines motherhood) and the constraints placed on the trade-off between the allocation in divorce of family property and claims to maintenance previously exercised in the courts.

ACTIVITY 7

Examine the details given about lone mothers, employment and childcare. What economic problems might a young lone mother face in trying to combine employment and childcare?

Using this section and your notes on Activity 2, explain why some mothers would prefer not to rely on former partners for financial support.

In what ways don't the Social Security Act 1990 and Child Support Act 1991 support the financial independence of women?

4.5 IMMIGRANT WORKERS

Another group of workers affected by the changes in the social security system in conjunction with other changes in the law are members of minority ethnic groups. In their case the government is not so concerned to support a particular model of the family: the changes in the immigration laws already discussed suggest that the right of spouses to live together and with their children is rather lightly regarded. Rather it appears that the UK is developing a system of guest-workers. The rights of some immigrants, although lawfully settled here, are limited by the system of sponsorship. The Social Security Act 1986 confirmed and increased these limitations. Children, elderly parents and other relatives entering the UK may be sponsored by a relative already living here. If they have entered either under the terms of the Immigration Act 1971 or after May 1980, the sponsor is liable to maintain them. The 1986 Act sets no time limit on that liability and makes it very clear that the sponsor will continue to be liable to maintain them, thus excluding them from eligibility to claim Income Support and probably Family Credit too. The immigration rules introduced in August 1985 explicitly included Supplementary Benefit in the 'public funds' on which sponsored immigrants should make no demands.

The scope of the sponsorship system was also extended. Foreign fiancé(e)s and spouses are admitted to the UK on condition that they make no claims on public funds either before the marriage or for a period of twelve months. They are usually given indefinite leave to stay after twelve months but each remains liable to support the other and their dependants. This can make it extremely difficult for a young wife to leave a violent husband. In other words, although lawfully living here, those who originally came under the sponsorship system will be treated differently from the rest of the population and the more benefits that become means-tested and discretionary, the greater the difference will be. There is already evidence that black claimants may be required to produce additional information such as a passport to confirm their British citizenship. There is also liaison between the DSS and Home Office if there is any doubt about that status.

5 CONCLUSION

It has not been possible in the space of one chapter to go through every area of private and public law which contain within them assumptions about family relationships and responsibilities. Many more could have been discussed. For example, the United Kingdom introduced a system of independent taxation in 1990 but that does not mean that all assumptions about family life have disappeared – the Married Couples Allowance continues to exist, for instance. The legal framework which determines women's and men's access to reproductive technology also contains assumptions about 'normal' fatherhood and 'normal' motherhood (see, for example, Warnock, 1984). Many of the judgements made about domestic violence do so (see Dallos and Foreman, 1993), although the courts are beginning to recognize rape within marriage as an offence.

This chapter has shown that the interaction of different aspects of private and public law is often complex and their impact on different members of families may be contradictory. Nevertheless some assumptions have persisted. In particular, men are still expected to provide financial support for their children *and* the mothers of those children. What has changed is that this is so even if there has never been a legal relationship between them. Conversely, women are expected to be dependent upon the fathers of their children: the law both in principle and in practice discourages mothers from achieving independence of men either via the labour market or via the benefit system. Women's status as mothers rather than as wives now affects their access to state benefits. In the past the converse was the case.

The level of resources available to local authorities and central government departments (such as the DSS) affects the extent to which the different systems can respond flexibly to the varying circumstances in which people actually live their lives. An overriding concern of government in the 1980s was to cut public expenditure on welfare. Another overriding concern was to sustain work incentives, particularly of men and young people, and so the benefit system has been used quite deliberately as an instrument to drive down wages. As a result, those dependent on state welfare have less choice about how they live their lives – with whom they live and the work they do. The law both reflects and attempts to sustain certain patterns of behaviour and responsibility within families. It remains to be seen whether the reforms of the 1980s accord with men's *and* women's expectations, experience and ideas of fairness. If they do not, these changes in the law will not have the intended outcomes.

NOTES

1 The Law Commissions were established in 1965 to advise the government on law reforms. There is one for Scotland and one for England and Wales.

2 Some useful studies of the history of family law include appendices by Finer and McGregor, another Scottish Law Commission in Finer Report (1974) *Report of the Committee on One Parent Families,* vol. 2, Cmnd 5629, London, HMSO; Holcombe, L. (1983) *Wives and Property,* University of Toronto Press; O'Donovan, K. (1985) *Sexual Divisions in Law,* Weidenfeld and Nicolson.

3 A wife has been able to pledge her husband's credit for necessary household purchases unless it is known that he had forbidden her to do so or that his housekeeping allowance is inadequate. This right is derived from the concept of 'common household agency' and is not restricted to spouses.

4 *Reform of Personal Taxation* (1986) Green Paper, Cmnd 9756, London, HMSO; *Reform of Social Security* (1985) Social Security White Paper, Cmnd 9691, London, HMSO; *Children Come First,* vol. 1 *Proposals* and vol. 2 *The Background* (1990) Cm. 1264, London, HMSO; Law Commission (1986) *Family Law Review of Childhood: Child Custody,* Working Paper no. 96, London, HMSO; Law Commission (1988) *Family Law Review of Child Law, Guardianship and Custody,* Report no. 172, HC 594, London, HMSO; Law Commission (1982) *Family Law, Illegitimacy,* Report no. 118, London, HC 98; Scottish Law Commission (1990) *Parental Responsibilities and Rights, Guardianship and Administration of Children's Property,* Discussion Paper 88, Edinburgh, HMSO; Scottish Law

Commission (1984) *Family Law, Matrimonial Property*, Report no. 86, HC 467, Edinburgh, HMSO; Law Commission (1988) *Facing the Future – A Discussion Paper on the Grounds for Divorce*, no. 170, London, HMSO.

REFERENCES

Allbeson, J. (1985) 'Seen but not heard: young people', in Ward, S. (ed.) *DHSS in Crisis*, London, CPAG.

Atkins, S. and Hoggett, B. (1984) *Women and the Law*, Oxford, Blackwell.

Audit Commission (1986) *Making a Reality of Community Care*, London, HMSO.

Bradshaw, J. (1990) in *Bulletin,* no. 2, London, Family Policy Studies Centre.

Bradshaw, J. and Millar, J. (1991) *Lone Parent Families in the UK*, DSS Report no. 6, London, HMSO.

Brophy, J. (1990) 'Custody law: childcare and inequality', in Smart, C. and Sevenhuijsen, S. (eds) *Child Custody and the Politics of Gender*, London, Routledge.

Bryan, M. (1991) 'The Social Security Act 1990: from benefit claim back to the maintenance enforcement', *Journal of Child Law*, January/March.

Committee of Public Accounts (1990) *DSS: Support for Lone Parent Families*, HC 249, London, HMSO.

Craig, G. and Glendinning, C. (1990) *The Impact of Social Security Changes: the view of young people*, Barnados, Essex.

Currie, E. (1990) *What Women Want*, London, Sidgwick and Jackson.

Dallos, R. and Foreman, S. (1993) 'Domestic violence', in Dallos, R. and McLaughlin, E. (eds) *Social Problems and the Family,* London, Sage/The Open University.

Deech, R. (1984) 'Matrimonial property and divorce: a century of progress?', in Freeman, M. (ed.) *State Law and Family*, London, Tavistock.

Department of Employment (1988) *Employment for the 1990s*, Cm. 540, London, HMSO.

Department of Environment (1991) *Annual Report*, Cm. 1508, London, HC.

Department of Health and Social Security (1974) *Report of the Committee on One Parent Families,* vol. 2, *Appendices*, Cmnd. 5629–I, London, HMSO.

Department of Health and Social Security (1985) *The Reform of Social Security*, vols 1–4, Cmnd 9519–20, London, HMSO.

Department of Social Security, *et al.* (1990) *Children Come First*, White Paper, 2 vols, Cm. 1264, London, HMSO.

Edwards, S. and Halpern, A. (1992) 'Parental responsibility: an instrument of social policy', *Family Law*, March.

Finer, M. and McGregor, O. R. (1974) 'The history of the obligation to maintain', Appendix 5 in DHSS (1974).

Freedman, J. *et al.* (1988) *Property and Marriage: an integrated approach: property, tax, pensions and benefits for the family,* Report no. 29, London, Institute for Fiscal Studies.

Gibson, C. (1991) 'The future for maintenance', *Civil Justice Quarterly,* October.

Joshi, H. (1991) 'Obstacles and opportunities for lone parents as bread-winners in Great Britain', in *Lone Parent Families: the economic challenge,* Paris, OECD.

Kahn-Freund, O. and Wedderburn, K. (1971) 'Preface' to Eekelaar, J., *Family Security and Family Breakdown,* Harmondsworth, Penguin Books.

Law Commission (1986) *Family Law Review of Child Law: child custody,* Working Paper no. 96, London, HMSO.

Law Commission (1988) *Facing the Future – A Discussion Paper on the Grounds for Divorce,* no. 170, London, HMSO.

Lister, R. (1992) *Women's Economic Dependency and Social Security,* Manchester, Equal Opportunities Commission.

Lord Chancellor's Department (1993) *Looking to the Future: Mediation and the Ground for Divorce,* Cm 2424, London, HMSO.

Macfarlane, A. (1986) *Marriage and Love in England 1300–1840,* Oxford, Blackwell.

MacLean, M. and Wadsworth, M. (1987) 'Children's life chances and parents' divorce', *International Journal of Law and the Family,* vol. 2, pp. 155–66.

Murray, C. (1990) *The Emerging British Underclass,* London, IEA.

National Audit Office (1990) *Department of Social Security: support for lone parents,* London, NAO.

Office of Population Censuses and Surveys (1991) *Population Trends,* Autumn, London. HMSO.

Raynesford, N. (1990) 'Housing conditions; problems and policies', in Macgregor, S. and Pimlott, B. (ed.) *Tackling the Inner Cities,* Oxford, Clarendon Press.

Scottish Law Commission (1974) *Memorandum,* in DHSS (1974), Appendix 6, London, HMSO.

Social Security Committee (1993) *The Operation of the Child Support Act,* H269, Session 93–94, London, HMSO.

The Children's Society (1987) *Young People Under Pressure: somewhere to live,* Briefing Paper no. 2, London, The Children's Society.

Titmuss, R.M. (1974) *Social Policy: an introduction,* London, Allen and Unwin.

Treasury (1979) *The Government's Expenditure Plans 1980–81,* Cmnd 7746, London, HMSO.

Warnock Report (1984) *Report of Committee of Enquiry into Human Fertilisation and Embryology,* Cmnd 9374, London, HMSO.

APPENDIX:
MAJOR LEGISLATION IN THE 1980s–'90s

Social Security Act 1980

Matrimonial and Family Proceedings Act 1984

Family Law (Scotland) Act 1985

Housing Act 1985

Social Security Act 1986

Sex Discrimination Act 1986

Law Reform (Parent and Child) (Scotland) Act 1986

Family Law Act 1986

Family Law Review Act 1987

Finance Act 1988

Social Security Act 1989

Children Act 1989

Human Embryology and Fertilisation Act 1990

Social Security Act 1990

Child Support Act 1991

CHAPTER 4
PATTERNS OF DIVERSITY AND LIVED REALITIES

RUDI DALLOS AND ROGER SAPSFORD

CONTENTS

INTRODUCTION

As we have seen in the previous chapters, the terms 'the family' or 'family life' are likely to evoke images of the heterosexual nuclear family. In this chapter we will continue the task begun in Chapter 1 and look at the extent to which people live in something approaching a nuclear family and also at the extent to which there is a diversity of family lives. Either through choice or accident, many people find themselves living in ways which do not correspond to the stereotypes of the nuclear family. The choices facing us about the nature of the type of relationships we want are complex, and we may decide to live together without formal marriage, for varying periods of time, perhaps with partners of the same rather than the opposite sex, simultaneously with more than one partner and with children who may or may not be biologically related to us.

Our intention in this chapter is to consider the extent to which lived realities frequently differ from the nuclear family and the nature and range of some of the variations of family life that have been tried. We will do this by looking at some statistics on the variety of family forms existing in the United Kingdom at present and make some brief cross-cultural comparisons. The chapter will also look at how people in these various family forms experience their lives and how they are held together by a network of expectations and perceived duties and obligations. Diversity can be described from the outside in terms of *structure*: the people in a household, their sexual relationships, roles, economic contributions and responsibilities, relationships to the children and so on. At the same time a family is defined internally in terms of its *belief systems*, which includes the meanings that are attached to the structure and the patterns of expectations, duties and perceived obligations. The range of these obligations is prescribed in turn by the culture, the local community, the intergenerational traditions of a family and the family's own idiosyncratic dynamics, negotiations and internalizations of the beliefs and values of its surrounding culture. The chapter will include a range of sketches and personal accounts of life in some of the different varieties of family life. One intention is to encourage you to be able to see 'ideology in action': how, whatever form of family life people have chosen, they are guided by the prevalent ideologies of their culture. In industrial countries these are usually based upon, or are a reaction to, the nuclear family model.

Following on from a description of the diversity of family life in terms of statistics and personal accounts, we will consider some arguments for and against the nuclear family. These arguments – focusing on gender inequalities, child-rearing practices and sexuality – will serve to illustrate the pressures on people to conform to particular versions of the family. The pressure is applied ostensibly for their own benefit but, arguably, also works for the benefit of the dominant groups in society or – which comes to the same thing – to maintain the *status quo*. An argument that is frequently used to support particular versions of the family is that, regardless of culture, there are some inevitable or 'natural' aspects of relationships, so that something not all that dissimilar to our nuclear family emerges in most societies. Alternatively, can we perhaps argue that the family is essentially a social construction and that there is a potentially infinite variety to the ways in which people could live together and children could be brought up? This tension about the extent to which there are universal features of family lives will run through this chapter and you should try to bear this in mind as you read it. A second pervasive tension in the discussion, which you should also keep in mind, lies between the lived realities discussed here and the assumptions and norms discussed in Chapters 2 and 3 of this book which underlie public policy and the law.

The main aims of this chapter are as follows:

1   To offer some statistics to paint a picture of the variety of contemporary family life in the United Kingdom.

2   To contrast *objective* and *subjective* definitions of family life.

3   To examine some of the arguments for and against the conventional white heterosexual family.

4   To consider the variety as opposed to universality of family lives – for example, whether there are fundamental tasks facing all human groupings that guides the evolution of something like the nuclear family.

5   To consider arguments, some of which have been raised in the previous chapters, about who benefits and loses within the nuclear family as compared to other forms such as lone-parent or communal arrangements.

I   VARIETIES OF FAMILY LIFE: SKETCHES

We are continually bombarded with images of family life from the media, education and religion. Though the influence of religion in some cultures has declined, it still plays an important role in symbolizing entrances and departures from a family and continues to foster beliefs in family duty, responsibility and sexual morality. Yet even these 'traditional' attitudes to family life have changed, with resulting shifts in family form. The advent of effective contraception has challenged sexual mores but has also resulted in the growth of negative attitudes to large families. In contrast to Victorian times, large families are now likely to be stigmatized as irresponsible, deviant or pathological, particularly if made up of working-class or ethnic minority people or headed by a single parent.

ACTIVITY I

Pause here to consider what you see as being *three* of the major criteria that would lead you to call a group of people a 'family' as opposed to a 'relationship' or 'grouping' of people?

DISCUSSION

The dominant image is of a nuclear family and this might include the following:

Objective criteria

a heterosexual couple	sexual orientation
two parents and their children	biological relatedness
predominantly monogamous	sexual fidelity
joint space and possessions	private property
together for an extended period of time	permanence
etc.	

Subjective criteria

A shared view and commitment to being a family

An acceptance of a set of mutual obligations, duties, roles

A commitment to staying together

etc.

We can see that it is not always easy to distinguish a 'family' from, say, a couple who say they have a 'relationship' and are 'living together' but do not see themselves as a 'family'. We will consider later some of the varieties of 'family life' and how they accept or challenge some of these criteria.

We can use the following simple framework and our criteria of 'family life' to consider some of the attempts that have been made to construct forms of family life or relationships that challenge 'conventional' family life:

Lone parent	Nuclear family	Extended family	Communes and kibbutzim

As you read these short sketches of varieties of 'family life', consider which of our earlier criteria they appear to accept or challenge.

1.1   LONE-PARENT FAMILIES

Lone-parent families are usually defined as: one parent, frequently the mother, living alone with her children, with the greater proportion of responsibility for caring for the children financially and emotionally; the lone parent may be in her own accommodation and head of her household but in many cases may be forced to share her living space with others, or to live with her relatives at least temporarily, in which case the lone-parent family becomes part of a wider extended family. The main challenge to the nuclear family is in terms of the central unit being not two parents but one. Other criteria such as a commitment to heterosexuality, monogamy, private family property may remain intact.

> I split up with my husband because it wasn't working. I had started an affair while I was with him and then took my son [Harry] and moved in with my lover. It was all right for a while but I started to realise that I needed to be free and make my own decisions – though it was a bit hard having to cope on my own, and money is still tight. I live on my own now with Harry and have some good friends, men and women. Other women sometimes help out with child-minding but I can't get out all that often. I get pretty lonely sometimes especially on Sundays when my friend, who is in a permanent relationship with someone, usually goes out with her family. My parents offer some support but they don't really approve of the way I live and would like to see me getting settled down. I take Harry over to them sometimes which gives me a bit of a break but then they start saying I am not bringing him up right and going on at me.
>
> I'm not sure that I want to live permanently with anyone again. I like my independence. I have boyfriends occasionally but I am wary of upsetting Harry by having anyone move in with us again. I think Harry wants me all to himself now and he can get a bit out of control sometimes. I probably could do with a man around to help with him sometimes and some of my men friends do help. It would be nice if his father could see him more often. He writes and telephones him sometimes but because he's angry with me he avoids contact with Harry which is sad, especially for Harry.
>
> (Personal account, given to author)

In describing the experience of becoming single parents, women frequently indicate that they go through initial periods of doubt, uncertainty and anxiety that they will not be able to manage. Following this, however, they tend to have feelings of increased self-confidence and a positive sense of freedom:

> I like my independence and I wouldn't like to go back. It's hard. I think you take a lot of knocks, and some of them take a hell of a lot of getting over, and you think, you're not gonna get over them, but somehow you do.
>
> I don't have to worry about meals. We can have what we want. I don't have to wash and iron shirts and trousers. Oh, it's heaven! At the end of it all you can turn round and think, 'I've brought these children up, or child up, on my own', and you can look and think, 'Well, I've done it!'
>
> (Shaw, 1991, pp. 147, 148)

Emerging from such accounts by women is a sense of being in control of their lives, of a new-found feeling of autonomy.

To some extent 'lone parenthood' may express women's choice. The statistics suggest that marriage has become less popular in the last two decades: the proportion of single people marrying has halved since 1971, as has the proportion of divorced people re-marrying, while the proportion of people describing themselves as 'cohabiting' is steadily increasing. Illegitimacy rates also continue to rise, with nearly 30 per cent of babies born to unmarried parents in 1990 (OPCS, 1991). Some of these couples will later marry, and some are in settled patterns of cohabitation (see Chapter 1 section 2), but some will reflect a woman's decision to raise her child without continuing in a relationship with the father. The majority of lone-parent households still result from death, divorce or desertion, however, with divorce being the largest single cause.

The lone-parent family is not in itself a problem but the term has, in a similar way to step-families, become embedded in pathology. There is a sense that both mother and child are somehow losing because they can't achieve the ideals of a nuclear family. There is some evidence that children of divorced parents are more liable to emotional problems, under-achievement and delinquency (MacLean and Wadsworth, 1988), but attendant factors such as greater poverty, housing problems and tensions between the divorced parents contribute to this, rather than simply the fact of living in a step-family or lone-parent family. Contrary to popular supposition, there is some possibility that remarriage and step-

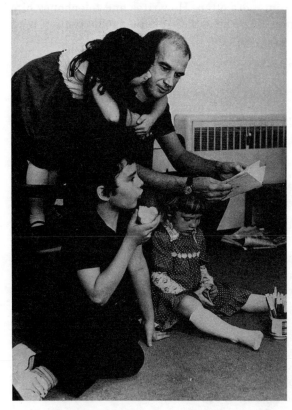

In the minority of lone-parent families: a father with his children

parenting may in fact be more disruptive to children than being raised by a lone parent. A recent analysis of data from the National Child Development Study, following up 17,000 children born in 1958, suggests that substantially more step-children than children of lone parents leave school at 16, leave home by 18 because of friction in the home, experience learning difficulties, fail to obtain educational qualifications and/or (in the case of girls) marry young in order to leave home.

1.2 EXTENDED FAMILIES, COMMUNES AND KIBBUTZIM

Extended families consist of biologically related family members of three generations living together under the same roof. Usually this will be children, parents and grandparents but may also include more distant relatives such as uncles and aunts.

The co-residence of other adults may fundamentally change the nature of family life, supplying the household with additional resources (e.g. childcare), though not all 'extended families' benefit in this way: some may consist of a couple, children and a bed-ridden elderly or disabled relative who constitutes yet another set of tasks for the household. It may also widen the range of relationships available to children in the household, lessening the tight grip of parental oversight. The lived experience of extended families may therefore be very different from what is experienced in nuclear families. Nevertheless we still tend to see them as 'families' – their 'public image' is very similar to that of the nuclear family.

Communes, at the extreme, may be a collection of unrelated people or couples with each couple having some boundary around it but, nevertheless, sharing some common activities. In some communes the sexual liaisons and pairings may shift (group marriage) so that it is hard to discriminate clear family forms, apart from children and their biological parents – and even this can also be in some doubt in some cases. A particularly interesting and more formally organized system of communal living is to be found in the Israeli kibbutzim. Some communes and kibbutzim can be seen as deliberately created alternatives to family living, as radically different ways for men and women to live together and for children to be reared. We shall discuss both in more detail in section 3.2. Here let us note simply the existence of communal alternatives to both nuclear and extended families, their rarity, and the fact that they do in practice share some problems with 'families', as we shall see.

1.3 GAY AND LESBIAN RELATIONSHIPS

Cutting across our simple typology of families is the question of sexuality and sexual orientation. The predominant challenge to the nuclear family here centres around sexual orientation. Other features such as the central unit being an adult couple, permanence, private family property, commitment to a permanent relationship may be in evidence in gay families.

The gay liberation and feminist movements have played a significant role in the development of the freedom of people with homosexual as opposed to heterosexual orientations in being able to 'come out', that is openly declare their homosexuality and to have the freedom to live together. This may be experienced both in terms of a sense of freedom and liberation and also as a time of tension and conflict with their own families:

> My mother accepts it now, although I still think she hopes it's a phase ... I feel totally at ease now they know. Everything used to be bottled up inside me. I just wanted to tell the world that I have found love in a woman. I got bad tempered because I couldn't. (Female)

> At first they were okay, then they recommended mental treatment. (Male, 19)

> Mum was upset. My dad kicked me out of the house and disowned me ... They feel the same now as when I told them. (Female, 18)

> (Trenchard and Warren, 1984, p. 41)

There is a strong sense of liberation and hope expressed when people are able to declare their gay and lesbian orientations but this is often a difficult issue, especially for young people, because their parents may not easily be able to accept it. Some of the fears that parents have are based on anxieties, misunderstandings and ignorance of what a gay male or lesbian family life is like. When there are children involved there may be a focus on perceived problems such as ridicule at school, difficulties the children may feel about bringing friends home, social isolation and lack of awareness of some of the potentially positive aspects of a gay family:

> I have a daughter and a son. The memory of their childhood years, storms and all, remains a joy to my life. Raising two children together with my lover, Frances, balancing the intricacies of relationship within that four-person inter-racial family, taught me invaluable measurements for myself, my capacities, my real agendas. It gave me tangible and sometimes painful lessons about difference, about power, and about purpose.

> (Lorde, 1988, pp. 42–3)

The accounts from children raised in homosexual relationships can be positive, as can the relationships between a lesbian mother and the children's father. The following is taken from accounts by Jane, her lover Miriam, Jane's ex-husband Edwin and their three children. Here Jane talks about an earlier relationship when she realised she was a lesbian:

> *Jane*: I knew I was [a lesbian] when I was about thirty ... I fell hopelessly in love ... It was the sort of thing one had heard about and seen on films ... The fact that I had a husband and three children made it difficult to accommodate. I told my husband about it. As always, he was totally gentle, kind and equally thrown, but he didn't

show it ... He put his arms around me and I put mine around him and we held each other very, very tight. I don't think we said anything else ...

Edwin: I wanted to be supportive. I didn't feel sorry for her. I felt sorry for her pain ... I felt it was something we were both involved in. I hoped I'd help her get over it ...

Much later, Jane fell in love again – this time with Miriam, a young woman who had come to stay with the family temporarily. They had a relationship for over seven years while living in the family home.

Edwin: She [Miriam] was more of a daughter to me. When the thing became permanent, I felt I'd better do the best I could.

Miriam: ... I've known the children since very young ... I've always got on with all three children. I love them like brothers and sisters. ... So long as I was near Jane, space didn't matter. As long as she was there, I didn't care where I was. I loved Edwin in the way I would expect to love a father, had I known mine.

Jane eventually moved out to live nearby with her lover Miriam and the children stayed with their father. The children described the break-up and the new family formation:

Rae (13): Mum was arguing with Dad more often ... I didn't begin to resent Miriam until she moved out and took my Mum ... Then Mum and Dad told me the facts. After the talk I didn't resent Miriam ... She'd helped us all to decide what to do. Mum moved out with Miriam. Then Sue [older daughter] moved out to Maxine [Sue's lesbian partner]. Dad, Miles and I moved to a smaller house. Everything was perfect. We were still a family, but living in three different houses.

Miles (18): I detested her [Jane – his mother] until a year and a half ago, when she moved out ... When I found out she was gay, ... it didn't make me feel any better about the mistreatment I had from her. Apart from being a son she didn't want, which I always knew, I was also a man ... I always felt I was the one who was picked on, especially when Rae could do no wrong ... I think I'm a far better person than I would have been if I had got the love I wanted ... I think there is nothing wrong with a lesbian mother if you want to be a mother. Those who say that lesbians shouldn't have children because they may be boys ... should not say that sort of thing unless they've experienced it ... or talk to those who have been in that situation ... I don't believe in the family concept of a father and a mother ... I believe in the concept of two parents. I don't see why they should be different sexes. I think it's totally irrelevant what sex they are, as long as they can provide for the needs of their children – material needs, love, discipline.

Sue (19): When I found out [her mother's being gay], it was like a light bulb exploding in my head and suddenly I knew why she'd behaved the way she had ... It had never occurred to me that I might be gay ... In fact, because Mum was, I didn't really want to be. No way did I want to be a carbon copy of Mum. People said we were so alike in many ways, even though I looked like Dad ...

(extracted from Hanscombe and Forster, 1982, pp. 125–32)

There have been significant discussions within and between the lesbian and gay movements and the extent to which the nuclear family is challenged varies. It is extremely difficult to draw generalizations here, but some of the significant differences centre around the commitment to monogamy and permanence of the relationship. Both lesbian and gay couples in many cases have children by previous relationships or have adopted children. Thus apart from their sexual orientation they may not wish to significantly challenge the norms of the nuclear family. A significant dimension as we have seen above, where children are involved, is the extent to which the relationship is temporary or permanent. One of the possible differences here may be that, since there is a common expectation that children stay with their mothers, it is more likely that lesbian couples will have children than gay men and this may in part serve to promote a more monogamous form of relationship. However, generalizations here are dangerous and there is considerable diversity, as there is in

An alternative type of family, one not always accepted by society

heterosexual families, as to how life is organized and the extent to which there is a deliberate attempt to be different on some or all the criteria of 'conventional' family life.

Challenges to the conventional form of family life may encounter resistance and be perceived of as a threat but it is possible that challenging of the sexual mores has aroused most anxieties:

> Homosexuality has always posed a threat to these dichotomies (private and public). It does not fit easily into the usual neat divisions between home and work. The characteristic forms of picking up, social interaction and erotic relating of most male homosexuals and many lesbians radically cut across conventional forms of courtship and sexual partnership … It seems that public displays of gay men still arouse fear and anxiety.
>
> (Weeks, 1985, p. 20, writing about his male gay experiences)

The anxieties aroused may in part lead to people assuming that homosexuals challenge or pose a threat to all the other criteria of family life; this , as we have seen, is not the case. Children do not simply follow in their parents' footsteps: gay parents do not necessarily produce gay children just as heterosexual parents do not invariably produce heterosexual children. The extent of rejection of the conventional family model varies with the political stance of the partners. The presence or absence of children does appear to be a crucial factor in determining, for example, whether a relationship will be permanent, monogamous, involve sharing of property and income. Yet, as we will see later, even in situations such as communes where there is the possibility of multiple-parenting and where there is less practical need for or moral pressure on permanent, monogamous coupling, there tends to be a drift towards nuclear family forms. This raises questions about the natural universality of family forms or the possibility that, whatever 'experiments' people attempt, they will invariably be drawn back to the basic social and emotional programming offered by society and their own families.

1.4 CHANGE AND THE FAMILY LIFE-CYCLE

From these accounts and brief descriptions we can see that families change and evolve. Even the nuclear family form is not the same throughout a family's lifetime. Many couples now cohabit prior to marriage, then spend a period of time together without children and are likely to spend considerable time alone together when the children have left home. One or other of them may also spend time living with their children again when they are old. It has been suggested that families face a number of tasks – such as child-rearing, intimacy, preparing children for the outside world – and that there are key transitional points where families need to make major changes – such as the birth of a child or when someone leaves the family (see Chapter 1 of Dallos, 1991). Within the 'conventional' white nuclear family in the United Kingdom there is a 'natural' progression:

Courtship – cohabitation – marriage – children – children at school – leaving home – mid-marriage – grandparenting – bereavement

At each stage a family is required to reorganize itself, sometimes dramatically, as when a couple have their first child. The family life-cycle, however, is more than a description of what normally happens; it also contains a set of socially determined ideologies about what *should* happen in families – when, with whom and how. A key example here is that white British families expect that their children will leave home in their late teens/early twenties. If this does not happen, they may see themselves and be seen as somehow deviant. Likewise, they expect that their children will marry and start to have families so that parents may feel disappointed if they have not had grandchildren by the time they are in their fifties.

Non-conventional families on the other hand may not go through these stages in the same sequence or may miss some of the stages. A lone-parent family, for example, may not have gone through a form of marriage and one of the parents will have separated from the child much earlier than in the typical nuclear family.

ACTIVITY 2

Consider the stages that a step-family may go through and the various forms of family life that they may have experienced at various points in their life.

DISCUSSION

In a step-family one or both parents may have had the experience of being single parents prior to embarking on their current marriage, a nuclear family if they have children from this new family, being a childless couple and so on. They are also likely to have moved through the transitional stages in a different order. For example, they may have had little time together as a courting couple before having been confronted with each other's children. Possibly they have been through their children leaving home and had not expected to go through it again nor to go through the stresses of having babies waking in the middle of the night and so on; in fact they may find themselves to be repeating some of the stages.

In other words, when we speak of 'the family' we are in reality describing not an object but a process – a social grouping which at any given time has a predictable history and a predictable future. The norm to which we refer when we speak of 'the family' progresses from unattached young people of opposite genders (themselves emerging from families) via courtship and

couple-formation to marriage, the conception, birth and raising of children, the years together after the children have left home, to (probably)
years of living alone after the death of one partner. The norm conceals a
wide range of variations, however. People may not form couples until later
in life, they may 'form up' with people of the same sex, they may or may
not solemnize their relationship through marriage, they may or may not
have children, they may or may not stay together during or after the
raising of the children, children may or may not leave home, and so on.
After divorce or the death of one partner, the process may or may not start
again, through remarriage or a second cohabitation. The conceptually
simple 'life-cycle' conceals a wide range of variations. It also tends to
conceal the extent to which each change of status is the result of choices
which people make – constrained choices, undoubtedly, but choices
nonetheless.

Increasingly, as varieties of family life and even attempts at ways of living
which set themselves to some extent in opposition to 'family life' (such as
communes and lesbian and gay relationships) become more and more
acceptable, people have to make choices. It could be argued that in Victorian times the question of choice was less pronounced: people simply got
married. Now people of all ages may think, reflect upon, plan and discuss
issues such as whether they will live together, part-time or full-time,
marry, have children, be monogamous, live with their parents, whether
they wish to be heterosexual, homosexual or bisexual, and so on. The
concept of the family life-cycle helps us to focus on how the choices become
critical at certain phases in people's lives. Evidence from clinical work
also illustrates how it is precisely at these decision-points that stress
seems to accumulate and various 'problems' may develop, especially
where viable solutions are not practical for 'structural' reasons.

SUMMARY

1   Forms of family organization in the United Kingdom can currently be conceptualized as a typology ranging from lone parents to
extended families and communal alternatives to families.

2   Family forms that look similar from the outside may in fact be
dissimilar from the inside and we need to know about how people
experience their life and the wider social context of the family.

3   Families can be seen to have a life-cycle – they change and evolve
– so when we talk about, for example, the nuclear family we need to
clarify the stage that the particular nuclear family is at: couple on
their own, with young children, as grandparents etc.

4   Whether people live in a nuclear family form or not exerts a
powerful influence in offering a set of ideals of family life that are
likely to be used to evaluate people's experiences of their particular
form of family life.

5   The ideology of the nuclear family perpetuates a myth that family members can 'get things right' if only they try hard enough; this obscures the reality that families exist in a wider social context with varying levels of support.

6   It also conceals the disjuncture between the lived experiences of a range of people and the single set of assumptions and pressures around which law and social policy tend to be built.

2   PATTERNS OF DIVERSITY

2.1   STATISTICS

We shall start by asking just how statistically common the 'normal family' is. Table 1 shows that a quarter of all households in Britain consist of people living alone (about three-fifths of them are people of pensionable age). A further third are households of adults only (including grown-up offspring in about 40 per cent of cases). Only 30 per cent of households contain dependent children, and a fifth of these households are lone-parent ones. Looking at it another way, three-fifths of households consist of married couples; of these 47 per cent have no children (but might have them in the future or might have had them in the past), and a further 13 per cent have adults living in the house who had previously been dependent children. In one sense, therefore, the married couple with children which constitutes 'the family' of the stereotype is a relatively rare form of household. In another, and taking into account families which have not yet achieved children and families with grown-up offspring, nearly two-thirds of households can be seen as conforming to the stereotype.

ACTIVITY 3

As you examine Tables 1, 2 and 3 consider what picture of the variety of family life they present. Is there evidence that nuclear forms are now a minority or does the basic pattern of married-with-children still predominate in UK society?

Thus family life of the married-with-children variety (including couples at an earlier or later life-stage, before or after the period of childcare) does seem to be a statistically very common domestic arrangement. It appears also to remain popular even with those who have tried it and decided to withdraw. Of the marriages existing at the beginning of 1987, one in eighty was broken by divorce before the end of the year; on the other hand, in a third of all marriages contracted during 1987, one or both partners had previously been divorced (OPCS, 1990).

Table 1   Households by type in 1990–91, Great Britain (percentages)

Single person	
Pensionable age	15%
Other	11
Two or more unrelated adults	3
Married couple	
No children	28
Dependent children	24
Non-dependent children only	8
Lone-parent	
Dependent children	6
Non-dependent children only	4
Two or more families	1

Source: Continuous Household Survey data; taken from
Social Trends, no. 22, 1992, 2.4, p. 41

Table 2   Divorce, cohabitation and remarriage, 1970 and 1987, United Kingdom (numbers and percentages)

	c.1970	1987
Number of divorces per 1,000 marriages (1970)	4.7	12.6
Proportion of women cohabiting prior to marriage for the first time (early 1970s)	7%	48%
Proportion of remarriages involving at least one divorced partner (1971)	21%	36%

Source: Coote, Harman and Hewitt, 1990, pp. 14, 15

Table 3   Living arrangements of children under sixteen, 1985, United Kingdom (percentages)

Children living with both natural parents (married)	78%
Children living with both natural parents (cohabiting)	2
Children living with lone mother	10
Children living with natural mother married to step-father*	7
Children living with natural mother co-habiting with 'step-father'	2
Children living elsewhere (e.g. lone father, adoptive or foster parents, relatives, special home or school)	2

Notes: Percentages add to more than 100 due to rounding.
*This may include some natural fathers who have married the mother since the birth.
Source: Coote, Harman and Hewitt, 1990, p. 16

The figures in Table 2 support some widely accepted preconceptions that divorce, cohabitation and step-family formations are on the increase. The increase in cohabitation is quite striking and highlights the difficulty of attempting any static definition of family life. Many of these relationships become families but the couples may not meet the criteria to be defined as formally cohabiting, nor subjectively experienced as marriage or even family life by the participants.

The pattern of remarriage also shows how, although people may appear to be still living in what looks like a nuclear family form, they are quite likely to be starting a marriage/family with someone who has been through it all before; again this is not the stereotype of the nuclear family.

We can look at this diversity from the children's point of view in Table 3. In 1985, 20 per cent of children were *not* living with both their natural parents. The vast majority of these children were living with the natural mother – alone in half the cases, and married to a 'step-father' in a large proportion of the remainder. It is estimated that there were between one and one and a half million step-families in 1985 and that 7 per cent of all children were living with their natural mother and a step-father. In the other direction, cohabitation is becoming increasingly common. In 1981 about 8 per cent of women were cohabiting in a relationship not formalized by legal marriage; by 1987 this had increased to 17% (Coote *et al.*, 1990). In the immediate preceding years some 50 per cent of single men and some 40 per cent of single women admitted to cohabitation before marriage, with the proportions being higher among those who had previously been divorced (Haskey and Kiernan, 1989, p. 25). The *average* length of cohabitation relationships was twenty-two months for single men and twenty months for single women, but around a quarter of the relationships had lasted for 5 years or more (ibid., p. 27).

Even within marriages and 'steady' cohabitation arrangements resembling marriages, there is considerable variation. In some (probably the largest category), the mother is mostly available to the children (not being in paid employment, or having employment whose hours are compatible with those of schools), while the father is available only at evenings and weekends. There are many others, however, where it is the wife who works further away from home and the father nearer to the home or even in the home, so that the children's experience will be the reverse. Where a partner has to travel to paid employment, the amount he or she is 'available to the family' will depend on the location of the work and the quality of transport provision, and there will be large regional and local variations. In the London region, journeys to work of up to two hours are not uncommon, which would mean that young children would probably not see the travelling parent at all during the week. Many people also work away from home in a more emphatic sense. Travelling sales staff, fishermen, naval and army personnel etc. would normally be away from home for long periods at a time. This is also not uncommon in certain kinds of middle-class family, where the spouses work in different towns, and is not unknown in working-class families where the husband travels to find work (common in the construction industry, for example). Distance from kin also differs a great deal between families, as does the extent to which the extended kin-group are involved in the life of the family even if they are geographically available.

Overall, then, something like a nuclear configuration of married parents with children does still appear to be statistically normal but this conceals considerable real diversity. Statistics suggest that the married status is more popular among some 'ethnic groups' than others. Looking at the population as a whole, people of 'British white' or Asian origin are the least likely to be single (the women less so even than the men), while people of other origins (particularly Afro-Caribbean) are substantially more likely. People of Afro-Caribbean or African origin also show the highest incidence of divorce or separation. Partly the differences are due to the different age structures of the groups. Partly, however, they are cultural in the sense of being arrangements commonly adopted by people of a given origin; families where the only continuously present adult is a woman are most common among people of Afro-Caribbean or African origin, and least among people of Indian, Chinese or Arab origin (Haskey, 1989, p. 13): see Table 4 and Figures 1 and 2.

The statistics show some fairly marked variations in the types of family organizations adopted in the UK by different ethnic groups. Afro-Caribbean families are far more likely to live in lone-parent households than any other race (Table 4 and Figure 1). In contrast, Asian and Chinese families are most likely to live in extended families. What might from the outside be classified as similar family forms in fact can represent different lived family realities, duties, expectations and obligations.

Furthermore it is necessary to have an understanding of the social and historical context of family forms. This issue has been of concern, for example, to family therapists and social workers who found that they were dealing with ethnic families in culture-bound or ethnocentric ways. As an example, the absence of fathers in some Afro-Caribbean families or the powerful influence of grandparents in the parenting of grandchildren were seen as problematic and in need of adjustment. Such an assumption may have some basis with white families but ignores the cultural location of family life.

Some of the issues are highlighted in the dilemmas that faced Afro-Caribbean families who emigrated to the United Kingdom. Broadly three types of family form have co-existed in the Caribbean:

(a) the conventional nuclear household or 'Christian marriage' which was found amongst the more wealthy, upwardly mobile families who were aspiring to Western values and success;

(b) the common-law household (i.e. long-term relationship between a man and a woman);

(c) the mother household in which a woman, usually the grandmother, is very influential in the management and decision-making in the family and often the sole, stable household head.

Whatever form of family the immigrant Afro-Caribbeans came from, they inevitably experienced a variety of problems often associated with the

Table 4 Household type: by ethnic group of head of household, 1984–1986, Great Britain (percentages)

Household type	Ethnic group of head of household						
	White	All ethnic minority groups	West Indian or Guyanese	Indian	Pakistani or Bangladeshi	Other ethnic minority groups	All groups (incl. bit stated)
One person households	24	14	18	6	5	21	24
One family households (with or without other persons)							
Couple							
with no children	26	11	11	10	6	14	26
with dependent children[1]	29	47	28	59	68	41	29
with non-dependent children only	8	4	5	5	2	4	8
Lone parent							
with dependent children[1]	4	11	23	4	4	8	4
with non-dependent children only	3	3	6	2	2	2	3
Two or more family households with children	1	6	2	11	10	2	1
Other households[2]	4	5	5	4	3	8	4
All households	100	100	100	100	100	100	100

Note: 1 Aged under 16 years of age, or under 19 years of age and never married and either in full-time education or else on a government scheme.
2 Households which contain either two or more families with no children or two or more persons not in a family.

Source: Labour Force Surveys, 1984–86 average. Office of Population Censuses and Surveys; table taken from Social Trends, no. 19, 1989, 2.7, p. 38.

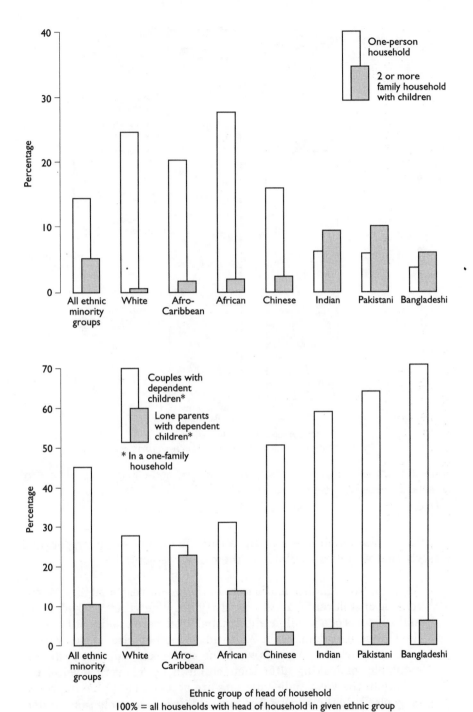

Figure 1   Proportion of all households containing certain family types by ethnic group of head of household, 1985–87, Great Britain

Source: OPCS, *Population Trends*, no. 57, 1989, Figure 6, p. 14, London, HMSO

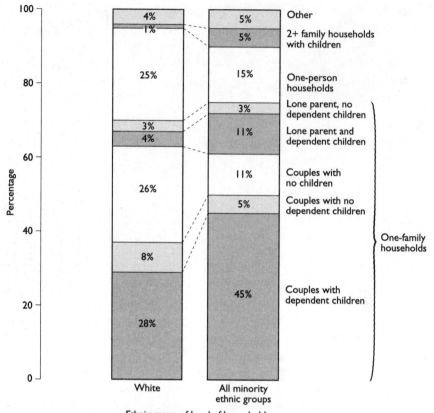

Figure 2   Families within households, by family type and ethnic group of head of household, 1985–87, Great Britain
Source: OPCS, *Population Trends*, no. 57, 1989, Figure 5, p. 13, London, HMSO

conflicts between their assumptions about the kind of social support and lifestyle that would be available to them and the actuality:

> As in the West Indies, mothers took the major responsibility for the rearing of children in all the family types. When they worked, informal supports of a familiar and trusted kind were readily at hand. In the United Kingdom, when West Indian mothers are forced by economic pressures to go out to work, no such social support system is available for looking after their children ... At every level of the society in the West Indies parents are accustomed to having somebody else help them look after their children. This help takes different forms in the different family types – from paid help in the conventional nuclear family to grandmothers, aunts, older siblings and neighbours in the other two groups. The care of these children provided by kinfolk is as good as that provided by their mothers ... there are always two or three older women talking to the young

Afro-Caribbean families are often matriarchal in form

> children ... As the children are generally in groups of eight to ten
> there is good peer group socialization as well as good adult relation-
> ship ... the warmth and enormous love and care with which they
> surround their children are taken for granted.
>
> (Barrow, 1982, pp. 224–5)

How effectively a family functions and what it means to live inside it
cannot be assessed simply by a description of its structure. It is at the
same time defined in terms of the beliefs held by the people inside it and
by the cultural context it is located within.

On the other hand, it is worth looking at structural factors in order to get
some idea of how Afro-Caribbean life in the UK is *different* from that in
the West Indies. There was indeed a strong tradition of entrusting the
children to another woman if the wife was in paid employment – probably
a paid worker if the woman was middle-class, and a female relative if the
woman was a peasant. When working-class couples came to the UK in the
1940s and '50s as part of the great 'wave of immigration', they could not
bring their support networks with them. Some brought their children but
also had to take paid employment, because such jobs as were available to
immigrants were not as well paid as had been suggested to them, and
living costs were high. Others left their children in the West Indies in the
care of relatives and had to take paid employment in order to send money
home for their support. (Further family problems tended to emerge when
they tried to bring these children to the UK to re-unite the family. With

the passing of the 1962 Immigration Act, teenage children were often seen not as permitted dependants but as prospective unemployed workers.) Thus Afro-Caribbean family traditions and levels of racism within the host society combined to make their lives difficult. Their experience of family life in the United Kingdom was structurally different from what they had experienced in the West Indies. The experience of their children, growing up in two cultures and in economic circumstances which are different again, will resemble their parents in some respects but differ quite markedly from them in others.

In thinking about Afro-Caribbean and other cultures it is important not to be trapped in a Eurocentrist perspective. Afro-Caribbean families, for example, may be different in many ways to white, British nuclear families, but it would be a mistake to regard these differences as an attack on 'family life'. In fact the reverse could be argued: there is often a strong sense of family life and respect for it, and moreover the family can represent or offer a 'haven' for black people from the racial prejudice they may experience in white society.

2.2 NORMS

While by no means everyone lives in 'a family' at any one time, most of us in the UK are in nuclear families at some stage of our lives. (Even among those minority ethnic groups where the extended family – three or more generations living together under the same roof – might be expected as a norm, nuclear families are more common in the United Kingdom than in the country of ultimate origin; one reason might be that the UK housing stock does not lend itself to extended-family households.) Nine out of ten people marry at some time in their lives (although this proportion is declining), and nine out of ten couples have children. Marriages are also more durable than discussion of divorce statistics would suggest: two out of three marriages are ended by death rather than divorce. Cohabitation *before* marriage may be becoming more common, but there is little good evidence (apart from in Sweden) for a strong trend towards cohabitation *instead of* marriage (FPSC, 1990; Coote, Harman and Hewitt, 1990).

The majority of children are still brought up in nuclear families: although one child in eight lives in a lone-parent family, four children out of five live with both their natural parents. Because lone parents frequently remarry, it is highly likely that those children who are currently in lone-parent families will be in a nuclear family again before they reach adulthood – most probably consisting of the natural mother and a step-father: in 1985 only 5 per cent of children aged 0–4 were in this kind of family, but 12 per cent of children aged 10–15 (FPSC, 1990). Even orphans and those whose care has been handed over to state or charitable institutions are very likely to spend a portion of their childhood in something resembling a nuclear family, given current preferences for fostering and adoption over long-term institutional care.

Thus those who describe the nuclear family as a statistical norm would seem to have some justice in their claim. We should not suppose that the other features of the stereotype of 'the family' necessarily hold, however – wives staying at home to care for children while husbands act as bread-winners, for example. In 1988 some 60 per cent of married women were in paid employment outside the home – 33 per cent of women with their youngest child aged 0–2, but 73 per cent of women with their youngest child aged ten or over. (Even then, some of the work is part-time, fitted in with childcare 'duties': 65 per cent of employed women with very young children are in part-time work, and 59 per cent of women with children aged 10+ (FPSC, 1990).)

One conclusion that we might be tempted to draw from such statistics of the apparent changes and diversity is that, with the increases in the numbers of people living in non-conventional family arrangements, there might be more favourable attitudes towards alternatives such as lone-parenthood and step-families. This does not appear to be happening so readily and, despite young children now being far more likely to have friends who are from divorced families, the nuclear family ideology still seems pervasive, never more so than amongst children experiencing the break-up of their family:

> The hope, the wish and sometimes the expectation that parents would reunite is at its height at the time of separation, and was a vivid fantasy for over half of the children. In their games, no single child in the entire group [research sample of children from divorced families] played separate homes or even separate bedrooms for the divorcing parents. Children happily restored the family in the play-house by placing father and mother in one bed, together, with their arms tightly woven one around the other. Other children tried, sometimes directly, to bring about or even force the reconciliation they desired.

(Wallerstein and Kelly, 1980, p. 47)

SUMMARY

1   There are considerable variations within UK culture in what might constitute family life.

2   The variations can be seen in terms of cultural differences, historical changes and geographical and other variations.

3   Families are not static but are continually changing as children grow and leave home and consequentially a person, even in the typical nuclear family, only spends a relatively small portion of their lives living under the same roof with their dependent children. The patterns also vary between the sexes with women (because of their

greater life expectancy) being much more likely than men to end their days living alone or possibly again living with their children or other relatives.

4   Despite the changes and variations most children – nearly 80 per cent in the UK – still spend most of their lives in a nuclear family form, which appears to be still the predominant form of family life in the UK.

5   In describing and forming generalizations about family life, we have to be careful to differentiate between men's and women's family lives: for example, far more women are likely to be lone parents, live on their own when they are old, divide their time between childcare and work and so on.

Thus it might legitimately be argued, as Diana Gittins does in *The Family in Question* (1985), that the concept of 'the family' is an analytic device and an ideological tactic. People live together in a wide variety of different domestic or non-domestic (institutional) arrangements, and the range is so great that what unifies them is not immediately obvious. The supposedly 'normal' family is a tool of public policy (as we saw in Chapter 2), an ideal towards which people are supposed to strive, and a pattern of structured inequality whose nature this taken-for-granted striving conceals:

> ... the family has become a vital and central symbol to notions of authority, inequality and deference. The symbolic importance of the family cannot be underestimated, for it goes beyond political allegiances of left or right and has arguably come to be seen as the most important institution of modern industrial society. The problem, however, is that it is seen as an institution grounded in reality rather than as a symbol-system or ideology. What orators *say* about the family is frequently very far removed from how men, women and children actually live out their lives.
> (Gittins, 1985, pp. 58–9)

One aspect of the ideology of the family which has been crucial in UK public policy, as we saw in Chapter 2, is the concept of the family as a 'private place'. This belief is largely an illusion: the state is able to penetrate the family whenever doing so is considered desirable, and indeed it does so extensively in matters of child-rearing and children's health and education. At the same time, the state is able to disclaim direct responsibility for anything 'within the private sphere' which it does not wish to control directly. The maintenance of wives and children is the business of husbands, in this view, and law and state welfare intervene only in a subset of the cases where husbands fail in this business. The care of children is the business of mothers, and again the state intervenes only *in extremis*. Thus state provision of income support becomes a 'grace', not a duty of the state or a right of those who seek it: 'By presenting social policy in this framework, governments have consistently been able to claim that they are not interfering in family life, whilst at the same time sustaining the boundaries of those family obligations which are thought to be important' (Muncie and Wetherell, in Chapter 2 of this book).

Another reason for considering 'the family' as an ideological and normative construction is because what actually happens is so often at variance with the rhetoric which justifies it. From the middle of the nineteenth century, for example, the labour movement pressed for 'a family wage' – a wage sufficient for a man to support a family – and justified the need in terms of equity within a structure in which men carried the responsibility for 'their' dependants. The net effect, however, was to keep women's wages low and to put more money in men's pockets. There was not then, and there is not now, any guarantee that the 'family wage' would be distributed equitably within the family. The Conservative party would describe itself as 'the party of the family' and frequently expresses concern that its policies should have the effect of strengthening 'the family', as we saw in Chapter 2. If we look at tax changes over the period 1978/9– 1990/1, however, we find that the changes to the tax system during successive Conservative governments have indeed favoured married couples more than single people, particularly if husband and wife elect to be taxed separately. However, the size of the improvement *decreases* if the couple have children, roughly in proportion to the number of children, and a couple with four children who are unable to have themselves taxed separately would actually have been better off in 1978/9 (Field, 1990). Chapter 2 of this book discussed the ideological images underlying welfare practice.

3 AGAINST THE FAMILY

3.1 AGAINST FAMILIES

The family has come under criticism at various historical points. For example, in Victorian times the loose living and vices of parents were seen to be responsible for producing criminal and immoral children. More recently in the 1960s the family came under considerable attack as an emotionally stifling and potentially damaging place (Laing, 1971; Cooper, 1972). 'Anti-family' movements such as the communes developed which made a deliberate attempt to counter what were seen as some of the damaging effects of families. These included questioning the sexual role of family life and monogamy, the 'selfish' preoccupation of families with maintaining the self-interests of their members at the expense of others, the assumed naturalness of the transfer of wealth through inheritance, and the inferior positions of children and women in families. Advocates of communes argued that many of the ills of society, such as exploitation and materialism, were fermented and perpetuated by nuclear family structures. Some of these arguments echoed the arguments made by early socialists in the USSR and the attempts to weaken the influence of family through the state provision of nurseries:

> Attacks on the family are typical of revolutionary periods. Christ told his disciples to leave their parents and families and to follow him. The French, Russian, and Chinese revolutions all undermined the traditional family structure in those countries in an attempt to speed the progress toward a new social order. The Israeli kibbutz is another example of the same process.
>
> Russian laws bearing on the family during and after their revolution illustrate this process. In the 1920s, laws regulating marriage, divorce, and abortion tended toward the dissolution of the family. But in the 1930s, when Russia was moving toward the crystallization of its newly established societal norms, laws were changed to support family continuity.
>
> (Timasheff, 1960, quoted in Minuchin, 1974, p. 48)

The challenges to the taken-for-granted 'naturalness' of the nuclear family have continued. Many people have come to see 'family life' as not inevitable, that they might live alone, part-time with one or more partners or in a lesbian or gay relationship. This raises further questions about the nature of sexuality: for example, whether heterosexual unions, though they may be more 'normal' in the sense of statistically more common, are not necessarily natural or morally superior. One attempt to resolve these complications in defining family life is to assert that there is a difference between relationships and various sexual liaisons and the 'family'. This incorporates a difference between *objective* and *subjective* definitions of the family. People may choose to refer to themselves as a family even when their arrangements do not conform to legal or religious definitions: for example, members of communes have in some cases referred to the commune as a family. A distinction also emerges here between households and families: one of the main criteria for a group's being defined as a family is that the relationships are blood ones, whereas a household is defined in terms of living space shared by a group of people who may not be biologically related.

3.2 ALTERNATIVES: COMMUNES AND SEXUALITY

Deliberate attempts at alternatives to the conventional family can tell us a considerable amount about family life and the two major areas of sexuality and gender roles. Communes have been set up with the stated intention of breaking down many aspects of family life such as possessive monogamous sexuality, and constricting gender roles and to enable people to opt out of the 'rat-race'. Frequently it is not until an establishment like the family is challenged fully, in the sense of attempting to live

Decision-making by consensus in a commune in Oregon in the United States: at the end of weekly meetings, tensions are soothed by holding and kissing of hands

alternatives, that the unstated patterns of expectations and obligations are revealed:

> We don't think of ourselves as drop-outs but rather as 'drop-ins' … We believe we are pioneers in a movement that will soon have to include most of civilization. The orthodox culture that we confront is fatally and contagiously diseased.
>
> (Houriet, 1973, pp. 9–10)

> Since men and women had the same household and childcare duties, we were able to do away with some of the socially determined division of labour according to sex … in organizing our everyday life together, we learned that there is no biological distinction between men and women in the desire and ability to cook, dance, choose clothes or express the need for affection …
>
> (Bookhagen et al., 1973)

> From the women's point of view kids can be a real drag, although one loves them. They are particularly a drag when there are no other children to play with. In a commune there are other kids and other adults share the burden.
>
> (Rigby, 1974, p. 272)

In communes where the equalization of men and women was an objective this did not always work out in practice and frequently the pre-existing socializations continually caused problems. Gender roles are difficult to eradicate, for example, when it comes to matters such as housework: 'There was no overlooking the fact that while the men sat around doing politics, the women were doing the cooking' (Bookhagen *et al.*, 1973). Some women found it very hard not to encourage their children's personal attachment to them and men often did not consider that childcare was really their responsibility or they felt an allegiance only to their own children. Sometimes the gender roles and socialization showed up in unusual ways, as one woman who has lived in a commune/co-operative describes:

> Though there were a few exceptions to the rule, it seemed that women were much better at living in a commune than men, they were more co-operative and were far more considerate and tolerant … the other thing that struck me was that male non-parents tended to be either very nice to all of the children, treating them all the same and generally kindly, alternatively they tended to ignore them. It was most of all the male parents who were extremely possessive and discriminatory towards their children … when the kids squab-bled, whilst the women would tell all the children off the men would take sides or tell off other people's children … The family it seems to me from this is far more important to men than women, contrary to what we are always led to expect. The men always seemed to be trying to get their own families into one room and to exclude the others.

(Personal communication from a former commune member)

These alternatives often challenged the norms of sexual possessiveness directly with a form of 'group marriage' or a loose extended family form. Some, on the other hand, pretty well kept to heterosexual pairings, but 'defensive monogamy' was discouraged and tended to be seen as breaking up the solidarity of the commune. Also, the ideals of non-exclusive sexual relationships caused considerable personal anguish with many people who were struggling with ideals of monogamy or feelings of jealousy and would feel abandoned and rejected if their 'partners' engaged in sexual relations with other members. Above all, the greater sexual freedom often came to be seen as in fact an extension of the conventional 'male as sexual predator' role, with the various sexual partners in the commune chalked up as 'conquests'.

A more systematized form of communal living is represented by the Israeli kibbutzim, communities of workers set up originally on socialist lines and aiming at economic self-sufficiency and social reform at the micro-level. One aim of most kibbutzim was to equalize conditions between men and women – to make all the jobs in the kibbutz equally accessible to both genders, and to relieve women from the burdens of child-rearing. In one of the main varieties of kibbutz the latter was implemented at one time by housing children apart from their parents and severely restricting the hours which parents spent with their own children.

Both aspects of the original aims have broken down to some extent (Spiro, 1979). As time went on, women began to assume a greater proportion of the child-related work, and later generations of parents insisted on a greater personal share of their children's time, including having them sleep with them rather than in communal dormitories. This insistence has in fact put very considerable strain on kibbutz economies, as living quarters originally constructed for couples had to be re-built with extra bedrooms, financed by money borrowed at the height of Israeli hyper-inflation (personal communication from a recent visitor).

Nonetheless, the kibbutzim have persisted as distinctive, communally run institutions in which the 'business of the family' is done in a different way. Minuchin compares and contrasts the experiences of a 'typical' American family living in the Midwest with that of a family in a kibbutz. There are some important differences between life in a kibbutz and a normal family. Childcare in a kibbutz is a shared activity and not the sole responsibility of the parents. Loyalty is to the other members of the kibbutz and not predominantly to the family:

> ... sometimes a number of members claimed that we two [young heterosexual couple] withdrew into ourselves too much and there-fore we drifted apart from the collective. So this was one of the problems we had to face and overcome – to bring ourselves back into the collective ... [T]he social pressure is very strong and you must prove they are wrong. These pressures affect both partners and make it difficult for them.
>
> (Personal account in Minuchin, 1974, p. 70)

There is less emphasis on private property and personal space. In some kibbutzim gender roles were less clearly differentiated in that women worked on an equal basis with the men and did not have such a burden of responsibility for the children. However, given these differences (which have to some extent been diluted to economic, political and military press-ures on the kibbutz), Minuchin identifies a number of core tasks that a family in the kibbutz shares with a typical nuclear family. One of these is the formation of *boundaries*. For both families the question is about the level of loyalty to the family versus the group. A kibbutz family may receive social disapproval if they become too family-centred, in contrast to a nuclear family which may experience criticism if they are not family-centred enough. Likewise, there are similar issues to do with the estab-lishment of hierarchies, roles, patterns of intimacy and sexuality. A given community or society may have different ideas about where on a con-tinuum a family should fall but there may be fundamental tasks of human living that they share.

3.3   MEN, WOMEN AND 'THE FAMILY'

One view would see 'the family' as a target and means of social control. Historically we can trace back the origins of modern attitudes to domestic living to not much earlier than the second half of the nineteenth century. The modern stereotype of 'the family' as an enclosed unit of husband and wife, with the husband providing economic support and the wife domestic labour and childcare, appears to have been promoted with three purposes:

(a) to assure the survival and the physical and moral development of 'the nation's children' (the idea of 'the national stock of labour power' and the state's legitimate interest in it was new in this period);

(b) to deal with those in poverty, and particularly the poverty of mothers, without their becoming a charge on the state;

(c) to discipline working-class men and bring them under control as responsible husbands and fathers.

(For a fuller discussion of this, see Abbott and Sapsford (1988).) Thus in structural terms 'the family' can be seen as a means of reproducing labour relations, both in society as a whole and in the microcosm of the couple:

> The modern nuclear family continues to regulate the actions of men, but its most obvious impact is on women. One valid way of looking at marriage is to see it as a particular form of labour relationship between men and women, whereby a woman pledges for life (with limited rights to quit) her labour, sexuality and reproductive capacity, and receives protection, upkeep and certain rights to children.
>
> (Leonard, 1980, p. 5)

The ideology of the family gives ultimate control to men, in their role as fathers; it is they who are ultimately responsible for the behaviour (and the debts) of family members, and they who have the authority within the family in the last resort, even if they do not exercise it in day-to-day matters. (Hence the description of the nuclear family as 'patriarchal'.) Major decisions – about the location of the household and major items of expenditure, for example – are 'naturally' referred to the father in most families. Even if both parents have paid employment outside the home, it is generally the man's job which is seen as of primary importance, and if childcare matters mean that one parent has to be absent from work, this is generally the woman. If mothers take paid employment – and doing so is a necessity for many, if the family is to have a reasonable style of life – then they acquire a dual role which amounts in essence to two full-time jobs: working outside the home does not generally lighten the burden of housework and childcare which the woman carries. That the husband/ father is generally the main wage-earner is not coincidental; the structure of the nuclear family is built around economic dependency.

The labour market is also structured with 'the family' in mind. The jobs which women do are on average of lower status and offer lower rewards than men's jobs, over the whole range of the occupational distribution

(Table 5). Seven per cent of men are in professional or managerial employment, but less than two per cent of women. Women predominate in 'skilled non-manual' posts (secretarial and clerical); men are more commonly in skilled manual or technical work or the professions. Within each job classification women fill the lower rank: they are more likely to be employed than self-employed professionals, more likely to be in junior than in intermediate non-manual occupation, more likely to be in semi- or unskilled manual work than to be supervisors or classed as skilled, and more likely to be farm labourers than farm owners or managers. There are occupational classifications that appear more or less reserved for one gender or the other: 35 per cent of men are in manual work classed as skilled, compared with 9 per cent of women, while over 40 per cent of women are in skilled non-manual work, compared with 12 per cent of men. (If we were to break these figures down in more detail, we should find that the non-manual positions held by women were mostly different from those held by men, even within the same broad category of work.) If we compare the average earnings of men and women in full-time employment, we find that the women earn substantially less than the men. Women's mean annual earnings are on average only 60 per cent of what men in the same occupational class earn, irrespective of which class we choose to examine (Marshall *et al.*, 1988). Given how little people of either gender earn who are in unskilled manual or in clerical work, this means that it is a rare woman in a job of less than professional or managerial status who earns sufficient to be comfortably able to support children and a mortgage without the support of a male salary.

Table 5   The labour market in 1988, by gender

Class of occupation	Men %	Women %	Ratio of men to women
Professional and management	6.9	1.5	5.95
Intermediate and technical	26.1	23.5	1.48
Skilled non-manual	12.5	40.4	0.41
Skilled manual	34.9	8.6	5.36
Semi-skilled	14.9	18.8	1.05
Unskilled	4.7	7.2	0.85

Source: OPCS (1991)

Married women are also disadvantaged by the uneven pattern of employment which their family responsibilities entails. Although most women are in paid employment for the majority of their employable years and show no less commitment to the labour market than men (Martin and Roberts, 1984), a substantial proportion of them leave employment on the birth of their first child, go back to part-time (and often poorly paid and low-status) work when the children reach school age, and only later resume full-time employment. This pattern of 'career breaks' often means that they rejoin the labour market at best at the same level as the one from which they left, or at a lower level because their skills have become outdated, while comparable men have meanwhile obtained promotion. (It also disadvantages women when they come to rely on the benefits system, as we saw in Chapter 3.) However, it is not just *married* women for whom the labour market is effectively 'gendered'. *All* women tend to be seen as likely to marry and have children, whether or not they have in fact done so, and so promotion and training tend to go the men because employers feel that giving them to women would be a waste of resources.

Thus the nuclear family is structured around financial dependence, determined by and also giving rise to a gendered inequality in the rewards available in the public labour market. We have noted other gendered inequalities already in this book – in women's position under the law, for example – and we have also noted how social policy and the provision of social benefits assumes that women are dependent on a male. For example, as we saw in Chapters 2 and 3, the original construction of the welfare state assumed that 'during marriage most women will not be gainfully employed' (Beveridge, 1942, p. 50) but that in marriage a woman 'gains a right to maintenance by her husband' (p. 44). It also assumed that the number of women with children but no husbands would remain insignificant. (Where a single woman is living with a man, that man is assumed to be financially responsible for her by the benefits system, whatever they perceive their relationship to be.) All of this amounts to a degree of social control over women through the medium of family organization.

The patriarchal nuclear family also controls women's lives in more subtle ways. Because children grow up within families where these forms of dependence exist, boys and girls acquire different expectations for their future during their early socialization. Broadly, boys are brought up to think in terms of work outside the home, and girls to think in terms of marriage and children; this is less true than it was, but still very common. Boys and girls are differently admonished within the home for boisterous or unruly behaviour; girls tend to be constrained by their parents (and their peers) to behave in feminine ways – which means, in practice, being passive rather than active. Boys and girls are also differently constrained by the real or supposed dangers of the public world. Girls (and women) are less free to wander abroad than boys, particularly at night, for fear of sexual assault, and they are therefore more firmly imprisoned within the home and under parental surveillance. (For a discussion of these forms of 'informal social control', see Heidensohn (1985).)

Thus a case can be made that 'the family' is an essentially *ideological* object. It may be seen as a form of domestic organization which is presented as normal and to be desired, as working for the interests of all its members, while in fact it creates, maintains, reproduces and justifies a set of labour relations which embody very strong gendered inequalities. It may be seen as an instrument through which men exert control over women, wittingly or unwittingly. (In so doing they are also themselves controlled and constrained to participate in and maintain the social order.)

3.4   CHILDREN AND 'THE FAMILY'

It is a central part of the concept of 'the family' that the nuclear family is
the proper form of domestic arrangement for child-rearing, for the sake of
the children. We tend to believe that children brought up in other settings, with one parent, or in a communal arrangement, or in institutions,
must be psychologically damaged by this in some way. This faith in the
benefit of 'the family' for children is so firmly entrenched in our local
belief-system that we tend to take it for granted as true, and it seems
strange to question it. Its truth *has* been questioned, however.

The arguments for the benefits of the family for children, surprisingly, are
not really about families at all but about mother–child attachments. It is
now almost common sense to believe that a child separated from his or her
mother will be emotionally damaged in some fundamental way. Some of
the evidence which has been employed to support these beliefs was
inspired by the need to examine the effects of children separated in the
Second World War due to evacuation from the cities. Freud's theories had
stressed the importance of the early attachments of the child to the
mother through breast-feeding and physical contact. At the same time,
studies had been emerging from ethology, the study of animals in their
natural settings, that there was an instinctive tendency for young animals to 'imprint' – that is, to form an extremely strong attachment to
whoever took care of them during a critical early period in their lives.
These observations, combined with a need to remove women from the
workforce after the Second World War in order to give the returning
troops a chance of employment, coalesced into a convenient ideology of the
importance of motherhood and the need for women to stay at home with
their children. Bowlby (1946, 1951) conducted a series of influential
studies which offered some evidence of psychological disturbance among
children who had been raised in orphanages and deprived of their
mothers. Further to this, he looked at children in child guidance settings
which showed that children who had experienced prolonged separation
from their mothers in early infancy tended to show incomplete socialization and to become socially disturbed in adulthood. Bowlby's work
influenced government ministries of the time (see Chapter 2) and was
widely disseminated.

Much of the basis of these studies is frequently misunderstood. Bowlby
(1951) later put much more emphasis on the quality of the mother–child
relationship rather than simply the absence of the mother (see also Winnicott, 1964). Others, such as Anna Freud, were advocating stimulating
nursery environments and positive separation and experience away from
mother rather than simply continual contact. Furthermore some of the
roots of the theory underlying Bowlby's work have been ignored. He was
influenced by the work of Melanie Klein (1952) who emphasized that at a
very early age the child experiences ambivalent feelings of love and hate
and the mother's presence is essential to deal with and help to resolve
both of these feelings. This is *not* quite equivalent to some of the plati-

tudes that can permeate discussions about the importance of 'mother love'.

Nevertheless, it is fair to say that this view has persisted even though recent evidence has shown that children can cope with having a number of caretakers and it is the quality of the relationships which is important (Rutter, 1972; West, 1969; Knight and West, 1975). Bowlby (1979) himself modified his views and made clear that he thought fathers and others could become attachment figures and children could certainly be left for periods with other people without adverse effects. Also, other factors such as poverty, poor housing, lack of play facilities and of other children to play with have been found to be more significantly associated with delinquency than any psychological characteristic of the children or family factors – or at least with *officially identified* delinquency.

However, there is a twist to these debates about attachment. Almost at the same time as the theories of the effects of separation were evolving, so were theories about the dangers of enmeshment or over-involvement in families. A number of therapists had suggested, for example, that schizoid conditions (highly disturbed psychological states) were associated with excessive parental contact and parental 'enmeshment' with the children – that such states could be induced by mothers who continually fussed over their children, put thoughts into their heads and generally would not allow them to develop as separate autonomous people (Bowen, 1960; Bateson, 1972). Thus women apparently have to tread a very fine line in order to get things 'right' for their children. The position of lone-parent mothers here can be seen as extremely delicate: it is very difficult for them to go out to work in practical terms and, if they do, they are likely to feel that their child is being emotionally deprived. If they do not go out to work, they may feel that they are over-involved with their child and confusing the child's sense of identity and independence. This belief that the child will suffer if brought up by a number of carers is not borne out by evidence. However, it may serve to morally coerce women into enmeshed roles with their children and possibly this, rather than material deprivation, may cause them both to suffer psychologically.

Underlying both these lines of reasoning is an implicit assumption about the importance of the mother's role. Yet, this again has been further questioned. Studies of the effects of divorce indicate that the most important factor in whether children will adjust well to the divorce is continued positive contact with both parents (Wallerstein and Kelly, 1980). Likewise in step-parent families there is a recognition that the single parent, usually a woman, needs to have someone, a partner, to give her a break from the endless responsibility of childcare. This introduces the idea that the father or someone like a father is important. However, it also suggests that it can be the relationship between the adults in the first place that is most likely to cause problems for a child. This has been borne out by research and clinical work where it has been shown repeatedly that a child may demonstrate problems as a response to conflicts between its parents – 'conflict detouring' (see Dallos, 1991; Haley, 1976). Extreme conflicts are, however, more likely where there is poverty, poor housing, lack of opportunity or stimulation for one or both of the partners. In short, it is very likely that parents in a nuclear family will have conflicts and, when extreme, it is very likely that these will affect the child's emotional development. Wallerstein and Kelly (1980) point out that even though parents may in turn be extremely positive with the children their conflicts will almost certainly be picked up and disturb their development.

Perhaps these should not be surprising findings: the norm of the nuclear family and the belief in its superiority as an arrangement for child-rearing is a very recent and culturally specific invention. Being brought up mostly by nurses or a nanny was a norm among the English aristocracy until comparatively recently and still is a norm in the Royal Family. About a quarter of a million children live mostly in an institution of one kind or another – orphanages, children's homes, boarding-schools, hospitals etc. There are many households with children which are headed by a lone parent, because of the death, divorce or desertion of one parent, just as there were in the working class in times past, and there are 'ethnic' trends in this: British children of Afro-Caribbean origin, for example, are more likely than 'indigenous' whites and much more likely than children of Asian, Turkish or Greek origins to live in a household where the mother or grandmother is the head and there may be no male consistently present. The range of child-rearing arrangements to be found in the United Kingdom is far more diverse than the concept of 'the family' would have us believe.

It is claimed that family life and childcare are also associated with poor mental health for the women who manage them (Brown and Harris, 1978; Bernard, 1982). It has been argued (Laing, 1971; Laing and Esterson, 1970) that small tight-knit family structures are inherently suffocating – that rather than providing comfort and security, what they provide is the necessity of mediating parental conflicts, which is likely in some cases to lead to mental disturbance, as the child tries to incorporate conflicting beliefs and values. David Cooper (1972) emphasizes the age hierarchy of families, coupled with the gender hierarchy which we have already considered, and looks on the family as the place where we learn a degree of subservience and dependence as children which carries through into our adult lives. The social anthropologist Edmund Leach (1967) has argued that some of the problems of modern society stem from people having to work out in their public lives the strains and tensions engendered within family life. Nancy Chodorow (1978) has suggested that the fact that within the traditional nuclear family both boys and girls have a woman (their mother) as the major figure of their social world and see their father less often may be responsible for many of the differences she perceives between men and women in later life, in their mode of interaction and their degree of independence.

The family home is also the place where children are most likely to come to physical harm, generally at the hands of their parents or step-parents.

'New Age' travellers: Brig Oundale with young friend, Blaze. Such children often spend time with a number of adults apart from their biological parents.

Statistics of reported child abuse kept by the NSPCC suggest that over 15,000 children were reportedly abused in 1986 – about three-fifths of them physically assaulted, the rest sexually molested (Creighton, 1986). Given that not all such cases are reported, or believed if reported, the true incidence of violence or sexual 'misuse' of children in the home is probably far greater. 'Self-report' surveys of violence have suggested that up to 15 per cent of children are attacked each year; surveys of sexual abuse in the UK suggest that up to 12 per cent of girls and up to 8 per cent of boys have been molested in some form (Taylor, 1989). Problems of definition are very great in this area, of course. The line between affection and sexual molestation is a fine one, as is the line between violent attack and 'physical discipline'; we allow behaviour in parents (undressing children against their will, striking them when they misbehave) which might lead to criminal prosecution if carried out by an outsider. There are well-established class and cultural differences in the 'normal' use of violence against children as a part of discipline: strict discipline is more common in the English working class than in the middle class (Newson and Newson, 1974, 1978), and some cultures (for example, in West Africa) are far stricter than the English working-class norm as a matter of taken-for-granted normality (Ellis, 1978). It may not be fair to characterize family life as particularly violent or abusive, given the scandals which come to light from time to time concerning institutions such as children's homes; children seem to be at risk *wherever* they are. However, the family is a particularly 'fine and private place' with regard to such behaviour.

4   FOR THE FAMILY

And yet ... We have covered some of the arguments for looking at 'the family', as an ideological tool, a concept which acts as a form of social control, rather than as any kind of 'real object'. However, there is no doubt that the notion of 'the family' is a very strong one in our society and one which appears natural as a way of talking about domestic organization. We might write this off as 'false consciousness': part of the force of the notion of ideology is that ideological propositions are those which we are taught to regard as natural and beyond dispute, and which we therefore seek to reproduce in our own lives, but which in essence serve other people's interests rather than our own. There is undoubtedly an element of this in the way in which we cling to the notion of the family as natural and desirable. It may be, however, that the arguments against the concept overstate their position to some extent and overlook real advantages that the concept brings to those who try to live by it. In this part of the text we shall look at two counter-arguments: the extent to which family life really is statistically normal, and the extent to which family organization provides various kinds of support which would otherwise be absent.

4.1   FAMILIES AND SUPPORT

One obvious fact about nuclear families is that they are set up as reciprocal systems of support. The stereotype has a woman caring for a household and for children – her's and her husband's – while the husband provides the household's economic support. As we have seen, there are many other domestic arrangements which may take place between husband and wife, but they tend to have in common that paid childcare only becomes possible without a gross decrease in standard of living if the wages and/or labour of *two* people are available. The wider family – the kin group – may also provide useful services. Nuclear families also help each other: neighbours within a community can offer services to each other which make life easier for all. One should not exaggerate the amount of help that mothers receive from kin or from the community, however. An interview study of mothers (Abbott and Sapsford, 1987), comparing mothers of children with learning difficulties with other mothers, found that of even the mothers of 'normal' children only 60 per cent had received substantial help from the 'extended family' or from neighbours (and the mothers of children with learning difficulties had received less help from neighbours). Reversing the emphasis, however, we may note that 60 per cent *did* receive substantial help.

Within the nuclear family itself, about 30 per cent of the husbands were described realistically as giving substantial help with childcare and household chores. This parallels other research: Boulton (1983) found that 50 per cent of husbands are only minimally involved in childcare, and Edgell's (1982) study suggests that very few husbands indeed are substantially involved in housework. Nonetheless, some support is provided, in some cases. (See also Figure 3 in Chapter 1.) Where husbands do not contribute to the work of the household, indeed, the reason may be

'Your dinner's ready, dear': learning to be a 'normal' family?

precisely that the family conforms to the stereotype and the husbands are away from home for most of the day. In Kathryn Backett's (1982) study of couples where the husband was in paid employment and the wife staying at home, husbands did far less than 50 per cent of the work even where they were perceived by their wives as doing so, but the willingness to be involved when they were present in the home was perceived as 'taking an equal share'. It is probably the case that being perceived as sharing the load is just as important as the amount of work actually done.

Looked at more widely, 'the family' can usefully be characterized from the point of view of its members as a pattern of long-term obligation. One level of obligation is 'obvious': adult members of a nuclear family see themselves as having a duty to care for each other and for their children – including, generally, children of one parent who are not the 'biological' children of the other (step-children). Beyond this, however, the younger generation also feel an obligation to the older generation (and one which is often presumed on by the state, in working out provision for the care of elderly people). This network of obligation is the subject of current research in the University of Lancaster, by Janet Finch and her colleagues (Finch, 1987, 1989; Finch and Mason, 1992). What seems to emerge is that obligation is felt to support and care for the older generation according to whether the elderly person concerned is one's own relative or the relative of one's spouse, but this is modified by the gender of the person feeling the obligation. Broadly, women are more likely than men to feel an obligation, to elderly people from either side of the family. Given that the *prima facie* obligation is to personal care rather than mere financial contribution – to taking the person into one's household, or supporting them in their own by a variety of personal services – it is generally also the woman who is liable actually to carry out the obligation. Before the event there is a certain amount of confusion in people's understanding of 'their obligations', with one set of prescriptions coming to the surface immediately during interview – that they would not expect the younger generation to care for them, on the part of parents, and that they *would* expect to be called on, on the part of children – and contradictory responses coming to light as interviews progress – parents being able to name the family member who is most 'obliged' to care for them, and children being able to name other family members who would be in a better position to do so (Hayes, 1989). The concept that *someone* in the family has such an obligation is seldom questioned, however. Under certain circumstances such obligations may persist even after divorce out of the family of the elderly person and even re-marriage into another family (Finch and Mason, 1989).

4.2   FAMILY AND IDENTITY

Another reason which has been put forward for the popularity of the family as an institution, among those who constitute it, is that it may act as a protection of the individual against the societal. As we saw in Chapter 1, this view of the family is widely associated with the new right: writers such as Ferdinand Mount (1982) have argued that one major function of families is to act as a point of resistance against the encroachment of state authority. However, similar views have also been put forward from the left (see, for example, Lasch, 1977) and some black writers (such as Carby, 1982) have seen it as a focus of resistance against the racism of the surrounding society (see Chapter 1).

This kind of function alone would not seem sufficient reason for the family's popularity, but we might see it as a special case of a more general tendency to treat family life as a place into which one can retreat from the rigours of public life. 'The family' of the stereotype is one in which all members regard each other with affection and are supportive of each other. It is somewhere which can compensate for what goes wrong at work and can add depth and colour to otherwise drab and routine lives, through what might be regarded as one of our age's greatest social experiments – the attempt to live with one person for a lifetime and know and be known by that person in a way not possible in casual social exchanges. For children 'the family' is a set of people who continue to like you when no-one does in the outside world, and somewhere which remains constant and comfortable while the outside world is constantly new and frightening; it is somewhere you can retreat when your experiments at living and growing up are not going well. The real family, the families in which people actually exist, seldom lives up to all or even much of this set of ideals. People grow to take each other for granted, and they bring their outside problems home and 'work them out' on the captive audience of other family members. Parents do *not* always love their children; despite the ideology which says that parental love is natural and inevitable, it is in fact often something which has to be worked at and which can break down under stress. People change and so find that what was satisfactory when it started is less satisfactory ten or twenty years later; in particular, children change and in the end often come to use their parents as a focus of their discontents. The privacy of the family home can sometimes make it a dangerous place for children and for women, as the statistics on family violence and sexual assault testify. Nonetheless, the ideals are a goal built into the institution, something which we seek to find in it, and sometimes something which we do try to build into it.

Finally, the institution of the family helps us to achieve our own identities, in four related ways:

1 To the extent to which it provides emotional support and social stability, it is one place where a settled sense of one's own identity, capability and acceptability is achieved. (It is not the only place, as is sometimes suggested – children have school and peer-group activity, and adults have work and leisure involvements – but it is an important and continuing source of identity nonetheless.)

2 When family relationships work they act to promote a sense of solidarity, of being part of a group rather than alone and vulnerable. As such, families can act as sites of resistance to public pressure, 'places' where alternative ways of seeing the social world can be tried out and reinforced by the support of other family members.

3 It provides a set of roles which enable us to locate ourselves within the social order – as wives, husbands, children. These roles carry values which enable the adults in families to mark and recognize their own adulthood. To be a husband or a wife is an achieved status, and one which people want to achieve. To be a husband (or the male in a settled relationship outside marriage) is to establish in the world's eyes and one's own that one has achieved adult male sexuality; bachelors of a certain age are often regarded with some suspicion. To be a wife, and even more to be a mother, is to establish one's normality and desirability as a woman. These are both forms of social control, but also goals which people desire. It is the desirability of the goals which gives family ideology its force; people reproduce the family as an institution by their own deliberate actions, following the goals which family ideology establishes. (For children, 'being in a family' also establishes a social status, and an inferior one. 'Leaving home' becomes an important transition into adulthood, and this again helps to maintain the family as nuclear.)

4 The experience of family life helps to establish our social identities in a wider sense – to establish us within a gender, a class, an ethnic group. This is something which will be discussed at length in Part 2 of this book.

5   CONCLUSION

This chapter has reviewed the ideological stereotype of 'the family' which dominates law, public policy and political rhetoric and has tried to contrast it with people's structural positions on the one hand and how they *experience* their lives on the other. We have examined some of the diversity of family life in terms of statistical descriptions of the frequencies of different family forms and some descriptions of the experiences from the inside of these forms. One general conclusion that we can make is that, regardless of the form of family in which we live or whether we live in a family at all, our experience is likely to be shaped by the dominant ideology of family life which in the UK is still the nuclear family. People may experience living in a different form such as a step-family as problematic, not just because our society is not equipped or prepared to offer such families much assistance – for example, in the form of education, advice, counselling about some of the likely tasks, difficulties that they are likely to face and so on – but also because they may feel 'deprived' or that their alternative form does not live up to the ideals of the nuclear family. Even people who have made a deliberate decision to reject the nuclear family model, such as those who have chosen to live in communes, seem to find it very difficult to break away from it totally. The media, education and experts on the family have contributed to this pervasive influence of the nuclear family. There is evidence that communes, for example, do not produce disturbed children and adults, but by and large such evidence is ignored in the face of the relentless emphasis on the nuclear form.

Yet the lived reality of the nuclear family represents quite a disturbing picture if we consider the exploitation of women, abuses of children, not to mention the isolation of families that are likely to occur. These disadvantages are themselves quite widely recognized, but though the statistics indicate some changes, they do not suggest that nuclear forms are becoming less popular. Instead, the conclusions many people appear to make is that if only they work harder they can get it right, or perhaps that next time, after a divorce, they can find domestic bliss in re-marriage. Cross-cultural comparisons shed some light on these beliefs by revealing that family forms are intimately linked to the culture and how the family functions within it. It could be argued in this way that a lone parent struggling to cope in the UK might find it much easier to live in another culture where a lone-parent form is more widely accepted and receives greater levels of support.

The discussion of different forms of family life has suggested that there are some fundamental tasks facing people living in any grouping: child-care, regulation of sexuality, establishing a sense of identity and boundary as an individual, patterns of intimacy as a couple and as some form of family unit, negotiating roles in terms of divisions of duties and decision-making and defining some rules about the patterns of mutual obligations or duties. What defines a family, then, can be seen to be the negotiation and completion of these tasks. This suggests a dynamic definition of family life as a process. That is, it is the continuing attempts to solve these tasks which embody family life rather than the particular form – nuclear, lone-parent, step-family, extended family or commune – that emerges as an attempted solution. The solutions that people can and are allowed to attempt are constrained by the culture, but such a dynamic model frees us from the trap of trying to define any one form of family life as 'the family'.

6 EVIDENCE AND ARGUMENT: A BRIEF NOTE

As a final point in this chapter, we need to think briefly but critically about the nature of the evidence which we have considered here and to review the nature of arguments in general in the social sciences. There has been a fair amount of history in the preceding chapters. You should note that what is presented is not a neutral description of times past, but a selective reappraisal of their history. We pick out events and trends as significant in relation to some *argument* which we want to pursue; they are judged as significant because they can be used to support or refute some claim about how the past has shaped the present.

Similarly, we point out cross-cultural similarities or differences not to describe other lands but to make some point about our own social system or about social systems in general. Indeed, even 'descriptive statistics' are not neutrally descriptive. The statistics themselves may be neutral, but *which* statistics we choose to collect and/or present is determined by the arguments which we desire to explore.

What matters is the starting-point. Any argument starts by defining terms, explicitly or implicitly, and four points can usefully be made about this process:

1 The discourse within which an argument is set – the terms we use to conduct it – determines the kind of answer which can be produced. If we are talking about 'the problem of prostitution', for example, we can explain the problem as an outcome of social structures, or as an expression of 'human nature', or as a product of human evil, or any combination of the three. Within an argument structured in this way, however, it is difficult to suggest that prostitution is a normal commercial transaction, no different from the sale and purchase of food or houses – we have already rejected this viewpoint when we started to consider it 'as a problem'.

2 In the example, it is almost equally difficult to try to redefine what the nature of 'the problem' is, as many feminists have tried – as a particular aspect of the more general problem of power relations between the genders. To do so may seem to be twisting the argument beyond its natural scope and introducing questions irrelevant to what is under discussion. What is 'relevant' or 'irrelevant' is discourse-defined, however: it is not

something which 'stands to reason', but something imposed by the terms of the argument.

3   'Capturing the discourse' is a natural way of winning arguments. In a political discussion of prostitution, for example, the battle is almost won once we have agreed to consider it 'a problem' and discuss it in the same terms as crime and delinquency; it then becomes something to be abolished or controlled. Someone who wanted to argue that it should be preserved would have to do so in other terms – perhaps by turning the argument towards propositions about the liberties of the individual and the inappropriateness of legal interference in the private sphere. (A comparable example might be the arguments over gun-control in the United States, and the way that 'the liberty of the individual' wars against 'the murder of the innocent' to control the direction that the argument will take.)

4   Thus we should always be wary when accepting arguments, even on the basis of valid evidence, and consider what conclusions and constraints on our thinking have been built into the discourse within which the argument is set. However, using the concept of discourse in this way is a form of *analysis*, not a form of criticism. To identify a dominant belief as discourse-defined is not in itself to refute it, because when we formulate the argument differently, our reformulation will *also* be discourse-defined. It is not the case that our opponents use discourse while we speak truth. On the contrary, it is impossible to speak about anything except in some discourse.

REFERENCES

Abbott, P. and Sapsford, R. (1987) *'Community Care' for Mentally Handicapped Children*, Milton Keynes, Open University Press.

Abbott, P. and Sapsford, R. (1988) 'The body politic: health, family and society', Unit 11 of D211, *Social Problems and Social Welfare*, Milton Keynes, The Open University.

Backett, K.(1982) *Mothers and Fathers*, London, Macmillan.

Barrow, J. (1982) 'West Indian families: an insider's perspective', in Rapaport, R. N. *et al.* (eds) op. cit.

Bateson, G. (1972) *Steps to an Ecology of Mind*, New York, Ballantine.

Bernard, J. (1982) *The Future of Marriage*, New Haven, CT, Yale University Press.

Beveridge, W. (1942) *Social Insurance and Allied Services*, Cmnd 6404, London, HMSO.

Bookhagen, C., Hemmer, E., Raspe, J. and Schultz, J. (1973) 'Kommune 2: child-rearing in the commune', in Dreitzal, H.P. (ed.) *Family, Marriage and the Struggle of the Sexes*, New York, Macmillan.

Boulton, M.G. (1983) *On Being a Mother: a study of women with pre-school children*, London, Tavistock.

Bowen, M. (1960) 'A family concept of schizophrenia', in Jackson, D.D. (ed.) *The Etiology of Schizophrenia*, New York, Basic Books.

Bowlby, J. (1946) *Forty-four Juvenile Thieves*, London, Baillière, Tindall and Cox.

Bowlby, J. (1951) *Maternal Care and Mental Health*, Geneva, World Health Organization.

Bowlby, J. (1979) *The Making and Breaking of Affectional Bonds*, London, Tavistock.

Brown, G.W. and Harris, T. (1978) *Social Origins of Depression*, London, Routledge and Kegan Paul.

Carby, H.J. (1982) 'White women listen: Black feminism and the boundaries of sisterhood', in Centre for Contemporary Cultural Studies, *The Empire Strikes Back: race and racism in '70s Britain*, London, Heinemann.

Chodorow, N. (1978) *The Reproduction of Mothering: psychoanalysis and the sociology of gender*, Berkeley, CA, University of California Press.

Cooper, D. (1972) *The Death of the Family*, Harmondsworth, Penguin.

Coote, A., Harman, H. and Hewitt, P. (1990) *The Family Way*, Social Policy Paper no. 1, London, Institute for Public Policy Research.

Creighton, S.J. (1986) *Annual Update of Statistics*, London, NSPCC.

Dallos, R. (1991) *Family Belief Systems, Therapy and Change*, Milton Keynes, Open University Press.

Edgell, S. (1982) *Middle-Class Couples: a study of segregation, domination and inequality in marriage*, London, Allen and Unwin.

Ellis, J. (ed.) (1978) *West Indian Families in Britain*, London, Routledge and Kegan Paul.

Family Policy Studies Centre (1990) *Factsheet 1: The Family Today – continuity and change*, London, FPSC.

Field, F. (1990) 'Budget 1990: The need for a family impact statement', *Family Policy Bulletin*, vol. 8, pp. 1–2.

Finch, J. (1987) 'Family obligation and the life course', in Bryman, A. *et al.* (eds) *Rethinking the Life Cycle*, London, Macmillan.

Finch, J. (1989) *Family Obligations and Social Change*, London, Polity Press.

Finch, J. and Mason, J. (1989) 'Divorce, remarriage and family obligation', paper presented to a British Sociological Association Conference, Plymouth Polytechnic.

Finch, J. and Mason, J. (1992) *Negotiating Family Responsibilities*, London, Routledge.

Gittins, D. (1985) *The Family in Question*, London, Macmillan.

Haley, J. (1976) *Problem Solving Therapy*, New York, Harper Row.

Hanscombe, G.E. and Forster, J. (1982) *Rocking the Cradle: lesbian mothers, a challenge in family living*, London, Sheba Feminist Publishers.

Haskey, J. (1989) 'Families and households of the ethnic minority and white populations of Great Britain', *Population Trends*, vol. 57, pp. 8–19.

Haskey, J. and Kiernan, K. (1989) 'Cohabitation in Britain: Characteristics and estimated numbers of cohabiting partners', *Population Trends*, vol. 58, pp. 23–32.

Hayes, L. (1989) 'One of us would do something: gender and the long-term obligations of young people to the family', paper presented to a British Sociological Association Conference, Plymouth Polytechnic.

Heidensohn, F. (1985) *Women and Crime*, London, Macmillan.

Houriet, R. (1973) *Getting Back Together*, London, Routledge and Kegan Paul.

Klein, M., Heimann, P., Isaacs, S. and Riviere, J. (1952) *Developments in Psycho-analysis* (New York, Da Capo Press, 1982, reprint of 1952 edn).

Knight, B. and West, D.J. (1975) 'Temporary and continuing delinquency', *British Journal of Criminology*, vol. 15, p. 43.

Laing, R.D. (1971) *The Politics of the Family and Other Essays*, London, Tavistock.

Laing, R.D. and Esterson, A. (1970) *Sanity, Madness and the Family*, Harmondsworth, Penguin Books.

Lasch, C. (1977) *Haven in a Heartless World*, New York, Basic Books.

Leach, E. (1967) *A Runaway World*, London, BBC Publications.

Leonard, D. (1980) *Sex and Generation: a study of courtship and weddings*, London, Tavistock.

Lorde, A. (1988) *A Burst of Light*, London, Sheba Feminist Publishers.

MacLean, M. and Wadsworth, M. (1988) 'Children's life chances and parental divorce', *International Journal of Law and the Family*, vol. 2, pp. 155–66.

Marshall, G., Rose, D., Newby, H. and Vogler, C. (1988) *Social Class in Modern Britain*, London, Unwin Hyman.

Martin, J. and Roberts, C. (1984) *Women and Employment: a lifetime perspective*, London, HMSO.

Minuchin, S. (1974) *Families and Family Therapy*, London, Tavistock Publications.

Mount, F. (1982) *The Subversive Family*, London, Cape.

Newson, J. and Newson, E. (1974) *Seven Years Old in the Home Environment*, London, Allen and Unwin.

Newson, J. and Newson, E. (1978) 'Cultural aspects of childrearing in the English-speaking world', in Richards, M. (ed.) *The Integration of a Child into a Social World*, Cambridge, Cambridge University Press.

Office of Population Censuses and Surveys (1990) *Social Trends*, no. 20, London, HMSO.

Office of Population Censuses and Surveys (1991) *Population Trends*, no. 66, London, HMSO.

Rapaport, R.N., Fogarty, M.P. and Rapaport, R. (1982) *Families in Britain*, London, Routledge and Kegan Paul.

Rigby, A. (1974) *Alternative Realities: a study of communes and their members*, London, Routledge and Kegan Paul.

Rutter, M. (1972) *Maternal Deprivation Reassessed*, Harmondsworth, Penguin Books.

Shaw, S. (1991) 'The conflicting experience of lone parenthood', in Hardey, M. and Crow, G. (eds) *Lone Parenthood: coping with constraints and making opportunities*, London, Wheatsheaf.

Spiro, M.E. (1979) *Gender and Culture: kibbutz women revisited*, Durham, NC, Duke University Press.

Taylor, S. (1989) 'How prevalent is it?', in Stainton Rogers, W., Hevey, D. and Ash, E. (eds) *Child Abuse and Neglect: facing the challenge*, Milton Keynes, The Open University.

Timasheff, N.S. (1960) 'The attempt to abolish the family in Russia', in Bell, N.W. and Vogel, E. (eds) *A Modern Introduction to the Family*, Glencoe, Free Press.

Trenchard, D. and Warren, H. (1984) *'Something to Tell You': the experience and needs of young lesbians and gay men in London*, London, London Gay Teenage Group.

Wallerstein, J. and Kelly, J.B. (1980) *Surviving the Break-up*, London, Grant McIntyre.

Weeks, J. (1985) *Sexuality and its Discontents: meaning, myths and modern sexualities*, London, Routledge.

West, D.J. (1969) *Who Becomes Delinquent?*, London, Heinemann.

Winnicott, D.W. (1964) *The Child, the Family and the Outside World*, Harmondsworth, Penguin Books.

PART 2
INTERACTIONS AND IDENTITIES

CHAPTER 5
CONSTRUCTING FAMILY LIFE: FAMILY BELIEF SYSTEMS

RUDI DALLOS

CONTENTS

INTRODUCTION

What we take to be 'the family' and 'family life' is influenced by the ideologies and discourses inherent in the society in which we live at a particular historical point. An analysis at the level of society and culture (see Chapter 1) suggests that 'family life' is shaped by dominant ideologies or discourses about what family life should be like. We can see families as reproducing themselves, both literally and ideologically. For example, although the roles of men and women in families and other living arrangements have changed significantly in the last thirty years, by and large women still take most of the responsibility for childcare, while men are expected to be the main breadwinners; and most of us (in Western cultures) live for the majority of our lives in an arrangement not too dissimilar from a nuclear family (see Chapter 4). Above all, for many of us the image of the nuclear family still governs our behaviours, expectations and feelings. We may be 'for' or 'against' the nuclear family, but either way, it has – until recently at least – set the agenda of our thinking, feeling and choices.

Yet within Western (and other) societies there is clearly a diversity of ways in which people may 'choose' to live together. Some of these choices are 'variations' on the nuclear family model, while others are quite deliberate and explicit attempts to reject it, such as communal and some lone-parent relationships. If we accept that many people make such choices, the question remains of how people go about constructing their own varieties of 'family life'. How do they decide how 'normal', as opposed to how 'deviant', they will be? To take a conventional example, a heterosexual couple needs to decide when or whether to marry; whether to have children and, if so, how many; how to divide up the family tasks such as childcare; whether they should divorce; whether they should marry again; how they should relate to any step-children they might have; and so on.

Above all, these decisions suggest the possibility that families do not simply absorb ideologies and discourses wholesale, but that they translate them within their own 'family culture', that is, the traditions and current dynamics within their own family. Between society and the individual is a set of shared premises, explanations and expectations: in short a family's own belief system. Metaphorically this can be represented as a deck of cards offering a range of options from which particular choices can be made. These 'cards' or options are derived mainly from personal experiences, family traditions and societal discourses. Continuing the metaphor, each family can be seen as having its own unique set of 'cards' which offers choice but also serves to constrain their perceived options and consequently the choices they make: family members make choices, but not simply in circumstances of their own choosing.

The ideas underlying this chapter have been inspired by work with families in therapeutic settings. Hence there is an emphasis on the development of problems and therapeutic change. However, such ideas have a wider implication for the study of 'family life', suggesting that it should be seen as dynamic, with family members continually influencing, and being influenced by, each other. Continuous change and development is regarded as essential and problems are seen to be related to 'stuckness' or an inability to find effective solutions to transitional tasks. The chapter concludes by proposing that in many cases this 'stuckness' may be a result of the internalization by families of wider ideologies, such as rigid notions of gender roles, which constrain the solutions that families are able to contemplate.

The belief systems approach described in this chapter tries to embrace two aspects of family life which at first sight might appear contradictory: on the one hand, people do appear to make autonomous decisions about their lives; on the other, family life is characterized by repetitive, predictable patterns of actions. These divergent features are accounted for by two psychological theories: the first, personal construct theory (Kelly, 1955), derives from humanistic and constructivist psychology in stressing that people create systems of meanings and courses of actions for themselves; the second, systems theory, emphasizes patterning and interdependence of action. This chapter attempts to show how these two approaches can be integrated by exploring the ways in which the beliefs held by family members guide their choices and serve to shape patterns of 'family life'. This approach has been variously termed a 'family belief systems' model (Dallos, 1991), 'family construct psychology' (Procter, 1981), 'second-order cybernetics' (Hoffman, 1985; Keeney, 1979), or 'constructivist family therapy' (Hoffman, 1990; Anderson and Goolishan, 1986).

One of the central themes guiding this chapter is that families are inevitably faced with various 'tasks' – difficulties and problems which they have to find ways of managing. These tasks alter as they proceed through their developmental cycle. The chapter starts with a discussion of the concept of the 'family life-cycle' which charts some of the major changes or transitions that family life presents, such as the birth of children, older children leaving home and bereavements. It is argued that families need to adapt and adjust continually in order to deal with such tasks; this is particularly the case at these moments of critical transition. Each family is seen as developing ways of dealing with the tasks facing them and attempting solutions. In turn these attempted solutions are seen to be shaped by the beliefs they hold as individuals, as a family and those they hold in common with wider society. The recursive combination of tasks, attempted solutions, outcomes and beliefs constitutes the family system.

I INTERNAL AND EXTERNAL RELATIONS

It can be argued that choices and the beliefs underlying them, operate at three distinct but interconnected levels:

1 *The social–cultural* – what is perceived as acceptable and desirable in any given society.

2 *The familial* – how people in families jointly negotiate decisions, based partly on the internalizations of cultural discourses and partly on their joint evolution of a set of shared beliefs.

3 *The personal* – each family member has a more or less unique set of personal beliefs: for the parents this may emanate from their accumulated experience prior to forming a family; for all members personal beliefs also develop from contacts outside the family, and so on.

These three levels need to be considered simultaneously to provide a comprehensive picture of 'family life'.

Each family or grouping can be seen as to some extent creating a unique interpersonal system of meanings and actions, a version of family life which develops from the amalgamation of its members' negotiations and choices based upon their personal and shared beliefs and histories. Though this process is creative, involves a wide variety of complex issues and is widely thought of as unique, it can nevertheless be suggested that there are some fundamental themes common to any social grouping:

(a) Relationship to the 'outside' world:

Family members may develop a set of perspectives or beliefs about themselves as a 'family', that is, what kind of a family they are – close vs distant, argumentative vs harmonious, formal vs informal, traditional vs modern and so on. But families also need to establish ways of interacting with a variety of 'external' systems, such as schools, workplaces, local community (neighbours, friends and extended family), in-laws and so on. Families vary in the beliefs they have about such boundaries: some believe that a rigid separation is required, stressing family 'privacy' and self-determination; others believe in a looser more permeable boundary, with easy access – 'open house'.

Family identities are not simply constructed internally but in some cases rigid definitions may be imposed (for example, some ethnic minority families or those containing members who have a 'disability', such as mental health problems, learning disability and so on).

(b) Internal relationships:

(i) *Power, intimacy and boundaries* Whilst family life is complex and varied, these three key issues continuously surface and require families to develop a set of beliefs enabling rules and procedures to be formed (Dallos and Procter, 1984; Minuchin, 1974; Haley, 1976). The issue of power requires the development of beliefs about responsibilities, decision-making, duties, obligations and commitments. The issue of boundaries includes beliefs about personal space and privacy

– the boundaries of the 'self' or private vs shared activity in the family. The issue of intimacy embraces a complex array of psychological emotional tasks and needs that have to be met, such as affection, sympathy, support, sexual intimacy and so on.

(ii) *Roles and tasks* In order to function, a family or any other social grouping has to establish some 'ground rules' and also develop some organization so that the basic physical and material necessities are met.

(iii) *Gender* Cutting across these dimensions of family life there is the central issue of gender roles and expectations. The development of gender-specific roles, division of labour, identity, patterning of activity and so on, will be affected by how the issue of gender is negotiated.

These areas of family life – the internal 'private' world and the interface with the wider community – will in turn be influenced by dominant ideologies and discourses. For example, the division of responsibilities within a family is guided by prevailing discourses about appropriate gender roles so that, until recently at least, boys have grown up believing that their role in families would be to provide and make major decisions, and girls that they would be mothers and run the domestic arrangements. More broadly, families are also expected to undertake certain duties, such as the 'appropriate' socialization of children. Similarly, the recurring public 'panics' about the family 'being in crisis' and in moral decline, falling apart, not shouldering its responsibilities and so on, are likely to be absorbed by family members and further regulate a family's internal activities and external relations. Each family will develop a set of beliefs governing the boundary between its private, internal world and that of a public external outside. Some families, for example, appear to hold to the belief that whatever happens 'under their roof' is essentially private and should be free from outside interference, whilst others expect, and even invite, outsiders to help manage their affairs or are keen to interact with other families and the local community.

2   THE FAMILY LIFE-CYCLE

Each family will contain in some form a set of beliefs covering these internal and external relationships. These in turn will embrace ideas about development and change. These have been encapsulated in the concept of 'family life-cycle development' by family therapists and researchers. Indeed much of this material on family life has been derived from the field of family therapy.

Until relatively recently the principle of the privacy of family life meant that we had very little information about what actually happens within families. Most of our knowledge was largely anecdotal and came either from personal experience or from literature and drama. Family therapy evolved in the 1960s out of the dissatisfactions that many therapists felt in working with individual forms of treatment. Therapists working with children in particular started to note that often the 'child's problems' appeared to be related to what was happening at home (Haley, 1976; Minuchin, 1974). However, without seeing families together, in the clinic or at home, therapists had little firm idea, apart from speculations, about exactly what went on between members of a family. As these therapists started to invite families along with their children for assessment and treatment, or in the case of adults along with their partners and children, a rich vein of information started to be mined. For the first time a systematic mapping of the internal dynamics of family life could be attempted. These observations led to the formulation of a range of models of family life, many of which stressed the predictability and repetitive patterning of family dynamics.

2.1 TASKS AND DIFFICULTIES

Families exist in environments which alter continuously. A family is an organic entity which maintains some form of identity and structure whilst at the same time continually evolves and changes. Apart from day-to-day variations and adaptations necessary for family life, it is also evident that families may be faced at times with massive demands for change ('tasks') such as when members arrive – births and marriages – and depart – divorce and death. There may also be external demands such as local social upheavals and major cultural changes. Duvall (1977) extended the idea of the individual life-cycle model to the idea of a 'family life-cycle' (FLC). The implications of this model for the practice of family therapy were first set out by Jay Haley (1981) in his book describing the therapeutic techniques of Milton Erickson. He describes how Erickson had noted that problems were often associated with critical periods of change and transition in families. For example, psychotic episodes in late adolescence were seen to be related to difficulties for the family over the departure of the son or daughter to set up his or her own home. Haley described certain events as critical, transitional stages for families (see Figure 1).

Erickson's concept of family development emphasized a life-long process of socialization, adjustment and learning within families. Hence socialization did not end with child-rearing but involved a reciprocal process whereby parents were also continually learning and adjusting to their children. Haley did not expand greatly on the subject, but he made clear that the model assumes that there exists a common set of values and norms inherent to Western society to which families are expected to comply. For example, he describes how young people 'need' to practise courtship skills in order to successfully find a suitable mate. Disruptions to this process, for example through involvement in family conflicts, can create problems for the young if they lead to disengagement from their peers.

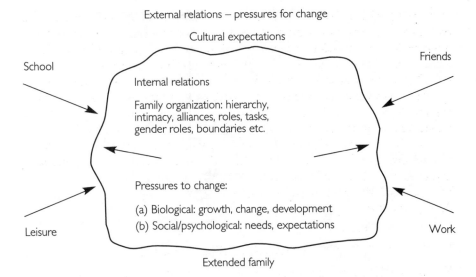

Family life-cycle stages: *Transitions*

The external and internal demands for change are *continuous*, but become critical at transitional points in a family's life:

• courtship

• early marriage

• birth of children

• middle marriage

• leaving home

• retirement and old age

Tasks: external and internal demands for change

Attempted solutions: ways of meeting the tasks, solving demands for change

Figure 1   Family life-cycle: change, tasks and attempted solutions

Source: Adapted from Dallos, 1991, p. 12

Carter and McGoldrick (1980) have offered some elaborations of the FLC model by additionally noting the significance of inter-generational traditions. They propose a two-dimensional model (see Figure 2).

Carter and McGoldrick describe their model as follows:

> The vertical flow in a system includes patterns of relating and functioning that are transmitted down the generations in a family ... It includes all the family attitudes, taboos, expectations, and loaded issues with which we grow up. One could say that these aspects of our lives are like the hand that we are dealt: they are a given. What we do with them is the issue for us.

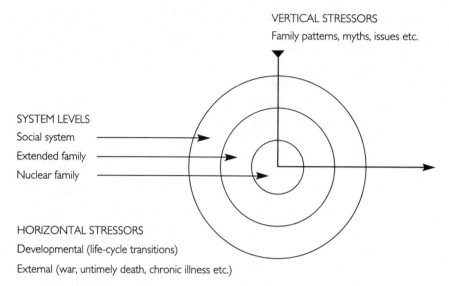

VERTICAL STRESSORS
Family patterns, myths, issues etc.

SYSTEM LEVELS
Social system
Extended family
Nuclear family

HORIZONTAL STRESSORS
Developmental (life-cycle transitions)
External (war, untimely death, chronic illness etc.)

Figure 2   Developmental influences on the family

Source: Carter and McGoldrick, 1980, p. 10

> The horizontal flow includes ... both the predictable developmental stresses, and those unpredictable events, 'the slings and arrows of outrageous fortune' that may disrupt the life-cycle process.
>
> (Carter and McGoldrick, 1980, p. 10)

ACTIVITY I

Take some time to consider your own current family or your family of origin. To what extent did your experience coincide with the life-cycle stages identified above? Did you proceed through them in this order? What issues arose for you as a result of any deviations from this nuclear family sequence? To what extent, even if you chose to proceed in different ways, do you think this model shaped your expectations, feelings and ways of finding solutions to the issues that arose?

Despite such elaborations, the concept of the family life-cycle has attracted critical attention especially on the grounds that it takes an overly normative view of family development and focuses on the nuclear family which, in its pure form, is not now the most common arrangement. The experiences of step-families, for example, can involve complex overlapping of these stages. A 'new' couple may find themselves in a courting, romantic phase, whilst at the same time having to deal with adolescent offspring from their partner's previous marriage. With this model there is also the danger of underestimating the diversity of choices people may feel are available: adults may choose to live in a lone-parent arrangement or in a commune, but these choices are less available to a child although, as Haley (1981) argues, parents' 'eccentric' choices can have considerable ramifications for the child in terms of being rejected by his or her peers and becoming labelled in various ways.

The life-cycle approach offers a framework for considering a wide range of issues concerning family life. It recognizes the influence of a broad set of rules, norms and expectations from within and outside of the family. In this way the crises associated with the various stages are related to moments of rupture between a family's beliefs and actions and those of the wider society. For example, parents may experience various forms of pressure if they 'cling' to an adolescent child too strongly. This is especially the case if the child demonstrates problems of various sorts which elicit interventions – such as advice from school, the doctor or social workers to 'allow their child more independence' in keeping with wider cultural norms. Such 'ruptures' are vividly illustrated by the experiences of some Asian families, for example, where a close and continuing involvement with the family is expected, which may create problems where the children have been brought up in British schools where a conflicting set of values prevail.

In particular, young adults in this period of transition can be seen as the family's 'research assistants'. They are usually spending more time away from the family, sampling new social groups and thereby exploring and testing the relevance of the family's beliefs in a variety of outside settings. This naturally leads to some questioning of the family's accepted ways of seeing things. For some families this questioning and challenging of the saliency and validity of their beliefs can be particularly threatening, especially if they are having to deal with other pressures.

2.2   ATTEMPTED SOLUTIONS

Families find various, often creative ways of solving the task or difficulties that face them during these transitional periods. For example, parents may start to spend more time together to prepare for change, they may make various arrangements to assist and maintain contact with their child, but in some cases they may attempt to delay the transition. These 'solutions' are seen as emerging from a combination of their circumstances, resources, beliefs, emotional needs, external circumstances and so on. In some instances the solutions are formed in a conscious and planned way, in others more emotively and intuitively. As Figure 1 indicates, there are likely to be a complex range of interacting factors involved.

The solutions generated and attempted will be shaped by the prevailing beliefs held. One important source of direction for these beliefs comes from family traditions going back several generations, and in some cases hundreds of years. One example of this can be seen in episodes of storytelling in a family, such as 'how Uncle Dave left home and things worked out for him after some period of struggle and hardship'. These anecdotes provide a store of experience generated by the traditions of family experimentation. These traditions have been conceptualized in terms of family scripts (Byng-Hall, 1985) which serve to guide how successive generations of children come to regulate their family lives. A powerful example is provided in cases of families who have a tradition of calling in outside agencies at difficult times:

> The belief system of a family is formed by, and in turn sustains, its patterns of behaviour. For instance, take a family that throughout the generations has maintained its balance during a crisis by calling upon a social work agency to temporarily remove one of its members. This family may well be seen as conforming to a belief that expulsion of a member is the only solution to a crisis. The more the family believes that expulsion is the only solution, the more the family uses expulsion, and so on through the generations.
>
> (Burnham, 1986 p. 21)

The family life-cycle model also draws our attention to the interplay between the images of family life available within a society and the family's own interpretation and internalizations of these. The dominant images are made more compelling by the fact that even if people are not in a true nuclear family (that is, living with partner and own children), the structure of a heterosexual couple living together with children is still the most common form of family experience and most of us will experience this for the greater part of our lives. However, this presumed uniformity obscures the complexity of the roles and experiences that face many families. In a step-family, in which both parents have been married before, and where they have children from their previous marriages as well as the current one, there is at any given moment a variety of ways in which people can regard themselves: each parent may at times experience themselves as being in a lone-parent family (with their children from the previous marriage); being a step-parent; belonging to a nuclear family with their new 'joint' children; or as a member of a step-family. At different times one definition may predominate over others or the experience may be confusing, contradictory and fragmented. Needless to say, the experiences of individuals are not simply personal but are related to the demands of other members of the family.

It is also possible to identify different and complex sets of kinship relationships, such as ex-spouse's mother/father and new partner's parents as grandparents-in-law. Significantly we have very little in the way of concepts or even language with which to label these relationships. Such changes are frequently accounted for as a result of the growth of divorce in the late twentieth century. However, historically the high mortality of mothers at childbirth has given us a long legacy of step-parent configurations. It is arguable that the lack of acknowledgement of such diversity is consistent with an ideological attempt to maintain the nuclear model as the image to be strived for. A widespread acceptance of alternatives remains widely perceived as 'radical' and as a challenge to one of the most basic foundations of Western and other societies. Yet:

> Attacks on the family are typical of revolutionary periods. Christ told his disciples to leave their parents and families and to follow him. The French, Russian, and Chinese revolutions all undermined the traditional family structure in those countries in an attempt to speed the progress toward a new social order. The Israeli kibbutz is another example of the same social process.
>
> (Minuchin, 1974, p. 48)

2.3   CEREMONY AND RITUAL

In most societies the transitions involved in life-cycle stages are demarcated and assisted by various forms of ceremonies and rituals: the end of courtship and entry into marriage by the wedding ceremony; the arrival of children by christening; bereavement by the funeral ceremony; not to mention various forms of graduation ceremonies, confirmations, retirement presentations and so on. Ceremonies and rituals play an important part in signalling change, perhaps erecting boundaries around a newly married couple or restating the relationship between the nuclear family and other parts of an extended family. The congregation of all the family members at ceremonies and rituals allows these redefinitions to be announced to all the members at one time, hence making it easier for them to become established. Selvini-Palazzoli *et al.* (1978) make the point that ceremonies and rituals are a very powerful form of implicit communication. For example, those who stand closest to the couple in the wedding picture may at the same time be implicitly displaying and reaffirming, for all to see, the new nature of the family organization.

The examination of rituals and ceremonies reveals how families are inextricably connected to the wider social world. Society contains ideas not only about how families should be, but how they should develop and change. In other words, rituals and ceremonies provide 'rites of passage' modes of order, not only for individuals but for the whole family.

2.4   GENDER AND SHIFTING INEQUALITIES OF POWER

Relationships in families may be considered a matter of give and take. But who gives and who takes varies during the course of a relationship. The balance of power can be seen to be determined by global considerations, such as the general balance of power between men and women – access to jobs, education and so on – and also by local conditions – the relative balance of power between partners. One way of conceptualizing power is in terms of the *resources* that each partner possesses (Blood and Wolfe, 1960; Homans, 1961). The most obvious and objective resources are income, education, physical strength and occupational status. But there are also a range of relative resources, such as physical attractiveness, love, affection, humour, emotional dependency, skills and so on. The latter are more open to negotiation and are to some extent constructed within the relationship, so that one partner may have considerable power because the other is deeply in love, emotionally dependent, feels inferior and so on. Which resources are dominant and how they are to be employed is, however, also to some extent dependent on culturally shaped sets of obligations. For example, partners are 'supposed' to provide for each other financially, emotionally and physically. Failure to provide, or withholding these basic resources, may be taken as grounds for complaint or for ending the relationship.

Gender differences in resources are also partly culturally determined. For example in Western cultures women have generally been valued if they possess beauty, charm, nurturance and supportive attributes. However, many of these not only have little exchange value, but are short-lived. Beauty in particular is seen as a central resource and women are encouraged to emphasize their looks. Western culture tends to define female beauty as youthful, fit and slim. As women age, this resource inevitably diminishes. Likewise, a woman's 'resource' is determined by her role as a wife and mother, but as children grow up she is less needed to care for children. The value of the role of wife may also be transient and lost through separation or divorce, in that it is contingent on being in a relationship and being appreciated in that relationship. Indeed many women, who have described their relationships as egalitarian, are shocked to realize the extent of their inequality and dependence when that relationship disintegrates and they become aware that much of their power was contingent on that of their partner, and the particular nature of their relationship (Foreman, 1994; Williams and Watson, 1988).

A number of researchers and therapists (Homans, 1961; Haley, 1976; Madanes, 1981) have suggested that satisfaction in relationships is related to an equitable distribution of rewards in the relationship. The power each partner possesses lies in the range of resources they have available that can be applied to influence their partner or other members of the family. It is also suggested that the distribution of power in a nuclear family alters during the life-cycle (Hesse-Biber and Williamson, 1984; Haley, 1976; Carter and McGoldrick, 1980). Typically, it can be argued that men and women have relatively equal power during courtship. Even if there are differences, the effects of this may be less marked since structures of dependence arising from living together have not been established. With the birth of a first child, and incrementally with the birth of each additional child, a woman's power is likely to decrease. It is common for a woman to stop working or to reduce her commitment to work. She thus becomes increasingly dependent upon a husband, and the more children she has the longer she may need to withdraw from a job or career, thus losing out on experience, promotions and so on. In contrast a husband is likely to be based outside the home and he may even work longer hours in order to meet the extra costs of the family. This may help *his* career to develop but is also likely to exacerbate the power inequalities in the relationship. As the children start school, and when they leave home, a woman's power may increase if she is able to return to work. At the same time a man's career may be starting to level off. As a couple move towards retirement the balance of power may appear to become more equal, but cultural norms may still perpetuate power inequalities.

2.5 NORMATIVE ASSUMPTIONS OF LIFE-CYCLE MODELS

Families exist within a cultural context and one of the key ways that this regulates family life is through a set of normative assumptions about how family life should progress through a number of key stages. The family life-cycle model suggests an image or norm of what people believe family life 'should' be like. Inherent in this image are beliefs about the form that the family should take; how a family should develop, solve problems, communicate with each other; how the members should feel about each other; and when it is appropriate for 'children' to leave and start a new family of their own. In one sense the concept of the family life-cycle merely maps out a formal set of assumptions that people in a given society hold about a particular form of family life.

At the same time the concept of the family life-cycle embodies the ideological assumptions and imperatives which designate the nuclear family as a goal to be strived for, especially in terms of offering the most satisfactory form of nurturance for children. Given the high rates of divorce now prevalent in most industrial societies, this model potentially serves as a form of implicit condemnation for many step-families who may feel obliged to continually struggle to contort themselves into a nuclear family configuration. As with many models in the social sciences, attempts to describe and categorize phenomena, such as the stages that families are likely to proceed through, can lead to the model becoming prescriptive. It has been proposed in contrast that we should fully acknowledge diversity and talk of 'life-cycles' plural rather than of one 'superior' or 'normal' version. This necessitates that we recognize that events, such as divorce, be 'viewed as normal rather than abnormal phases of the family life-cycle and that this can be reframed in positive terms, such as a couple being "ready for a new relationship" or children "being the lucky possessors of two families instead of one"' (Morawetz, 1984, p. 571).

3 SYSTEMS THEORY

The discussion of the family life-cycle so far has suggested that families need to adapt continually by developing attempted solutions to the tasks that face them. On the other hand families also develop stability and coherence in the face of such continual change. Therapeutic work and research with families required a model which could embrace both these aspects of family life. This section explores the contribution that systems theory has made and how this model has been developed to embrace people's potential to act autonomously on the basis of their beliefs and understandings.

Originating in the biological and engineering sciences, systems theory was developed as a model to describe and explain the dynamic properties of 'systems'. A system is seen as a number of interconnected components or elements which mutually and continually influence each other:

> A system is a set of 'objects' together with the relationship between these objects and their attributes ... Every part of a system is so related to the others that a change in one part will cause a change in the other parts and in the total system. A system is not a composite of independent parts but a coherent and inseparable whole.
>
> (Hall and Fagan, 1956)

In the human body, for example, our body temperature, though continually varying, is maintained within safe and tolerable limits. This is termed a 'closed' system which operates to correct deviations or 'errors' from a desired setting. In contrast a system can be 'open' whereby it progressively escalates, as in forms of excitement or arousal. Bateson (1958, 1972) and Jackson (1957) first suggested that the twin concepts of *escalation* and *stability* could be employed to map social processes.

3.1 LINEAR VERSUS CIRCULAR CAUSALITY

Systems theory stresses the interdependence of action in families and other relationships. Each person is seen as influencing the other and their responses in turn influence the first person, whose response influences the other's and so on. Any action is therefore seen as also a response and a response as also an action. In effect the question of looking for a starting-point – 'who started it' – is seen as unproductive. In families, even if we can identify who appeared to start a particular sequence (such as an argument), this may in turn have been a response to a previous episode. Paul Watzlawick and his colleagues (1967, 1974) coined the term 'circularities' to capture the essentially repetitive patterns of interaction that can be found. This represents a fundamental shift from how relationship difficulties had previously been explained. Two simple examples are offered to illustrate this idea: see Figure 3.

A circular view of problems stresses how the action of each person of the pair in Figure 3 influences the other and their behaviour in turn influences them. This is radically different to linear explanations. Each partner's behaviour in these examples can be seen to be maintained by the actions of the other. So John's anger may serve to fuel Mary's apologies or placatory behaviour which in turn leads to more of the same from John. Likewise, Doris's dependent actions may serve to fuel attempts by George to withdraw and become detached. Often linear explanations are couched in terms of invariant personality traits, such as John's angry personality, George's level of detachment, Mary's apologetic nature or Doris's dependency. Whether, Doris, for example is more or less insecure than other people is less relevant than the fact that her level of insecurity is maintained by the interaction between her and George. Likewise, George's

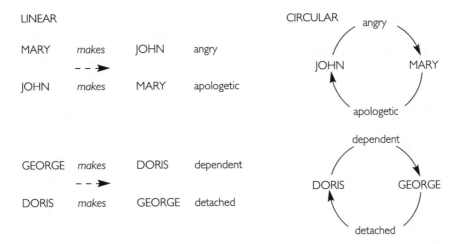

Figure 3   Linear versus circular causality
Source: Adapted from Dallos, 1991, p. 16

level of detachment can be seen to be maintained by Doris's behaviour. Although the gender positions reflected in these examples may be reversed in some couples, these are common gender patterns. This suggests that, though interpersonally maintained, such cycles are also shaped by dominant cultural gender roles.

In the above examples the patterns are liable to escalation but over time a regularity and repetition can be detected. In larger groups this regularity, or *circularity*, is more readily apparent:

Sandra: Can I stir that, Mummy ?

Diane
(mother):   Not just now. Be careful you'll burn yourself ...

Sandra: (climbing on to a chair near the cooker) What's that ? Can I put some sugar in? ...

Mother: You can cut up some pastry, don't drop it ... All right, don't worry. Don't wipe it, we'll use some more ... (exasperated) John do you think you could do something with Sandra?

John
(father):   Doesn't she want to help you ? ...

Sandra: Look she is going to burn herself ... I've asked you before ...

John: Come here Sandra, get down ... Let's go out to the workshop, we can do some hammering.

Sandra: (ten minutes later, Diana thinks she has heard Sandra cry and comes to the workshop) ... Oh God, John, she's cut her finger. Can't you see? I thought you'd watch her ...

John: It's just a scratch. She's OK ... I couldn't get this screw out ...

Diane: It's all right sweetie, come on I've made some more pastry ...

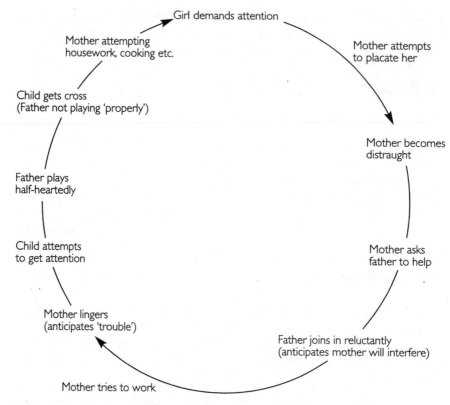

Figure 4   Circularity encapsulating a 'peripheral' father role
Source: Adapted from Dallos, 1991, p. 17

The behaviour of this family (also illustrated by Figure 4) can be seen to be repetitive and we can predict how they might interact in a variety of different situations such as bedtime, bathing, going to the park and so on. The presence of these regularities in behaviour make it look, to an outsider, *as if* the family is following a set of rules which seem to be necessary to maintain some form of equilibrium (Jackson, 1957). As observers, we can see regularities in the actions of members of a family and we can go on to infer a set of rules that might give rise to such regularities. These are, however, only inferences in the minds of us as observers.

ACTIVITY 2

Can you think of examples from your own family life, from other families you know or other social situations – work or leisure – of such repetitive patterns?

(a) Write a description of the sequence of actions or steps that seem to take place. You might like to map these as a diagram or circularity as in Figure 4.

(b) Note down the explanations that the participants offer for their actions. (If you have no idea what these are, take a little time to 'speculate' or hypothesize what they might be.)

(c) Finally, in what way do the explanations and attributions given appear to maintain the patterns?

Family rows, in particular, display the feature of being highly stereotyped but the participants' ability to detect the patterns, and their own contribution to maintaining them, is often clouded by emotions of anger, fear or sadness. In a circular manner the interactions are seen as producing the emotional states which in turn perpetuate the patterns. Minuchin (1974) has provided some experimental evidence on the extent to which the physiological reactions of people in families are interdependent and related to structural disturbances. He suggested that conditions such as asthma, diabetes and anorexia nervosa could be aggravated by the emotional climate in the family. He demonstrated, for example, that blood-sugar levels in children suffering with diabetes were directly related to the emotional conflict that was experimentally activated between the parents.

3.2   FEEDBACK AND REFLEXIVITY

A central concept in systems theory is that of *feedback* – the capacity of a system to adapt its functioning based upon information regarding the effects of its output. The concept of feedback is widely used to mean receiving information about how well we have achieved our intended aims, plans, what people think of us and so on. Early theorists (Bateson, 1972; Jackson, 1957) suggested that relationships could be described as reflexive systems which operated on the basis of two types of feedback: open systems in which feedback serves to produce escalation (for example, an argument between two people which runs out of control and leads to physical conflict and perhaps the termination of a relationship); and closed systems, which employ feedback to correct any deviations from a setting or a norm. The latter therefore tend to reinforce stability and the maintenance of existing patterns. In order for a relationship to function or be viable as a social unit, it needs to show both patterns. Functioning as an open system allows change and adaptation to alterations inside or outside the system (as long as the escalation does not proceed so far as to destroy the system). Alternatively, a system which is rigidly closed is unable to adapt to novel demands and changes in the environment.

The concept of reflexivity is central to systems theory – a system has the capacity to monitor or reflect on its own actions. It is possible to build simple mechanical systems to demonstrate some adaptability (for example, a central heating system or robots), but in human relationships the notion of a system contains the idea of cognition, for example assessing what the needs of a particular situation or relationship are and adjusting to deviations in attaining these. Don Jackson (1957) suggested that relationships which contained 'pathology' could be seen to function as closed systems. These operated so that any change in the symptomatic member would be met by actions in the others which would have the sum effect of reducing, rather than encouraging, change. Despite family members expressing a desire to change, it was argued that in some sense the symptoms had been incorporated into the relationship dynamics; and the habitual behaviour in relation to the symptoms served to maintain, rather than change, the problems.

3.3 PATTERNING OF BELIEFS

The use of the concept of 'circularity' provides a powerful way of describing the mechanisms whereby problems may be 'unwittingly' maintained despite the obvious distress that all the members of the family may be experiencing. However, there is a need to reconcile a view of families as composed of human beings with the potential to make free, autonomous choices with the recognition that their choices often appear to fuse together into repetitive and predictable patterns. Part of the predictability is to do with families living in a wider culture, which expects certain regularities in bed-times, meal-times, accepted forms of behaviour between parents and children, men and women and so on. However, families, though sharing the common dimensions of living, also develop idiosyncratic patterns of beliefs and behaviour that are, to some extent, unique.

> In the case of the family, interactions are always framed by a rich, rather stable symbolic context, specific to the human condition, that reminds the participants how reality should be constructed and creates, anchors, and reminds of, family rules. In fact, each member of a family, is defined as such as a member of a particular family, because he or she shares with the rest a rather specific way of organizing reality, an ideology. The family member's sense of belonging to a collective derives from the experience of consonance emanating from shared reality-organizing constructs.
>
> (Sluzki, 1983, p. 472)

The description of circularity tends to be limited to the analysis of behaviours. There is a need, in addition, to consider the following propositions in order to take account of people's beliefs, understandings, abilities to formulate attempted solutions and to make choices. These form the basis of the rest of this chapter:

1   Understandings in families are patterned and shared in an analogous way to their patterns of behaviour.

2   Understandings can be seen to consist of a limited number of shared constructs or dimensions of understanding

3   Members of a family may use a variety of terms to explain/describe their understandings, each of which may be subjectively constructed/interpreted and thus not immediately accessible to outside observers.

4   Members may employ a variety of different terms which effectively cover the same range of events. In other words the basis of their understandings or belief system may 'boil down' to a few major or 'core' constructs or dimensions.

This view does not simply imply that families are in continual agreement, far from it. It does imply, though, that members do share some beliefs, often implicitly, about what is worth agreeing or disagreeing about. To take an example: a family may 'share' a set of beliefs that it is important and valuable to be fully educated, widely read and interested in academic and cultural matters. Coupled with this there may be a perception of people who avoid education as ignorant or to be pitied because of their lack of intelligence. It is unlikely that every person in the family will whole-heartedly endorse such a set of beliefs. However, it is likely that education will be a highly salient issue for all of them. In fact the topic of 'education' may act as a sort of a cue or trigger which activates a range of family processes. An adolescent in this family, for example, may 'know' that he or she can exert considerable power and disruption by threatening to 'drop out' of school and take a menial job. The topic of education can come to represent the arena in which numerous struggles are conducted. Likewise, for a family with a child displaying symptoms of anorexia, a key family issue may become 'food' and the topic of health would then be used to carry the underlying family conflicts.

3.4   COMMUNICATION

An important question concerns how family beliefs become established and maintained. Systems theory is fundamentally also a theory of communication and emphasizes that patterns of action are constructed through continual communication, much of which takes place at a non-conscious level. This in some ways resembles psychoanalytic ideas of a dynamic unconscious (see Chapter 7), but proposes, instead of a historical focus, the idea that family members continually express and receive messages from each other at an non-conscious level. It is these current, 'here and now', communicational processes, and non-conscious influences, which are regarded as predominantly shaping their thoughts, feelings and actions, rather than experiences in childhood or in their past interactions.

Communication is seen as continuous and inevitable; any behaviour in the presence of others can be seen to be a potential communication:

> Activity or inactivity, words or silence all have message value: they influence others and these others, in turn, cannot not respond to these communications and are thus themselves communicating ... the mere absence of talking or of taking notice of each other is no

exception … The man in a crowded lunch counter who looks straight ahead, or the airplane passenger who sits with his eyes closed, are both communicating that they do not want to communicate to anybody or to be spoken to, and their neighbours usually 'get this message' and respond appropriately by leaving them alone.

(Watzlawick *et al.*, 1967, p. 49)

Secondly, for communication to occur there must be both a sender and a receiver. Just how an action is interpreted depends not only on the disposition of the sender or the receiver, but on the interchange between them. The meaning of the communication is seen as arising from a process of negotiation involving a further exchange or meta-communication (that is, communication about communication). Communication is viewed as a never-ending/never-beginning flow and it is argued that it is always possible when we search for a starting-point to identify some previous antecedents which acted as a potential communication (Watzlawick *et al.*, 1967). Also, a broad view of communication is taken, regarding it as multi-faceted and including non-verbal as well as verbal actions. Non-verbal communication is seen to convey important information about feelings and emotions. The verbal part of a message can at times be relatively ambiguous without the non-verbal component to clarify intention. When there is ambiguity or incongruence between the verbal and non-verbal components, an attempt at clarification or meta-communication may be attempted: for example, a mother might say to her son 'you don't seem *very* enthusiastic' or 'you seem a *bit* fed up'. As a result, young children lacking the verbal ability and power to engage in such clarification may become confused and disoriented in times of emotional upheavals in a family.

3.5 PUNCTUATION

Watzlawick *et al.* (1967) suggested that this flow of communication and action is divided up into meaningful units or chunks. The term *punctuation* was coined to describe how people develop a set of *self-fulfilling* perceptions or beliefs about their relationship which can interlock, like the pieces of a jigsaw puzzle, to produce repetitive patterns. The concept of punctuation introduces the idea of systems as not simply mechanistic, but as governed by patterns of beliefs or constructs. Over time, members of a family come to form predictions, not only of each other's actions, but also of each other's thoughts, beliefs and feelings. Since they spend considerable time together, share similar experiences and communicate continually with each other, they come to form a web of mutual anticipations. These serve both to explain and predict each other's behaviour and thoughts, but also to construct and maintain them. Members of a family might be surprised if, for example, one of them expresses beliefs or shows emotions which they regard as unusual; and these signs of surprise will serve to attenuate such deviations.

This is consistent with George Kelly's (1955) emphasis on the interdependence of action and construing. He argued that our constructs (cognitions, perceptions, expectations etc.) serve to guide our actions and the outcome of our actions in turn serve to validate or refute our constructs. As such, action and constructs are seen to be mutually linked (see Figure 5).

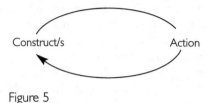

Figure 5

In relationships each person's actions form the basis for the other's constructs and so on. It is this interlocking of beliefs and actions which can be seen to underlie the patterns of behaviour or circularities described earlier. One example is that of a cycle of approach–avoidance (see Figure 6).

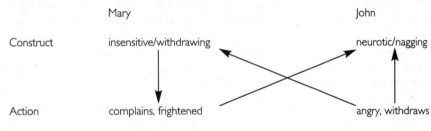

Figure 6

This cycle is mutually maintained by each partner's punctuations or beliefs: Mary may perceive John's behaviour at a moment in time – perhaps reading the paper, watching television or leaving the room – as indicating that he is withdrawing, ignoring her and so on. This perception subsequently leads her to make some indirect attempts to contact him such as asking him to do some jobs around the house or asking him where he is going. More than likely these will be made in a slightly tense tone since what will follow is already anticipated. John may then construe Mary's actions as indicating that she is 'nagging' or trying to get at him. Since he doesn't like this and thinks she shouldn't go on at him, he withdraws further. Mary might then become angry, attack him verbally and he may obstinately withdraw further. By now each partner may think that their perceptions have been confirmed. Yes, Mary feels she was right, he was withdrawing. Likewise John thinks he was right, she was trying to nag him – again.

The cycle can in this way become self-validating. It can be extremely hard for either partner to see what contribution they are making to the cycle. Insight into this pattern by either partner might not invariably help. In the above example, if Mary for instance becomes aware of this sequence between them and attempts to explain it to John, this may be seen as further nagging! Likewise an insight and 'explanation' from John about this might be regarded by Mary as further evidence of his 'smart-ass, detached, uninvolved, over-rational withdrawing'! Such sequences are by no means restricted to marital relationships. A similar situation can be seen in parent–child relationships, for example, where a father and son may be caught in a cycle of reprimand–misbehaviour. The father may punctuate their cycle as his having to reprimand the boy continually for his frequent misdemeanours. However, the son may punctuate it as his misbehaving in order to get back at his father for continually reprimanding him. Watzlawick goes on to suggest that such 'struggles' over the definition of the relationship and each other's actions underlie many relationship problems.

Communication and beliefs are interdependent, particularly in the sense that what we experience the other person to be communicating is partly determined by what we 'expect' to hear. Furthermore these expectations can serve as self-fulfilling prophecies, as in the examples above; once a pattern is established it is virtually meaningless to attempt to define who started it. Punctuation not only involves dividing up a cycle in a particular way but then involves inferring causes and reasons about why people are acting in these ways. In some situations the mutual punctuations may be in agreement: for example, a couple may be in agreement that they are making love. There may still be some differences in how each interprets the other's motives, however.

There may also be cases where people are interacting on the basis of profoundly incorrect assumptions about each other's punctuations. As a joke, the psychologist Paul Watzlawick (1977) asked two of his friends who were psychiatrists (unknown to each other) to assess a middle-aged man 'suspected of suffering from a delusional psychosis', i.e. that he was a famous psychiatrist. Suitably briefed, the two psychiatrists were put in the same room and proceeded to interview each other. Their mutual protestations, justifications and attempts to prove their professional expertise served to convince each other of the severity of the delusion! It took some time before one of them started to become suspicious, not because of the other's behaviour, but because he remembered having heard of a 'real' Doctor Don Jackson and started to 'smell a rat'.

In this and the previous examples, people appear to be attempting not only to 'read each other's minds', by assuming they know the other's reasons for acting, but, furthermore, are attempting to extort evidence to confirm this by 'putting ideas' into the other's mind. Laing (1966; and Esterson, 1964) suggested that a variety of coercive processes operate in families. One example of this is the process of induction whereby children in the family may be implicitly and subtly 'instructed' into certain beliefs about the world and about themselves:

Mother: Are you not feeling well ?

Daughter: No. I just don't want to do this ...

Mother: (looking to grandmother and smiling) I think she's a bit off colour ...

Daughter: I'm all right ...

Mother: I'll make you a drink, it'll settle your tummy ...

(Dallos, 1994)

Here, rather than accepting that the child does not want to do something, a punctuation or explanation of 'illness' is imposed. In order to avoid further harassment the child might comply with this, thereby confirming to her mother that she 'really' was ill and perhaps leading to confusion in the child about the validity of her own thoughts and feelings.

Parents have power over their children, hold their trust and respect and consequently such 'instruction', especially if a child is never allowed to openly express her wishes, can construct a convoluted and perhaps symptomatic form of family interaction. The pattern of beliefs induced in this way can construct conscious and non-conscious expectations which lead to self-fulfilling effects (Rosenthal and Jacobson, 1986; Watzlawick, 1984). Frequently we may hold implicit expectations or make interpretations during an interaction which are only partly conscious but which predispose us to act in certain ways. These reactions can influence how the interaction proceeds, since we may alter our behaviour in subtle ways and thereby help to produce our expectations.

3.6   BELIEFS AND ACTIONS IN TRIADS

As suggested earlier, an important contribution of systems theory is its emphasis on examining interactions beyond the narrow focus of the dyad. One important observation, which stimulated a move towards considering the triad as the significant unit of family life, derived from the work of clinicians who were involved with child-focused problems. It was observed initially that when parents were consulted, for example to gain further information about the problems, frequently the parents themselves were in considerable conflict or distress. It appeared that often the parents' marriages were far from harmonious or stress-free, and clinicians, such as Haley (1976) and Minuchin (1974), suggested that children were in effect 'scapegoats'; their symptoms, such as tantrums, crying, sickness, headaches, school-refusal and so on, were serving the function of distracting or avoiding the conflicts between the parents. They noted further that in some cases the conflicts were 'open' and fairly easy to detect and discuss. In other families the conflicts were disguised or denied, and were mainly indicated by the disagreements between the parents about how to deal with the child's problems. This process, whereby a third person is 'pulled' in to the conflicts of a pair, was termed

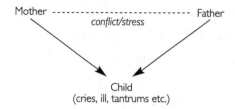

Figure 7   Conflict detouring/triangulation
Source: Adapted from Dallos, 1991, p. 97

conflict-detouring or *triangulation* (Haley, 1976; Minuchin, 1974) (see Figure 7).

The development of conflict detouring was seen to involve a form of 'learning by trial and error'. A young child might experience the stress and tension between his or her parents and respond to the raised voices, banging of doors or violence by crying, losing his or her concentration on what s/he is doing, feeling sick and so on. One or other of these behaviours may be enough to capture the parents' attention and distract them from their struggle in order to focus on the child. This temporarily produces a cessation of conflict between parents; following several repetitions of this process, the child's behaviour or symptoms can become programmed into the family dynamics and function to maintain the situation. This basic pattern can be constructed in a variety of ways and circumstances. The parents may not be in conflict with each other but may be stressed, tired or depressed due to pressures at work or unemployment. The conflict can cut across generations, for example between lone parents and their parents or in-laws, between the parents and the child's school and so on. The child's symptoms can in a sense be seen as *benevolent*, for example offering a distraction for stressed parents from their own worries.

Triangulation also involves the construction of an agreement about the situation in a family. There is likely to be an agreement that the child is the main cause of the family's current concerns and difficulties. The construction of such an explanation is an example of a family 'myth' (see section 5). This is in effect a falsification or distortion of reality since the child's problems can be seen as resulting from, not as causing, the conflict. The belief that the child is the source of the family's problems has resonances with psychoanalytic concepts in that the distortion can be seen to serve as an emotional defence. Once established, this myth can become increasingly painful to confront. For example, if the child's symptoms become severe, the parents may feel extremely guilty, believing that their conflicts have in a sense been the cause. However, this picture tends to minimize the child's role as merely responding to the conflicts. In reality most young children at some stage discover the 'power' that a symptom of 'illness' confers, such as being able to avoid school, unpleasant duties, gain sympathy and attention and so on. Therefore a child may start to collude with this state of affairs and continue to display symptoms in part because of the apparent advantages he or she gains. This in turn can

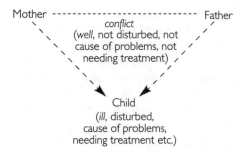

Figure 8 Examples of constructs/beliefs encapsulating conflict detouring/triangulation

Source: Adapted from Dallos, 1991, p. 99

serve to confirm for the whole family – including the child – the belief or myth that he or she is the source of the problems.

There may be a variety of constructs to describe the child's problems but the net effect of these is that the parents are described as similar to each other, and different to the child, in not having or being the cause of the 'problem' (see Figure 8).

In reality, the situation is often more complex than this. Parents may disagree on how to treat the child (for example, discipline vs sympathy) and may shift positions, taking turns to side with the child. These 'shifting coalitions' can be extremely confusing for a young child and have been implicated in causing or aggravating more severe problems, such as anorexia and schizophrenia (Palazzoli *et al.*, 1978). Psychiatric and other agencies may also perpetuate conflicting views about such conditions, which families then come to internalize and act out in their internal dynamics.

3.7 GENDER AND TRIANGULATION

The conflicts and arguments in a family about the child's symptoms and how to deal with them also display some important patterns, however. As seen in the previous examples of family dynamics, it is frequently the mother who is predominantly involved in 'caring' for the child. Many fathers occupy a largely peripheral position and are expected to provide mainly a disciplinary or practical role. Both parents therefore potentially occupy conflicting roles: mothers are expected to care and offer 'love', but at the same time may be implicitly 'blamed' for the child's problems. Likewise, a father may collude with this and blame the mother, but may in turn be accused of 'not doing enough'. At the interactional level, parents may oscillate between blaming their relationship for the child's problems and finding temporary relief from guilt in the idea that they did not cause it since it was really the child's problem. This may in turn be untenable since it triggers concern about the child.

As suggested earlier, a related issue is the relatively powerless position of women within the family. From an initial relationship which may be relatively equal, the woman is likely to become extremely dependent and relatively powerless when she has children. A combination of the awareness of increasing dependence and the consequence of the large amount of time spent on childcare may result in a close relationship between the mother and the child. This attachment in turn may provide a source of power and help to balance the inequality of power in the relationship. Caplow (1968) argues that, as the child grows, this coalition between mother and child can eventually become powerful enough to be capable of 'defeating' the father. On the one hand, this patterning fits with conventional societal gender expectations about family life, but it also perpetuates the positioning of fathers as peripheral in childcare. This configuration has posed considerable problems for family therapists. Attempts to 'engage' fathers may be regarded as desirable and necessary, but at the same time this ignores the ways in which close mother–child attachments may provide a vital source of female identity and power. Intervening to request a father to become more involved potentially implies that the woman is a 'failure' and further erodes her sources of power (Williams and Watson, 1988; Perelberg and Miller, 1990).

4 THE CONSTRUCTION OF MEANING

In the discussion so far, it is apparent that, in order to manage family life, people need to have some agreement about how they see the world as well as some understanding of each other – to have some understanding of how others see things. The following two sections will consider how families mutually create both versions of reality which give meaning to their actions and lives together and also distortions, myths or unrealities. The concept of conflict detouring, discussed earlier, is one such example which denies conflict in the parental relationship by means of the myth of the child's symptoms as the sole source of problems.

4.1 NEGOTIATING MEANINGS: AGREEMENT AND EMPATHY

George Kelly (1955) referred to two key processes governing relationships: on the one hand, there is a recognition of *commonality* in which each partner perceives that they both appear to be looking at the world in a similar way; on the other, *sociality* is the extent to which each person has an understanding or empathy regarding how the other person sees the world. So, in addition to developing a common frame of reference, sociality involves an ability to predict how the other person will use such constructs. For example, whilst two people might both be vegetarians, they may come to realize that one of them is vegetarian predominantly for health reasons whereas the other is a vegetarian on moral grounds. The growth of sociality involves the ability to make increasingly sophisticated predictions about the other's construct system (Dallos, 1991).

Couples, families and other groupings appear to develop a set of shared – *core* – constructs or beliefs. It is likely that there will have evolved some shared ways of seeing a variety of events concerned with their relationship – how they see each other, their relationship, how their relationship contrasts with that of other couples they know. As Duck (1988) suggests, there will also be some initial agreement or mutual validation of each other's construct systems as part of the initial courtship and 'filtering' process involved in making the decision to continue the relationship.

Procter (1981, 1985) has added that family members not only hold individual and personal construct systems, but over time come to form *shared* construct systems (SCS). He suggests that to take part in a group such as a family requires each person to have a set of constructs about the relationships between the members. Secondly, it is necessary for there to be some agreement or shared way of seeing events. Obviously if there is total disagreement about the interpretation of events, a group or couple would fall apart. He emphasizes that the agreement is about the domain of choices seen to be possible, not about the specific choices made at any one time. For example, an adolescent may come to argue passionately against his or her parents' materialistic values, but that very passion confirms his or her commitment to acknowledging that a construct of, say, materialism vs spiritualism is important.

4.2   NEGOTIATING SHARED CONSTRUCTS

The basis of a family is usually a couple whose relationship is shaped by a combination of influences – historical, cultural and inter-generational family traditions. Initially there are likely to be 'strategic' processes – attempts to deliberately convey certain impressions in order to 'look good' or to elicit sympathy (Goffman, 1970). What each person is attempting to convey contains their beliefs about what is acceptable and desirable and thereby also reveals information about themselves. A couple therefore have two important sources of information about each other: what they perceive to be each other's constructs and what they construe to be the beliefs held in each other's family of origin. These patterns of emerging constructs can be summarized in terms of a *similarity–dissimilarity* construct.

As a couple start to form a relationship, they can be seen to develop a set of constructs about their own relationship and, in particular, how it is similar or different to their parents' relationship. The couple's initial disclosures involve them forming constructs about how much similarity there is between them and each other's families. What each of them will remember is selective and coloured by their family's constructs system. In turn it is likely that as they tell each other their already edited stories, there is a second process of editing whereby what they both hear from each other is again interpreted within their respective family of origin's construct systems. The two sets of memories – the person talking about their family and the partner's edited version of this story – go into the 'cooking-pot' of the couple's new construct system. Subsequently, one partner may selectively recall a part of the other's story as a tactic in negotiations: for example, Harry may say to Doris that she is being 'bossy – just like her mother'. Since this is probably based on what Doris has told Harry, this is likely to be a very powerful tactic. She may protest or attempt to rewrite this version of her story, thereby possibly adding further material that Harry could use in this way. These exchanges of stories need not always be employed in such malevolent ways; our intention here is merely to illustrate how the processes of rewriting family history can occur. These reconstructed memories can become very powerful, to a point where each partner may become confused even about the simple factual details of what actually did happen in their past.

Once couples have traded information about themselves and have sometimes told each other about the 'bad' things that have happened, there is a danger that they have 'labelled' themselves. They have provided a set of enduring constructs about themselves couched in the language of the family of origin's construct systems. There may be complex strategic processes operating about what they choose to disclose, such as attempts to solicit sympathy or to be 'rescued' from the roles that their families have put them in. These essentially concern shifts from one to the other pole of constructs, but what is most important is that they communicate their core constructs emanating from the families of origin, that is, the range of choices in their pack of 'cards'.

4.3   SHARED SOCIETAL CONSTRUCTS

A serious problem with analyses of family belief systems has been that little attempt had been made to include an analysis of the wider social context within which relationships grow. These include the influence of other family members, peer groups and changing social norms about relationships and about what are regarded as desirable characteristics in a partner. In order to function in any given society a person needs to have a set of beliefs covering the following areas:

(a) a construction of the prevalent constructions of that culture;

(b) the extent to which a person chooses to hold constructions common to that culture; this will define the extent to which they remain within or outside any particular part of that culture or sub-culture.

In order to participate in relationships in our culture, we need both to have some idea about the common constructs – beliefs, attitudes, expectations about relationships – and at least to some extent to agree to operate within them. There may be local variations in this, such as religious groups, role-defined groups (e.g. married vs single people, professional classes vs manual or unemployed people), sub-cultures (such as hippies, gay or lesbian groups) and so on. However, each sub-group is likely to have a more or less coherent set of common constructs which are adhered to and at least some awareness of how these differ from the wider community (Reiss, 1980). Relationships which are very idiosyncratic or eccentric are likely to experience considerable pressure and stigma to conform (new age travellers, for example). As relationships develop and change, partners will make transitions between these various groups, for instance from single – to courting – to married.

4.4 HIERARCHIES OF MEANINGS

Relationships can be seen to be operating at several levels of meaning simultaneously: each partner's own construct, their perspective of the other's construct, and their idea of how they imagine the other person imagines their construct. Pearce and Cronen (1980) emphasize that at any particular time a communication derives its meaning not only from the content of the communication, but also from the context in which it is uttered. In turn, the context is defined by the previous history of the relationship. From the history of their previous interactions, a couple have available a repertoire of memories embodying a set of constructs which they employ to anticipate present and future interactions between them. These anticipations may be very influential: for example, a wife may anticipate that her husband will make sexual demands irrespective of her feelings and this may set up a self-fulfilling prophecy whereby she responds in a cold and wary way to any signs of overtures of affection from him. Over time they may both come to anticipate this kind of interaction. Attempts to behave differently or suggest a different definition of each other's behaviour may be thwarted by this context. On the other hand, a warm, more positive context can serve to tolerate, or forgive, a certain amount of 'bad' behaviour.

Pearce and Cronen (1980) suggest that relationships can be seen, like Chinese boxes, as successively contained within levels of contexts (see Figure 9). Any particular action in a relationship derives its meaning from the context of the episode, which in turn derives its meaning from the overall meanings based on the shared history of the relationship; these in turn are defined by family scripts and finally by the cultural context. To take the above example, a couple may find themselves arguing and this might be given a meaning of 'going through a bad patch' or as 'a crisis for the couple'. How it is defined depends on the wider definition of the relationship. If the couple are married as opposed to co-habiting this might provide a more tolerant context, i.e. marriages are relatively permanent and expected to have 'ups and downs' (cultural constructs). However, there may be a family/life script, such as previous broken relationships, that provides a context in which conflicts are seen as dangerous and to be avoided. The various levels of contexts may offer contradictory interpretations which may promote attempts at change to achieve consistency. There may also be contradictions between various competing cultural constructs: for example, more 'modern' conceptions of marriage expect greater satisfaction and hold less tolerance for conflict, or a common discourse that 'good' relationships are 'spontaneously compatible', in which any conflict may be seen as a sign that the relationship is not working and should be terminated.

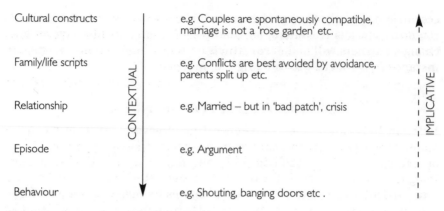

Figure 9   Layered meanings and relationships

There are also implicative forces so that meanings are given from the lower to the higher levels. The present experience of a relationship – for example, having a joke or being intimate – can provide evidence that the relationship is good. Likewise, if a couple 'make up after a conflict', this can provide evidence that conflicts need not always be avoided. Therapeutic interventions are often directed at altering the higher contextual definitions by persuading couples to attempt patterns of behaviour previously avoided as 'too dangerous' (Dallos, 1991).

4.5   SHARED HISTORIES

Pearce and Cronen's (1980) model not only emphasizes the importance of looking at levels of meanings and contexts but at relationships over time. The history of the relationship is seen to provide a context within which current actions are interpreted. So the attempts by one partner to be 'nice' may be distrusted if there has been a history of conflict. On the other hand some unpleasant behaviour may be tolerated if the relationship is defined as 'good'. A problematic situation can occur when there is a fine balance between these definitions, i.e. there has been considerable conflict but also some satisfaction. An ambiguity may occur so that a particular action, such as 'teasing', can be defined as vindictive if the negative aspects are focused on, or alternatively can be seen as 'fun'. However, a couple may also attempt to use the current action to define the relationship, i.e. we are having 'fun' so our relationship must be good. Each person may also define the present action and the relationship differently. People tend to refer to such states as 'not knowing where we're at', 'being at a crossroads' etc. The higher levels of contexts – the family and cultural scripts – can help to stabilize such reverberation, but for people who have had contradictory and ambiguous experiences in previous relationships and in their families (life scripts), the reverberation may continue to the higher levels, so that problems in their relationship may imply that the world cannot be trusted. Possibly this offers another way of explaining so-called 'insecure' personalities and relationships.

An important contribution of Pearce and Cronen's (1980) model is that it starts to offer a way of integrating meanings created within relationships with wider societal beliefs, attitudes, norms and values. People in relationships are seen as creating meanings with 'one eye' on the meanings, definitions and expectations of relations prevalent in their local and wider societal context.

5 CONSTRUCTIONS OF UNREALITY: MYTHS AND DEFENCES

The previous sections offer a picture of families as engaged in the mutual construction of patterns of behaviour and beliefs, jointly building a shared reality. Concepts, such as conflict detouring discussed earlier, on the other hand, suggest that in some circumstances families build constructions which appear to distort their reality. Another way of saying this is that they can be employed in the construction of unreality. This can take various forms, such as denying what is to others patently true, projecting inaccurate feelings onto each other or constructing myths. These processes can be seen to be related to the emotional life of families. Psychodynamic theories offer a useful starting-point for an analysis of such contortion of beliefs. Central to Freud's psychodynamic model (see Chapter 7) is the idea that cognitions and the rational processes are directed by emotional forces – 'ego in the service of the id'. Freud proposed that a variety of defence mechanisms operate, such as denial, projection, repression and projection, whereby unpleasant emotions attached to certain memories and thoughts are blocked from consciousness. In other words, if reality is unacceptable then we can attempt to distort it into something which is less unacceptable or push it out of our mind. The main implications are that a consideration of family beliefs requires some consideration of how the beliefs are related to the family's emotional life.

5.1 FAMILY MYTHS

Ferreira (1963) suggested that unconscious fantasies and conflicts operated not only at the level of the individual but also could operate as a collective unconscious fantasy or 'family myth'. Aspects of a family's past, especially traumatic or distressing events experienced by the parents, grandparents or even more distant relatives, can become shrouded in defensive myths which serve to cover up memories which are too painful for them to accept. This can involve not only denial but the fabrication of stories or myths, a sort of rewriting of history. Such myths can become debilitating, however, when they serve to continually falsify and mystify experience in the family, leading to spirals of denial and fabrication:

> The term 'family myth' refers to a series of fairly well-integrated beliefs shared by all the family members, concerning each other and

their mutual positions in the family life, beliefs that go unchallenged by everyone involved in spite of the reality distortions which they may conspicuously imply ... The family myth describes the roles and attributions of family members in their transactions with each other which although false and mirage-like, are accepted by everyone as something sacred and taboo that no one would dare to investigate, much less challenge.

(Ferreira, 1963, p. 457)

The function of family myths is to preserve the family stability or homeostasis, to avoid the possibilities of disruption or disintegration of the family or relationships within it. It represents a response to real or perceived threats to the viability of the family. A family myth can be seen to represent to the family what a defence mechanism is to the individual:

Seemingly, the family myth is called into play whenever certain tensions reach predetermined thresholds among the family members and in some way, real or fantasized, threaten to disrupt ongoing relationships. Then, the family myth functions like the thermostat that is kicked into action by the 'temperature' in the family. Like other homeostatic mechanisms, the myth prevents the family system from damaging, perhaps destroying itself. It has therefore the quality of a 'safety valve', that is, a survival value.

(Ferreira, 1963, p. 462)

An important point about family myths is that there is little awareness that there is any distortion of reality in the family. This is very like Freud's concept of defence mechanisms such as denial, projection and repression. Considerable emotional energy is invested in maintaining the myth and attempts to expose it are met with great resistance (Laing and Esterson, 1964: Laing, 1966).

Ferreira's work marks an extremely important bridge between systems theory and psychodynamic accounts of families. It starts to offer a way of looking at processes in families which includes not only an analysis of behaviour but also an integration of beliefs and emotions. It suggests that emotions and beliefs are inevitably interlinked: emotions are connected to cognitions and vice versa; in other words, an emotion involves some cognitive discriminations of events. I may feel angry about something a colleague said to me, or sad about the loss of a friend. Likewise, I may perceive a certain physiological state in my body and give a meaning to it. In short, cognitions lead to emotions and emotions lead to cognitions.

Myths are seen as social constructions which serve to avoid the family having to confront painful tensions and conflicts which are perceived as potentially threatening the viability of the family. Another way of putting this is that myths may emerge as a tactic to maintain the family homeostasis, or coherence, in the face of requirements for change, as in critical life-cycle transitions. The idea of a constructed unreality was first presented by two French psychiatrists a hundred years ago in the famous paper 'Folie à deux':

> The problem is not only to examine the influence of the insane on the supposedly sane man, but also the opposite, the influence of the rational on the deluded one, and to show how through mutual compromises, the differences are eliminated.
>
> (Lasegue and Falret, 1877, p. 4)

Ferreira argues that a family exists in relation to a local community and is required to adjust and integrate with other systems. A family myth, such as that 'we are a happy family' or that a step-parent loves a step-child even more than their 'natural' child, may be driven by an attempt to conform to socially acceptable values. Of course, not only the family, but also society can create a model of family life which is based on a shaky foundation of myths in the form of unrealizable expectations. One of the periods when families are confronted with the needs for change and consequently some reappraisals of what they are and should be as a family is at the time of major transitional stages in the life-cycle. Faced with what they may perceive to be expected of them as a family, but which they may not be able to face or which are contradictory, one solution may be to turn away from reality or, more likely, to attempt to maintain a version of reality which was reasonably appropriate in a previous stage of the family's existence. Pollner and Wikler (1985) present an example of such a process of denial in a family:

> The family ... was initially encountered at a large psychiatric institute to which they had turned in their search for a remedy for five and a half year-old Mary's unusual behaviour. Family members stated that Mary was a verbal and intelligent child who malingered and refused to speak in public in order to embarrass the family. Extensive clinical examination revealed Mary to be severely retarded and unable to perform at anywhere near the level of confidence claimed by her parents and two older sibs ... Initial viewings of the videotapes suggested that family members' transactions were permeated by subtle, almost artful, practices that could function to create the image of Mary as an intelligent child.

The authors describe six strategies whereby the family operated in a concerted way to attribute intelligence to Mary's actions. The attributions in effect ascribe 'agency' and purpose to her actions which to outside observers was blatantly missing. The authors note and describe a number of strategies employed to distort the reality of their situation.

ACTIVITY 3

This activity is intended to help you to integrate some of the ideas in this chapter.

Read the following summary of the techniques employed in Mary's family to 'deny' her disability. Then consider the following questions:

(a) From a family life-cycle perspective discussed earlier:

    (i)   What transitional stages did this family appear to be negotiating?

    (ii) What tasks faced them?

    (iii) How did Mary's abilities present them with unusual difficulties?

    (iv) How could their actions be viewed as attempted solutions?

(b) What beliefs and discourses 'external' to the family appear to have shaped their beliefs and ways of acting?

> Framing – this involved the construction of a frame such as a game of 'catch' wherein virtually any activity that Mary displayed could be attributed with intelligent meaning. If she stood passively and let the ball drop out of her hands, it could be framed as deliberately dropping the ball or not wanting to play.
>
> Postscripting – was the reverse in the sense of giving meaning to Mary's actions after the event. The family tracked any action that she might emit and weaved a meaningful story on to it such as if she was acting in a goal-directed way. For example, at one point Mary's sister dropped a block on the floor while Mary was banging a block on the table. As Mary sat down her sister said 'OK, let's find that block'.
>
> Semantic crediting – here a range of reflexive behaviour responses, such as a startled reaction to a noise, were integrated by the family with simultaneous verbal requests to Mary. Though she was in fact responding to the non-verbal stimuli the family interpreted her response as showing a comprehension of verbal instructions.
>
> Puppeteering – in some instances rather than waiting for Mary to do something as a basis for the implementation of an attributional strategy the family might subtly manipulate her physically towards an object. This would be accompanied by a verbal instruction and touch or positioning themselves so that she was forced to move in a particular direction. The result could appear and would be credited as Mary making deliberate planned actions.
>
> Putting words into Mary's mouth – this involved the construction of a dialogue or episode wherein each utterance such as a gurgle emitted by Mary was interpreted by one member of the family at a time. As an example, in one sequence she was encouraged to talk by asking her to say her name and age for $5. Her following gurgles were interpreted for her as 'she's bargaining for more money'.

Explaining in the bright direction – despite the previous strategies it was possible that at times Mary's behaviour was obviously inadequate. Such inadequacies were explained away by an overriding incorrigible belief that she was 'intelligent' and so therefore these were lapses explained as being due to her 'not wanting to play', 'teasing, 'pretending' or 'malingering'.

(Adapted from Pollner and Wikler, 1985)

From a family life-cycle perspective this can be seen as an inability to come to terms with the fact that Mary would not develop as expected. The recognition that a child is seriously disabled has been likened to a process of bereavement for a family (Black, 1987). There is a need to face up to the pain that the child will not develop as expected and that this will involve some possible difficulties for the family. Most basically, it destroys the belief that they are a 'normal, happy, trouble-free' family. Some of the tasks at this stage for a family would be to foster Mary's development, encourage education skills, encourage some independence; for Mary's parents, to readjust their lives to having more time for themselves through the day, possibly a return to work for Mary's mother; for Mary's siblings, to adjust to treating Mary as an equal, another child not as a baby and so on. However, in this family, due to Mary's difficulties, many of these expected tasks could not be fulfilled. Instead, a more complex and demanding set of tasks are presented, such as adjusting their lives to caring for a child whose abilities will delay these expected developments and require all the family to invest considerable amounts of their time in caring for her.

The primary attempted solution in this family can be seen as an attempt to deny that there is a problem by constructing a 'myth' of normality. The practices in the family served to maintain the myth that Mary was 'intelligent' and that there was nothing wrong with her. The process can be seen as the family's attempt to deal with the process of 'mourning' described by Black (1987) in families when they come to recognize that their child is severely disabled. The family's behaviour was in some ways appropriate for the treatment of a child of below two years of age, which was roughly the level of Mary's actual functioning. Rather than constructing a false belief system anew, they can be seen to be attempting to hold on to a previously appropriate frame which no longer tallied with the external reality.

It is possible that this family had high expectations of their child which were embedded in ideologies of 'normal' development and progress. The greater the extent of a family's acceptance of cultural norms, the greater is likely to be their experience of frustration, guilt, embarrassment and loss. It is also possible that in some cases professionals involved with a family in such a situation may collude to minimize or distort the truth.

The concept of family myths goes some way towards offering a picture of the inter-linking between the actions, beliefs and emotional aspects of family life. It is possible that when a family is unable to cope with the combination of emotional demands, demands for organizational change and demands for the revision of beliefs inherent in a life-cycle transition, it may try to manage by the construction of various myths such as that one of them is 'damaged' or 'sick'. This represents a myth that 'we are all OK except for the fact that one of us is ill, sick or crazy' and were it not for the stresses and strains involved with 'looking after' the patient, they could all lead 'happy and fulfilled lives'. Alternatively, as above, they may attempt to deny that one of them is in fact disabled by constructing a façade of normality. Finally, the family myth is usually eventually presented for external validation, for example to various professionals who embody wider consensual realities, ideologies and discourses. Acceptance of the myth can serve to maintain or strengthen; rejection can result in crises and disintegration, but frequently results in further withdrawal and spirals of denial and isolation. Therapeutic or other interventions with families under such distress have to weave a sensitive path between these two possible scenarios.

6 DISCUSSION AND CONCLUSIONS

The family systems approach stresses the way in which a family's beliefs are recursively linked to their actions. Beliefs and actions are seen to be linked so that predictable patterns of action, feelings and thoughts emerge. The question remains, though, of the extent to which families simply internalize, as opposed to create, new versions or adaptations of the discourses or ideologies of our culture. Work with families in therapeutic settings can reveal something about the beliefs that they hold, how these relate to common widely held discourses, and how these patterns of beliefs shape their lives together. Therapeutic work with families has provided important information about families' internal worlds – their patterns of beliefs, hopes, expectations, reasoning and the resulting patterns of actions. However, voices of criticisms have also been raised. For example, family therapy has been taken to task for serving to maintain gender inequalities, partly as a consequence of the insensitivity that some therapists have shown to their existence in families. Alternatively, it could also be suggested that family therapy can have, and possibly has had, a subversive function. Many families come for therapy with firm ideas about what 'appropriate' family life is, and should be like. The process of therapy can explore the implications of their beliefs and encourage a consideration of alternatives which may challenge widely held discourses.

One of the most prevalent of the beliefs that are likely to be challenged is that the 'problem' is simply residing in one member of the family. However, it might be a mistake and arrogant to assume simply that a family has 'got things wrong', just as it is to assume that they are simply acting out conflicts caused by inequalities of power or inconsistencies embedded in wider social discourses. It can be argued from a family beliefs systems perspective that families do at least to some extent create their own versions of reality. This version is influenced by wider discourses, especially of gender which is, arguably, inevitably a central axis of family life. How the societal discourses are internalized and acted upon, however, is not simple. It is true that in many families fathers are peripheral, but not in all. Neither do women inevitably adopt the prescribed roles of mothering. Not all couples display a stereotypical pattern of male dominance/female subservience. Therapy and research with families suggests that some degree of creativity is possible arising both from the unique combinations of each partner's personalities, previous histories, and also from the deliberate attempts to negotiate versions of family life which suit them. Returning to the start of this chapter, family members do appear able to negotiate belief systems which either accept or directly challenge conventional models of family life.

REFERENCES

Anderson, H. and Goolishan, H. A. (1986) 'Problem determined systems: toward transformation in family therapy', *Journal of Strategic and Family Therapy*, vol. 4, no. 4, pp. 1–13.

Bateson, G. (1958) *Naven*, Palo Alto, CA, Stanford University Press.

Bateson,G. (1972) *Steps to an Ecology of Mind*, New York, Ballantine.

Black, D. (1987) 'Handicap and family therapy', in Bentovin, A., Barnes, G. C. and Cochlin, A. (eds) *Family Therapy: complementary frameworks of theory and practice*, London, Academic Press.

Blood, R.V. and Wolfe, D.M. (1960) *Husbands and Wives: the dynamics of married living,* New York, Free Press.

Burnham, J. (1986) *Family Therapy,* London, Tavistock Publications.

Byng-Hall,J. (1985) 'The family script: a useful bridge between theory and practice', *Journal of Family Therapy*, vol. 7, pp. 301–7.

Caplow, T. (1968) *Two Against One: coalitions in triads*, Englewood Cliffs, NJ, Prentice Hall.

Carter, E. and McGoldrick, M. (1980) *The Family Life-cycle: a framework for family therapy,* New York, Gardner.

Dallos, R. (1991) *Family Belief Systems, Therapy and Change*, Buckingham, Open University Press.

Dallos, R. (1994) Examples from current research and practice.

Dallos, R. and Procter, H. (1984) *Family Processes*, Unit 2, D307, *Social Psychology*, Milton Keynes, The Open University.

Duck, S. (1988) *Relating to Others*, Buckingham, Open University Press.

Duvall, E. (1977) *Marriage and Family Development,* Philadelphia, PA, Lippincott.

Ferreira, A. J. (1963) 'Family myths and homeostasis', *Archives of General Psychiatry,* vol. 9, pp. 457–63.

Foreman, S. (1994) (in prep.) *Inequalities of Power and Sexual Problems in Couples,* Buckingham, Open University Press.

Goffman, E. (1970) *Strategic Interaction,* Oxford, Blackwell.

Hall, A. D. and Fagan, R. E.(1956) 'Definitions of systems', in Hall, A. D. and Fagan, R. E. (eds) *General Systems, Vol. 1,* New York, Bell Telephone Laboratories.

Haley, J. (1976) *Problem Solving Therapy,* San Francisco, CA, Jossey-Bass.

Haley, J. (1981) *Uncommon Therapy,* New York, Norton.

Hesse-Biber, S. and Williamson, J. (1984) 'Resource theory and power in families: life-cycle consideration', *Family Process,* vol. 23, no. 2, pp. 261–70.

Hoffman, L. (1985) 'Beyond power and control: toward a "second order" family systems therapy', *Family Systems Medicine,* vol. 3, no. 4, pp. 381–96.

Hoffman, L. (1990) 'Constructing realities: the art of lenses', *Family Process,* vol. 19, no. 1, pp. 1–13.

Homans, G. (1961) *Social Behaviour: its elementary forms,* New York, Harcourt Brace Jovanovich.

Jackson, D. (1957) ' Three questions of family homeostasis', *Psychiatric Quarterly Supplement,* vol. 31, pp. 79–90.

Keeney, R. (1979) 'Ecosysemic epistemology: an alternative paradigm for diagnosis', *Family Process,* vol. 18, pp. 117–29.

Kelly, G. A. (1955)*The Psychology of Personal Constructs,Vols. 1 and 2,* New York, Norton.

Laing, R.D. (1966) *The Politics of the Family and Other Essays,* London, Tavistock.

Laing, R. D. and Esterson, A. (1964) *Sanity, Madness and the Family,* Harmondsworth, Penguin.

Lasegue, C. and Falret, J (1877) 'La folie à deux, ou folie communiqué?', *Annals Medico-Psyhologique,* vol. 18, November 1877. (English translation by R. Michard (1961) in *American Journal of Psychiatry,* supp. to vol. 121, no. 4, pp. 2–18.)

Madanes, C. (1981) *Strategic Family Therapy,* London, Jossey-Bass.

Minuchin, S. (1974) *Families and Family Therapy,* Harvard, Harvard University Press.

Morawetz, A. (1984) 'The single-parent family: an author's reflections', *Family Process,* vol. 23, no. 4, pp. 571–7.

Pearce, W.B. and Cronen, V. E. (1980) *Communication, Action and Meaning,* New York, Praeger.

Perelberg, R. J. and Miller, A. (1990) *Gender and Power in Families*, London, Routledge.

Pollner, M. and Wikler, L. (1985) 'The social construction of unreality', *Family Process,* vol. 24, no. 2, pp. 241–59.

Procter, H. G. (1981) 'Family construct psychology', in Walrond, S. Skinner, R. (ed.) *Family Therapy and Approaches,* London, Routledge and Kegan Paul.

Procter, H. G. (1985) 'A personal construct approach to family therapy and systems intervention', in Button, E. (ed.) *Personal Construct Theory and Mental Health*, London, Croom Helm.

Reiss, D. (1980) *The Family's Construction of Reality*, London, Routledge.

Rosenthal, R. and Jacobson, L. (1968) *Pygmalion in the Classroom: teacher's expectations and pupils' intellectual development*, New York, Holt, Rinehart and Winston.

Selvini-Palazzoli, M., Cecchin, G., Prata, G. and Boscolo, L. (1978) *Paradox and Counter Paradox*, New York, Jason Aronson.

Sluzki, C. (1983) 'Process, structure and world views: towards an inegrated view of systemic models in family therapy', *Family Process*, vol. 22, pp. 469–76.

Watzlawick, P., Beavin, J. and Jackson, D. (1967) *Pragmatics of Human Communication*, New York, Norton.

Watzlawick, P., Weakland, J. and Fisch, R. (1974) *Change: principles of problem formation and problem resolution,* New York, Norton.

Watzlawick, P. (1984) *The Invented Reality,* New York, Norton.

Watzlawick, P. (1977) *How Real is Real?*, New York, Vintage Books.

Williams, J. and Watson, G. (1988) 'Sexual inequality, family life and family therapy', in Street, E. and Dryden, W. (eds) *Family Therapy in Britain*, Buckingham, Open University Press.

CHAPTER 6
SOCIAL STRUCTURE, IDEOLOGY AND FAMILY DYNAMICS: THE CASE OF PARENTING

MARGARET WETHERELL

CONTENTS

INTRODUCTION

This chapter is concerned with relationships, experiences and the psychological dimensions of family life. But, in contrast to Chapter 5, Chapter 6 develops a detailed case-study of just one stage of the family life-cycle, and examines how family interactions and identities are structured through social rather than interpersonal processes. We will focus on mothering and fathering and will argue that the *private* experience of becoming a parent cannot be understood independently of the *public* context in which parenting takes place.

A major aim of this chapter is to develop an alternative line of argument which will both extend and debate aspects of the systems approach developed in Chapter 5. We will move from the concepts of family systems theories and family therapy to the concepts of social psychology and sociology, and will look at cultural and social constructs rather than personal or family constructs, at social roles and social positions rather than positions within family coalitions, and at how power relations in society as a whole may construct the lines of dominance within families. The chapter argues that to fully understand the way in which families function, family life needs to be seen as an ensemble of social relations as well as a network of personal relationships.

The sociologist Bob Connell (1987) has noted that when studying family life a strong sense emerges of 'something people fetch up against' – a sense of social conditions, structures and constraints which work beyond individuals. This chapter will try to explicate the 'something' the social context provides and the ways in which individual choices, family identities and family dynamics become organized within this context. Although there are advantages in treating families as relatively self-contained and self-regulating systems, we will try to show that families must also be seen as part of a social totality.

We focus in this chapter on mothering and fathering for several reasons. First, because these experiences are so common-place; the majority of people in the UK become parents. Second, because, in commonsense ideology, the transition to parenthood is seen, rightly or wrongly, as the moment when new families are created. People talk, for instance, of 'starting a family'. Mainly, however, the birth of a child is a time when the relationships between social forms and idealized and actual family forms become particularly salient as new parents try to manage the changes in their lives.

Chapter 6 draws not just on social psychological and sociological analyses of family life, it also relies to a very large extent on feminist theory and research. More than any other social theory, feminist theory has dictated the agenda for social scientific work on mothering and fathering in recent years. Feminist social scientists have been in the forefront of attempts to describe the ways in which power relations in the public sphere organize relationships in the private world of the family.

Chapter 8 on the history of feminist analyses of family life provides some useful context and background for the arguments and theories developed in this chapter.

1   MOTHERING AND FATHERING IN CONTEXT

As a mother holds her new baby in her arms she ... experiences a sensation of emotional and physical fulfilment that here at last is what she has been waiting to see and she is also emotionally fulfilled by producing a child for the man she loves.

(Bourne, 1979, p. 8, cited in Marshall, 1991, p. 69)

The very ideas of 'the housewife' and 'the husband' are fusions of emotional relations, power and the division of labour. The gender regime of a particular family represents a continuing synthesis of relations governed by the three structures.

(Connell, 1987, p. 125)

The birth of a first child has been described variously as a transition, as a crisis, and as just one further developmental stage in the life of the individual. Some of these characterizations are more apocalyptic than others, but there is general agreement that something significant has occurred. And, as the extract from Gordon Bourne's popular manual on pregnancy suggests, this transition is seen as particularly significant for women. Mothering, to a greater extent than fathering, is surrounded by powerful sets of ideologies and cultural expectations about identity and feelings.

In the first year of first-time parenthood, both mothers and fathers will be engaged in trying to negotiate a new modus vivendi for their family life. The relationships which surround new mothers and fathers undergo profound changes as both struggle to cope with the additional physical and emotional demands of parenting. Both fathers and mothers are likely to experience a scarcity of free time, and are more likely to conflict with each other over the allocation of that time. Much of the emotional work following the first birth will be taken up with re-defining and re-negotiating roles in the light of these new responsibilities.

To become a mother or a father in whatever type of family context is to acquire a new set of experiences, a new set of relationships and a new sense of self. The case-study developed in this chapter focuses on these changes and will try and unravel the three 'structures' which Connell notes – power, the division of labour, and the emotions – and show how they intertwine. We will argue that to understand the identities new mothers and fathers assume and the new relationships and family dynamics which emerge, the following questions must be addressed:

1   Who does what, both inside and outside the home, and how does this change?

2   How are resources (material, economic, emotional and social) distributed within families?

3   What ideas about mothering and fathering are dominant in the person's culture?

We will try to describe how social structures and social divisions, social roles and social expectations, ideologies and cultural conventions, power inequalities and conflicting interests, contribute to the making of mothering and fathering. The family lives that individuals create are not all the same and we hope to show how social factors combine in different ways to form diverse patterns.

Our case-study will be guided by several assumptions. First, that families are both active and reactive. We will assume, to re-work one of Marx's most famous aphorisms, that families actively make their own history, but they cannot construct this history just as they please. Our aim is to indicate some of the circumstances and conditions with which mothers and fathers must work and the ways in which families are both responsive to these circumstances and generative of solutions.

Secondly, we assume that, although it is difficult, it is indeed possible to generalize about family life. No family is, of course, ever entirely 'typical'. Each family presents an individual case. Mothers and fathers (including lone mothers and fathers) are engaged in flexible compromises between economic needs, available opportunities for paid work, childcare provisions, and individual desires and wishes. We need to study the nature of the balancing acts families make and the effects of these diverse strategies.

But, on the other hand, it is possible to find strong commonalities within and across social classes and ethnic groups. Any particular family's responses will be a complex mixture of cultural and structural influences, and there are regularities in both these aspects. As Westwood and Bhachu (1988) have pointed out, Muslim Asian mothers, for example, share many cultural and economic factors in common. And there are some similarities in the circumstances of all minority mothers (whether Asian, Afro-Caribbean, Cypriot, Turkish or Chinese, for instance) who are first-generation migrants. It is clear, too, that mothers, in whatever social or ethnic group, share major concerns, notably around childcare arrangements and childcare provisions. And it is certainly the case that fathers will have a great deal in common, as men, regardless of their ethnic and social class backgrounds.

The review of research on mothering and fathering which follows will try to indicate some of the main trends across different social groups, some of the differences due to ethnic and class position, and the variable ways these construct family life. As Anne Phoenix (1988) reminds us, it is important to remember in this context that the actions of white British families are also influenced by cultural conventions. It is not simply minority families whose practices can be explained through cultural patterns. Cultural beliefs and practices can be seen as established reactions to the structural (social, historical and material) circumstances of people's lives. On some occasions family patterns clearly relate to immediate economic circumstances; at other times it will prove more useful to refer to beliefs and values in order to understand family choices.

Our case-study will assume, thirdly, that an individual's identity or psychology (their emotions, motives, attitudes, and to some extent their personality and temperament) can to a large extent be understood through an analysis of their social roles. We will draw upon *role theory* (cf Biddle, 1979) to understand the psychological and interactional aspects of mothering and fathering. Role theory was developed within sociology and social psychology as a means of explaining the relationship between individual psychology and the social context. The central argument is that a person's behaviour, their identity, their sense of self and their personal characteristics can be predicted from their social position. With this focus on the social determination of individual behaviour, role theory can be contrasted with other theories of identity and psychological development which focus, for example, on biological causes or individual differences in personality traits to explain patterns in people's lives.

The term 'role' refers to the social expectations and prescriptions (the *social scripts*) which go with different occupations and social positions. It is argued that when a person comes to occupy a new social position such as 'father' or 'mother', their social behaviour becomes modelled on social prescriptions concerning how those who occupy this niche should behave. In essence, role theory tries to describe how a person's individual biography and private experiences of family life become structured by collective ideologies and cultural conventions and by the person's social position within a stratified and organized social system. It is claimed that any regularities in people's choices, senses of identity and conduct can be explained by these regularities in the social context.

Role theorists examine the way in which people become 'socialized' into roles through childhood learning and imitation of parents and other models. It is assumed that most people, throughout their lives, will behave in a manner which meets social expectations because, first, there are strong pressures and sanctions against alternative behaviour, second, because there are considerable rewards and social support for performing appropriately, and, finally, because these prescriptions become internalized and 'second nature', becoming seen as the only reasonable way to behave.

In exploring the effects of social constraints on family choices and the generality and diversity of experiences of mothering and fathering, this chapter will thus be reviewing and evaluating the key premises of role theory. Our aim is to develop the argument that people's choices and experiences can be seen as a direct reflection of available social materials, their social positions and the social scripts for these positions.

The next section of this chapter describes how work and family life are typically organized in families with small children, and how the sexual division of labour, which is cross-cut by an ethnic division of labour, differentially affects the resources of women and men and the micro-politics of domestic life. Section 3 then describes some of the ideological context surrounding mothering and fathering. We shall look finally, in section 4, at what happens to identity and individual psychology in this social context, arguing that the 'emotions' (that is, senses of identity and people's experiences of family life) will be strongly influenced by typical divisions of labour and public ideologies.

2   NEGOTIATING THE PUBLIC AND THE PRIVATE

2.1   CHILDCARE AND PAID WORK

Children demand time, care and labour. Yet their caretakers also require money to maintain themselves and their dependants. The way this combination – childcare and paid work – is organized will probably be the single largest factor influencing the experience of mothering and fathering and family relationships. Mothers and fathers construct their lives within an entrenched sexual division of labour which assigns women primary responsibility for childcare, and which also marks out enclaves of 'women's work' and 'men's work' in both the domestic sphere and in the public world of paid work.

For the 1950s' family, the compromise usually resulted in the wife and mother staying at home as the primary caretaker. Women are still the primary caretakers but in increasing numbers they combine paid work with domestic responsibilities. According to the most recent General Household Survey (for 1989), four in ten mothers of children under five now go out to work. Twelve per cent of these mothers work full-time, the rest part-time. As the age of dependent children increases, so does the proportion of women involved in the paid workforce. Thus three in four mothers with children aged ten or over work outside the home (31 per cent of these mothers work full-time and 43 per cent part-time).

Despite this increased participation in paid work, the economic activities of mothers generally tend to fall into a pattern of two peaks and a trough (Warrier, 1988), although there is considerable variation across ethnic groups, and differences between lone mothers and mothers with partners. One peak occurs before children are born, with the other peak once children cease to be dependent. As the figures from the General Household Survey confirm, most mothers' working lives vary across the life-cycle of their families.

Surveys of men's economic activity suggest that, in contrast, very little changes in the majority of men's working lives when they become fathers.

For some men, of course, such as lone fathers, or those small numbers of men who take on primary responsibility for childcare, the effects will be significant. But these groups are exceptions. Men, with or without children, are still much more likely than women to be in paid employment. In 85 per cent of cases husbands put in more paid work hours than their wives (Martin and Roberts 1984); 88 per cent of men with dependent children are involved in paid work (General Household Survey, 1984).

As Moss (1980) has pointed out, men often tend to work longer hours and are actually more likely to work full-time when they have young children. This is partly because family formation generally coincides with the time in their 20s and 30s when middle-class men are trying to establish their careers, but also because men across social class and ethnic groupings need to compensate for the loss or partial loss of their partner's income.

What differences occur for mothers across ethnic groups? A number of surveys have suggested that Afro-Caribbean and non-Muslim Asian mothers have the highest rates of economic activity, followed by white mothers, while Muslim Asian mothers from countries such as Pakistan and Bangladesh have the lowest, although women from this last group may be substantially involved in home working, making piece goods for payment (Westwood and Bhachu, 1988).

A typical scenario for a large number of white mothers is to move from full-time to part-time work on the birth of a child. For most women – black and white – mothering is also associated with shifts across different employment (industrial and service) sectors. The break in employment associated with parenting, and particularly this tendency for white mothers to return to part-time rather than full-time work, means that, for many, mothering is associated with downward occupational mobility and deskilling (Martin and Roberts, 1984).

The shift from full-time to part-time work as a way of coping with childcare responsibilities is, however, much less typical for black women (Bruegel, 1989). Afro-Caribbean and Asian mothers are much more likely to continue to work full-time. Prospects, income and the quality of work available vary greatly between white women who work full-time and white women who work part-time, but this difference is not so marked for black women.

What do these differences across ethnic groups reflect? Some of the causes are clearly structural or economic rather than cultural. Due to the effects of racism on employment prospects, black households are poorer and more dependent on women's earnings. Black women are thus more likely to seek full-time work from economic necessity despite their poorer prospects. Bruegel (1989) notes that the full-time work of black women is more likely to be in the lowest paid sectors. Black women, for example, are much more likely to work in manufacturing, especially food processing and clothing, and in transport, and much less likely to work in banking, insurance and finance than white women. Black women are also more likely to be unemployed and Bruegel notes that black women graduates in

London earn on average only 71 per cent as much a week as white women graduates.

Cultural differences are important too, however. Racism and disadvantage are experienced by Muslim Asian households as well as by Afro-Caribbean and non-Muslim Asian households. The reasons why there are fewer Muslim Asian women in the paid workforce outside the home involve Islamic traditions. But as, Bruegel notes, once a black women (Asian or Afro-Caribbean) has decided to work, then the majority, regardless of cultural background, do choose to work full-time.

Not only are racism and disadvantage important influences on the choices and family experiences of black mothers, for many the circumstances of migration have also proved crucial, and here there may be differences across generations. For example, according to Shrikala Warrier (1988), mothers in rural Punjab, Gujarat, Pakistan and Bangladesh worked both inside and outside the home but much of the work outside the home was unpaid and a great deal of economic activity centred on production within the home. For women migrants from these areas, therefore, migration brought many changes, described as both 'baffling and exciting' (Wilson, 1978). First, family life became for some women more strongly separated from paid work; secondly, since work became paid, there were more opportunities for an independent economic existence; and, finally, women moved from the agrarian, non-industrial sector to manufacturing and service sectors.

Many ethnic minority mothers are employed within what has been described as the ethnic economy (Phizacklea, 1988) or have been employed as homeworkers producing goods for piece payment at home. In these cases, as Westwood and Bhachu (1988) note, it becomes more difficult to separate productive from reproductive work and the private and the public become intermingled in a way they are not for most white mothers who work outside the home and family. Many Cypriot, Chinese and Indian women migrated on the basis that they would be employed within a family firm, or a relative's business. The labour power of women, sometimes unpaid, was one way in which male migrants could pool together resources to carve out a niche in a hostile economic environment. These circumstances for some communities (such as Greek Cypriot migrants) were strengthened through ideologies about the position of women and family honour.

The changing pattern of internal dynamics and interactions within families when they acquire children, and the ways women and men understand their new identity as mothers and fathers, will all depend on the way in which the public and private are structured and organized after the birth of children. We have tried to indicate some of the regularities in this structuring but also how choices will differ. Women and men can call upon very diverse resources and this diversity increases when we consider ethnic and class position, and whether mothers and fathers are lone parents.

ACTIVITY I

Using your own experiences as a reference point, or the experiences of your parents or friends, you might find it useful to make some notes at this stage in the chapter of the changes you and/or others experienced in economic circumstances and occupational history as a result of the birth of a child. What happened to paid work patterns, for example, in the cases with which you are familiar?

How do any changes fit with the general patterns just described? Try to describe, too, the effects (if any) of these changes on the division of domestic tasks within the home.

2.2 THE DIVISION OF LABOUR WITHIN THE HOME

To a large extent, how things are organized within the home after the birth of a child can be predicted from the patterns for paid work just discussed. Fathers in general are considerably less involved in domestic work and in the nurture of children than mothers. Within this pattern, however, there is considerable variation. Some couples, for example, arrange shift-work around childcare; in other households the person with the best chance of reasonable employment goes out to work. There is also general agreement that things have changed, that fathers are no longer so traditional, and have become 'new men'. This impression may be particularly marked for women in ethnic minority households – such as this Sikh grandmother – when they compare the old and the new:

> Look at my son, he changes the baby's nappy and feeds him every day. He also cooks sometimes for his son and wife. He was even present at the birth of his son. My daughter-in-law just expects him to do all these things. I would not have dreamed of asking my husband even to fetch a glass of water or take care of the children when they were babies, not even when they were ill. My mother and sister helped then, not him.
>
> (quoted in Bhachu, 1988, p. 93)

According to investigators, any changes which have occurred, however, have been restricted to particular areas of family life: there has been an increase in paternal involvement around the time of childbirth but despite some exceptions little difference for most men in the performance of routine chores such as nappy changing (Lewis and O'Brien, 1987, p. 3). Lewis (1986) argues that fathers have always been involved to some extent in child-rearing and, interestingly, historical records suggest that nearly every generation assumes that the fathers in their generation are in some way less traditional than previous generations.

On the basis of an intensive investigation of a sample of fathers, Russell (1983) has argued that they seem to fall into four types. Russell's research was conducted in Australia with 309 mainly white, English-speaking, two-parent families from a range of social backgrounds, but his findings match those of similar studies in the UK of white fathers across the social classes (Lewis, 1986). Russell describes one type as the 'uninterested and unavailable' father who is rarely at home. A second type is the 'traditional father', who spends more time at home, playing with his children, but who takes minimal responsibility for their day-to-day care. Thirdly, there is what their female partners described as the 'good father'. These fathers would perform some basic childcare tasks, and were seen as good because they were willing to help their partners. Russell describes the final type as the 'non-traditional highly participant father' who defines himself as sharing care with the mother. These fathers carried out 46 per cent of childcare tasks each week. But Russell points out that even in these cases

Are men's roles changing?

mothers were mainly seen as taking overall responsibility for the child in terms of deciding the routine and organization of the child's life.

Studies which have looked at the ways in which couples use time and at the allocation of work, leisure and parenting within marriage, have found that overall there have been only marginal increases in fathers' participation in childcare and domestic work in recent years (e.g. Land, 1983). Detailed studies of white families in the 1960s and the '70s, when women once again began to enter paid work on a large scale, note that the employment status of wives makes very little difference to men's domestic contribution. The most remarkable feature of husbands' domestic work-time is how little it changes, even in quite detailed activities, in response to changes in wives' working patterns, with the only notable increase in any domestic work activity being in time spent cooking and/or washing up by men with full-time employed wives (Thomas and Zmroczek, 1985, p. 115).

The general pattern can be seen in Figure 1. Women take primary responsibility for domestic work and childcare (activities which obviously increase on the birth of a child) while men take major responsibility for household repairs (which do not tend to change). The consequences for the leisure time of women who work are also clear in Figure 1. Whereas male employees experience around 10.2 hours of free time per weekend day, and 2.6 during the week, for female employees the figures are 7.2 during weekend days and 2.1 for week days (Henwood, 1987).

Owing to their ability to define the limits of their involvement in caring and domestic work, most men are able to retain responsibility for just one predominant social role, that of breadwinner, while many women juggle a number of social roles, coping with childcare and domestic work in addition to their paid-work commitments.

As Russell (1983) notes, few fathers, even those most involved in childcare, take over the role of the working mother completely. Few, for example, carry out domestic chores in addition to childcare, and much of the domestic work is still left to the mother to complete on her return from work. As La Rossa and La Rossa (1981) observe, men tend to choose those parenting tasks which are highly visible, involve less engagement of time and attention, and fall towards the play end of the work/play childcare continuum.

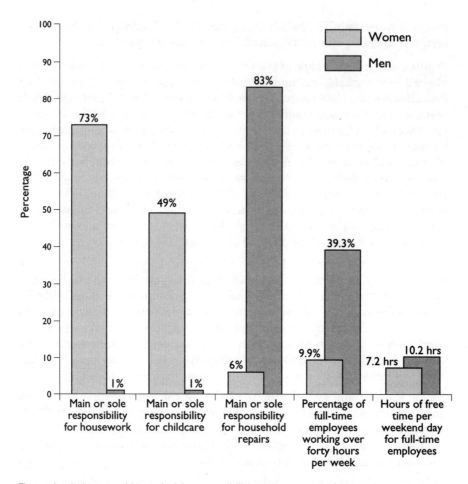

Figure 1   Leisure and household responsibilities

Note: Diagram only shows main responsibilities for domestic work and childcare; it does not indicate where such tasks are shared and percentages do not therefore add up to 100.

Source: Henwood, Rimmer and Wicks (eds) (1987), p. 67; data from Department of Employment/OPCS, *Women and Employment*, HMSO, 1984; Jowell and Wither-spoon (eds) *British Social Attitudes, the 1985 Report*, Gower, 1985; CSO, *Social Trends 17*, HMSO, 1987.

The daily paternal commitment to both housework and childcare remains small compared with their spouse's involvement, and women continue to retain overall responsibility for the domestic sphere even when both partners work outside the home. It is possible to conclude that women's increased participation in the paid workforce over the last thirty years has not been paralleled by a comparable increase in men's domestic responsibilities. Significant changes in women's roles in the public world of work have thus not been matched by equivalent changes in the private world of the family.

2.3   POWER, INEQUALITY AND THE DIVISION OF RESOURCES WITHIN FAMILIES

Power and powerlessness are difficult to assess and can be contradictory in the sense that many family members will experience both (sometimes simultaneously). Power within families covers many spheres. Power depends on social status, on knowledge and competence, on the capacity to accumulate and control resources, on the threat and capacity for violence, on established habits and traditions, and on ideology and cultural beliefs which will legitimate the authority of some family members over others. Power may be expressed in the ability to command respect and obedience, in feelings of autonomy and control over one's life, in the capacity to regulate one's dependency on others, in the power to decide where the family lives and whose career is given priority, and in the freedom to be able to leave difficult family situations.

In understanding power relations within families, we need to consider the type of household: nuclear families will obviously differ from lone-parent families and from joint households structured by hierarchical relationships between generations. We also need to consider how material resources are divided, and people's perceptions of the appropriateness of this division. In general, the forms of power mothers and fathers can exercise and their sense of identity and autonomy will be largely determined by the way they are placed within the division of labour described above. This division of labour marks out contrasting areas of competence and knowledge for women and men and structures their financial resources.

For many mothers power derives from their control over the daily routine and their children's lives, their domestic knowledge and competence, and also from the emotional relationships women build with their children and their partners. Many fathers and men are dependent on their female partners not just for care and nurturance, cooking, cleaning and general looking after, but because they value the personal and sexual relationships built up in the home. Without these, life could be isolated, lonely and difficult. One white, male engineer's clerk interviewed by Charlie Lewis in his study of fathers, put it like this:

> I suppose I've been surprised at my emotions, but … yeah, to me, without the kids, you know, I don't know what I'd do … And things like this … and if anything ever happened to them I'd crack up, actually … you know, that sort of emotion … you're probably just as dependent on them as they are on you.
>
> (1986, p. 165)

Many men, then, are dependent on their families and this dependence can create areas of powerlessness. Lewis and other writers on fathering have noted a paradox in many men's lives. A father may be recognized as the powerful 'head of the house' but may often feel somewhat excluded and detached from the central family relationships and thus out on a limb.

Men often use their incompetence within the house and lack of domestic skills as a justification for not getting more involved in housework and childcare. But this incompetence is double-edged because it also excludes men from building the type of relationships with their children which mothers can achieve, and deprives them of some of the pleasures of child-rearing. Some sense of this contradictory gain and loss can be seen in the following comments from a white, male managing director whom Lewis interviewed, explaining why he never bathed his small son:

> I'm probably too clumsy ... I suppose it goes back to the original awkward feeling ... Um, I feel the way they are, how small they are ... remarkably delicate ... And since I know I'm not going to do it full-time I might as well let the experts get on with it and leave the amateurs out.
>
> (1986, p. 100)

Many feminists have argued, however, that the lack of power fathers experience in the family is minor compared to the powerlessness of mothers. This perspective points out that the sexual division of labour, and the ways in which the public and private are typically managed in families, skew dependency relationships in favour of fathers. The bias is particularly noticeable in men's greater access to financial resources and their control of these, and reflected in the potential threat of domestic violence.

The division of financial resources within any particular family will reflect a complex interaction between earnings, social customs and con-ventions, and power. The solutions families reach vary across economic circumstances and across ethnic groups. Although many mothers work, and thus have some financial independence, women in general are typi-cally concentrated in low-paid sectors. Most men earn considerably more than their female partners. One survey conducted in 1984 suggested, for example, that married women earn only about half their husband's earn-ings, with only 7 per cent of married women earning the same as or more than their husbands (Martin and Roberts, 1984).

Most white mothers and fathers live within nuclear family structures and generally assume both incomes should be seen as contributions to the maintenance of the household and that money should be shared. One study (Stone, 1983) of a sample of white mothers found that the majority knew how much their partners earned and either had a shared bank account or received a housekeeping allowance. This sharing or pooling, however, needs to be seen within the context of the equally prevalent assumption that it is appropriate for the main breadwinner (usually male) to decide the overall allocation of resources. Sharing does not necessarily imply equal access.

Recent studies by Wilson (1987) and Brannen and Moss (1987) have found that whereas mothers, particularly in low-income families, are often assigned the task of managing family finances, men are more likely to control access to resources and to decide on the relative distribution of family income. Thus fathers decided what proportion of family finances should be allocated to food and household expenses, while mothers ensured that this amount, however limited, provided for the family's needs.

When men retain financial control, they can decide who is to benefit from expenditure and can, if they wish, distribute resources in ways which will benefit them in preference to other family members. When money becomes scarce, women and children may well receive a smaller proportion. The importance of male control over financial resources is underlined by Graham's (1987) study of lone mothers in which she found that some mothers in her study were objectively better off, in financial terms, as single parents, although their household income had fallen, precisely because they now had control over their income:

> Ronald didn't like me buying anything for the children. If I went out and bought them a pair of shoes and he wasn't with me, there was hell to pay when I got home. He just didn't like me spending money without his consent. If he wanted to go out and buy things that was different. He was very keen on photography and he bought a lot of photographic equipment. What things he wanted to buy was OK but the basics and things I needed to get for the children, he thought was unreasonable.

(Graham, 1987, p. 63)

These patterns, however, which suggest that the sexual division of labour differentially empowers men within families need to be qualified for many Afro-Caribbean families. Karen Stone (1983) has argued on the basis of an interview study with thirty-one Afro-Caribbean mothers that quite a different ethos and distribution of resources occurred in these cases. The Afro-Caribbean women she interviewed, unlike the white mothers, stressed the value of separate incomes and financial independence for women, and the importance of earning their own money so that they could regulate their income and choices apart from their male partners. The majority of Stone's Afro-Caribbean respondents had not told their partners how much they earned and did not know their partner's earnings. This pattern is commensurate with the fact that many Afro-Caribbean mothers may well be the financial heads of their households. This distribution of resources needs to be seen, however, not as an aberration, but as an alternative norm which may be associated with strong family relationships despite white British cultural assumptions.

For Asian mothers and fathers a very important determinant of their relative power and the distribution of financial resources will be the form their household takes. Many Asian couples with small children live in three-generational, joint households with their parents or parents-in-law, pooling resources across this grouping. These households may be structured hierarchically with several adults, often the most senior, taking responsibility for running the family economy (Ballard, 1979). This household form is more common among Gujerati and Muslim Asian families and less common among Sikh families (Bhachu, 1988).

Stone (1983) found that, as with the white mothers she interviewed, the twenty-two Asian mothers she talked to saw their earnings as making an essential contribution to a shared family income. However, in a greater proportion of cases, these mothers saw it as appropriate and desirable for husbands or parents-in-law to directly control their income, with the woman receiving money at the husband's discretion. Compared to Afro-Caribbean mothers, for example, very few of the Asian women in Stone's study wished to emphasize financial independence as a motive for working.

Patterns change, however, as economic necessities change. Parminder Bhachu (1988) has argued that the picture often painted of Asian mothers as passive and powerless victims of patriarchical and hierarchical family structures needs careful qualification. The paid work of Asian women has had a considerable impact on the organization of the domestic domain. The pooling of resources within a joint household also empowers older women, and these family forms have been a major source of support for Asian women and men in the face of racism and consequent disadvantage.

There seems to be a trend, in Asian families, particularly in the Sikh families Bhachu studied, for the move from joint to nuclear households to be associated with decreased male dominance as women take responsibility for generating and controlling financial resources. The power women and men can wield within the domestic sphere is closely related to their power outside that sphere. Bhachu argues, for example, that Sikh women's participation in the paid labour force combined with the changes associated with migration

> ... [have] led to actual changes in the structure of the household, in the expenditure and authority patterns within it, which have favoured them – or, rather, have strengthened their power base within the domestic domain. Exposure to the external world of waged employment has led to internal changes within the household which are reflected in structural changes within the organization of the Sikh community. For example, this is reflected in a kinship system which is much more loosely organized and much less patriarchical than in the past.
>
> (1988, p. 79)

But, as a sign of the complexity of the interactions between cultural and economic factors, Bhachu also notes that the wages of many Sikh women are now increasingly used as a springboard to propel the family into self-employment and the setting up of independent businesses. Women, then, move from the paid workforce into unpaid roles within the family business and, as a result, may become once again financially dependent.

Section 2 has tried to describe some of the social processes which structure the lives of families with small children. We argued that understanding this social context is indispensable to understanding the way personal relationships develop within families. The kinds of rules and constructs families create and the kind of system a family becomes will depend on these social raw materials. What mothers and fathers actually do – their practices – will depend on their social positions and these positions, as we have seen, are shaped by economic and cultural considerations.

3   'GOOD MOTHERS' AND 'GOOD FATHERS'

It is clear already that, as role theory suggests, the experience of parenting is bound up with social and cultural expectations about appropriate forms of behaviour. The lives of mothers and fathers are regulated by ideas concerning maternal and paternal characteristics, feelings, attitudes and priorities. We turn now to look at some of the ideologies surrounding the *identities* associated with mothering and fathering, focusing particularly on stereotypes and the way in which 'good mothers' and 'good fathers' are conceptualized.

The use of the word ideology in this context suggests that we assume there will be connections between these ideas concerning good and bad mothers and fathers and power relations in wider society. Feminists have argued that expectations of maternal and paternal behaviour reinforce and maintain gender inequalities and marginalize the mothering and fathering practices of ethnic minorities. So far in this chapter, we have talked mainly about cultural conventions to describe the effects of people's beliefs, values, habits and practices on their lives. Ideology, as Chapter 2 noted, has a more specific reference. The term covers the same territory – the meanings through which people make sense of their lives – but implies, in addition, that we are not just drawing attention to differences but also taking a more critical perspective on prevalent ideas and assumptions.

ACTIVITY 2

Pause for a moment and try to anticipate the main themes in popular ideologies of motherhood and fatherhood. What do people typically expect from their relationship with their children? What do you and the people around you normally mean by the terms 'good mother' and 'good father'? To what extent do your ideals conflict with or mesh with the conventional expectations of white British culture?

3.1 THE 'ANGEL IN THE HOUSE' AND THE 'STURDY OAK'

The reasons people give for having children vary across history and across cultures. In Western societies, and certainly among white families in the UK, people's reasons for becoming parents tend to conform to an individualistic ethos. Emphasis is placed mainly on personal rather than communal or social advantages.

People look to their children to provide them with a sense of personal growth, achievement, and some purpose in life. Children are seen as providing an opportunity for developing a new set of affectionate relationships and, most importantly, children validate adult identity and are a sign, particularly for women, of becoming a proper independent person. As Anne Woollett (1991) notes, in our relatively pro-natalist society, motherhood and fatherhood, if not mandatory, are seen as highly desirable, normal and part of the natural progression through life:

> The only people I can say I love with any sense of confidence are my children. I can say that because I feel more security about my feelings for, and obligations to, them than I do about anyone else.
>
> (Wandor cited in Woollett, 1991, p. 56)

> It's made me feel more fulfilled. It's given me something in life; I feel that I have achieved something now. Whereas before, I mean work and everything, maybe it was the jobs I had, but I always felt I was in a rut and was never achieving anything. But I feel as though I have done something useful: and if I can turn her into a nice person and put her in the world I'll feel I've really achieved something.
>
> (mother cited in Oakley, 1980, p. 263)

As Woollett notes, childlessness has a strongly negative image which is particularly difficult for those with fertility problems or those who have chosen to remain childless.

The strength and nature of the values involved suggests some of the powerful effects the transition to parenthood is likely to have upon identity. To become a mother or a father involves grappling with a pervasive set of social expectations about the 'good mother' and the 'good father'. To the extent that parenthood becomes defined as form of personal growth and as a personal achievement, the actions and reactions of parents will become signs of their success or failure as a person. Again, this is particularly so for women and the expectations vary across ethnic and class positions.

Researchers in this area have identified several elements in contemporary ideas about the 'good mother' found in childcare manuals (which are usually addressed to white, middle-class mothers), in the professions most closely associated with teaching parenting skills (who will deal with a range of mothers), and in the words of (usually white) mothers and fathers themselves (cf Dally, 1982; Urwin, 1985). One predominant conception is that the 'good mother' should be what Leonard and Speakman (1986) describe as the warm centre of the private domain – the 'angel in the house':

> There is an ideal of the 'good' mother towards which all mothers should strive. A good mother is one who is always available to her children; she gives time and attention to them, listens to their problems and questions and guides them where necessary. She cares for them physically by keeping them neat and clean and providing them with adequate food and clothing and emotionally by showing them love. She is calm and patient, does not scream or yell or continually smack her children. The cardinal sin of motherhood with its associated guilt is to lose one's temper with a child. Self-control should be exercised at all times. Even in extenuating circumstance such as when a baby screams with colic for days or when the mother has no emotional or physical support in her task, she must at all times be in complete control of her own emotions.
>
> (Wearing, 1984, p. 49)

An enormously high standard is set in this popular ideal. To be a 'good mother' demands unceasing selfless devotion to the child under all and any circumstances, requiring the mother to put the child's interests above her own. In reaction to the stringency of the ideal many, following the lead of the psychoanalyst Winnicott (1964), have talked instead of the 'good enough mother'.

But even a 'good enough mother' is seen as the one who is primarily responsible for her children's welfare, with the implication that she must subordinate her own needs and ambitions to those of her family, absorbing the stress of parenting and protecting others from its negative outcomes. In addition, 'good enough mothers' must take responsibility for the quality of their parenting experience regardless of the degree of social and relational stress which they experience.

'Good mothers' are expected to able to expand their own personal resources and to 'cope', that is to meet the needs of the situation whatever the personal cost and to make their work invisible by absorbing stress. This can be achieved by prioritizing childcare and down-grading other areas of mothers' lives, for example by lowering housekeeping standards and cutting down on leisure interests and sleep.

The effect of coping, as Hilary Graham (1982) has argued, is to render the work and stress of mothering invisible and to reinforce the belief that it is relatively easy and can be performed unaided. Failure to live up to the ideal of 'good motherhood' can result in maternal guilt and feelings of failure. Women, Graham points out, are the subject of both personal and public censure if they cannot 'cope', however difficult the task. If they fail to do so, they perceive themselves to be bad mothers:

If after the 3.00 am feed he had one of those gemmy times when he wouldn't settle, I'd get irritable with him and I felt dreadful about it. I said to Stan 'I'm a bad mother', you know because I was picking him up and shouting at him. I felt awful about it.

(mother quoted in Graham, 1982, p. 113)

Ehrenreich and English (1979) have noted the widespread belief in the bad or 'pathological' mother who is the dark side of the good mother. Bad or unnatural mothers are assumed to be those who react negatively to motherhood and who fail to find fulfilment. Since mothers in general tend to be held responsible for all the negative aspects of their child's behaviour even in adulthood, there is considerable scope here for maternal guilt. A bad mother seems to be one who not only experiences but articulates her stress, thus making her work visible, and directly challenging the social construction of motherhood as easy and naturally satisfying.

It seems clear that assumptions about the 'good mother' are both more circumscribed, narrow and more emotionally charged than those concerning the 'good father'. The expectations of fathers are much more varied. Several models are available, each of which create their own stresses and demands. Good fathers may be patriarchs, disciplinarians, their children's 'best friend', moral leaders, educators about the ways of the world, or substitute mothers. Here are some of the responses Russell (1983) obtained from his sample of white Australian fathers:

'The male is expected to be the disciplinarian, to work and be the backbone of the family. He does physical work around the house and plays football and cricket with his son.'

'To work and do odd chores. Go to the pub on the way home with his mates. Drink and watch TV while waiting for dinner to be ready.'

'Work and provide, to be an authority figure. He is someone to look up to for leadership. Dad is usually at the top of the family pyramid.'

(Russell, 1983, p. 27)

Fathers, as Lewis and O'Brien (1987) put it, are expected to be the 'sturdy oaks' of families – distant, powerful, strong, reliable and consistent. Fathers are frequently idealized for their capacity to be above the domestic fray, able to intervene to offer 'a wider and less emotional perspective' on family problems. As a result of this ideological pressure, men who are unemployed may feel that their masculinity and fathering abilities are challenged. While, paradoxically, men who take a very active role in childcare and housework may find they are accused of being 'good mothers' but 'bad fathers'.

It is important to note that the celebration of the virtues of mothers and fathers evident in the 'angel in the house' and 'sturdy oak' type of imagery depends greatly on who is doing the mothering or fathering. While politicians across the spectrum have been concerned to preserve the family, many have also supported immigration laws and procedures designed to keep black families apart – husbands from wives, and parents from children (Amos and Parmar, 1984). Politicians, too, have been typically more concerned about the effects upon children of *white* mothers going out to work than black mothers, and more concerned about absent white fathers than absent black fathers.

Similarly, the importance of mothering, and becoming a 'good mother', has been particularly emphasized historically in times of concern about the 'fitness of the white race' and the importance of 'breeding the right type of Englishman' (Leonard and Speakman, 1986). Mothers of the 'best stock' and 'pedigree' were encouraged to give their all to child-rearing, while others – working-class women for example – were actively discouraged from having children or encouraged to consider sterilization. It has been argued that the contraception and abortion policies within the NHS continue to operate within this frame, with young, single, black women under most pressure to have abortions, or to have contraceptive injections such as Depo-Provera (Mama, 1984; Rocheron, 1986). Phoenix and Woollett (1991) note, too, how more health education leaflets on contraception have been translated into Asian languages than on any other health issue.

Women with disabilities, too, find that they are often regarded as inappropriate mothers, and find their motherhood is rarely viewed positively: 'Each time I announced I was pregnant, everyone in the family looked shocked, dropped their forks at the dinner table – not exactly a celebration' (35-year-old, white, married woman, mother of two who contracted

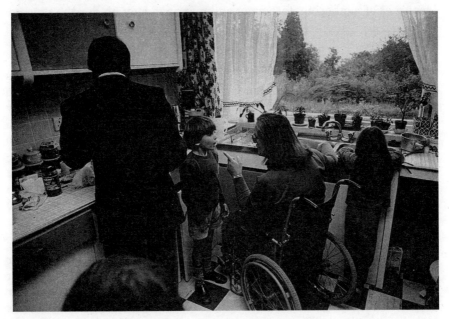

Exercising the right to mother

polio at age 5) (Asch and Fine, 1988). Disabled women report finding it difficult to obtain adequate counselling on pregnancy and childbirth, and have similarly found themselves either urged or coerced into sterilization or inappropriate contraception.

The ideologies of the 'angel in the house' and the 'sturdy oak' present particular problems for mothers and fathers with disabilities. Fathers with disabilities, for example, are often perceived as like another child and seen as emasculated through their disability. But the effects are especially disadvantaging for women with disabilities. American research (cf Asch and Fine, 1988) demonstrates that disabled women are considerably less likely to be married or in long-term relationships than either disabled men or non-disabled women (49 per cent of disabled women were married compared to 60 per cent of disabled men). Difficulties generally seem to be more tolerated by female partners than male partners: one American survey demonstrated, for example, that 90 per cent of female alcoholics are left by their spouses compared to 10 per cent of male alcoholics.

Asch and Fine argue that these differences are due to the perception of the idealized good wife and mother – not just warm, compassionate, and caring of others, but also mobile, capable, and continually active around the house – and the stereotyping of disabled women as meeting none of these requirements. Explorations of the perceptions of men without a disability suggest that they see disabled women as needing care and thus as unable to fulfil the traditional role of caring for male partners and meeting their needs both emotionally and practically. Some men and women with disabilities may not wish either to parent, or to be involved in heterosexual relationships. For those who do, however, contemporary ideologies of mothering, fathering and marriage may hinder the process.

3.2   REGULATING 'NORMALITY'

We have placed most emphasis on ideas about mothering because debates about the principles of parenting in general are usually addressed only to mothers in actuality. And it is mothers who tend to be seen as ultimately responsible for the welfare, achievements and failings of their children. Ideologies about the good mother become influential when they begin to regulate mothers' actions either through self-discipline and self-censorship or through the actions of state agencies and those professionals (such as health visitors) who work with mothers. Ideologies also become powerful, as the findings for disabled people suggest, when they come to dictate what is seen as 'normal'.

To a large extent assumptions about how parents should mother or father depend on psychological theories about the nature of children and their needs. There is general agreement among white mothers and fathers, for example, that the first five years of a child's life are crucial for their psychological development and for this reason small children need their biological mothers. These assumptions were strongly reinforced by the popularizing of psychological theories concerning maternal deprivation in the 1950s. Contemporary empirical research suggests, in contrast, that children are capable of forming attachments to many people and, depending on the circumstances, are unlikely to suffer ill-effects from mothers working (Mischel and Fuhr, 1988; Tizard, 1988).

Karen Stone's research suggests that, in comparison to white mothers, Afro-Caribbean and Asian mothers are much less likely to agree that the early years are vital; the Asian mothers, however, tended to agree with white women that small children are best cared for by their biological mothers, while only half of the Afro-Caribbean women were of this opinion, believing that children can receive good care from a range of people.

In recent years a new 'norm' for parenting has become established in the psychological literature. Psychologists and the writers of childcare manuals have become concerned about the importance of what they describe as 'sensitive mothering'. As Marshall (1991) notes, childcare manuals tend to give contradictory messages. On the one hand, great emphasis is placed on flexibility and convenience and ostentatiously not laying down rules:

> So even though this book is not designed to tell mothers how to rear their babies, but how their babies develop, and therefore what they need, I hope it will help mothers to find ways of doing the job so that life is as satisfactory as possible for the infant and therefore as easy as possible for themselves.
>
> (Penelope Leach, *Baby and Child*, 1988, cited in Marshall, 1991, p. 73)

Yet, on the other hand, within this notion of how babies develop is contained relatively strict prescriptions about maternal behaviour. Modern middle-class women, the readers of babycare manuals, are instructed that they should now try to be 'sensitive mothers'.

'Sensitivity' implies being tuned in to the baby's needs, understanding the baby's mental abilities, and being responsive to cues about changing needs. The sensitive mother is defined in these accounts as one who continually aids her child's development by 'scaffolding', in psychological terminology, that is, constructing the environment as a learning experience, a scaffold through which the baby can grow.

ACTIVITY 3

To gain some perspective on these pedagogic assumptions, consider the following two extracts from a study conducted by Tizard and Hughes (1984) which has been critically re-analysed by Walkerdine and Lucey (1989). You could use these extracts as a stimulus for investigating your own views on how parents should interact with small children. How responsive do you think mothers should be and what are the gains and costs of this responsiveness?

Walkerdine and Lucey introduce these extracts by noting that here are two ordinary pre-school girls – Amanda and Dawn – around four years old each having lunch with their mothers. In the extracts 'C' refers to the child and 'M' to the mother. Walkerdine and Lucey ask their readers, first, which mother do you think is sensitive and, then, why do you think this question is being asked by psychological researchers?

AMANDA AND HER MOTHER

C: Is ours a sloping roof?

M: Mmm, we've got two sloping roofs, and they sort of meet in the middle.

C: Why have we?

M: Oh, it's just the way our house is built. Most people have sloping roofs, so that the rain can run off them. Otherwise if you have a flat roof, the rain would sit in the middle of the roof and make a big puddle, and then it would start coming through.

C: Our school has a flat roof, you know.

M: Yes, it does actually, doesn't it?

C: And the rain sits there and goes through.

M: Well, it doesn't go through. It's probably built with drains so that the water runs away. You have big blocks of flats with rather flat sort of roofs, but houses at the time this house was built usually had sloping roofs.

C: Does Rosie [*friend*] have a sloping roof?

M: Mmm. Rosie's house is very like ours. In countries where they have a lot of snow, they have even more sloping roofs. So that when they've got a lot of snow, the snow can just fall off.

C: Whereas, if you had a flat roof, what would it do? Would it just have a drain?

M: No, then it would sit on the roof, and when it melted it would make a big puddle.

DAWN AND HER MOTHER

C: I got the wrong straw. [*She has a white cup and yellow straw, while her sister has a yellow cup and white straw.*]

M: Huh?

C: I got the wrong straw.

M: Why's that?

C: That side that colour, that. [*Points to cups.*]

M: What colour's that then? [*Pointing to Dawn's cup.*]

C: That one?

M: What colour is it then?

C: Red.

M: White.

C: White.

M: What colour's Sue's [*sister*] then?

C: Blue.

M: Your dress is blue.

[*Dawn then takes Sue's white straw to match her white cup.*]

M: Give her back her straw before she hits you. [*M gives the white straw back to Sue.*]

C: That must be mine. [*Pointing to white straw.*]

M: Well, go without then.

C: I want that one. [*The argument continues.*]

DISCUSSION

In some ways it is difficult to compare these two conversations. Amanda is asking her mother for information while Dawn seems to be asking for an object that has been given to her sister. Both mothers, however, seem to try to use the conversation to do some teaching, in Dawn's case of colour concepts. It is this last aspect which concerns Walkerdine and Lucey and which was the focus of the psychological investigations they wish to criticize.

Walkerdine and Lucey point out that in the original studies of these two mother–child interactions, Amanda's mother was described as a 'sensitive mother' and the lunch-time episode was described as 'a remarkable attempt by a child not yet four to explore an abstract topic' (Walkerdine and Lucey, 1989, p. 19). Amanda's mother was thought to aid her daughter's development by adjusting her replies to her daughter's level, providing detailed explanations, and building a basis for understanding concepts.

In contrast, the exchange between Dawn and her mother was described as failing to achieve mutual understanding. The psychologists who studied Dawn commented, '[Dawn] was unable to express the concepts in terms which her mother would understand, such as "I should have the white straw to go with my white cup". This difficulty was compounded by her mother's lack of sensitivity or lack of patience' (Walkerdine and Lucey, 1989, p. 19).

It now seems commonsense that all mothers (and fathers) should try to be sensitive to their growing children's needs. It is difficult to question the obviousness of this assumption and many mothers (and fathers) have been very influenced by the doctrines involved. While parents in the past were exhorted to be concerned about discipline and obedience and were told to encourage distant and respectful relationships with their children, modern parents are exhorted to be amateur teachers and psychologists, actively nurturing their child's growth. While it was once assumed that children had relatively fixed personalities and characters and would develop almost regardless of parents' actions, it is now assumed that parents have a decisive influence. These changes are in line with the general emphasis on the quality and form of personal and intimate relationships in Western societies.

Walkerdine and Lucey argue that it is particularly crucial to critically evaluate the assumptions about 'sensitive mothering' because psychologists have argued that 'sensitivity' is linked with social class. Working-class parents (such as Dawn's mother) have been found to be the least 'sensitive' and middle-class mothers (like Amanda's) the most 'sensitive'. Studies suggest that working-class mothers emphasize the separation of household work and educative play, are more likely to insist on children learning to play by themselves, to focus on getting domestic work done, and tend to use parental power more overtly to enforce discipline (Zelkowitz, 1982).

Does this mean that working-class mothers with these goals should be described as 'bad parents'? While agreeing that children need to be treated with respect, care and consideration, Walkerdine and Lucey and other feminist psychologists (Woollett and Phoenix, 1991) want to contest the arguments for the 'sensitive mother' and this assumption about working-class mothers. They dispute whether it is necessary for mothers to be engaged in constant pedagogy and patience, unfailingly responsive to their child's needs. Is it necessary, they ask, or even desirable for mothers to turn all routine household tasks into moments of learning for the child so that even putting the shopping away becomes an opportunity for teaching colour and number concepts?

The feminist response to the 'sensitive mother' covers several dimensions. Woollett and Phoenix (1991) note that there is little compelling evidence that 'sensitive mothering', defined as unfailing responsiveness and constant pedagogy, benefits children. Most mothers and fathers, across social classes, are probably sensitive some of the time by these criteria and lack patience at others. Walkerdine and Lucey argue that the strategies working-class mothers adopt make sense in terms of the financial resources and time available. 'Sensitive mothering' is extremely demanding, not just on the nerves, time and energies of mothers, but also in terms of resources. As Woollett and Phoenix note, there are good reasons why mothers living in bed and breakfast accommodation, for example, might be unwilling to encourage 'water play'. Indeed, feminist psychologists have argued that extreme child-centredness is actually oppressive for mothers. In no other relationship would individuals be expected to behave in such an other-orientated and self-sacrificing way.

Walkerdine and Lucey argue that central to the concept of the 'sensitive mother' is the claim that children are best disciplined through fostering an 'illusion of autonomy'. That is, it is best for children to believe that they are complying with their mothers because they want to rather than because they have been forced to. Again middle-class mothers are more likely to use indirect disciplinary strategies, to try and avoid overt conflict, and battles of will, and tend to describe the child's resistance and frustration at authority as 'bad feelings' or 'silliness' rather than as a genuine conflict of wishes. Walkerdine and Lucey wonder whether the actual power relationship between children and their parents should be disguised in this way and whether it might be fair to say that there is more actual democracy in the kitchens of working-class mothers. They argue that the directive strategies adopted by most of the working-class mothers they studied tended to result in more space for expressions of aggression by the child and were less oppressive for the mother, in the sense that children were presented with clearer boundaries and limits.

While it is very important not to undervalue sensitivity or the essential supportive experiences young children need, and although the debate

about how best to rear and discipline children will continue, it is crucial, too, that ideologies of the 'good mother', whether she is seen as the 'angel in the house' or the 'sensitive pedagogue' are critically examined. A focus on ideology suggests questioning the effect of these concepts as they come to define ranges of normality. Phoenix and Woollett argue that some 'norms' and fashions of child-rearing can marginalize black and working-class mothers. There is a danger that what is seen as different will also be seen as pathological and 'abnormal', and thus requiring more state surveillance. They note, that as a consequence, mothering can be a lot less 'private' for certain social groups, and the relationship between the public sphere and the separate domestic world of the family becomes more blurred.

Psychological studies of parenting typically use white, middle-class mothers as their subjects. Mothers are easier to obtain than fathers, white women are seen as more 'normal' and 'unexceptional' than black mothers, and many middle-class women are more likely to have the time, connections and interests which result in them becoming part of a psychological investigation (Woollett and Phoenix, 1991). Phoenix and Woollett argue that the consequence, therefore, is that the cultural practices of one social group become the ideologies which are used to assess and disparage the cultural practices of other social groups.

Very similar points have been made concerning the disadvantage lesbian mothers experience. Although studies suggest that children who grow up in lesbian households suffer no ill-effects (Hanscombe and Forster, 1981), these children also report the difficulties they experience at school and from peer-group assumptions about the 'normal family'. Any disadvantage seems to result from public social expectations rather than from their private experiences of family life.

Walkerdine and Lucey's analysis, and ideologies of mothering and fathering more generally, have been described in detail in this section because they pick out another important aspect of the social context in which any particular mother or father will construct their sense of identity and parenting practices. The ideologies we have described have important implications both for this experience of parenting and for the ways in which children are positioned to enter the public world of school and work.

4   INTERACTIONS AND IDENTITIES

We have described the diverse economic circumstances under which mothering and fathering occur, the division of labour inside and outside the home, and aspects of the ideological context. And we have noted some of the consequences for interactions and identities. Section 4 will attempt to pull together this discussion and, drawing particularly on feminist analyses, will try to summarize some of the psychological effects of the social context described in sections 2 and 3.

4.1   THE PSYCHOLOGICAL CONSEQUENCES OF GENDER ROLES

Many have argued that women and men are enabled and constricted by their gender roles in different ways. Men acquire the competencies and skills required for the public domain but at the cost of emotional expressiveness and social skills, while women's roles in the family are thought to encourage precisely the reverse pattern of psychological strengths and weaknesses. Fathers are typically accused of competitiveness, distance, disengagement from family problems, failures of intimacy, inattentiveness to others and brutality (Lewis and O'Brien, 1987). Women are typically accused of refusing to think for themselves, and avoiding the 'strain involved in undertaking an authentic existence' because 'lounging back into a tub of tepid water' (namely, family life) is easier than developing skills of independence and assertiveness (Leonard and Speakman, 1986).

These portraits of femininity and masculinity are polarized and polemical but mesh with the gender differences which consistently emerge in psychological studies. They mesh, too, with the finding that women and men display very different patterns of mental illness. Men are more likely to be diagnosed as experiencing personality disorders or having problems with substance abuse, such as drug dependency or alcoholism. And, men, in general, are much less likely to admit they have a problem. In contrast, women are more willing to admit to difficulties, are more likely to be diagnosed as suffering from depression and neurotic illness, to be prescribed psychotropic drugs, and to be admitted to mental hospital.

Recently many men, in autobiographical accounts, have begun to document the pressures that social expectations of masculinity have created in their lives (e.g. Jackson, 1990). But feminists have argued that, although both men and women are afflicted by gender roles, the psychological consequences are more severe for women, with the social position of mothers described as particularly oppressive. This claim, which we will take up in detail, is built on several lines of argument. Feminists have looked to the nature of what has been culturally defined as 'women's work' and its psychological correlates, and to the psychological costs associated with the position women occupy in the sexual division of labour.

Studies of housework and mothering (e.g. Boulton, 1983; Oakley, 1974; 1979; Sharpe, 1984) and of the activities involved in caring for dependants, out of love and necessity rather than money (Graham,1983), have argued that if this work were regarded as a job and compared to other possible occupations, the disadvantageous features would quickly become evident. Mothers, these studies suggest, cope with working conditions that are known to be associated with stress and ill-health in the paid workforce.

This is particularly true for the mothers of babies and pre-school children. Not only can the work of caring for small children be monotonous, repetitive and isolating, the hours are long and mothers have little control over their working day. While caring for dependants, and mothering in particular, has its compensations in terms of the rapport between carer and care-giver, caring also demands constant flexibility. Carers must constantly adapt to the needs of the other. Such demands can make it difficult for mothers to impose their own structure on their working day, or to rely on periods of uninterrupted sleep or leisure, contributing to feelings of fatigue and depression. Unlike paid work, there is no clearly scheduled time off from mothering and it is difficult for mothers to withdraw voluntarily:

> He seemed to want constant attention day and night. When he dropped off I would put him down and just slump across the table thinking, 'Please don't wake up.' I would hear him cry and my whole body would scream, 'please, please don't wake up.'
>
> (mother quoted in Phillips, 1983, p. 36)

> Every gesture requires an effort of will. The flat quickly sinks into chaos, dishes are washed under the tap as they are needed, and the airing cupboard stinks of urine because I have dried Carl's pants out instead of washing them … Worst of all that oasis in the afternoon when Carl is asleep and I can at last get down to my books, I waste destructively by going to bed. I have usually reached that point of tiredness where it takes some moment of fumbling to fix a light in its socket and there is an area of buzzing and shimmering between me and what I am trying to do.
>
> (Gail, 1985, p. 106)

Mothers across ethnic groups and social classes have pointed out that one of the major reasons why they wish to work outside the home, apart from economic necessity, is to avoid the isolation and boredom of working inside the home. Yet, it is also true that the experience of paid work for women can be such that motherhood and home life can in turn seem preferable. Sallie Westwood (1988) has described how both Gujerati and white women in a sample of factory-workers she studied often romanticized motherhood as a way out of work and perceived mothering as a much superior lifestyle. The reality for many women is that working conditions both within the home and outside the home will be unsatisfactory.

In coping with the disadvantageous aspects of mothering and housework, women often rely on informal support networks of family members and other mothers who share their experience, help pass the time, and can confirm and validate both the best and the worst aspects. Some of the worst features of mothering as work seem to be intensified when the work of caring takes place within a nuclear or lone-parent household compared to joint or extended households. Shrikala Warrier (1988) has pointed out that this contrast was particularly noticeable to the migrant Gujerati women she studied:

Although most women had been full-time housewives in East Africa, few had experienced a sense of isolation as a strong and effective support network operated among the women, which frequently cut across the boundaries of caste and kin ... several women in the sample mentioned the practice of a group of neighbourhood women (often unrelated) getting together to cook special dishes, and to exchange news and gossip ... Eight women who had lived in joint households pointed out that the problem of loneliness had never existed for them there. In Britain, on the other hand, the separation of households and the distances separating close friends and relatives, prevented women meeting during the day. Women who stayed at home in such circumstances generally found it very lonely, depressing and isolating.

(Warrier, 1988, pp.140–41)

The rare studies of men who take on the primary responsibility for child-care, either while living with a female partner or as a lone father, suggest that the psychological consequences of women's working lives are likely to be experienced by anyone placed in the same social position. Lone unemployed fathers are particularly vulnerable to isolation, stress and poverty, although Grief (1985) notes that some lone fathers can also receive a great deal of social support and admiration for their activities, and tend to be placed on a pedestal. His studies with white, American lone fathers suggest they are also more likely than lone mothers to involve their children in housework.

A second strand in feminist arguments for the debilitating consequences of mothering points to other features of mothers' experiences which are also recognized indicators of stress and ill-health. Feminists have noted studies suggesting that, in general, women and men who are under-resourced, powerless, who experience a loss in social status, and who lack leisure time are more likely to suffer stress and impaired mental health. They note that mothers very frequently fall into all of these categories. A study by Horwitz (1982) demonstrated, for example, a clear correlation between relative lack of power and lack of access to resources within the family and the prevalence of psychiatric disorders among women. Research links the incidence of depression some mothers experience to the social isolation in which mothering is carried out, particularly for mothers who have neither access to social contacts through paid work outside the home, nor a close and confiding relationship with their spouse.

From a feminist perspective, therefore, given the characteristics of women's and men's social roles, it is not surprising that married women seem to have higher rates of mental illness and, in one study, were 1.68 times as likely as men to receive psychiatric care in hospital (Gove and Tudor, 1973). It is also not surprising that a great number of studies suggest that, while marriage is associated with improved mental health for men, it is associated with impaired mental health for women

(Cochrane, 1983). Married women suffer much higher rates of mental illness than married men. Indeed studies suggest that it is single women with no children and married men who are best protected against mental illness. Feminists argue that women appear to be carrying the family's psychological burden, caring for and nurturing family members, at the expense of their own sense of well-being.

Mothers' chronic depression, particularly evident following childbirth, has been seen as evidence of women's chronic oppression (Nicholson, 1986). Depression and feelings of sadness, apathy, stress and frustration have been regarded as an understandable response to the changes which the role of mother brings. These are normal reactions, feminists argue, to the loss of status and personal autonomy, to the stress of childcare as work, and to the social isolation in which mothering is practised.

The ambivalence and stress expressed in many mothers' accounts of their experience reflects the contradictory status of motherhood in contemporary culture. Popular media images of motherhood depict happy, affluent mothers and clean, immaculately dressed and untroublesome children. While mothering is culturally defined as a vital and necessary task, and mothers as selfless and praiseworthy individuals, mothers are effectively marginalized in contemporary society through the exclusion of young children from places of work and entertainment, and the consequent isolation of mothers in the home. This has led a number of authors, among them Wearing (1984), to argue that while motherhood as a concept is accorded high ideological and moral status, mothering as a task has remained a hard, lonely and low status occupation.

4.2   NEGOTIATIONS AND FAMILY DYNAMICS

In introducing our case-study of parenting, section 1 of this chapter argued that the relationships surrounding new mothers and fathers will undergo profound changes as both struggle to cope with the additional physical and emotional demands. We noted that much of the emotional work following the first birth is taken up with re-defining and re-negotiating roles in the light of these new responsibilities. Feminist researchers have argued that, as with the psychological consequences of gender roles, the outcomes of these negotiations are similarly deleterious for women, and are typically skewed in favour of men. One effect, they suggest, of the social context in which family life is constructed is that women start from a position of weakness in family negotiation.

ACTIVITY 4

Take a look at the following extracts which have been taken from a range of studies of mostly white mothers and fathers talking about the way they manage their activities. These extracts indicate some of the broad context in which family negotiations take place. With each extract, try to note down the beliefs and assumptions which are evident concerning the division of labour and gender roles.

1   'I think he's very good really, em, because he comes in and he's had a very brain-filled day which can be much more exhausting than pick and shovels. And, er, they (children) just crawl all over him like ants, and he puts up with it, which I think is quite good.' (mother quoted in Backett, 1987, p. 83)

2   'He works six days a week so I don't want him to spend his one day off working around the house. He'd rather go out or he likes the garden. I think his one day off should be a day off, not a day doing *my* work.' (mother quoted in Boulton, 1983, p. 155)

3   'I usually bath and wash the kids' hair on Sundays. And that's the sort of thing a man can't do. You can't expect a man to do it. It's not in a man, to manage hair and things like it is in a woman.' (mother quoted in Boulton, 1983, p. 158)

4   'Women have better instinct. They know better. They know the difference between crying and crying. A man couldn't do it.' (mother quoted in Boulton, 1983, p. 158)

5   'The mother will inevitably be in much closer contact with the children. And this is not just my particular job, many fellows in my position because of the demands of their job they are not in as close contact with the children as they could be or should be. So that your presence is required only in extremis.' (father quoted in Backett, 1987, p. 80)

6   'It's not that he's not willing to, I think he's just, he's one of these distractable people, he's always kind of off somewhere else. Uh, not that he's neglectful, but I think, like Leo's nappy needs changing now, and I'll go and do that whereas he'll just kind of not realize till the last minute.' (mother quoted in Croghan, 1991, p. 233)

7   'He probably could have helped a lot more than he did in fact, that's not his fault. He's a very very heavy sleeper and he didn't even hear him. He would wake up the next morning and say, "That was good, he didn't wake at all last night" and I would say, "Did he hell! I was up nine times last night".' (mother quoted in Croghan, 1991, p. 235)

8   'Well it may just be the fact that I'm an uptight person with limited tolerance for situations (in) which I am not the controlling factor. But Sharon is not like that. She is generally a more peaceful and tranquil person with or without children. But what I am saying is, that as far as she and I are concerned, she is certainly better suited for a broad range of the necessary functions, where I just go off the deep end. And that's not a sexist thing. I mean, hell I do more than my share.' (father quoted in La Rossa and La Rossa, 1981, p. 193)

9   'I mean I participate when I feel like it, but if I feel like burying my head in the newspaper I do, or if I feel like ignoring the disturbances that are going on, then I can do it.' (father quoted in Backett, 1987, p. 83)

10   'If Karl gives him a bath or gets his food ready, I'll tend to say, "thanks for doing that". We've talked about it a lot because Karl doesn't say thank-you to me when I do things. And I do feel if I say thank-you, maybe he'll do it more often. Praise him. It's kind of subtle ... managing men.' (mother quoted in Croghan, 1991, p. 238)

11   'I don't complain because if I complain he'll think, "she doesn't appreciate it, so I won't do it".' (mother quoted in Croghan, 1991, p. 237)

DISCUSSION

As we noted earlier, role theorists argue that one way regularities in the social context come to affect individual lives is through *social scripts* or the patterns of expectations and beliefs people develop about appropriate and inappropriate behaviour. Social scripts provide people with what have been called 'vocabularies of motives', that is, with ways of making sense of their own and others' actions, and making sense, too, of the social context in which individual biographies must be lived out.

The scripts or themes which have been noted by feminist researchers in the extracts above are relatively clear. First, they point to the assumption evident in several cases (such as extracts 1 and 2) that the only proper form of work is paid work. Women's work in the home thus tends to become invisible and seen as less demanding, of less value and of lower priority. Time off and leisure-time in families also become defined in relation to paid work. But if the boundaries between domestic work in the home and leisure become blurred in this way, then it becomes difficult for women working in the home to see themselves as having a right to be 'off duty', in the way that time at home often becomes defined as time off work for men. These extracts thus put flesh on the figures for male and female leisure-time quoted in section 2.2 and indicate how social scripts and social structures become translated into family constructs which reproduce social patterns.

Other extracts (such as 3–8) suggest that women tend to be seen as 'naturally' more competent at domestic tasks, either through instinct, greater experience and closer contact with children, or because of the kind of people they are. Both mothers and fathers in these extracts make sense of unequal divisions of labour organized around gender through talking about differences in *individual* personalities and preferences. Things are seen to be the way they are because of the characters of the particular women and men involved rather than as a feature of the broader organization of society.

Whatever the source of women's greater perceived competence in the home it obviously can become a way of justifying and legitimating the double burden some women experience of paid work (part-time or full-time) and domestic work, as well as creating dilemmas for men who wish to work in the home, who want to be more responsible for their children or who are unemployed. Increasingly, in recent years it seems that whereas women have become seen as 'good workers' in the sphere of paid work, men have not been seen as 'good workers' in the home to an equivalent extent. And indeed are sometimes seen as congenitally unable to perform domestic tasks.

The final three extracts (9–11) draw attention to the way in which men's contribution within the home can become seen as voluntary and as a optional favour or gift which 'good husbands' will provide for their wives but which is not strictly necessary, or an obligation which could be demanded by women by right. One of the women interviewed, for example, talks of thanking her husband for 'helping out'. Again this assumption is asymmetrical with paid work, since paid work by women outside the home is not typically seen as a favour which women do for men but as something which is done from economic necessity, for greater mutual benefit, or for individual fulfilment.

Much negotiation within couples takes place within the assumption of the 'companionate marriage'. Marriage is seen as a partnership of equals, sharing goods and resources, where the emphasis is on affection, mutuality and emotional support. It is difficult to square this emphasis on sharing, mutuality and equivalence with the actual division of labour within many households and the actual division of resources in many families. In practice, therefore, companionate marriage and parity often become interpreted within a notion of 'equal but different', with men and women seen as making *complementary* contributions to family welfare. This assumption of 'equal but different' can obviously help obscure the fact that for many women the situation may be one of inequality rather than parity.

Feminist researchers (such as Croghan, 1991) have argued that the assumption of mutual benefit and mutual support, combined with the kinds of social scripts in the extracts noted above, make it particularly difficult for women to negotiate alternative divisions of labour, and to express their inequality along with any dismay they may experience at their workload and lack of support. To question these things, and social inequalities more generally, become equivalent to questioning and attacking a central emotional relationship, and a particular individual with whom one is closely linked.

Croghan argues that one consequence of this social and ideological pattern is that many mothers are placed in a situation where they can only interpret any distress, particularly in the early years of motherhood, as a sign of their own inadequacy or as a personal failure to accommodate themselves to the maternal role. Women and men in general are more likely to blame themselves and look to individual causes of problems rather than explain their difficulties in social terms. Many mothers transform their anger and grievance into feelings of guilt and self-blame.

Feminists suggest, therefore, that one important interactional and psychological consequence of the way in which mothering and fathering are socially structured is that women mistakenly see their family lives in terms of *personal* failures to live up to their own internalized standards, when perhaps they should be questioning those standards, and attributing difficulties to male power and inequalities in social relations. In this view, social scripts both reflect and sustain the power differences between women and men.

In conclusion, it seems important that these general insights about the way social patterns, ideologies, and cultural conventions become translated into family constructs and family scripts are used in combination with the tools described in Chapter 5, derived from family systems research and family therapy. In understanding any particular family interaction, we need to know the origins of the raw materials which couples use to negotiate and construct their family life as well as be able to make sense of the course that family dynamics and family interactions are likely to take as a consequence.

5   EVALUATION

This chapter has tried to indicate some of the social processes involved in the construction of the interior of family life, through a detailed case-study of mothering and fathering. Our analysis of the importance of economic circumstances, divisions of labour, ideologies, cultural conventions, and social roles for family relationships and interactions has, like all accounts of family life, been developed within a particular frame and set of values. We have emphasized feminist perspectives on mothering and fathering and the oppressive features of family life for women. Section 5 now turns to an evaluation of this feminist perspective and the concepts through which we have explicated the social construction of family life.

5.1   QUESTIONS OF IDENTITY

There has been a major shift in feminist thinking from studies in the early 1970s which questioned the value of family life and the basis of women's roles within the family to studies which began to emphasize instead the importance of mothering (see Chapter 8). Feminists continued to be concerned about the oppressive nature of the social conditions in which women mother, but also wanted to stress the joys of motherhood and mothering as a crucial sphere of power and authority for women.

Clearly, the analysis developed in this chapter has focused on oppressiveness rather than satisfactions. It is perhaps inevitable that a concern from a feminist perspective with the way social circumstances structure family life should lead to this emphasis. But have the difficulties of mothering (and fathering) been over-emphasized? Given that the experience of gender roles is sometimes rather grim, why do women continue to choose to have children, especially since in objective economic terms parenthood seems an irrational choice. How do we explain the continuation of family life and its popularity?

One answer to this question might be that women have no choice in the matter, not because of biology, but in the sense that social conditions define a woman's lot and it is beyond one individual to resist the life patterns, constraints and opportunities presented. We could also argue that women (and men) are dupes of the ideologies of motherhood and companionate marriage. Since the dominant ways of making sense of experience take women and men's roles as natural and fulfilling, women become persuaded into mothering in a context which disadvantages them.

Undoubtedly ideologies are powerful in guiding individual's actions. This answer, however, seems to ignore the pleasures that women and men receive from parenthood and family relationships. These pleasures and the popularity of family life suggest that there may be more involved than simple conformity to social demands. It suggests that we need to flesh out our account of gender relations within families with a more complex analysis of identity and the development of femininity and masculinity as psychological traits. And we need to explore further how ideologies of motherhood, fatherhood and companionate marriage might mesh in with that psychological development.

This question of motivation and identity strikes, in essence, at role theory (introduced in section 1) and its adequacy as an explanation of the connections between personal experience and social situation. Does role theory adequately describe how ideologies and work arrangements in the public sphere become translated into the personality, aptitudes and personal values displayed by individual women and men in families? Can role theory explain the complicated motives of individual mothers and fathers? It is important to remember that role theory does not pretend to be a psychological theory; it provides a simple framework for connecting together individual identity and social expectations. But, as Segal (Chapter 8 of this volume) points out, the history of feminist analyses of family life indicates that when we begin to look more closely at people's motives and emotions, the connection between the individual and the social becomes more and more complex.

Role theory has considerable advantages. It can connect everyday experience and people's biographies with broad economic and cultural patterns. The accounts mothers and fathers give, for example, can be seen as 'social scripts' which go with their social roles. And it is clear that ideologies of the 'good mother' and the 'companionate marriage' discussed in this chapter can become personal narratives guiding the perceptions, feelings, thoughts and actions of individual women and men. But many roles and scripts seem to be deeply contradictory. Motherhood is both pleasure and pain; mothers and fathers may simultaneously love and hate their assigned tasks. And it is difficult to see how role theory can work with these contradictions. How many different scripts can be associated with a particular social role? Is the formula of social position plus a set of social expectations flexible enough to cope with the fragmentary nature of people's feelings and reactions?

Masculinity and femininity are not like a set of clothes in a wardrobe which can be put on and off with ease. These identities feel more like a skin which can not be shed. Lynne Segal concludes as a consequence that:

> ... role theory analysis, which sees people as inevitably conforming to the social expectations surrounding them, cannot adequately explain the over-riding significance we each attach to our sense of gender identity, its force and power over us, despite all the personal confusion and insecurities which surround it.
>
> (1987, p. 120)

Role theory does not seem to do justice to the complexity of society and social interaction and the sheer variety of ways in which someone can behave and still be recognized as a mother or a father. Look back, for example, at the conversations between mothers and daughters studied by Walkerdine and Lucey. To what extent does it help make sense of the subtle and complex interactional processes operating in these conversations if we describe these women as simply acting out the role of 'mother'?

Finally, role theory cannot explain why in practice people seem so resistant to social change, and find instituting changes in their personal lives so difficult. The flexibility of human nature and its malleability in the face of social pressures are stressed in role theory. If people are like blank slates on which any set of social expectations can be written, then why is change so difficult?

For these and other reasons, many researchers in the field of gender relations have argued that gender identity is perhaps more complex than a simple internalizing of the role expectations of the social context. The reproduction of gender identity involves complex and contradictory emotions, desires and motives as well as the relationship patterns associated with the division of labour. These researchers have turned increasingly to psychoanalysis as an explanation which could incorporate all these elements. And, for this reason, Chapter 7 will take up the psychoanalytic challenge to role theory.

5.2   DEALING WITH DIVERSITY

Diversity has been a major theme in this chapter and, indeed, has presented a substantial challenge to feminist and other social and psychological theories of family life. Diversity is particularly testing because it requires the development of concepts which can accommodate movement up and down a sliding scale from homogeneity of experience to complete heterogeneity. The tension between universality of experience and specificity is an uneasy one.

On the one hand, universality must always be questioned. The boundaries set by the social divisions of 'race'/ethnicity, gender, class, sexuality, generation and disability must be respected and every family and every family member needs to be positioned carefully within this context. But even within these conventional social categories it is important not to assume commonality, to assume, for example, that all Muslim Asian women in a similar social position will feel the same way. Yet social scientists must generalize, not just because social science works through the identification of patterns and regularities but because there are also real commonalities in the lives of women and men which run across 'race'/ethnicity, disability/able-bodiedness, gender, social class, sexuality and generations, or combinations of these. June Jordan has made this point forcefully:

> I think there is something deficient in the thinking on the part of anybody who proposes either gender identity politics or race identity politics as sufficient, because every single one of us is more than whatever race we represent or embody and more than whatever gender category we fall into. We have other kinds of allegiances, other kinds of dreams that have nothing to do with whether we are white or not white.

(Jordan, quoted in Parmar, 1989, p. 61)

Generalization, however, will always be complicated by the fact that the pattern of commonalities will change across topics of investigation. Alliances discovered, for instance, in studies of male and female sexual experience, might need to be disbanded and reconstituted when paid work is investigated or feelings around childcare provision explored.

In the face of diversity it is tempting to focus only on specificity and to describe unique patterns of identity relying on the voices of those familiar with the experience. Diversity can lead to the questioning of authenticity and speaking rights: who has the right, for example, to speak on whose behalf? In analysing family life it is necessary to both look for commonalities and yet remember that experiences may be so different that speech on behalf of another may seem like a form of colonialism.

The task of understanding is made more difficult by the bias, particularly in psychology but also in other social science disciplines, towards studies of the experiences of white, heterosexual, nuclear families. Much is known, for example, concerning white women's experiences of motherhood, or concerning the interactions of white fathers and their sons. The ways in which gender relations structure family life are becoming well understood. Much less attention has been paid to the commonalities and differences with ethnic minority families and other family forms.

Amos and Parmar (1984) have argued that much of the work which is available often reproduces crude stereotypes of strong matriachical Afro-Caribbean women, for example, and passive, downtrodden Asian mothers and daughters confined within arranged marriages. They argue for studies of family life which will locate the experiences of black families within the historical experiences of black people more generally. Most importantly these studies, as Ann Phoenix (1988) emphasizes, must be sensitive to the position of black people within the UK, rather than relying on anthropological work in Pakistan, Jamaica and other countries of origin.

6   CONCLUSION

The argument in this chapter does not dispute the importance of the analyses conducted by family systems theorists (see Chapter 5 of this volume). It is vital to understand, from the inside, how a family organizes its activities and the logic of interpersonal relationships. But it is also important to explain the broader patterns in family negotiations and why they have a tendency to go in one direction rather than another. Why it is, for example, that men are more likely to resort to violence under stress while women become depressed, and why power is unevenly shared in families in regular and predictable ways.

A social perspective on the construction of family life tries to explain the sources of those differences which result from cultural and structural positioning; it also tries to connect the constructs and belief systems of families to ideologies, social expectations, and to the division of labour. Those are its major strengths. We have seen, however, that an elaboration of the social context in which families construct their lives can be at the expense of the psychological subtleties. Chapter 7 returns to those subtleties and also describes some further attempts to synthesize the psychological dimensions of family life with the social dimensions.

ACKNOWLEDGEMENT

This chapter was based on a review of material on feminist perspectives on mothering and fathering supplied by Rosaleen Croghan.

REFERENCES

Amos, V. and Parmar, P. (1984) 'Challenging imperial feminism', *Feminist Review*, vol. 17, pp. 3–19.

Asch, A. and Fine, M. (1988) 'Introduction: beyond pedestals', in Fine, M. and Asch, A. (eds) *Women with Disabilities: essays in psychology, culture and politics*, Philadelphia, PA, Temple University Press.

Backett, K. (1987) 'The negotiation of fatherhood', in Lewis, C. and O'Brien, M. (eds).

Ballard, C. (1979) 'Conflict, community and change: second-generation South Asians', in Khan, V. (ed.) *Minority Families in Britain: support and stress*, London, Macmillan.

Bhachu, P. (1988) 'Apri Marzi Kardhi: home and work: Sikh women in Britain', in Westwood, S. and Bhachu, P. (eds).

Biddle, B. (1979) *Role Theory*, New York, Academic Press.

Boulton, M.G. (1983) *On Being a Mother*, London, Tavistock.

Bourne, G. (1979) *Pregnancy*, London, Pan.

Brannen, J. and Moss, P. (1987) 'Fathers and employment', in Lewis, C. and O'Brien, M. (eds).

Bruegel, I. (1989) 'Sex and race in the labour market', *Feminist Review*, vol. 32, pp. 49–68.

Cochrane, R. (1983) *The Social Creation of Mental Illness*, London, Longman.

Connell, R.W. (1987) *Gender and Power*, Cambridge, Polity Press.

Croghan, R. (1991) 'First-time mothers' accounts of inequalities in the division of labour', *Feminism and Psychology*, vol. 1, pp. 221–47.

Dally, A. (1982) *Inventing Motherhood*, London, Burnett Books.

Ehrenreich, B. and English, D. (1979) *For Her Own Good: 150 years of the experts' advice to women*, London, Pluto Press.

Gail, S. (1985) 'The housewife', in Malos E. (ed.) *The Politics of Housework*, London, Allison and Busby.

General Household Survey (1984) *Office of Population Censuses and Surveys Report on 1982 Data*, London, HMSO.

General Household Survey (1990) *Office of Population Censuses and Surveys, Preliminary Results for 1989*, London, HMSO.

Gove, W.R. and Tudor, J.F. (1973) 'Adult sex roles and mental illness', *American Journal of Sociology*, vol. 78, no. 4, pp. 812–35.

Graham, H. (1982) 'Coping: or how mothers are seen and not heard', in Friedman, S. and Elizabeth Sarah (eds) *On the Problem of Men*, London, The Women's Press.

Graham, H. (1983) 'Caring: a labour of love', in Finch, J. and Groves, D. (eds) *A Labour of Love: women, work and caring*, London, Routledge and Kegan Paul.

Graham, H. (1987) 'Being poor: perceptions and coping strategies of lone mothers', in Brannen, J. and Wilson, G. (eds) *Give and Take in Families*, London, Allen and Unwin.

Grief, G. (1985) *Single Fathers*, Lexington, Lexington Books.

Hanscombe, G. and Forster, J. (1981) *Rocking the Cradle: lesbian mothers, a challenge in family living*, London, Peter Owen.

Henwood, M. (1987) 'Family care', in Henwood, M., Rimmer, L. and Wicks, M. (eds) *Inside the Family: changing roles of men and women*, London, Family Policy Studies Centre.

Horwitz, A.V. (1982) 'Sex role expectations, power, and psychological distress', *Sex Roles*, pp. 8,606–23.

Jackson, D. (1990) *Unmasking Masculinity: a critical autobiography*, London, Routledge.

Land, H. (1983) 'Poverty and gender: the distribution of resources within the family', in Brown, M. (ed.) *The Structure of Disadvantage*, London, Heinemann.

La Rossa, R. and La Rossa, M. (1981) *Transition to Parenthood: how children change families*, Beverly Hills, CA, Sage Publications.

Leonard, D. and Speakman, M. (1986) 'Women in the family: companions or caretakers', in Beechey, V. and Whitelegg, E. (eds) *Women in Britain Today*, Milton Keynes, Open University Press.

Lewis, C. (1986) *Becoming a Father*, Milton Keynes, Open University Press.

Lewis, C. and O'Brien, M. (1987) 'Constraints on fathers: research, theory and clinical practice', in Lewis, C. and O'Brien, M. (eds).

Lewis, C. and O'Brien, M. (eds) (1987) *Reassessing Fatherhood: new observations on fathers and the modern family*, London, Sage.

Mama, A. (1984) 'Black women, the economic crisis and the British State', *Feminist Review*, vol. 17, pp. 19–33.

Marshall, H. (1991) 'The social construction of motherhood: an analysis of childcare and parenting manuals', in Woollett, A., Phoenix, A. and Lloyd, E. (eds).

Martin, J. and Roberts, C. (1984) *Women and Employment: a lifetime perspective*, DE/OPCS, London, HMSO.

Mischel, H. and Fuhr, R. (1988) 'Maternal employment: its psychological effects on children and their families', in Dornbusch, S. and Stroeber, M. (eds) *Feminism, Children and the New Families*, New York, The Guildford Press.

Moss, P. (1980) 'Parents at work', in Moss, P. and Fonda, N. (eds) *Work and the Family,* London, Temple Smith.

Nicholson, P. (1986) 'Depression following childbirth', in Wilkinson, S. (ed.) *Feminist Social Psychology*, Milton Keynes, Open University Press.

Oakley, A. (1974) *The Sociology of Housework*, Oxford, Martin Robertson.

Oakley, A. (1979) *Becoming a Mother*, Oxford, Martin Robertson.

Oakley, A. (1980) *Women Confined: towards a sociology of childbirth*, Oxford, Martin Robertson.

Parmar, P. (1989) 'Other kinds of dreams', *Feminist Review*, vol. 31, pp. 55–65.

Phillips, A. (1983) *Your Body, Your Baby, Your Life*, London, Pandora Press.

Phizacklea, A. (1988) 'Enterpreneurship, ethnicity and gender', in Westwood, S. and Bhachu, P. (eds).

Phoenix, A. (1988) 'Narrow definitions of culture: the case of early motherhood', in Westwood, S. and Bhachu, P. (eds).

Phoenix, A. and Woollett, A. (1991) 'Motherhood: social construction, politics and psychology', in Woollett, A., Phoenix, A. and Lloyd, E. (eds).

Rocheron, Y. (1986) 'The Asian mother and baby campaign: the construction of ethnic minority health needs', *Critical Social Policy*, vol. 17, pp. 4–23.

Russell, G. (1983) *The Changing Role of Fathers*, Milton Keynes, Open University Press.

Segal, L. (1987) *Is the Future Female? Troubled thoughts on contemporary feminism*, London, Virago.

Sharpe, S. (1984) *Double Identity*, Harmondsworth, Penguin Books.

Stone, K. (1983) 'Motherhood and waged work: West Indian, Asian, and white mothers compared', in Phizacklea, A. (ed.) *One Way Ticket: migration and female labour*, London, Routledge.

Thomas, G. and Zmroczek, L. (1985) 'Household technology: the "liberation" of women from the home', in Close, P. and Collins, R. (eds) *Family and Economy in Modern Society*, London, Macmillan.

Tizard, B. (1988) 'Employed mothers and the care of young children', in Woollett, A., Phoenix, A. and Lloyd, E. (eds).

Tizard, B. and Hughes, M. (1984) *Young Children Learning*, London, Fontana.

Urwin, C. (1985) 'Constructing motherhood: the persuasion of normal development', in Steedman, C., Urwin, C. and Walkerdine, V. (eds) *Language, Gender and Childhood*, London, Routledge.

Walkerdine, V. and Lucey, H. (1989) *Democracy in the Kitchen*, London, Virago.

Warrier, S. (1988) 'Marriage, maternity and female economic activity: Gujarati mothers in Britain', in Westwood, S. and Bhachu, P. (eds).

Wearing, B. (1984) *The Ideology of Motherhood*, Sydney, Allen and Unwin.

Westwood, S. (1988) 'Workers and wives: continuities and discontinuities in the lives of Gujarati Women', in Westwood, S. and Bhachu, P. (eds).

Westwood, S. and Bhachu, P. (eds) (1988) *Enterprising Women: ethnicity, economy and gender relations*, London, Routledge.

Wilson, A. (1978) *Finding a Voice*, London, Virago.

Wilson, G. (1987) *Money in the Family: financial organisation and women's responsibility*, Aldershot, Avebury.

Winnicott, D. (1964) *The Child, the Family, and the Outside World*, Harmondsworth, Penguin.

Woollett, A. (1991) 'Having children: accounts of childless women and women with reproductive problems', in Woollett, A., Phoenix, A. and Lloyd, E. (eds).

Woollett, A. and Phoenix, A. (1991) 'Psychological views of mothering', in Woollett, A., Phoenix, A. and Lloyd, E. (eds).

Woollett, A., Phoenix, A. and Lloyd, E. (eds) (1991) *Motherhood: meanings, practices and ideologies*, London, Sage.

Zelkowitz, P. (1982) 'Parenting philosophies and practices', in Belle, D. (ed.) *Lives in Stress: women and depression*, London, Sage.

CHAPTER 7
THE PSYCHOANALYTIC APPROACH TO FAMILY LIFE

MARGARET WETHERELL

CONTENTS

INTRODUCTION

More than any other tradition, psychoanalysis has had a radical and, some would say, disturbing effect upon our collective image of mothers and fathers, the needs and desires of children, family rivalries and the problems of sexual and gender identity. Many investigators have seen in psychoanalysis enormous potential for mapping the complex emotional interior of the family (Connell, 1987, p. 124). Others are entirely sceptical and regard psychoanalysis as an aberration, a tangential and misguided path in the analysis of family life.

The review of psychoanalytic theory in this chapter will try to cover, in section 1, the common core of psychoanalytic thought on identity and family life, and thus the elements that unite most psychoanalysts. Section 2 will then describe some of the variety in psychoanalytic accounts and the points of dispute which divide parts of the psychoanalytic community. These first two sections set the scene. Section 3 follows up in detail one school of psychoanalytic thought best described as 'feminist object relations theory'. This perspective attempts to combine psychoanalytic concepts with sociological analyses of family life and thus provides a good test-case for the claim that psychoanalysis can be both socially and psychologically astute. Section 4 evaluates feminist object relations work and broader psychoanalytic premises, focusing particularly on the treatment of diversity.

Sigmund Freud (1856–1939)

1   PSYCHOANALYSIS, IDENTITY AND FAMILY LIFE

As Chapter 6 demonstrated, the accounts of identity and family life found in role theories of socialization are often criticized for being pallid and unconvincing – insensitive to the turbulence of people's emotional lives and the subtlety of their responses to family life. The perspective that psychoanalysis offers as an alternative to these accounts is anything but bland. Indeed, psychoanalysts are often accused of presenting too melodramatic a view of the individual and the family – torn apart by conflict and sexual and aggressive terrorism but also held together by these things. For some psychoanalysts, the family is best seen as a hothouse of repressed emotions and unacceptable drives. And it is within this intense atmosphere that amorphous infants are (sometimes brutally) programmed to become social beings.

The core assumptions concerning identity and family life around which psychoanalysts cohere can be divided into three categories which will be discussed in turn below. First, there is a distinctive argument concerning the nature of identity, subjectivity and individual psychology, which stresses the role of the unconscious and contradictions in experience. Second, psychoanalysis suggests a particular set of tasks for family life. Families are seen as the mediator between the child, culture and society, and as the formative influence in the genesis of every individual. Finally, psychoanalysis suggests a dynamic but historical view of adult sexual relations and family life. Families involve relationships between adults whose identity is already constituted (and perhaps inevitably deformed) by their previous family experiences. The changing pattern of family relationships in the present thus resonates with material from the past history of the individual. Freud in a famous statement suggested, for instance, that six people are always involved when two people go to bed together – the couple and the ghosts of their parents contained within their psyches. For psychoanalysts, the construction of a successful family life in the present depends on a history of earlier positive experiences of family life.

1.1   THE SPLIT AND 'ALIENATED' INDIVIDUAL

The model of identity and individual psychology proposed by psychoanalysis has been central to its impact on family studies. Part of this effect derives from the ways in which psychoanalysis challenges strongly held beliefs about human nature. Psychoanalysis explicitly rejects the notion that humans are quintessentially rational and coherent beings. This approach questions the assumption that people's actions are organized by a central, directing consciousness which sums up the totality of mental life (Frosh, 1987, p. 85).

Much of psychology, commonsense, social policy, social work and indeed research on families takes for granted that people generally know what they are doing and why. People are thought to be guided most of the time

The psychoanalyst goes fishing

by reasonable and sensible motives, and are usually treated as if in control of their plans and lives. Psychoanalysis argues, however, that this rationality and sensibleness is mere superficial appearance. Rationality does not come naturally but emerges from an uneven struggle between the forces of the unconscious and the conscious control we try to exert in response. Psychoanalysts suggest that people are often unable to consciously understand or articulate the underlying reasons for their actions.

To understand this attack on conventional concepts of human nature, we need to understand the theory of mental life that psychoanalysis proposes and particularly this distinction between the conscious and the unconscious. The key claim has been succinctly summarized as follows:

> In talking about evidence for the unconscious, I'm talking about evidence for a submerged 'inner' world which lies like an iceberg mostly hidden under water, with the 'outer' world – the conscious self – showing only as the tip of the iceberg.
>
> (Minsky, 1990, p. 6)

As Rosalind Minsky's metaphor indicates, psychoanalysts suggest that our subjective experience is divided and split. Psychoanalysis proposes a 'depth' analysis of the human mind, with several layers or strata: some ideas, emotions, drives and motives are unconscious and inaccessible to conscious thought; other material might be preconscious, or on the boundaries, moving in and out of consciousness; while consciousness is our mundane awareness of passing thoughts, ideas, reactions and emotions.

This suggestion that self-knowledge might be partial, and that there may be more to our motivation and actions than we can be aware of, is a radical one. What evidence is there for unconscious thoughts and processes? In one respect, it is difficult to dispute the claim that our minds might contain events which are sometimes inaccessible to introspection. We are all familiar, for example, with experiences such as driving on 'automatic pilot' and arriving at a destination with no clear memory of the journey. These events suggest that although we were not consciously paying attention, our minds were nonetheless going through all the thought and action patterns required in the situation. Similarly, there is the experience of having a name on the tip of one's tongue but not being able to recall it, although perhaps an hour or a day later, the missing name emerges into consciousness.

There is a great difference, however, between pointing to mental processes like these which seem to chug along unconsciously, and the psychoanalytic concept of the unconscious. For Freud and other psychoanalysts, the term *the unconscious* refers to a set of highly charged and powerful emotions and desires which are actively held back or 'repressed' from conscious awareness. This unconscious material is truly dynamic in the sense that it is a source of motivation and a spur to action.

Psychoanalysts argue that any sustained introspection on our mental states and subjective experience will demonstrate signs and manifestations of the unconscious. We may notice, for example, strong, apparently irrational, reactions of liking or hostility towards others, fleeting and unaccountable feelings of anxiety, triumph or irritation, signs of nonverbal tension, dreams and neurotic symptoms such as phobias, obsessions and compulsions.

Freud saw, for example, the commonly experienced and sometimes inexplicable feelings of strong identification with another human being as unconscious attempts to substitute for a lost human relationship, or for one that was urgently needed and unobtainable (Guntrip, 1971). Developing this point, Guntrip notes how a child who is unable to develop a satisfactory relationship with a parent who may be too cold, aloof, aggressive or authoritarian tends to make up for the loss by identifying with or growing like that parent or through identifying strongly with others who embody the missing characteristics.

Wishful thinking, fantasy, projections and day-dreams are other common experiences which psychoanalysts would argue indicate unconscious processes: '... each one of us behaves in some respect like a paranoiac, corrects some aspect of the world which is unbearable to him [sic] by the construction of a wish and introduces this delusion into reality' (Freud, 1930, cited in Frosh, 1987, p. 39).

> Most of us are familiar with the following kind of behaviour. We feel anxious – guilty – or vulnerable, so we hit out at the people closest to us and act as if they were attacking us. This mechanism is known in psychoanalytic theory as 'projection'. We find a part of ourselves unacceptable (the thing we feel guilty about – our anxiety and insecurity, our vulnerability) and instead of allowing ourself to consciously feel and acknowledge the feelings we don't like, we project them onto other people and then feel under attack from these people. These same people then represent the alienated part of ourself we've thrown out. Feeling under attack we attack them (usually much to

their surprise!). At its simplest it's the 'kicking the cat' reaction (much as I dislike that expression). The point about projection is that it is one of the many defensive behaviours by which we protect ourselves from knowing about the contents of our inner world – our psyche ...

(Minsky, 1990, p. 4)

To accept the idea of the unconscious, therefore, is to accept that adults are fragmented and only partially aware of crucial aspects of their emotional lives. As Stephen Frosh (1987) has pointed out, the concept suggests that we are aliens to ourselves; psychoanalysis dismisses the claim that understanding our private worlds of consciousness is all that is necessary for self-knowledge.

1.2   THE TASKS OF FAMILY LIFE

The second distinctive line of argument shared by psychoanalysts concerns the role of the family in the constitution of the individual's mental life. The influence of family life is spelled out in the continuation of Rosalind Minsky's argument:

The unconscious of any individual seems to be structured by what goes on emotionally within his or her family whether it be nuclear, single-parent or extended. We all have to have parents or parent •substitutes to survive, whatever culture we're born into. The unconscious we end up with depends on the repression of events and conflicts set up in early childhood involving these people ...

(1990, p. 6)

Psychoanalysts disagree about how family life works on infants and children but all agree that the events and experiences of early childhood fix

the character and personality of the individual and lay down the bases from which future actions stem. It is the family which determines the balance and shape of the iceberg of the mind.

This argument is partly the well-known claim that families act as the main agents of socialization, transforming unsocialized infants into members of a society and culture who know the appropriate conventions and rules. But, more than this, psychoanalysis suggests that the formation of a divided individual, split between the conscious and the unconscious, is the consequence of the way society bears down, through family life, on children.

Freud, for instance, saw the process of development from infancy to adulthood as demanding a transition from a primitive anarchic state to a state of control where what he called the 'reality principle' would dominate. Family life was seen as crucial in policing this shift and as responsible for bringing it about. And one of the most obvious manifestations of the power of families is in the area of sexuality:

> The child, far from being an asexual innocent, begins life as a demanding, narcissistic, and auto-erotic animal who is gradually forced to accept the existence of others, and certain socially sanctioned organizations of its sexual needs. The child is forced to recognize the demands of an extra-psychic 'reality', in the form of the necessities of association with others and the attainment of a pattern of sexual objects and gratification ('genitality') which will make possible the reproduction of new members of the species, themselves in turn subject to social necessities and the needs of the species.
>
> (Hirst and Woolley, 1982, pp. 141–2)

The task of the family in dealing with, what Freud at least conceptualized as a 'perverse', destructive and unorganized individual, is clear. Basically family life lays down conditions and demands for repression: 'The child must swallow his/her desires in the face of the power of the real world' (Frosh, 1987, p. 36). The uncontrolled energizing forces of the unconscious must be brought under control and the child must move from an undifferentiated state of desires (and reactions to the frustrations of these) to the development of a conscious self (or *ego*) which can regulate conduct in more socially acceptable directions.

Under the pressure of family life, therefore, some emotions, thoughts and drives become pushed into the unconscious. Emotions and desires which cannot be expressed under prevailing social conditions become repressed and the child builds a reservoir of unacceptable material, a negative or shadow of the conscious mind, which becomes inaccessible to consciousness (Connell, 1987, p. 114).

Sexuality, sensual and erotic gratifications especially follow this rule and indeed in many psychoanalytic theories are seen as the main focus in middle childhood of efforts towards the channelling of the child's energies in conventional forms. Since incest is such a strong taboo, one of the main tasks of family life, according to psychoanalysis, is to re-direct and submerge sexual expressions directed towards the parents, specifically the parent of the opposite sex.

Freud assumed that fathers were particularly implicated in this powerful reworking of the child's basic state; other psychoanalysts, as we shall see, want to stress instead the power of the mother. As Frosh points out, in the Freudian theory of family life the father comes to stand as the principle of authority for the child:

> Thus, the father in the Oedipal structure is not just (or even) the child's real father, who may be threatening or appeasing, appalling or absent; he is the symbol of patriarchical authority and hence of all social authority under patriarchy, he stands in the position of the originator of culture and of sexual difference, of what is male and female, allowable and forbidden … The real father slips away in this; what emerges instead is a description of the impossibility of interpersonal relationships (child with object) that are not already structured by something outside them, the 'law' which society operates.
>
> (Frosh, 1987, pp. 48–9)

Psychoanalysis, therefore, presents us with a picture of family life as the nexus through which the individual confronts the power and authority of society. The task of the family is to channel this power, presenting the child with patterns of relationships which will generate identity and shape consciousness.

1.3   MAINTAINING FAMILY LIFE

In contrast to role theory accounts which seem to suggest that socialization is a relatively straightforward matter of the internalization of society's roles, rules and conventions, psychoanalysis emphasizes the difficult and conflict-laden nature of socialization and child development. Socialization involves an active struggle between children and society mediated through parents and parent substitutes. And the result may be an uneven and precarious integration of the individual into family life, since conventional social action may involve the active repression of desires and emotions which are important to individuals and still active unconsciously.

For Freud, most adults are like domesticated animals: our natural state and natural energies have been tamed, subdued and made respectable (Frosh, 1987, p. 46). Social life – or 'civilized' life in Freud's terminology – involves various forms of powerful distortion which result in different balances and temporary truces between the conscious and unconscious layers of the mind. There are some obvious implications here for the analysis of ongoing patterns of family life and this is the third concern psychoanalysts share.

As we have seen, the family theories reviewed in Chapter 5 stress patterns of negotiation in families and how the idiosyncratic system that a family develops may shape the actions and interrelationships of family members, sometimes with quite dramatic effects on their sense of identity and life chances. The approach of role theory, reviewed in Chapter 6, went on to describe how the social positions of the actors in family dramas also systematically influence outcomes. Psychoanalysis, however, argues that both these approaches miss the point that negotiations in families involve not just conscious levels of awareness and conscious interests but also the unconscious.

In this view there may be an emotional and irrational charge to sibling rivalries, for instance, or to intergenerational conflicts between mothers and daughters that cannot be understood just at the conscious level. Psychoanalysis would draw attention, for example, to the jealousies

Happy families?: Elizabeth Taylor and Richard Burton in the film of Edward Albee's play *Who's Afraid of Virginia Woolf?* Albee's drama vividly expresses Freud's sense of family life as a hot-house of emotional conflict and intense ambivalence.

experienced by first-born and other children at the arrival of new infants. They would note phenomena such as the repetition of earlier family experiences in the selection of sexual mates, and would want to speculate on the potential incompatibility of women and men because of the different ways in which their psychic lives have been constructed. Psychoanalysts would also want to investigate the contrasting forms of conflict between fathers and sons compared, for example, to mothers and sons. These conflicts would be seen as having unconscious origins and are thus not explicable simply through the differential social position of women and men or through the conscious constructs guiding family negotiation.

Shortly, we will examine in more detail one set of psychoanalytic arguments about these types of family relationships and family phenomena. But first, having described the core of psychoanalytic thought, we need to review some of the debates that divide psychoanalysts and dictate the different positions taken up on the development of identity and family life.

2   DIVISIONS WITHIN PSYCHOANALYSIS

2.1   INSTINCTS VERSUS OBJECT RELATIONS

One of the main divisions within psychoanalysis concerns competing positions on the contents of the unconscious and the nature of the pre-socialized infant who is the object of the family's interventions. Here we will compare two answers – Freud's position with the views of the 'object relations' school of thought which are taken up in more detail in section 3.

According to Freud, the infant at birth comes supplied with a set of innate instincts and it is the ideas associated with these instincts which become suppressed in childhood and repressed as the contents of the unconscious. Freud assumed that there must be some animating or driving force biologically built into human infants (Frosh, 1987). Without this source of energy at birth, we would be simple organic blobs with nervous systems contained in resting states. Some motivation to act comes from the external world but, according to Freud, the infant already also contains instincts or sources of energy which push towards certain forms of satisfaction. Instinctual life, however, is blind and outside time, a set of forces which recognizes no constraints, no feebleness of the body or limitations in resources (Frosh, 1987).

One obvious 'instinct' is hunger and this energizes the search for food. More controversially, Freud argued that sexual and aggressive instincts (instincts for life and death) were also inherent and present from the start. Infants have already present within them a force aimed at preserving life, sexual urges, and a force for destructiveness. These forces become associated, through the events of childhood and family life, with particular ideas and emotions. The 'death instinct' is a force which moves towards entropy, chaos and disintegration while the sexual or life instincts move towards integration, relationships with others and the continuation of life forms.

What kind of sexuality is this that Freud thought small children possessed? Children are viewed, in Freud's classic phrase, as 'polymorphously perverse', meaning that the sexual instinct built into humans is generalized and attuned to all forms of sensual gratification (Coward, 1983, p. 192). Children are not naturally heterosexual and focused on the opposite sex, or even naturally homosexual, they are simply sexual and driven towards pleasurable, sensual (erotic) experiences in a number of sites, receiving pleasure from eating, for example. Childhood sexuality is a form of sexuality which has not yet been organized socially into conventional forms or into deviations from these.

Although Freud puts stress on innate instinctual organization, he can also be interpreted as rejecting the suggestion that heterosexuality or femininity and masculinity are natural and biologically determined states. The infant simply contains a drive towards sexuality but the form that sexuality takes and whether the individual emerges as predominantly lesbian or gay, predominantly heterosexual, or predominantly oriented towards bisexual experiences will be determined by what happens within their early family history. Similarly, Freud did not wish to draw hard and fast distinctions between masculine men and feminine women. He seemed to regard masculinity and femininity as outcomes of early social relationships which may not necessarily conform with biological sex.

Sexuality, then, for Freud, is another site where socialization is not straightforward, automatic and inevitable. Indeed to explain the varied ways in which adults manifest sexuality, Freud believed it was necessary to see sexual development as a fraught and complex process which could go in a number of directions. The acquisition of a sexual identity, according to Freud, does not just involve the passive acceptance of feminine and masculine ideals and 'normal' heterosexuality but can involve resistance to these and the unconscious holding on to desires which contradict what is expected of women and men.

For Freud, then, the reason why the unconscious is dynamic and forceful and requires active repression is that it is structured around powerful instinctual energies and the initial, perhaps highly socially inappropriate, aims and objects of these instincts. Freud saw the infant as self-energized. His entire theory is based on the assumption that from infancy onwards the individual is in conflict with society. For this reason, as Stephen Frosh (1987) notes, it is perhaps inappropriate to talk of Freud as proposing a theory of identity since the term suggests more integration, singleness, consistency and unity to people's sense of self than Freud would wish to convey.

In contrast, object relations theorists such as Winnicott, Fairburn and Guntrip, whose work developed in the 1950s and '60s, envision (in some ways) a more peaceful beginning to life and hold a more optimistic view of the outcomes. This line of work is called *object relations theory* because, unlike Freud, Winnicott and his colleagues were interested not in the operation of instincts per se, but in the way in which infants build up relationships with the objects (people) in their environment. These theorists argue that an individual's sense of self, including both our conscious and our unconscious subjective experiences, are formed through early family relationships within the 'interpersonal field' provided by the family or family substitutes. The unconscious, in their view, is thus not structured by innate instincts but through the mental residues of these early relationships. The unconscious, in other words, is composed principally through social influences from the beginning.

Stephen Frosh has provided a very clear description of the object relations argument:

> Whereas Freud places sexual and aggressive instincts at the centre of mental life, object relations theorists emphasize the relational context of development. For them, the crucial point in considering individual psychology is not the biological 'drives' that underlie behaviour, but the quality of the relationships that are available to a person, and have been available during the formative period of very early life. These early relationships are understood to lay down basic psychic structures and internalizations which provide the template for later relationships; the quality of the early environment is thus crucial for the future conduct of a person's life.
>
> (1987, p. 4)

Our adult selves are thus seen as dependent on the kind of treatment – caring or inhumane, consistent or inconsistent, regular or disrupted – we received from our caretakers. As Frosh also points out, the object relations view leads to very different conclusions about normality and abnormality and the possibilities for human happiness in general.

Freud is generally described as developing a deeply pessimistic analysis of the human condition. He set, for example, somewhat minimal goals for his psychoanalytic therapy. For Freud, therapy could be described as successful when it achieved merely the reduction of the extreme forms of misery experienced by the few to the ordinary common unhappiness experienced by the majority (Freud cited in Frosh, 1987, p. 61). In a famous statement he saw life as principally about the avoidance of pain rather than the active seeking of pleasure. Happiness was not to be expected; indeed, 'unhappiness is much less difficult to experience' (Freud, 1930, cited in Frosh, 1987, p. 68).

The goal of his psychoanalytic therapy was simply, through insight, to allow individuals to be reconciled to their conflicts and become more able to manage these. Freud's pessimism rested on his perception of human nature as forever divided, contradictory and in conflict, split between the conscious tip of the iceberg and the submerged underneath. Freud argued that in an important sense we are all inevitably more or less 'neurotic'. Normality and abnormality are on a continuum, with 'normality' as an incomplete achievement. Everyone is in the same boat – dealing with strong but inadmissible emotions and drives, through a fragile ego, or sense of self, built around methods of containment and defence against unconscious material. No-one can, therefore, be entirely perfect, coherent or completely adapted to social conditions.

Object relations theorists take a very different view and stress that, given good initial family relationships and what Winnicott (1964) described as 'good enough mothering', that is, mothering which meets most of the basic needs of the child most of the time, there need be no unresolvable struggle or conflict. The unconscious and the conscious might become coherently combined in the stream of an individual's life and projects. In contrast to Freud, object relations theorists see the failure to adapt to family life and to social pressures as unusual and a sign not of normality, but of weaknesses and flaws in the relationships parents or parent substitutes offer children, such as deprivation, abuse, ridicule, excessive discipline or indifference. People will, of course, differ in their degree of psychic integration depending on the positive or negative nature of the environmental conditions experienced as children. But even bad early circumstances might be partially compensated for in later life.

ACTIVITY I

At this point you might find it helpful to summarize the main differences between the views of Freud and object relations theorists on the development of the psyche.

Which approach is *most* likely to describe the child as 'active' in its own socialization, initiating and provoking conflicts with others?

Why does a sharper distinction between neurotic and healthy forms of behaviour seem to emerge in object relations theory than Freudian theory?

2.2 SOCIAL AND NON-SOCIAL PSYCHOANALYSIS

It might seem, therefore, that object relations theory, with its more optimistic view of human potential and its emphasis on the child's reactions to relationships rather than active instincts, offers the most scope for integration with other social science research on family life, since social relationships, from the beginning, are seen as constructing the infant's sense of self. In general that has proved to be the case, although doubts remain, addressed differently by competing object relations theorists, about the biological basis to the drive to form relationships, which object relations theory does appear to assume even as it rejects Freud's panoply of innate drives. Several studies of early infancy (such as Richards, 1974, and Schaffer, 1978) seem to suggest that babies have an inbuilt sociality and display innate patterns of action and attention that predispose the infant towards connections with others. There is a symmetry, therefore, between the arguments of object relations theories and the findings of some experimental developmental psychologists about the biological basis of human behaviour.

But we shouldn't abandon Freud's theory just yet, however, as it too can be synthesized with sociologically oriented theories, and particularly with claims that social, historical and economic factors primarily determine the forms family life takes. Freud can be read in several ways, as Rosalind Coward has noted:

> ... recently it has been suggested that Freud's account of sexual construction is not, in fact, an account of a universal and timeless process which unfolds itself regardless of the culture or historical moment into which an individual is born. Instead it is seen as a theory of sexual construction within a historically finite period – a cultural period, loosely designated patriarchical. As such, it can be taken as an illuminating account of sexual construction within a delimited period.
>
> (1983, p. 189)

The ambiguity concerning whether Freud proposes a strongly biologically based account stressing universal instincts and a universal sequence of development which holds across all cultures and historical periods, or suggests a more limited framework which can vary according to social circumstances, explains why Freudian theory has appealed to conservative political theorists and Marxist thinkers alike.

Freud's main premise that the individual and society are in conflict can be taken in a number of directions. The conflict can be seen as taking the same form in every society since it is determined by the underlying structure of the unconscious which represents an unchanging human nature. Or it could be argued that the type of conflict which emerges and the types of individuals which result will depend on the particular family structures in operation, and these alter across societies, across culture and across time. As Coward notes, it is possible to argue that the forms of identity, particularly gender identity, found in contemporary society are simply those characteristic of patriarchy, that is, of a period of male domination. Radical changes in social structure, therefore, would produce radically different forms of human nature.

In Freud's grim assessment, 'civilization' is dependent on the repression and curtailing of individual needs and on individual renunciation of basic instincts and drives (Connell, 1987). Thus often it is those who are the most alienated from original and primitive states of desire who may appear to be the most adapted or most civilized (Hirst and Woolley, 1982). Without repression and active channelling of instinctual impulses, Freud thought that human life would become, in Thomas Hobbes' words, 'nasty, brutish and short' (*Leviathan*, 1651). Social life would be bloody, chaotic and libertarian in the extreme. In order for men and women to combine together in positive social relationships, basic human drives towards the immediate satisfaction of needs and destructiveness must be denied and early forms of pleasure curtailed.

However, even if we accept this general analysis of the human condition, there is still considerable room for social variation and the influence of social forces on the construction of individual psychology. Indeed it could be 'civilization' or the organization of a particular society that determines the degree and type of 'neurosis' experienced by its members. Women and men raised in very different family structures could, therefore, radically differ in the way they understand sexuality and gender identity, work, relationships with nature, children and the purposes of social life.

As this summary has tried to indicate, accounts and descriptions of Freud's work are bound to be contentious. Not only are there differences between Freud's earlier and later formulations, and inconsistencies which remain in his thought, but it is possible to provide many different readings and interpretations, depending on the interests of the reader. The crucial question is whether psychoanalysis can be used as a description of how individual identity might be constituted through varying social circumstances or whether the form which psychoanalytic arguments take is unable to incorporate a plurality of lifestyles and thus family forms.

The next section of the chapter takes up one object relations theory and will return to this issue of the social or non-social nature of psychoanalysis. The feminist object relations theory reviewed in section 3 attempts to spell out one set of connections between the social context and the formation of identity. As section 4 will demonstrate, however, critics of this approach have not been convinced that psychoanalytic accounts can do justice to the obvious ways in which family life is shaped by social processes.

The review of major themes and divisions within psychoanalytic thought we have developed in sections 1 and 2 has covered only the bare bones. We have not dwelt, for example, on some of the more familiar aspects of Freud's work such as the stages (oral, anal and phallic) through which children are thought to pass, or on the Oedipal and Electra complexes, the development of defence mechanisms within the ego or conscious self, or on the child's acquisition of a moral conscience and sense of guilt and shame (superego). Similarly, there are important divisions within psychoanalytic theory which extend beyond object relations versus classic Freudianism. (For more detailed reviews of the social and political implications of psychoanalysis, see Connell (1987), Frosh (1987, 1989), Hirst and Woolley (1982), Leonard (1984), Sayers (1986).)

The goal, however, was to begin to indicate why psychoanalysis has been seen as vitally relevant to the analysis of family life and how it might supplement or contradict approaches to family life based on systems theory (Chapter 5) or on role theory (Chapter 6 of this volume). We have seen that the main contribution of psychoanalysis lies in its description of the constitution of personality and identity within family life. Psychoanalytic theories try to describe how the events, crises and developmental tasks of infancy and childhood organize, formulate and fix the identity of the individual.

Psychoanalysis suggests that a historical dimension must be added to analyses of family life because the way individuals are formed in their first families will more or less shape the way they construct sexual relations in adult life and parent their own children. Primarily, however, psychoanalysis challenges the view that socialization is a simple matter of internalizing roles or the expectations associated with different social positions. The claim is that to understand identity and interaction in families, it is not enough to look at what society expects of its members; it is necessary to delve deep inside people's mental structures and psychological organization to look at both conscious and unconscious motives.

3 FEMINIST OBJECT RELATIONS THEORY

The development of a feminist version of object relations theory is primarily associated with the work of the North American feminist Nancy Chodorow (1978, 1989) and, in the UK, with the writings of Luise Eichenbaum and Susie Orbach (1982). Aimed at redressing the patriarchical bias of Freudian and other psychoanalytic perspectives, this version of object relations theory has become a standard account of the development of family life in social and political theory; it has also become popularized more generally (e.g. Lewelyn and Osborne, 1990) and incorporated, for instance, into lay opinion in the UK through Orbach's columns in *The Guardian*, other newspapers and magazines, and the development in London of the Women's Therapy Centre.

Depending on their orientation, critics have seen this success either as a sign that feminist object relations theory presents a watered down version of psychoanalysis (Minsky, 1990) or a diluted form of feminism (Spelman, 1988). This review will cover the main arguments of feminist object relations theory in two areas: the development of gender identity, which Chodorow links to the social reproduction of family life, and the psychological difficulties of heterosexual relations.

3.1 MOTHERS, FATHERS, DAUGHTERS AND SONS

Chodorow's theory of family life is wide-ranging in scope and attempts to integrate observations from across the social sciences: from anthropology, sociology, feminist political theory and psychology. Her central argument is that there are important causal connections between the sexual division of labour, found in much the same form in all societies, the fact of patriarchy or male dominance, and the psychology of gender identity. In contrast to Freud, she wants to argue that it is forms of *mothering* which

provide the link and which explain both the structure of society and the structure of women's and men's psyches.

Chodorow notes first that, although there are substantial differences across cultures in the way mothering and fathering are handled, there is nonetheless a universal human sexual division of labour whereby women take prime responsibility for child-rearing. It is women everywhere who do the main work of mothering, that is, the labour of nurturing and caring for small children.

It is also the case that women tend to be subordinated through this sexual division of labour. In Western societies there are clear inequalities in the financial, material and political resources of women and men, ideologies of male superiority and male dominance, and power relations character-istic of these divisions. Patriarchy is exemplified through male violence, the separation of the public world of work from the private world of the family, and the persistent devaluation of women's work in the domestic sphere.

Chodorow also notes that in Western societies there seem to be regu-larities in the way masculine and feminine identities are constituted. Women and men, she argues, seem to take up and value very different forms of identity. Crudely speaking, women and men seem to possess quite different senses of self and capacities for relating to others. Women seem more attuned to others' needs and more emotionally responsive while men seem underdeveloped emotionally but appear more able to take an autonomous and independent stance (see Chapter 6, section 4.1).

What are the links, then, between the fact that women mother, the fact of patriarchy and the fact that women and men seem to regularly differ in their motivations, desires and attitudes? And, crucially, how can we explain the pleasure that women take in mothering? If mothering is difficult and demanding and involves a loss of economic and social independence, why do women continue to do it? Chodorow argues that many women are intensely ambivalent about the costs and difficulties of mothering but also find genuine pleasure from this role, just as many men are ambivalent about their exclusion from family life.

Some of the inconsistencies involved are evident in women's autobiographical accounts of mothering:

> My children cause me the most exquisite suffering of which I have any experience. It is the suffering of ambivalence, the murderous alternation between bitter resentment and raw-edged nerves and blissful gratification and tenderness. Sometimes I seem to myself, in my feelings toward these tiny guiltless beings, a monster of selfishness and intolerance. Their voices wear away at my nerves, their constant needs, above all their need for simplicity and patience, fill me with despair at my own failures, despair too at my fate ...
> (Rich, 1977, p. 21)

> I wanted to call this book 'The Hell of Motherhood', but my publisher did not like it. He was quite right. Anything that brings as much joy, delight and happiness as being a mother could not possibly be hell.
> (Nicholson, 1983, p. 1)

Many mothers will not feel like this but nonetheless, as Connell (1987) has pointed out, an adequate theory of family life and the reproduction of the sexual division of labour must explain why people go along with the social order. We need to explain how the psychological gains of motherhood combine with, and sometimes seem to justify, the social and economic losses. Why is it that most women show such psychological investment in motherhood, despite the problems, and why do most men become so psychologically invested in masculinity?

 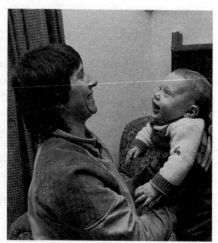

Madonnas and modern mothers: is mothering still over-idealized?

274

The depth and degree of feelings about mothering, femininity and masculinity led Chodorow to look towards psychoanalytic concepts and explanations. To explain why society continues in the form it does, with the apparent support of women and men, despite the costs to many women (and some men), psychological dimensions, satisfactions and rewards must be meshed in some way with the social dimensions.

> I continue to locate important experiences and oppressions of gender in emotional and intrapsychic life and in the arena of primary relations ... Psychoanalysis enables us to understand such experiences particularly well, to recognize their acute intensity and yet to analyse them in their full multi-layered complexity.
>
> (Chodorow, 1989, p. 8)

The first stage in Chodorow's argument is to accept the validity of the object relations argument that gender identity, character and personality are formed through the child's relationships in the early stages of life.

Chodorow argues that the child's sense of gender identity becomes established between the ages of 18 and 36 months, at the time when the core sense of self and personal identity are also formed. Crucially, however, given prevailing social conditions, these extremely important early relationships through which the self is defined will primarily be with a woman, usually, but not necessarily, the biological mother. For both boys and girls, it is their interactions, battles and loving relationships with their mothers which set the scene for the acquisition of character and personality:

> An account of the early mother–infant relationship in contemporary Western society reveals the overwhelming importance of the mother in everyone's psychological development, in their sense of self, and in their basic relational stance.
>
> (Chodorow, 1978, p. 76)

People, object relations theory argues, are formed through relationships, within a relational field. The relational field of early childhood is very different for girls and boys, however. Mothers (and fathers who become more important later on), consciously and unconsciously, set very different standards and have very different expectations of their relationships with their daughters and sons.

Chodorow, in common with other object relations theorists is not persuaded by biological arguments or the importance of prior 'instincts'. Children are male or female at birth but the contents of gender, the specific forms which masculinity and femininity take, she argues, are socially constructed. Biological sex differences alone do not predict adult identity. The significance and meaning given to anatomy are mediated through culture and social relations.

In essence, mothers tend to experience daughters as less distinct from themselves than sons. The consequence is a closer and more entangled mother–daughter bond. Similarly, daughters can identify more closely with their mothers and see themselves as like her in very basic senses. In contrast, boys must separate themselves from their mothers and develop a sense of themselves as different. Both boys and girls begin life with a strong attachment to their mothers; this attachment and identification can continue in a modified form for girls, but boys are expected to develop other forms of identification to become masculine.

Masculinity and femininity, then, both become problematic forms of identity. Chodorow argues that women and men gain strengths from their experiences of being mothered but are also maimed by it in characteristic ways. Women, for example, find it difficult to develop a sense of themselves as individuals, with a distinct identity. Femininity represents a failure to significantly move away from the mother and see oneself as not continuous or merged with her. Women's gains lie in their greater capacity, as a result, to relate to and become attached to others.

Masculinity, Chodorow argues, rests on the foundation of repressing early basic connections with the mother; this gives a stronger sense of boundaries between people, but is also a more insecure way of defining oneself. Masculinity is formed through a reaction against the mother. And, since in many nuclear families fathers are often distant figures because of their work commitments, a sense of masculinity may not be based on a close personal relationship in the way that femininity can be. Men gain autonomy at the expense of the capacity to care for others and the ability to make others' needs their own.

Chodorow, then, sees far-reaching effects from the fact that in our society (and in all societies) it is women who mother. On it hangs the identity daughters and sons will assume, and through it daughters become primed to look after others and repeat the mothering they received, while sons become primed for male dominance. The sexual division of labour reproduces itself. The connections Chodorow proposes between psychology, patriarchy and motherhood are thus dialectical or circular ones.

The existing patriarchical order puts women in the position where they must mother, often in isolation from the male world of work. Their mothering creates a new generation of women whose personality is such that they will want to become mothers themselves and will achieve satisfaction from creating relationships with their children. Simultaneously, a new generation of men becomes happy to let them assume this responsibility and seek their own satisfaction in the public world of work. Patriarchy is reconfirmed and women and men are fitted psychologically for their social positions.

Other features of the experience of mothering reinforce this circle. Firstly, the less complete, later occurring separation which girls experience results in more sustained, more intense maternal contact than sons obtain. There are thus more opportunities for the transmission of the dominant cultural ideologies about the role of women. Secondly, Chodorow argues, quoting the anthropologist Margaret Mead, that the experience of being mothered is one which induces misogyny in both women and men and a contempt for femininity:

> One result for children of both sexes is that since 'it is the mother's and not the father's voice which gives the principal early approval and disapproval, the nagging voice of conscience is feminine in both sexes'. Thus as children of either sex attempt to gain independence – to make decisions on their own that are different from their upbringing – they must do this by consciously or unconsciously rejecting their mother (and people like her) and the things she is associated with.
>
> (Chodorow, 1989, p. 34)

This rejection is much more profound in boys since the striving for independence in their case involves patterns of identification directed away from the mother. The consequence is to reinforce the dread and devaluation of women found in patriarchical ideology.

ACTIVITY 2

How does Chodorow theorize the formation of male and female identities?

What do you think she might predict would occur if fathers were entirely responsible for child-rearing?

We will turn later to criticisms of Chodorow's work, but you may find it useful at this point to begin formulating your own response to this line of argument.

Do you agree with Chodorow that women and men differ psychologically?

Do you think any differences can be adequately explained by mothers' contrasting relationships with their male and female children?

Why do you think women take on the main burden of childcare?

In your view are they more psychologically suited for this role?

What are the relative weights of the sexual divisions of labour, social conventions, psychology and biology in your opinion?

We turn next to look at the patterns that feminist object relations theorists predict for sexual relations between women and men. If the personalities of women and men are formed in the fashion Chodorow suggests, what are the consequences for relationships between adult women and men?

3.2   THE PSYCHOPATHOLOGY OF THE EVERYDAY HETEROSEXUAL COUPLE

Nancy Chodorow's work suggests a rather bleak picture of adult male and female characteristics, as Virginia Goldner has pointed out:

> In brief, growing up under these gendered social arrangements produces women with relatively permeable psychological boundaries, who fashion their identity in terms of other people, have a greater capacity for empathy, and are at greater risk of losing themselves. Men, on the other hand, emerge with relatively rigid psychological boundaries, disown their dependency needs and fear being engulfed, have relatively greater difficulty empathizing with others, and are better able to think for themselves. In other words, women and men emerge as psychological reciprocals, and both are psychologically hobbled.
>
> (1985, p. 21)

This image of mutually reinforcing psychological restriction and limitation has prompted the French psychoanalyst, Christiane Olivier (1989), to speak of the 'psychopathology of the everyday couple'. Olivier argues that heterosexual relationships based on love and romance run aground on the mutual incompatibility of masculine and feminine psychic strategies acquired through their experience of mothering.

In the first stages of infatuation, Olivier suggests, the woman and the man are driven by the same desire for symbiosis, a 'single identity for two people' (1989, p. 91), hoping for complementarity, a perfect understanding and unconditional adoration from the other – the qualities a mother offers her child. But the history of psychological development and the scars and lesions left by the contrasting trajectories of masculine and feminine socialization ensure, says Olivier, that the actual establishment of a heterosexual relationship produces different anxieties in the male and female partners.

Men become fearful of being enclosed, stifled and dependent, while women become fearful that they will not be loved enough. These incompatible, largely unconscious fantasies of the couple can fuel a spiralling dialectic. In Olivier's analysis, male retreat due to the fear of being trapped, produces female fear of abandonment and demand for proofs of love, this demand generates further anxiety in the man, and so on.

Olivier sees yet other dimensions to this dialectic. She claims, for example, that men in learning to separate from their mothers lose the capacity to voice affection and loving feelings. Acts, particularly sexual acts, replace the missing words. Further, men are impelled to dominate to avoid the danger of domination. Olivier argues that men relive in their adult relations with women the vulnerability and fear they experienced in relation to their mothers. The boy is powerless in the face of his mother, and the struggle to 'become a man', as we have seen, primarily concerns the establishment of separation and removal from her sphere of influence.

When you say 'LOVE', do you mean EROS or a need for instinctual satisfaction or object love or oedipal love or genital love or simple old-fashioned schmaltz?

Many men, Olivier suggests, experience ambivalence about women as desiring subjects, that is as active selves and agents, particularly when women express sexual desire. Women as *desired objects* become preferable, and thus men constantly wish, unconsciously, to position the women they have relationships with as powerless others rather than powerful agents. Perhaps it is for this reason that pornography and male sexual fantasies frequently portray women as submissive, available, powerless and controllable – generally representing women as static and manageable possessions and only active in the pursuit of desires when sanctioned by men (Friday, 1980; Griffin, 1981).

Women, on the other hand, Olivier states:

> ... look to love for that unity of the self which she has so far never known, since it was her lot to be first valued as a child and then desired as an adolescent. Through love she tries to reach a reunifying of 'subject who can be valued' with 'object who can be desired', so that at last she can feel herself to be a person. The woman eagerly grasps the chance offered her by the man so that she may be, at last, a 'satisfactory object' for someone.
>
> (1989, p. 97)

Olivier is suggesting here, in an analysis which complements Chodorow's account although with slightly different emphases, that women never receive from their mothers the sense of being a desired object. Adult women thus look to their relationships with others to supply this missing sense of self-hood (Eichenbaum and Orbach, 1982). They turn to others to gain, perhaps paradoxically, the recognition that they are both autonomous, powerful and active subjects in the world and desired and loved for themselves, rather than as part of their mothers. Boys, because of their different gender, can be seen by their mothers as both desired subjects and loved objects, and their path to maturity thus involves freeing themselves from their mother's love, seeing thereafter dangers in the adoring gaze of powerful women.

To summarize this analysis, men are seen as both dependent on women, wanting closeness, symbiosis and affection, yet fearful also of this dependence and intimacy because it threatens a hard-won sense of self as a separate and independent being. Women, on the other hand, faced with this male response frequently end up in the position of being able to be only desired objects and never desired subjects, of being feared to the extent that they are powerful and separate selves, and yet not being offered in return the qualities of nurture, support and intimacy they offer to men.

Eichenbaum and Orbach (1982) and other feminist psychotherapists argue that it is precisely this male failure which turns women towards their children and repeats the cycle. As men are unable to satisfy women's needs for attachment, women become 'needy' and project this need on to their children but especially their daughters. Women, Eichenbaum and Orbach suggest, begin to look to their children to supply or supplement the close affectionate relationships they desire but often fail to find with male partners.

The particular projection onto daughters is helped by the shared gender, which builds a closer process of identification. Unsatisfied themselves, women may (consciously and unconsciously) teach their daughters to repress the expression of their emotional needs. Some mothers may become confused about the boundaries and responsibilities of the mother–daughter relationship, expecting their daughters to mother them, not just in later life when the daughters have become adults and mothers have become elderly but even in adolescence and childhood. Women may both look after their daughters and unconsciously expect their daughters to reciprocate. Hence girls grow up emotionally deprived, but repress the expression of that 'neediness'. This pattern, according to Eichenbaum and Orbach, produces women who care for others because they have a 'pool' of unmet needs on which to draw – to the great advantage of adult males who, having been taught to repress all expression of their emotional dependency, are more likely to be taken care of by women.

This type of psychoanalytic story about male–female relations has emerged in many forms in recent years and not just within object relations analyses. The social psychologist Wendy Hollway (1983, 1989), for example, has connected this general pattern of masculine and feminine fears and vulnerabilities to the discourses or accounts women and men draw upon in talking about their relationships. She argues that women frequently use what she calls a 'have and hold discourse' in describing their relationships. That is, women often account for their relationships in terms of the importance of commitment, caring, mutual support, relationships and a sense of connection with others. Men, too, can describe their relationships in these terms but they frequently find that other ways of taking about relationships, such as a 'permissive discourse' and what Hollway calls the 'male sex drive discourse', are more congenial.

The permissive discourse, in contrast to the have/hold discourse, stresses personal fulfilment above the rights of others in relationships. This discourse celebrates sexual gratification and the importance of sexual experience per se rather than monogamy. The male sex drive discourse similarly stresses the importance and motivating power of sex for men. It is a discourse in which men become the active subjects, seeking out heterosexual relationships, while women become the objects of men's sex drive, and it is a discourse in which men describe themselves as driven to sexual relationships by their biological needs rather than by needs for caring and mutual support.

Hollway argues that boys and girls must construct their sexuality in relation to these dominant discourses and ideas about what it means to be 'macho' or feminine. For boys, the achievement of sexuality and adult status becomes defined as 'successful conquest' within the male sex drive discourse, and commitment becomes defined as entrapping and dangerous; whereas for girls, being attractive to boys, and thus identified as the *object* of male sex drive discourse, becomes the way in which sexuality is defined. Success for girls also becomes defined through the have/hold account as 'getting and keeping a man'. The expression of spontaneous sexual desire and active rather than passive sexuality becomes difficult for women, whereas, for men, the expression of commitment becomes difficult.

Hollway argues that gender identity is always contradictory and women's and men's relationships are characterized by ambivalence – by inconsistent desires. It is not the case that men, or women, always understand themselves, their motives and relationships within just one discourse. Hollway suggests that the contradictions are particularly intense for men and thus it makes sense to reverse Freud's puzzlement over femininity expressed in his question 'What does a woman want?' and ask instead 'What does a man want?'

According to Hollway, the contradiction for men occurs between their deep feelings about relationships, their fear of commitment and the dominant discourses in which they have constructed their emotional and sexual lives. Hollway describes several strategies found in the heterosexual couples she studied: from men who use sex as a cover for their desires for closeness and intimacy, to men who hide their dependency on their partners by projecting this dependency onto the woman ('She needs me rather than I need her'), to men who control their fears through constant multiple relationships and infidelity, and men who develop an oscillating pattern of movement towards their partner and the expression of their needs, followed soon after by movement away and denial of feelings.

The same general argument about heterosexual relationships can be found, too, in some earlier neo-Freudian work of the 1930s and '40s. Karen Horney (1967), for instance, sees similar ironies in masculine and feminine development. If the classic feminine pattern or feminine 'neurosis' leans towards masochism, self-effacing personality trends, and the desire for submergence in others, then the masculine 'neurosis' leans towards detachment, power-seeking and independence at any cost. These two forms of masculine and feminine 'neurosis' – men seeking power and women seeking power through others – can be complementary. But, notes Horney, this complementarity only works if the woman never gains empowerment, or a completed self, and the man never gains the benefits of properly relating to and caring for others (Westkott, 1986).

Similarly, it has been argued that the breakdown of relationships and infidelity affects women and men differentially. Male jealousy is more likely to be expressed through concerns with re-establishing sexual control in the relationship and may lead to sexual dysfunction, whereas female jealousy is bound up with an intense fear of separation, abandonment and desertion (Lewelyn and Osborne, 1990).

Sociolinguists who study the conversational strategies of couples have also come to similar conclusions, although without the paraphernalia of psychoanalytic terminology. Tannen (1991), for example, argues that communication involves a constant juggling act between the two goals of intimacy and independence – connecting with others and asserting oneself in relation to others. Men, on a number of linguistic levels, incline towards independence; women towards intimacy. Thus numerous studies (reviewed by Smith, 1985; Thorne and Henley, 1975) demonstrate that men display more dominant conversational strategies – interrupt others

more, take more conversational turns, hold the floor for longer; women, in contrast, spend more time in conversations establishing the basic framework for communication – asking questions, initiating topics and engaging in positive reinforcement (what are sometimes called back-channel noises – 'yes', 'mm', 'that's interesting', 'how fascinating', 'did you really?' etc.)

Tannen argues that women and men particularly come into conflict over asking for help and 'talking about troubles'. Women, she states, want the gift of understanding, men prefer to give the gift of advice. Women find it helpful to talk over their troubles and do not interpret the presence of these troubles as a sign of weakness. Men prefer to take a protective role in relation to their partners which can mean not disclosing difficulties. Tannen suggests that when told the troubles of others women tend to reply with troubles of their own (the 'I know just what you mean' response), but men find this reciprocity irritating, preferring to see their difficulties as unique and individual rather than communally shared problems.

The fact that some consensus emerges about the characteristics of men and women in relationships across a range of psychoanalytic, psychological and socio-linguistic sources does not mean, of course, that this account of the possibilities and difficulties of heterosexual relationships should be assumed to be correct. It is difficult to reconcile the pessimistic tone of much of this form of analysis with the indications of many successful heterosexual relationships, and women's and men's strong inclinations towards marriage and the establishment of new relationships. The various schools of thought account for this in different ways.

Karen Horney, for example, argues that, although our society and social conditions incline women and men to the neuroses she describes, healthy reactions and relationships are also possible. Psychoanalysts such as

Olivier would argue that most relationships are a compromise between fantasy and reality. Since both women and men derive so much pleasure from relationships, there are strong pressures to moderate and compensate for the negative dialectic of pressures for intimacy and fear of intimacy that Olivier describes. The ideal heterosexual relationship is built on knowledge of these psychic limitations and unconscious fantasies and works around them.

Other more feminist analysts such as Hollway might argue that relationships persist at women's expense and depend on their sacrifice. Heterosexual relations and conventional family forms continue in the way they do because women, in the phrase of one populist account, have indeed been conditioned 'to love too much'.

In this section we have focused entirely on heterosexual relations, not because similar issues of managing intimacy and independence may not arise in lesbian and gay relationships, but because psychoanalytic and other discussions of the psychological dimensions of relationships tend to assume heterosexuality as the norm and thus take heterosexual relations as their main focus. Much of this work has been developed in a therapeutic context and these facilities have often not been extended or made available to what have been seen as non-conventional relationships (Kitzinger, 1987). (See Hall, Kitzinger, Loulan, and Perkins (1992), Perkins (1991) and Silverstein (1991) for a discussion of the relevance of therapy and psychological theories for lesbian and gay relationships.) We shall return to the treatment of diversity in psychoanalysis in section 4.

ACTIVITY 3

As a way of summarizing this section, try to list the different fears that these analyses suggest women and men might experience in heterosexual relationships.

What do these approaches claim that women and men look for in relationships?

How do the theorists connect these hopes and fears to early child-rearing?

Julia Segal (1985) argues that, unlike some other psychological theories, the patterns that psychoanalysts find in behaviour should not be seen as rules or statistical generalizations which apply to all women and men. Psychoanalytic claims are insights which need to be tested out and modified in each individual case. There is thus no easy way of proving or verifying psychoanalytic statements, and Segal suggests the only sure test is to ask 'Does this insight make sense to me based on my experience?'. In Activity 2 you were asked to begin formulating your own response to Chodorow's work; you could now continue this process of evaluation for these arguments about heterosexual relationships.

---

4 EVALUATING PSYCHOANALYTIC PERSPECTIVES

The work of Nancy Chodorow and other feminist object relations theorists, along with the psychoanalytic approach in general, has been subjected to a number of different lines of attack. Consider, for example, the following comments:

> ... with the exception of some inspired but fairly restricted conquests, psychoanalysis is neither a natural nor a human science, but a self-confession by the bourgeoisie of its own misery and perfidy, which blends the bitter insight and ideological blindness of a class in decline.
>
> (Timpanaro, 1976, p. 224, cited in Frosh, 1987, p. 11)

> [Freud] was, without doubt, a genius, not of science, but of propaganda, not of rigorous proof, but of persuasion, not of the design of experiments, but of literary art. His place is not, as he claimed, with Copernicus and Darwin, but with Hans Christian Andersen and the Brothers Grimm, tellers of fairy tales.
>
> (Eysenck, 1985, p. 208, cited in Frosh, 1987, p. 6)

> 'Families', Chodorow says, 'create children gendered, heterosexual, and ready to marry' – or anyway they are supposed to. But do families have no racial or class or ethnic identity? Do they create children prepared to marry anyone, no matter the person's race, class, ethnicity, religion? ... If children are said to be prepared to participate in a sexually unequal society, why aren't they also said to be prepared to participate in a society where there are racial, class, and other forms of inequality?
>
> (Spelman, 1988, p. 86)

> The currently popular socialization theory of the type suggested by the American feminist Nancy Chodorow is inadequate because, although it quite rightly draws attention to the identifications we make with one or both parents (or substitutes), it leaves out the drama of the child in terms of its *desires* – which have a crucial bearing on its identifications and the formation of the unconscious.
>
> (Minsky, 1990, p. 7)

These comments capture some of the exasperation external critics display in relation to psychoanalysis, also demonstrated by critics of Chodorow's work from within feminism and psychoanalysis. In response to their critics, psychoanalysts often argue, provocatively and irritatingly, that those who mock are simply too squeamish to accept the facts of unconscious mental life and erect defences against the findings of childhood sexuality in particular.

The comments, however, also indicate some of the main themes in evaluations of psychoanalysis. Marxist and other social theorists, for example, such as Timpanaro (1976), have argued that psychoanalysis tends to create mysteries where there are none. Phenomena such as ambivalence which could easily be explained by the contradictions in people's social position, and phenomena such as wishful thinking which may simply compensate for areas of disadvantage and deprivation in people's lives, are referred instead to the operations of the unconscious. Timpanaro argues that one of the main weaknesses of Freudian psychoanalysis lies in its preference for complicated and laborious explanations of human motives. He questions, too, Freud's lack of humanism and his evident willingness to think the worst of human nature.

Timpanaro and others (e.g. Leonard, 1984) point out that Freud and other psychoanalytic theorists tend to work with undifferentiated models of society, described simply as 'civilization', for example. Although gender is discussed in great detail, there is no analysis of the very different social circumstances of different social groups. Psychoanalysis provides a subtle and detailed analysis of psychological manoeuvrings but the theory is weakened by the failure to complement this sophistication with an equally detailed social theory. Similarly, historical changes are neglected. Thus Freud, writing about his bourgeois patients in turn-of-the-century Vienna, tended to forget his (and their) concrete social and historical circumstances and write as though he had discovered a universal pattern of responses and neuroses. In response to Timpanaro and other Marxist critics, psycho-analysts suggest that social theories of all description tend to over-simplify psychological processes. People, they argue, in these accounts become defined merely through their class and other social positions.

We will take up the social critique of psychoanalysis in more detail in relation to Chodorow and the question of diversity. First, however, let us examine the methodological critiques that experimental psychologists develop and the points that family therapists might make in response to some of the general features of psychoanalysis.

Eysenck's comment above is typical of those who wish to distinguish between scientific psychology and unscientific psychoanalysis. According to Eysenck, a more scientific approach would make concrete predictions about observable events, would design experiments to test hypotheses, and would collect data in a more systematic fashion, focusing on quantitative and numerical records. From this perspective it is not enough to rely on insight. But, as Stephen Frosh has argued, this critique misses the point of the psychoanalytic enterprise:

> The object of psychoanalytic knowledge is subjectivity, the flowing, changing, productive and disjointed experience that each of us has of ourselves and the world and the pattern of linkages that this subjectivity has with external events. The criteria for evaluation of the correctness of theories in this area cannot be solely empirical or observational, because such approaches operate on the wrong level to conceptualize and measure subjective experience. Other criteria that deal with personal *meanings* are the appropriate ones for investigating the persuasive and conceptual power of psychoanalysis ...
> (1987, p. 9)

Frosh suggests that the affinity Eysenck sees between psychoanalysis and literary insight should be viewed as a major advantage rather than a disadvantage. There is no way of easily resolving this debate and perhaps by now you will have come to your own conclusions about the value of psychoanalytic investigation.

The critical points that family therapists and family systems theorists make are in many ways more apposite. From the point of view of the family therapist, psychoanalysis can be accused of taking an overly historical approach to family life and thus neglecting the interpersonal dimensions, or the micro-politics, of family interaction.

Although object relations theorists do stress the early relational context of child development, once identity is fixed, other people (apart from the therapist) tend to disappear from the psychoanalytic frame. Problems in later life, for instance, are treated through individual therapy, with the individual isolated from their immediate familial and social context. Psychoanalytic therapy becomes a conversation with the patient about the past, where the origins of difficulties in the present are traced back to early mother–infant interaction.

In contrast, family systems perspectives focus on how conflicts in families, identity problems and personal difficulties are the result of continuing family patterns and maintained through negotiations in which all family members may collude. It is an axiom of family therapy that the person presenting the most difficulties at the beginning of an investigation may be a cover for the more entrenched problems of another family member. This approach, therefore, might acknowledge that a theory such as Chodorow's provides a good account of the way in which broader gender relations such as the sexual division of labour impinge psychologically on family lives, a neglected area in family systems work, but they would argue that when it comes to studying the patterns and power relations *within* families, the concepts of family constructs, rules, negotiations and systems are more fruitful.

Chodorow and other object relations theorists are often accused of providing yet further examples of explanations which blame mothers for all the ills of the world, and particularly for any difficulties experienced by their children. It is true that Chodorow (and psychoanalysis more generally) focuses on mothers and on children's early relationships for which the mother is most likely to be responsible. However, this criticism also ignores the main thrust of Chodorow's argument. Chodorow is not blaming mothers as individuals but the social circumstances in which women come to mother and which mark out female and male psychology. To a large extent, she sees women (and men) as living out social scripts over which they have little control.

A much more pertinent question for evaluation is thus whether Chodorow actually succeeds in her goal of describing the links between broader social relations and individual psychology. Views are mixed. On the one hand, many social scientists agree with Chodorow that a successful theory of family life must embed psychological processes with social processes. And even Marxist critics concede the potential of psychoanalytic concepts to account for the complexity of the emotional patterns which hold families together and which can also create intolerable pressures (Leonard, 1984). There is broad agreement that a purely materialist analysis which would see economic changes as the key to changes in sexual politics will never adequately account for the tenacity with which people hold on to their sexual and gender identities. But do mothering and family relationships fall so neatly into the pattern Chodorow proposes?

> My own mother worked her twelve-hour professional day within a week of my birth. Cooking, cleaning, empathic skills – she has none, though she is an excellent surgeon and acclaimed gynaecologist. And as I have sought sympathy for my own 'unnatural' childhood, I have found everywhere evidence of the amazing diversity buried within the ideology of the familial: fathers who were present and caring, 'working' mothers who were strong and powerful within the home, daughters who bonded tightly with fathers or older brothers, mothers who could not love their sons, mothers who never accepted their daughters, mothers who identified with their sons, and so on. As Liz Heron comments... 'Each story belongs somewhere inside that general pattern [the public image of "the family"], yet none of them quite fits.'
>
> (Segal, 1987, p. 140)

Since Chodorow's analysis was, initially at least, presented as a 'grand theory' of the reproduction of mothering and the sexual divisions of labour, it is particularly vulnerable to the challenge of diversity. Chodorow describes not a range of mothering patterns, or the general conditions of mothering through which variety could be understood, but one developmental organization and one family pattern from which all else follows.

Spelman (1988) has noted the main weaknesses here. Family members may be black, white, working-class, middle-class, gay or lesbian, and living within nuclear, extended, lone-parent, foster family or step-family arrangements. How many families conform to the pattern of mother at home and father at work? Does the ideology of patriarchy hold equally across all families? In racist societies, Spelman asks, is it the case that all black men will have been imbued with an idea of superiority to all white women? Is not the ideology of male dominance, class and 'race' specific? Society is organized not simply through a sexual division of labour but also through ethnic divisions and through competing class relations. All of these things will interact to determine the forms in which family life will be reproduced.

In her more recent writings Chodorow acknowledges these limitations in her earlier work and extends the criticisms:

> Like all theoretical approaches within the feminist project, psycho-analytic feminism does specific things and not others. First, like the theory from which it derives, it is not easily or often historically, socially, or culturally specific. It tends towards universalism and can be read, even if it avoids the essentialism of psychoanalysis itself, to imply there is a psychological commonality among all women and among all men. Psychoanalytic feminism has not tried enough to capture the varied, particular organizations of gender and sexuality in different times and places, nor has it made the dynamics of change central. The dominant theoretical lexicon of psychoanalysis included gender but not class, race, or ethnicity. Accordingly psycho-analytic feminism has not been especially attuned to differences among women – to class, racial, and ethnic variations in experience, identity, or location in social practices and relations. Feminist the-ory and practice, of course, need to be culturally and historically specific, and it would be useful if psychoanalysis had the data and theory to differentiate genders and sexualities finely across history and culture. Psychoanalytic feminism would also be considerably enriched by clinical, theoretical, or psychoanalytically informed phenomenological and experiential accounts of gender identity, self, and relation among women and men of colour and of non-dominant classes.
>
> (1989, p. 4)

Chodorow now argues that her account should be seen as picking up just one of the ways in which patriarchy and some contemporary family forms are maintained. But she also wants to defend strongly the value of psychoanalysis. One way of doing this is to make a distinction between form and content. Chodorow (1989) suggests that the form of the human mind may be pretty much as psychoanalysis describes and pretty much universal. That is, people everywhere will have conscious and unconscious motives and fantasies. And, says Chodorow, everywhere the basic emotional lives of individuals will be structured through their early experiences and object relations. The content of those fantasies and unconscious desires, however, and the content and shape of early object relations will vary according to local circumstances and the family lives people can construct within those circumstances.

This seems a much more satisfactory argument. Psychoanalysis is seen as providing some of the intellectual tools to analyse family life but these analyses will need to clearly state their boundaries of applicability. We move from one universal theory of mothering to plural accounts. Chodorow's final argument for psychoanalysis is negative rather than positive but it is difficult to refute her logic:

> Until we have another theory which can tell us about unconscious mental processes, conflict, and relations of gender, sexuality, and self, we had best take psychoanalysis for what it does include and can tell us rather than dismissing it out of hand.

(1989, p. 4)

5   CONCLUSION

The main focus of this chapter has been on the arguments of psychoanalysis, on the debates within the field itself, and on some of the surrounding controversies. Psychoanalysis deals best with the individual and with questions of identity. It points to and attempts to explain the obvious fact that families are made up of members with distinctive personalities, demands and needs. Family life involves the working out of conflicts between strong characters and these may be resolved in ways that do not mirror social positions and power in the public sphere. The explanatory potential of psychoanalysis is weakened, however, by its constituency: it has been a largely white, middle-class activity. As Chodorow points out, the detailed accounts of other forms of subjectivity and other forms of identity required for more complex analyses are largely missing.

One important psychoanalytic insight we have not mentioned is the notion of 'over-determination'. Psychoanalysts argue that a psychological symptom such as a phobia, for instance, may have many determinants. The analyst cannot rest when one cause is found; an entire network of sometimes consistent and sometimes contradictory psychic events will be involved. There may be many explanations, and each one in itself may seem plausible and sufficient, but it is crucial to understand the totality of causes and connections.

It seems clear that the interior of family life can also be seen as 'over-determined'. Connell (1987) has neatly pointed to the surplus of explanations family life seems to require:

> Far from being the basis of society, the family is one of its most complex products. There is nothing simple about it. The interior of the family is a scene of multi-layered relationships folded over on each other like geological strata. In no other institution are relationships so extended in time, so intensive in contact, so dense in their interweaving of economics, emotion, power and resistance.
>
> (1987, p. 121)

The task for the future is to do real justice to this complexity. If there is a consensus among researchers into the internal dynamics of family life, it is that this research still has a considerable way to go.

ACKNOWLEDGEMENT

This chapter is based on some material concerning Chodorow's perspective supplied by Elizabeth Barrett.

REFERENCES

Chodorow, N. (1978) *The Reproduction of Mothering: psychoanalysis and the sociology of gender*, Berkeley, CA, University of California Press.

Chodorow, N. (1989) *Feminism and Psychoanalytic Theory*, New Haven, CT, Yale University Press.

Connell, R. (1987) *Gender and Power*, Cambridge, Polity Press.

Coward, R. (1983) *Patriarchical Precedents: sexuality and social relations*, London, Routledge and Kegan Paul.

Eichenbaum, L. and Orbach, S. (1982) *Outside In and Inside Out: women's psychology: a feminist psychoanalytic approach*, Harmondsworth, Penguin Books.

Eysenck, H. J. (1985) *Decline and Fall of the Freudian Empire*, Harmondsworth, Viking.

Freud, S. (1930) *Civilization and its Discontents* (Pelican Freud Library vol. 12, Harmondsworth, Penguin Books, 1985).

Friday, N. (1980) *Men in Love: their secret fantasies*, London, Arrow.

Frosh, S. (1987) *The Politics of Psychoanalysis: an introduction to Freudian and post-Freudian theory*, London, Macmillan.

Frosh, S. (1989) *Psychoanalysis and Psychology: minding the gap*, London, Macmillan.

Goldner, V. (1985) 'Warning: family therapy may be hazardous to your health', *Networker*, Nov/Dec, pp. 18–23.

Griffin, S. (1981) *Pornography and Silence*, London, The Women's Press.

Guntrip, H. (1971) *Psychoanalytic Theory, Therapy, and the Self*, New York, Basic Books.

Hall, M., Kitzinger, C., Loulan, J. and Perkins, R. (1992) 'Lesbian psychology, lesbian politics', *Feminism and Psychology*, no. 2, pp. 7–27.

Hirst, P. and Woolley, P. (1982) *Social Relations and Human Attributes*, London, Tavistock.

Hollway, W. (1983) 'Heterosexual sex, power and desire for the other', in Cartledge, S. and Ryan, J. (eds) *Sex and Love: new thoughts on old contradictions*, London, The Women's Press.

Hollway, W. (1989) *Subjectivity and Method in Psychology: gender, meaning and science*, London, Sage.

Horney, K. (1967) *Feminine Psychology*, New York, W. W. Norton.

Kitzinger, C. (1987) *The Social Construction of Lesbianism*, London, Sage.

Leonard, P. (1984) *Personality and Ideology*, London, Macmillan.

Lewelyn, S. and Osborne, K. (1990) *Women's Lives*, London, Routledge.

Minsky, R. (1990) 'The trouble is it's ahistorical: the problem of the unconscious in feminist theory', *Feminist Review*, vol. 36, pp. 4–14.

Nicholson, J. (1983) *The Heartache of Motherhood*, London, Sheldon Press.

Olivier, C. (1989) *Jocasta's Children: the imprint of the mother*, London, Routledge.

Perkins, R. (1991) 'Therapy for lesbians?: the case against', *Feminism and Psychology*, vol. 1, pp. 325–9.

Rich, A. (1977) *Of Woman Born*, London, Virago.

Richards, M. (ed.) (1974) *The Integration of a Child into a Social World*, Cambridge, Cambridge University Press.

Sayers, J. (1986) *Sexual Contradictions: psychology, psychoanalysis and feminism*, London, Tavistock.

Schaffer, H. R. (1978) 'The development of interpersonal behaviour', in Tajfel, H. and Fraser, C. (eds) *Introducing Social Psychology*, Harmondsworth, Penguin Books.

Segal, J. (1985) *Phantasy in Everyday Life: a psychoanalytical approach to understanding ourselves*, Harmondsworth, Penguin Books.

Segal, L. (1987) *Is the Future Female?: troubled thoughts on contemporary feminism*, London, Virago Press.

Silverstein, C. (ed.) (1991) *Gays, Lesbians and their Therapists*, New York, Norton.

Smith, P. (1985) *Language, the Sexes and Society*, Oxford, Blackwell.

Spelman, E. V. (1988) *Inessential Woman: problems of exclusion in feminist thought*, Boston, MA, Beacon Press.

Tannen, D. (1991) *You Just Don't Understand*, London, Virago Press.

Thorne, B. and Henley, N. (eds) (1975) *Language and Sex: difference and dominance*, Rowley, MA, Newbury House.

Timpanaro, S. (1976) *The Freudian Slip*, London, New Left Books.

Westkott, M. (1986) *The Feminist Legacy of Karen Horney*, New Haven, CT, Yale University Press.

Winnicott, D. (1964) *The Child, the Family and the Outside World*, Harmondsworth, Penguin Books.

CHAPTER 8
A FEMINIST LOOKS AT THE FAMILY

LYNNE SEGAL

CONTENTS

INTRODUCTION

Patriarchy's chief institution is the family. It is both a mirror and a connection to the larger society.
(Kate Millett, 1971, p. 55)

Above all, the second stage involves not a retreat to the family, but embracing the family in new terms of equality and diversity.
(Betty Friedan, 1981)

The pain and difficulties experienced by a generation of feminists who self-consciously attempted to construct alternatives to the family are a major social psychological source of the emergence of pro-family feminism, and one ... that may fuel the pro-family retreat from sexual politics.
(Judith Stacey, 1987, p. 231)

Fully two decades after the resurgence of feminist writing and struggle at the close of the 1960s, it is a good time to assess their impact within the academy. This chapter will look specifically at the effects of feminist thinking on our understandings of 'the family', suggesting that it has resulted in a number of fundamental shifts in scholarly, clinical and popular descriptions and explanations of contemporary family life.

I am writing from the position of a feminist psychologist and political activist who has attempted to map out the theoretical and political significance of different strands of feminist thinking around the nature of sexual difference, and the forces behind the persistence and tenacity of gender hierarchy. As a socialist feminist I have, as well, always stressed the ways in which gender hierarchy intersects with other axes of exploitation and oppression, suggesting that what is most significant about women's situation at any particular time or place may not always be understood simply through a focus on gender relations. I am well aware, therefore, that feminist contributions to any understanding of family life are themselves both shifting and diverse.

Indeed, at first glance, the feminist perception of the family over the last two decades, both polemical and scholarly, may seem to have moved full circle – from fierce criticism of the family to a celebration of women's role within it. The strident and joyful rebirth of feminism in the Western women's liberation movements at the close of the 1960s took off from a fundamental critique of 'the family'. What troubled feminists then was their perception of women's dependent, undervalued and frequently isolated and miserable existence inside the family – especially when engaged in full-time motherhood. The first section will therefore look at those early feminist criticisms of the prevailing ideology of the existing nuclear family as an unchanging, natural and necessary institution, challenging, in particular, what was seen as a hypocritical glorification of motherhood. It also introduces the feminist focus upon the inequalities of power within the family, and the possibilities for men's abuse of power, highlighting the levels of conflict and violence in many families.

Looking at trends in feminist writing on family life from the late 1970s, however, a decisive shift seems to occur. Section 2, therefore, deals with reflections by feminists observing, indeed beginning to celebrate, the importance and significance of motherhood, and women's maternal and domestic engagements in the family. Not only do we see here the characteristic feminist emphasis on highlighting women's specific experience as women, but a stress on the strengths of female bonding and 'maternal thinking'. The emphasis on the particularities of motherhood, however, was soon to generate a further interest in the distinctive contribution of fathers. Consequently, section 3 focuses on recent work on fatherhood, assessing its significance in shifting perspectives on the strengths and weaknesses of contemporary family arrangements.

It would be an oversimplification, nevertheless, to see feminist thinking on the family simply as shifting from an initial criticism of women's role within it to a greater celebration of its importance (as well as displaying at times a new interest in shared parenting and fatherhood). Theoretical shifts are never quite so linear or so simple as this, particularly when linked to the fortunes of a social movement, like feminism. Disputes and theoretical divergencies come from many sources. The fourth and final section thus deals with other types of theoretical conflicts and challenges within and around feminist thinking on the family.

One of these stems from the flowering of Black feminism in the early 1980s. It brought its own perspectives on the family, most of them critical of those of white feminists. A few white feminists, however, were now rejecting earlier critiques of the traditional nuclear family, while others were busy emphasizing the need for the recognition of ever greater diversity and difference in household and family arrangements. Indeed one form of feminist literature becoming fashionable in the 1980s was increasingly sceptical of *any* generalizations about 'women' or women's 'distinctive perspectives'. These feminist theoreticians were now questioning all types of fixed categories, identities and relationships, stressing what they saw as the complex, shifting and plural nature of the social meanings which construct, and allow us to speak of, our own experiences of gender, sexuality, parenting or any other aspect of our existence.

Outside feminist debate, however, the popularity and appeal of 'the family' is today as pervasive as ever. The disparagement, often condemnation, of those who live outside its traditional ideal – married couple, with male breadwinner and female caregiver – also persists. Meanwhile, feminists continue to debate and dispute, if more wearily, those early passionate attacks on 'the family' and women's place within it.

1 CRITIQUE AND DECONSTRUCTION OF THE FAMILY

To begin at the beginning of the re-emergence of feminism is to take on board the significance of the early women's liberation critique of the institution and ideology of the family as the major site of women's subordination to men. As we shall see, it would prove increasingly influential across the social sciences generally. The 1950s is rightly seen as a time when, following the disruptions of war, the Western world saw unprecedented attempts to reconstruct the family – and women's place at its centre. Ideologically and materially, the idea of the happy, healthy family was promoted by whatever means possible. Social scientists of all persuasions wrote of the institution of the family as universal and eternal, blaming any type of social or individual discontent on the 'problem' family. Hollywood, as well, at this time replaced its gangster and war movies, its popular *film noir* of the 1930s, with the domestic themes of family life. When youth rebelled 'without a cause', that cause was soon tracked down to the weak, permissive father, the self-centred, harsh and domineering mother. It was against the background of such monolithic concern with domesticity, described so well in the writings of Elizabeth Wilson (1980) or Denise Riley (1983a), that the first stirrings of the feminist critique of family life appeared.

The 1960s, with its upsurge of youthful protest movements and 'counter-culture', had spawned its own fierce rejection of the stifling, inward-looking, acquisitive, post-war suburban family. Those social scientists and psychiatrists who responded with attempts to understand the causes of the 'youth revolt' tended to blame status-seeking, over-demanding parents, but particularly to condemn the housebound mother attempting to live her life through her children. There was certainly nothing new about 'mother-blaming' (so prominent in the history of clinical and welfare work), but writers like David Cooper were to reach new levels of maternal denunciation: 'A young man has only to look a little cross with his manipulative, incestuously demanding mother to end up on a detention order as "dangerous to others"' (1964, p. 71). There would soon, however, be something quite new to hear about that particular domestic tyrant of the 1960s, once women themselves began, at last, to speak.

The ground was prepared in the United States in 1963 by Betty Friedan's *The Feminine Mystique*, where she described that 'underlying feeling of emptiness' many housewives experienced without any stake in the world outside their homes. Three years later, in Britain, Juliet Mitchell published an article entitled 'Women: the longest revolution', in which she declared that the 'true' woman and the 'true' family 'may both be sites of violence and despair ...' (1966, p. 19). That same year British sociologist Hannah Gavron documented the isolation and frustration of full-time housewives in *The Captive Wife: conflicts of housebound wives* (1966). But it was the early articles and books accompanying the appearance of women's liberation as a social movement at the close of the 1960s which first broadcast the analysis of women as an oppressed sex, with that oppression attributed, primarily, to their economic dependence within the family.

One of the very first and always the most controversial of these books, coming from the United States, was Shulamith Firestone's *The Dialectic of Sex: the case for feminist revolution* (1970). It would later serve to exemplify what has been described as the 'demon texts' of women's liberation, which feminists came to apologise for as they faced endless accusations that feminism was indifferent to the problems of mothers and children, and the importance of family life. What Firestone *had* stressed was the enormous pressure on women to fulfil themselves through, and only through, motherhood, and the dangers of mothering in familial contexts which made them financially dependent on a man, thereby placing them, in her view, at 'the tyranny of (their) reproductive biology'. In fact, Firestone's particular type of 'radical feminism' was from the beginning rejected by many, and in Britain by most, other feminists in the 1970s, who often called themselves 'socialist feminists'. (Radical feminists, like Firestone, believed that historically the first and basic oppression was that of 'patriarchy', men gaining control over women. It was this form of social exploitation and subordination which gave rise subsequently to all other social hierarchies, for example those of class or 'race'. Socialist feminists, on the other hand, tended to see class, 'race' and gender as all hierarchical axes of power currently serving the interests of a global 'patriarchal capitalism'.) Moreover, Firestone's own uniquely fanciful, Utopian suggestion that feminism must 'free women from their biology' through technologies of artificial reproduction was, even more decisively, dismissed early on by other feminists, like Michelene Wandor in Britain (1973), as both 'illogical' and 'inadequate'. Yet, no matter how many times it would be countered, and no matter how persistent the feminist campaigns and activities of the early 1970s around the needs and welfare of mothers and children (whether setting up and staffing community nurseries, campaigning for increased Child Benefit, more responsive pregnancy care, or childbirth conditions under women's control, and so on, and so on), the accusation that feminists ignored or rejected motherhood would persist. It was one of the most fundamental and successful ways in which men (and women) have attempted to divide women against each other. Even feminists themselves have at times used this accusation to dismiss early women's liberation critiques of the family (Hart, 1991, pp. 105–6).

What was happening in these years was indeed the exposure by Western feminists of many women's silent sorrow, at home, alone. But feminists were not inventing the complaints they so frequently recorded. As Sheila Rowbotham (1990) documents so well, in their own newsheets and publications – outside any institutional framework – women in the UK and elsewhere began to provide their own experiential accounts of their dissatisfaction with housework and its effects on consciousness:

> Waves of boredom, apathy and aimlessness descended, together
> with overwhelming guilt about the feelings. There were positive

feelings too, of pride and love and creativity, but somehow they were drowned by the knowledge that now my life revolved solely round pleasing people, my husband, my son, even my mother-in-law ...
(1990, p. 7)

These accounts quickly influenced the type of research feminists undertook inside academic institutions. For instance, Ann Oakley (herself a victim of motherhood blues or 'post-natal depression') interviewed 40 London housewives in 1971, reporting that 70 per cent of her sample were dissatisfied with housework as work, and that the most frequent complaints were of loneliness and low self-esteem (Oakley, 1974). Later that same decade, other sociological studies, like that of Brown and Harris (1978), would duplicate her findings, uncovering high levels of depression in full-time housewives, particularly amongst urban working-class populations. Similar research findings suggesting the psychological costs for wives in marriage were being reported by Jessie Bernard (1973), Pauline Bart (1971) and other feminist researchers in the USA in the early 1970s.

The discipline of psychology itself (with its emphasis on the 'individual' and its search for some universal set of potential attributes to explain the behaviour of this individual) has proved rather unreceptive to feminism (with its emphasis on the power relations of gender and the specificities of women's lives). Nevertheless, since psychology attracts very high levels of female students, and feminist ideas continue to influence many women, it is clear that both women psychologists and psychology students were likely to be seeking connections between feminism and psychology. One of the very first connections made between the two was the extensive critique of the influence of John Bowlby's 'maternal deprivation' thesis in clinical and applied psychology.

Mica Nava, for instance, who joined a women's liberation group in 1970, and wrote an early critique of 'the family', has suggested that the key event in her mobilization to feminism was a paper critical of Bowlby's work presented by a young North American child psychologist, Rochelle Wortis, at the first British Women's Liberation Conference in Oxford in 1970: 'Child-rearing and women's liberation'. Documenting societies where 'multiple attachments are the norm', Wortis rejected Bowlby's overriding emphasis on the mother–child attachment to the exclusion of all other social relations and environmental factors, stressing that what a child needs is a stable, sensitive, stimulating environment. Her paper both rejected the exclusive mother-centred focus of psychological work on child development, and summed up the early feminist critique of the family:

> If the undervaluation of women in society is to end, we must begin at the beginning, by a more equitable distribution of labour around the child-rearing function and the home ... Men can and should take a more active part than they have done until now.
>
> (Wortis, in Nava, 1983, p.70)

What is significant about this pioneering feminist research on family life is that it set the stage for future methodological and conceptual battles within the academy, as feminists struggled to expose the androcentrism of existing social scientific thinking. Like many in her wake, for example, Oakley (1974) emphasized the male-oriented nature of sociological concepts, which had never, for instance, registered the existence of housework as *work*; and of a male-based 'objectivity' which was never sufficiently woman-focused to perceive women's discontent in the home. Feminist methodology was therefore seen as one which would begin with the centring of *women's* experience, necessary to overcome their former invisibility.

What a feminist social scientist saw when she looked at the family in the early 1970s, therefore, was a very radical questioning of a woman's place within it. Further disclosures of men's domestic violence against women, of their sexual coercion and abuse of children in the home, and general control over resources and decision-making, all continued both to feed feminist calls for a women-centred orientation in the social sciences and to fan feminist fears of the potential dangers of family life for women (and children) throughout the 1970s, so firmly hidden in the all-pervasive familial ideology of the satisfactions of hearth and home.

What this meant within feminist theory was that the family could no longer be analysed as a homogeneous unit. Its internal structures and functions, and its wider economic, political and ideological significance, all needed to be untangled to reveal the power relations of men over women, and the patterns of individual costs or benefits operating along gender and generational lines. Feminist solutions to the inequalities they exposed between men and women in the family in the early 1970s, whether coming from the grassroots or from theoretical debates, usually involved extensive social – as well as personal – struggle and transformation.

Research therefore proceeded along a variety of different pathways. Some feminists explored the role of the state and welfare policies in creating and maintaining women's dependence on men in the family, while pursuing policy reforms and social provision which would both increase women's financial independence from men and relieve housebound carers of some of the burdens of care. Other feminists examined the links between the nature of women's waged and unwaged work, assessing the importance of domestic labour for the economy, and the problems of trade union bargaining on the basis of a 'family wage' for male workers.

Feminists also set out to uncover the ways in which men had historically gained a large measure of control over women's reproductive and sexual lives through the denial of contraception and abortion to women and the medicalization of pregnancy and childbirth, with reproduction legitimized only within marriage. This was studied in the more concrete context of women's long struggle to gain control over sexuality, childbirth and motherhood, and the less concrete context of the ways in which familial ideology served to stigmatize lesbianism, single motherhood and other types of non-traditional sexual or domestic patterns. Within psychology, feminists argued that girls' socialization, primarily for marriage and motherhood, created psychologically damaging patterns of under-achievement, dependency and subordination. These different strands of feminist ideas and activities share in common a critique of the existing sexual division of labour, and all promote ideas of women's greater economic independence, reproductive control and cultural and political activity through involvement in the world *beyond*, as well as *within*, the family. (Any historical overview of the women's movement can provide examples of these different approaches and tactics, for example Coote and Campbell (1982), Segal (1987) or Rowbotham (1990).)

Drawing out the links between the public and the private (between ideology, the state, employment, reproduction and personal life), however, also connected with a dominant feminist goal in the early 1970s to involve *men* more in the care of children and domestic work. Women and men, in feminist aspirations at that time, should each be able to participate equally in public life and waged work, alongside parenting and domestic work. As Elizabeth Wilson would summarize, over a decade later, when feminists looked at the family in those days, they did not reject motherhood (some, indeed, were already mothers), but they did demand that the conditions of motherhood should change: 'The socialization of housework, paid maternity leave, proper collective childcare, publicly funded, and decent paid jobs with shorter working hours were the solutions then advanced' (1989, p. 15). To this list, the feminist psychologist would have added her call for less sex-typing in children's socialization – from toys to textbooks or parental and social attitudes generally – assuming with, for example, Sandra Bem (1974) that more androgynous individuals were more psychologically healthy.

In the research of early 1970s feminism, it is of significance to note, the aim was always to explore family life, and its costs and benefits for women, in order to understand and overcome existing *inequalities* between women and men. Pauline Bart, for example, argued that her research showed that: '... it is the women who assume the traditional feminine role – who are housewives, who stay married to their husbands, who are not overtly aggressive, in short who "buy" the traditional norms – who respond with depression when their children leave home' (1971, p. 184).

From this she concluded:

> The women's liberation movement, by pointing out alternative life styles, by providing the emotional support necessary for deviating from the ascribed sex roles, and by emphasizing the importance of women actualizing their *own selves,* fulfilling their *own* potentials, can help in the development of personhood for both men and women.
> (1971, p. 186)

In the second half of the 1970s the goal of seeking ways of creating gender equality was gradually superseded by the goal of exploring and giving value to women's distinctive lives and experience, for their own sake – above all, describing and celebrating women's distinctive biological, maternal and sexual existence. Once again, however, this trend seemed to occur first, and most distinctively, in the USA.

2   RECONSTRUCTION AND THE CELEBRATION OF MOTHERHOOD

Half a decade before Betty Friedan would make her public recantation in *The Second Stage* (1981) – accusing feminism, and her own early work, of having been anti-family and mistaken in stressing women's need for autonomy while highlighting their dissatisfaction with full-time mother-hood – several important feminist texts on mothering were published which emphasized the overriding importance of women's maternalism. The turning-point was Adrienne Rich's *Of Woman Born* published in 1976, in which she clearly differentiated *mothering*, and women's maternal bodies, from *motherhood*, as a repressive, patriarchal insti-tution. Rich wrote of the revolutionary and transformative potential of women's bodies and the mothering experience, concluding:

> The repossession by women of our bodies will bring far more essen-tial change to human society than the seizing of the means of pro-duction by workers ... We need to imagine a world where every woman is the presiding genius of her own body. In such a world, women will truly create new life, bringing forth not only children (if and as we choose), but the visions and the thinking necessary to sustain, console and alter human existence – a new relationship to the universe. Sexuality, politics, intelligence, position, motherhood, work, community, intimacy will develop new meanings; thinking itself will be transformed.
>
> This is where we have to begin.
>
> (1976, pp. 285–6)

Two years later Nancy Chodorow, in *The Reproduction of Mothering* (1978), examined what she saw as the deep-seated psychological and social effects of the fact that it is *women* who mother. Rather like the psychologist Dorothy Dinnerstein (1976), two years earlier, she suggested that the sexual division of labour within the family entails differing childhood experiences for girls and boys which result in lasting and opposed gender-specific personality differences and emotional needs which perpetuate gender hierarchy and men's cultural devaluation and fear of women. Combining certain psychoanalytic ideas which stressed the significance of early mother–child bonding and sociological theories of sex-role socialization, Chodorow saw boys as having to repress their early identification with the mother (thus producing men's typical inability to

303

express caring, warmth and intimacy) and girls as having to remain throughout their lives – as they began – closely bonded with their mothers (thus producing women's apparent psychic dependency, defining themselves always only in relation to others). In order to enable both girls and boys to internalize less polarized and more egalitarian images of what it is to be either 'feminine' or 'masculine', Chodorow proposed the solution of shared parenting.

Two years later again and Sara Ruddick (1980) brought together the themes being advanced in the late 1970s by writers like Rich and Chodorow with her concepts of 'maternal thinking' and 'maternal practices', describing women's deep commitment to the mothering experience, often despite constraining and oppressive conditions. Some features of the mothering experience, she argued, are invariant and nearly unchangeable, like maternal concern with preservation, growth and the acceptability of the child. In the interests of preserving fragile life, fostering growth and welcoming change, maternal practices tend towards humility, humour, realism, respect for persons and responsiveness to growth (Ruddick, 1980, p. 83). Jane Flax, also from the USA, would argue in criticism of this work that the mother's sexuality, aggression and need and desire for an autonomous life are all ignored by Ruddick: 'Important things like rage, frustration, aggression, sexuality, irrational intense love and hate, re-experiencing one's own childhood, blurring of body boundaries, conflicts of demands of a child, one's mate, other children and other work are missing' (1984, p. 13). Nevertheless, what Ruddick's writing presented, as Ann Snitow (1992, p. 39) would aptly summarize over a decade later, was a 'song to motherhood'.

By the close of the 1980s this type of affirmation of women's maternalistic subjectivity had led to the psychological research of Carol Gilligan (1982), widely acclaimed for its emphasis on women's separate styles of moral reasoning, and Rose Lamb Coser's (1981) stress on basic cognitive differences between women and men, alongside Mary Belenky and colleagues' work on women's separate ways of knowing (1986). This trend had gone about as far as it could go with Phyllis Chesler's *Sacred Bond* (1990) in which she stressed the 'sacred' nature of the biological bond between mother and baby – a notion which would have filled feminists with dread just over a decade earlier. Chesler's goal, in this book, had been to defend the rights of the 'surrogate' mother in the famous 'Baby M' case. But whatever the very real dangers of exploitation of working-class and poor women involved in 'surrogate' motherhood, Chesler used this very particular case to assert a general return to naturalism. She thereby implicitly rejected the significance of the former feminist argument that 'motherhood' should be seen as a social construction, to present it as a 'natural' or biological category. Meanwhile, in counterpoint to this new pro-natalist trend *within* feminism, books have appeared from women calling themselves 'feminist' overtly hostile to every aspect of the earlier feminist search for women's social and political equality with men and scornful of all the former activities of the Women's Liberation Movement, including their campaign in the USA for the Equal Rights Amendment (ERA), which was derailed by Reagan (Hewlett, 1986).

Whilst the feminist mothering literature was always more popular in the USA than in the UK, greater attention was being paid to the details of maternal experience and behaviour in the UK as well from the late 1970s. (Feminist psychotherapists Luise Eichenbaum and Susie Orbach (1982), for example, also used object-relations psychoanalytic perspectives in their popular writing on mother–daughter themes.) There is no doubt, either, that the feminist focus on the significance – rather than simply the burdens – of mothering did serve to inspire and strengthen many women. Those active in political struggles in the 1980s, especially in the women's peace movement, often invoked motherhood to combine and celebrate women's pacific and nurturing goals, as in 'Families and Babies Against the Bomb'. Illustratively, one campaigner from the Greenham Common peace camp would declare:

> I think most women are really in touch with what life is about. You can't even contemplate having a child without considering the value of that life and the struggle people have bringing up children, putting in all those hours and hours of caring.

(quoted in Rowbotham, 1990, p. 290)

At the same time, however, continuing economic recession was to lead to a political downturn for any reformist policies of welfare expansion in the interests of dependent people or those caring for others in the home. The victories of the monetarist right-wing governments of Thatcher and Reagan would make feminist struggles for nursery provision or adequate child support not only increasingly hard to win, but seemingly impossibly Utopian even to conceive. Some feminists who worried about the declining stress on the importance of *social* provision for parenting, like Denise Riley in Britain, now felt it necessary to reassert in the early 1980s that for most women 'the truth is that to both work and have children is, as well as a pleasure, a bitterly exhausting fight' (1983b, p. 155). Certainly, recent surveys of women with pre-school children, like that of Mary Boulton (1983), continue to find that although most mothers express a sense of meaning and purpose in their lives as mothers, many of them nevertheless find childcare a predominantly frustrating and irritating experience, the majority still feeling isolated, guilty, overburdened and anxious. More frustrating again, indeed often desperately so, are the lives of those many people, mostly women, caring for elderly or disabled people, at home, alone, and so often unassisted by any state provision. The one in six women currently caring for elderly relations at home, for example, have been found to suffer from both physical and mental stress, a stress which is often shared, of course, by those being cared for (see Finch and Groves, 1983). The problems women may face in mothering are thus compounded in caring for the elderly, a type of caring often far removed from the joys of participating in the life of the growing child.

However, if the popularity of feminist texts celebrating the joys and passions of women's mothering experience was beginning to overshadow the significance of earlier work on women's ambivalent and conflicting attitudes towards mothering, it tended to remove from view altogether the former feminist critique that women's lives should *not* be defined primarily in terms of motherhood. For women who may choose to forgo the pleasures and pains of motherhood, or women unable to conceive or adopt children, feminism seemed to offer increasingly little support in their choice or circumstance of non-motherhood (see Snitow, 1992).

3 THE NEW EMPHASIS ON FATHERHOOD

The implications of feminist celebration of motherhood for analyses of family life, within and outside scholarly work, were diverse, and at times ambiguous. Stressing as she did the radical potential of the female body, Adrienne Rich said little about the nurturing father, suggesting that the 'tokenly' involved father offers not even an individual solution to the problems of a patriarchal world (1976, p. 211). Other feminists have written of the possibilities of a world without fathers, a world which, as in the feminist Utopia, *Herland*, women alone will rule, and all of life will therefore be imbued with the 'feminine principle' of caring and spirituality, freed at last from the 'masculine principle' of competitiveness, aggression and greed (Gilman, 1979). Ruddick, however, stressed that maternal ways arise from actual childcare practices: men may 'mother'. Indeed, like Chodorow, she stressed the social, psychological and political importance of assimilating men into childcare and, most importantly, argued that transformed maternal thought must be brought into, and hence change, the public realm (Ruddick, 1980, p. 90). Other writers, and in particular some men, began to use such feminist thinking to stress the importance of *men's* active engagement in fathering. So, in a sense, not only was mothering reclaimed in new ways by feminists in the second half of the 1970s, but, by its close, 'fathering' was being reclaimed and celebrated by men influenced by feminism, both in the home and in the academy.

Before the 1970s there was very little attention paid to fatherhood by anyone, although a few social scientists had worried about the effects of complete 'father-absence' on boy's sex-role socialization. From the late 1970s, however, and often drawing explicitly on the work of feminist writers like Chodorow, fathers' participation in infant care became a popular research topic. Ross Parke (1981), for example, wrote of the 'unique role of the father in fostering the infant's cognitive development', while other studies stressed the benefits for children of active fathering. Moreover, despite assumptions that men and women interact differently with babies and infants, psychological and sociological studies conducted within the last ten years or so have suggested that when both parents participate in active parenting, there are more similarities than differences in how they do it. As Graeme Russell's study of fathering suggests, fathers who are full-time caregivers display the same type of enhanced sensitivity to their infants as full-time mothers, while a mother's more typically greater sensitivity to her baby's needs does not generalize to a greater responsiveness to other people's children. Equally, Russell concludes from his overview of a wide range of research on reverse-role parenting, it is remarkable how little difference it seems to make to children, female or male, *which* parent parents (1983, p. 167).

The families where men are more likely to share the caring of children and housework, however, are those atypical families where both parents already have highly paid professional careers of equal importance to them, and where there is the additional assistance of (paid) nursery and childcare (see Ehrensaft, 1987). Most research has also suggested that men's actual sharing of housework and childcare falls far short of equal engagement, even when their partners have full-time jobs. Moreover men have tended to increase their participation in the pleasanter side of family life, like playing with the children, rather than its more mundane and physical side. Some researchers on fatherhood, like Charlie Lewis (1986), and certainly many feminists, have therefore concluded that the changes which have occurred in paternal behaviour are slight. A more rounded picture would seem to be that fathers today are more likely to have more intimate engagements with their children than they did, for example, a generation earlier, and that, as Lorna McKee (1987) suggests, there is a more 'open-endedness' to fathering nowadays, with many men still doing little in the home and some men taking an equal share. Those men who are sharing more equally are most likely to be the men for whom a combination of individual and social factors work together to make sharing a more acceptable, attractive and rewarding choice. Many men, for example, could not participate significantly in domestic work and childcare, even if their workmates, peer group and partners encouraged it (a situation which is far more likely to occur in relation to professional workers than blue-collar workers), because of the high levels of overtime they feel obliged to work – especially with young children in the family. One study in Britain, for example, found that married men under thirty work four times the amount of overtime as childless men of the same age (see Segal, 1990, pp. 33–7).

In terms of its effects upon women in the family, some studies show that married women with jobs and mothers of very young children are happier when their husbands perform more housework and childcare. Other psychological surveys, however, report that only a minority of women, whether employed or not, seem to desire greater parental participation in childcare. Women, it seems, fear losing their traditional authority in the home and their exclusive importance to children. This, perhaps, is not so surprising. For even if men's sharing of domestic work, where it does occur, seems beneficial to both women and children, it does little on its own to undermine men's overall social and cultural dominance. Many women may well feel they do not wish to relinquish what authority they do have, in the one place they are more likely to have it.

Looked at from a broader political perspective, it is also clear that the reassertion of fatherhood can serve to threaten some groups of women. Not coincidentally, it would seem, a growing stress on the importance of fathers in families has occurred at a time when men's actual power and control over women and children is declining. The father of the 1950s was necessary to his family (as Joyce saw it, 'a necessary evil'), but he was needed, it was thought then, for his financial support and the status and legitimacy he conferred on wife and offspring. Today's interest in the importance of fathering occurs at a time when women may feel more able to question any automatic assumption by men of paternal rights. Until the mid-1970s the social stigma and serious discrimination against unmarried mothers and illegitimate children, as well as the disgrace accompanying divorce, meant that few women could consider mothering outside marriage as a positive choice. Men, in their turn, would characteristically deny the paternity of their illegitimate children to avoid maintenance costs.

Many feminists of the 1970s, however, began to reject and criticize the institution of marriage as, legally and symbolically, enshrining men's authority over women and children. 'Why be a wife?', they asked, when marriage legally gave to husbands the right to control women's sexuality and fertility, by refusing to recognize women's choice to mother outside marriage. Politically, some feminists began to see some advantages to single parenthood, free from men's control. Economically, whether through jobs or welfare, more women were in a position where they could attempt to raise children on their own (though for most, not without the serious financial penalties that the loss of a superior male 'breadwinner' wage entailed). Since the late 1960s it has also become easier for women to seek to terminate a pregnancy if they conceive unintentionally (though abortion in the UK has never been available to a woman as a right). With more women able to obtain an abortion, more mothers choosing divorce or perhaps even to embark on motherhood alone, more women and men having children together but outside marriage and some women, particularly lesbians, choosing to conceive through artificial insemination by donor (AID), some men in recent decades have begun to worry about their loss of paternal rights. With more women beginning to question whether families need fathers, significant pressure groups have been working to assure them that they do (like Families Need Fathers, formed in 1974).

In response to men's anxieties, by the close of the 1970s, and for the first time ever, the Law Commission on illegitimacy was recommending the need to strengthen the rights of unmarried fathers (Smart, 1987). Illustrating the new anxiety over women's capacity to choose to mother independently from men, it proposed giving all biological fathers automatic parental rights (a proposal which was abandoned only because it would confer such rights on any successfully impregnating rapist). The legal bias against lesbian mothers was also being endorsed and sensationalized in media coverage at the close of the 1970s, with the *London Evening*

News, for example, viciously attacking lesbians seeking motherhood through AID.

At a time when men's hold on their traditional familial and paternal authority is becoming less secure than ever before, the new stress on fatherhood can thus serve very old familial rhetoric: the rhetoric which importantly negates feminist insistence upon the actual contemporary diversity of households with children, whether co-habiting single people, lesbian couples, gay men, women on their own, or women living with friends or other relatives. The force of choice or circumstance – perhaps stemming from sexual orientation, perhaps a response to domestic violence, or from a myriad of other possibilities – which may have led people to live outside nuclear families, can thereby once again be pushed aside in favour of unthinking allegiance to the traditional familial ideal. Before embracing the importance of fathers, therefore, we need to pay careful attention to just how easily the abuse of paternal power has been condoned or denied within traditional family life. There are real dangers that the pro-father, pro-family rhetoric so readily merges with the type of conservative moral backlash to feminism and gay politics which we have seen in recent times. It works through manipulating people's sexual fears and paranoia to stigmatize all over again non-familial sex and relationships – an easy thing to do when the harsher economic climate and the tragic reality of AIDS in the 1980s made many feel more vulnerable and search around for scapegoats.

Mindful of these possible dangers, however, I still believe feminists were right to suggest the importance of men's participation in childcare and domestic nurturing as one – although definitely only one – aspect of forging new, less polarized and oppressive meanings for 'masculinity' and 'femininity'. Nevertheless, in a world where men in general still tend to have more financial and social power than women, we need to tread warily, embracing the importance of fatherhood in ways which do not threaten women and undermine recognition of non-traditional household arrangements.

4   DIFFERENCE AND DIVERSITY

If feminist writing has veered between critique and celebration of women's domestic and maternal roles within families, while at times touching upon the complexities of women's more ambivalent attitudes, it has all the while mostly attempted to stress the diversity of family forms. This involved, in the words of Rayna Rapp, the effort 'to deconstruct the family as a natural unit and reconstruct it as a social unit' (1979, p. 181). But if most feminists continue to insist upon the diversity of family forms, and reject traditional family rhetoric, we may still need to question whether their approach has been diverse enough.

Black feminists, for instance, have criticized the ethnocentrism of white feminism for privileging sexism as the major source of women's oppression in families, downplaying the significance of racism and ethnic diversity in determining how women are oppressed. Following critiques like those of Bell Hooks (1984), the blindness of classic texts like Friedan's *The Feminine Mystique* to the fact that her bored and unhappy house-wives were white women, not black women, is now well known. Black women at the time, almost all working long hours in very poorly paid jobs, may well have longed for more time in the home.

More generally, what feminists wrote about the isolation and discontent of women in the home throughout the 1970s was based on the lives of white women, bearing perhaps little connection with other ethnic house-hold groupings. As many, like Parita Trivedi (1984), have since pointed out, Asian women are more likely to have other female relatives inside the household. Moreover, white feminists have often failed to emphasize the crucial role of Black and Asian family groupings in providing protec-tion against the surrounding racism of white-dominated societies. For these families, the immigration policies of the state have more often opposed rather than supported their attempts to unite or keep families together by bringing in dependants from outside the UK. In campaigning for welfare benefits or attacking the 'family wage', many white feminists have ignored the situation of Black or immigrant women in the UK who, while paying taxes, receive no benefit at all for the children they support abroad. The basic argument here is that Black feminists believe, and correctly, that white feminists have often developed perspectives on 'women's' situation in the family which distort the situation of Black women. In agreement with this criticism, for example, Michèle Barrett and Mary McIntosh (1985) were later to criticize their own book *The Anti-social Family* (1983) suggesting that 'our work has spoken from an unac-knowledged but ethnically specific position ... its apparently universal applicability has been specious' (1985, p. 25).

Today, feminists are more aware that if we are to describe the possible strengths and weaknesses of different family forms, then ethnic diversity must be tackled. It is true that in most societies today feminism will involve a struggle against some aspects of family life, whether it is against the material and social deprivation of single mothers in England, the ostracism of unmarried mothers in Ireland, dowry murders in India, or the struggle of Asian feminists in Britain against domestic violence. But the precise forms of critique and struggle will vary from one society, or specific social group, to another.

There has been further conflict, as well, within contemporary white fem-inist thinking on family life, with a minority calling for a return to a more conservative approach which rejects any emphasis on alternative family forms. In the USA, feminist philosopher and political theorist, Jean Bethke Elsthain, for example, has re-affirmed the traditional definition of family as the term 'having its basis in marriage and kinship'. She rejects the insistence on the diversity of families today as 'insulting to family men and women', individualistic and irresponsible (1982, p. 447). Assessing her work, Judith Stacey (1987), also from the USA, suggests that there has in fact been a gradual disappearance of the former feminist critique of the family in the attempt to preserve and celebrate women's motherhood. She attributes this to the pains and difficulties of women – particularly of ageing feminists in the right-wing climate of the 1980s – constructing the types of intimate relationships they might desire in a world where the possibilities for making choices around parenting and relationships remain more open for men, even as they begin to close down for women. Stacey sees three sorts of personal traumas as particularly widespread among these women who shunned traditional marriage and child-bearing arrangements, strengthening the appeal of a more conservative retreat from any sexual politics critical of the traditional family – lack of sexual relationships, involuntary childlessness and single parenthood.

Yet while feminists themselves may have become less vocal in their criticism of the traditional family, more people today do continue to choose to live outside them. For example, households of single parents with children increased by 75 per cent between 1971 and 1991, and recent surveys suggest that many of these single parents, who are mostly women, now prefer to remain single (Bradshaw and Miller, 1990). Moreover, with the ageing of the population, the single person household is the largest and fastest growing household unit in the UK. Those who live outside traditional family units, whether because they are lone parents, widowed, gay, lesbian, migrant workers, or simply choose alternative lifestyles, are still likely, however, to find themselves isolated or socially impoverished because of the continuing privileging of the heterosexual nuclear family form in welfare spending and ideological affirmation. Moreover, the support for the idea of the 'natural' family is all the more paradoxical at a time when the surge in reproductive technology and continuing high rates of divorce ineluctably undermine the logical foundation of any such notion.

Many of the debates now occurring around *in vitro* fertilization (IVF), surrogate motherhood and artificial insemination by donor (AID) arouse such passion precisely because of the ways in which they undermine any naturalist conceptions of the family. They separate out biological parenthood from social parenthood, and reproduction from either marriage or sexuality. Of course, this is no new phenomenon, when the high levels of re-marriage following divorce has often meant that parenting is undertaken as a social rather than a biological responsibility in 'reconstituted families'. But there are many who are still busily trying to demarcate from all these increasingly possible permutations of parenting and family life, what is 'natural' or 'normal' and what is not.

Another paradox exists in the fact that accompanying the increasing insistence on the importance of 'the family' throughout the Thatcher years, it was women caring for children and other dependants in the home who were consistently discriminated against during this period. Over the Thatcher decade all the legislation affecting women, whether around family policy or workplace issues, proved retrogressive for families with dependent persons. Although the number of women entering jobs continued to increase dramatically in the 1980s, the UK has now the lowest nursery care provision in the EC (excluding Portugal) and the worst maternity leave provision (with two out of three women, because they work 'part-time', excluded from maternity leave altogether), while the real value of family allowance or child benefit fell by 18 per cent during this decade (see Armstrong, 1991). Meanwhile, the burdens of caring for dependent adults in the home (undertaken by one in four middle-aged women without any financial reward) have vastly increased as an effect of the government's devolution of geriatric and mental care on the 'community' without back-up provision (see Coote et al., 1990). While affecting all people engaged in caring work in the home, these policies have hit some households far harder than others. Thus changes in benefits and income support systems have made it almost impossible for many lone parents to avoid poverty. Over the last decade, therefore, the household/family has become more than ever a site where dramatic social inequalities have been deepening and reproducing themselves.

In this situation, traditional voices continue – as ever – to insist upon the importance of the traditional, male-headed nuclear family, and to blame the victims of deepening social inequalities (like single mothers) for both causing their own immiseration and 'social decay' generally. Other voices, however, mostly those still inspired by the more materialist feminism of the early women's movement, continue to insist that 'the family' is not a natural but a social construct, and that it is the material circumstances, quality and commitment of relationships with children which matters, not their form. This more pragmatic and pluralistic approach to families is being pushed as the necessary basis for official welfare thinking in the UK by, for example, women, like Anna Coote, attempting to influence future Labour Party welfare programmes (Coote et al., 1990). They stress the crucial importance of recognizing the significance of the diversity of family forms precisely because the 1980s saw the growth of ever-widening material disparities between different types of households.

Indeed, many feminist theorists from the mid-1980s, influenced by French post-structuralist philosophy (usually identified as feminist postmodernism), began to place such emphasis on diversity between women, and on the instability, uncertainty and complexity of the category 'women', that they reject *any* attempts at universalizing women's experience. Illustrating this point, Nancy Fraser and Linda Nicholson argue that the assumption of shared, cross-cultural mothering experiences and effects, like those found in the theoretical approaches of Nancy Chodorow or Carol Gilligan, are 'essentialist' (1990, p. 9). They further reject the psychoanalytic idea of 'a deep sense of self', constituted in early childhood, different for women and men, and determining subsequent experience and behaviour.

5   CONCLUSION

Many theoretical conflicts have thus emerged in feminist scholarship in the 1980s which make it impossible to write of *the* feminist perspective, or even to identify clearly any particular number of feminist perspectives, on the family. Whatever shifts and manoeuvres different feminist positions on the family have taken over the years, however, I suspect that there are just a few formulations which would find favour with a significant majority today. Notwithstanding our anxieties (or lack of them) about the way appeals to 'family' have often served to deny legitimacy and support to those living outside its traditional frontiers, all feminists have always wanted to combine love and commitment, caring and freedom, in ways which might prove less oppressive to women than they have tended to in the past. Most feminists, as well, have recognized the extent of social, economic and political change which would be needed for there to be any profound change in the existing problems the majority of women face juggling family lives and employment. In pondering parenthood today, I think many feminists would feel able to endorse the sentiments of Catherine Stimpson (1989), from the USA, writing as a co-parenting lesbian on the new narratives of love and freedom which she feels she is a part of creating as she helps to raise her lover's children 'without using them or using ourselves up':

> I have a national policy for families ... Let no children starve – in mind or body. Let no child be beaten. Let parents speak their name, and have enough money and flexible public services to do their chores. Then – let me alone. I want privacy, not to hide some viciousness, not to perpetuate a false division between public and domestic life, but because I need the space in which to give texture to a language of love and care that is now gossamer.

Stimpson sees her policy as one 'as simple, as nontheoretical as a child's need for apple juice'. Maybe so. But it is one which we in the UK and the USA are, sadly, a very long way from realizing; indeed, perhaps further away then ever.

REFERENCES

Armstrong, I. (1991) 'Women and children last? Women under Thatcherism', in *Women: A Cultural Review*, vol. 2, no. 1, Spring.

Barrett, M. and McIntosh, M. (1983) *The Anti-social Family*, London, Verso.

Barrett, M. and McIntosh, M. (1985) 'Ethnocentrism and socialist–feminist theory', *Feminist Review*, no. 20, pp. 23– 47.

Bart, P. (1971) 'Depression in middle-aged women', in Gornick, V. and Moran, B. (eds) *Women in Sexist Society*, New York, Basic Books.

Belenky, M., Blythe, M., Goldberger, N., Tarule, J. (1986) *Women's Ways of Knowing: the development of self, voice and mind*, New York, Basic Books.

Bem, S. (1974) 'The measurement of psychological androgyny', *Journal of Consulting and Clinical Psychology*, vol. 42, no. 2, pp. 155–62.

Bernard, J. (1973) *The Future of Marriage*, New York, Souvenir Press.

Boulton, M. (1983) *On Being a Mother*, London, Tavistock.

Bradshaw, J. and Miller, J. (1990) *Lone Parent Families in the UK*, DHSS Report, May.

Brown, G. and Harris, T. (1978) *Social Origins of Depression*, London, Tavistock.

Chesler, P. (1990) *Sacred Bond: legacy of Baby M*, London, Virago Press.

Chodorow, N. (1978) *The Reproduction of Mothering*, London, University of California Press.

Chodorow, N. (1980) 'Gender, relation and difference in psychoanalytic perspectives', in Eisenstein, H. and Jardine, A. (eds) *The Future of Difference*, Boston, MA, G.K. Hall.

Cooper, D. (1964) 'Sartre on Genet', *New Left Review*, no. 25.

Coote, A. and Campbell, B. (1982) *Sweet Freedom*, London, Pan.

Coote, A., Harman, H., and Hewitt, P. (1990) *The Family Way: a new approach to policy making*, Social Policy Paper no.1, London, Institute for Public Policy.

Coser, R. L. (1981) 'On the reproduction of mothering: a methodological debate', *Signs*, vol. 6, no. 3, Spring.

Dinnerstein, D. (1976) *The Rocking of the Cradle and the Ruling of the World* (2nd rev. edn, London, The Women's Press, 1987).

Ehrensaft, D. (1987) *Parenting Together: men and women sharing the care of their children*, New York, Free Press.

Eichenbaum, L. and Orbach, S. (1982) *Outside In ... Inside Out*, Harmondworth, Penguin Books.

Elsthain, J.B. (1982) 'Feminism, family and comunity', *Dissent*, Fall, no. 447.

Finch, J. and Groves, D. (1983) *A Labour of Love: women, work and caring*, London, Routledge and Kegan Paul.

Firestone, S. (1970) *The Dialectic of Sex: the case for feminist revolution*, New York, William Morrow.

Flax, J. (1984) 'Theorizing motherhood', *Women's Review of Books*, vol. 1, no. 9.

Fraser, N. and Nicholson, L.J. (eds) (1990) *Feminism/Postmodernism*, London, Routledge.

Friedan, B. (1963) *The Feminine Mystique*, Harmondsworth, Penguin Books.

Friedan, B. (1981) *The Second Stage*, London, Michael Joseph.

Gavron, H. (1966) *The Captive Wife: conflicts of housebound wives*, Harmondsworth, Penguin Books.

Gilligan, C. (1982) *In a Different Voice: psychological theory and women's development*, London, Harvard University Press.

Gilman, C. Perkins (1979) *Herland*, New York, Pantheon (first published 1915).

Hart, N. (1991) 'Procreation: the substance of female oppression in modern society, Part 1: The True Proletariat', *Contentions: Debates in Society Culture and Science*, vol. 1, no. 1.

Hewlett, S. A. (1986) *A Lesser Life: the myth of women's liberation in America*, New York, William Morrow.

Hooks, B. (1984) *Feminist Theory: from margin to center*, Boston, MA, South End Press.

Lewis, C. (1986) *Becoming a Father*, Milton Keynes, Open University Press.

McKee, L. (1987) 'Fathers', *The Guardian*, 19 January.

Millett, K. (1971) *Sexual Politics*, New York, Avon Books.

Mitchell, J. (1966) 'Women: the longest revolution', reprinted in *The Longest Revolution: on feminism, literature and psychoanalysis*, London, Virago.

Nava, M. (1983) 'From Utopian to scientific feminism? Early feminist critiques of the family', in Segal, L. (ed.) op. cit.

Oakley, A. (1974) *The Sociology of Housework*, London, Martin Robertson.

Parke, R. (1981) *Fathering*, London, Fontana.

Rapp, R. (1979) 'Household and family', in Rapp, R., Ross, R. and Bridenthal, R., 'Examining family history', *Feminist Studies*, vol. 181, Spring.

Rich, A. (1976) *Of Woman Born: motherhood as experience and institution*, London, Virago.

Riley, D. (1983a) *War in the Nursery: theories of the child and the mother*, London, Virago.

Riley, D. (1983b) '"The serious burdens of love?" Some questions on childcare, feminism and socialism', in Segal, L. (ed.) op. cit.

Rowbotham, S. (1990) *The Past is Before Us: feminism in action since the 1960s*, Harmondsworth, Penguin Books.

Ruddick, S. (1980) 'Maternal thinking', *Feminist Studies*, vol. 6, no. 2, Summer, pp. 342–67.

Russell, G. (1983) *The Changing Role of Fathers*, London, University of Queensland Press.

Segal, L. (ed.) (1983) *What Is to be Done about the Family?*, Harmondsworth, Penguin Books.

Segal, L. (1987) *Is the Future Female?: troubled thoughts on contemporary feminism*, London, Virago.

Segal, L. (1990) *Slow Motion: changing masculinities, changing men*, London, Virago.

Smart, C. (1987) 'There is of course the distinction dictated by nature: law and the problem of paternity', in Stanworth, M. (ed.) *Reproductive Technologies: gender, motherhood and medicine*, Cambridge, Polity Press.

Snitow, A. (1992) 'Feminism and motherhood: an American reading', *Feminist Review*, no. 40, Spring, pp. 32–51.

Stacey, J. (1987) 'Are feminists afraid to leave home?: the challenge of Conservative pro-family feminism', in Mitchell, J. and Oakley, A. (eds) *What is Feminism?*, Oxford, Blackwell.

Stimpson, C. (1989) *Where the Meanings Are: feminism and cultural spaces*, London, Routledge.

Trivedi, P. (1984) 'To deny our fullness: Asian women in the making of history', *Feminist Review*, no. 17.

Wandor, M. (1973) Review of Shulamith Firestone's *The Dialectic of Sex* in *Red Rag,* no. 3.

Wilson, E. (1980) *Only Halfway to Paradise,* London, Tavistock

Wilson, E. (1989) 'In a different way', in Gieve, K. (ed.) *Balancing Acts: on being a mother*, London, Virago.

ENDNOTE: PUBLIC AND PRIVATE

ROGER SAPSFORD

Our conception of the social world as divided into 'public' and 'private' spheres is largely taken for granted and seen as a 'natural' way of viewing the social world. It is also, however, a powerful ideological tool, reinforcing as natural and inevitable a set of structured inequalities between groups of people – men and women, adults and children – and favouring the interests of some groups at the expense of others, as well as legitimating the dominance of some individuals over others at a more personal level.

The family is a crucial area of interface between these two spheres: it encapsulates and embodies the private sphere, but it is also an object in the public sphere open to manipulation. Families are held to account for matters which fall in the sphere of public policy – the health, development and behaviour of their children, for example, or the care of elderly relatives; these are seen as matters of private concern, though monitored in the public interest. At the same time there is increasing pressure for what occurs in the privacy of families – how wives are treated by husbands, how children are treated by parents – to become more open and accountable.

Concepts of 'public' and 'private' spheres and lives permeate our thought about the social world to perhaps an even greater extent than concepts of family do – and the two are closely related, though not identical. Like familial concepts, the 'public/private' concept is associated with power relations and structured inequalities, sometimes in ways which are not immediately obvious. Again like familial concepts, the public/private distinction is taken for granted as a natural way of describing social life, but it can sometimes be quite difficult to pin down precisely what we mean by it.

A first point to make is that it is very easy to think of 'the public' and 'the private' as *places* – to see them as part of the *structure* of our social lives. It is important for us to remember that they are also *processes* – something we *do* to ourselves and to each other. This is very difficult to keep in mind; for some reason we are much better at thinking about static structures than about processes and the way they mutate over time, and we keep falling back into structural analysis.

A second point is that the notion of public and private really does centre around the ideological stereotype of 'the family' – husband working in public and returning to his wife and children in the private home. Most stereotypes locate work and politics as public activities, and domestic life as private, with the 'average' man appearing most strongly in the public sphere, while 'average' women and children are confined to the private sphere. The place of leisure activities occurring outside the home is less clear. They are private sphere in that they are not part of work or politics – even the round of golf at which business or politics is carried on is seen as something different from the same discussions carried out in an office, officially. On the other hand, one goes out into public places in order to do them.

One powerful effect of the 'family' stereotype is that it leads us to think of the 'normal' adult as married. If the separation between public and private is more ambiguous than it first appears for familial settings, its application to the lives of unmarried (or 'uncoupled') people creates other problems. Think, for example, about how to define the 'private' sphere for those who live in the homes of others (e.g. single people living with their parents) or who share communal living spaces (e.g. multi-occupancy of flats or houses). Within such settings, there are different and shifting layers of public and private spaces. In communal settings, for example, the 'private' space of the household may itself be divided into 'public' rooms (shared by all members) and 'private' rooms in which individuals exercise a degree of separatism from the communal space of the rest of the house or flat. But, at different times, the communal spaces may be used as the space for private occasions (to entertain one person's visitors etc.).

Although the reference point for the public/private distinction is the married couple with children, such ambiguities about the division of life into public and private spaces and times can be found there as well. Each partner may work in a public sphere – in paid employment, say. They may have their 'public life as a couple' – for example at dinner parties. They have their lives with the children, in private and in public. They have their private lives together, 'off-stage', when the children are not present. Finally, they may each have a private life that does not involve other members of the family. We begin to see that the division of the social world into 'public' and 'private' greatly oversimplifies how people actually live and experience their lives. When this kind of oversimplification is found, we often look to see who benefits from having it described in these terms; in other words, we look for an ideological basis to the description. We have already noted how the distinction tends to privilege men over women. We might also note how it tends to take for granted that people will live in heterosexual pairings and ignores questions of how lesbians and gay men organize and experience their lives, classifying them instead as deviants from the familial norm.

We should note, perhaps, that the 'private sphere' was not particularly confined to the home during the period when it was being created and consolidated, the Victorian era.

> It is ironic that the new middle classes of the nineteenth century who so fervently preached the gospel of domestic bliss, the sanctity of the family, the woman's place in the home ... were able to place so much of the burden of their own domestic work on to the shoulders of working-class servants ... Most affluent middle-class women thus had a good deal of spare time to spend in calling on friends and kin ... Many also engaged in a variety of philanthropic and educational activities. These were not 'private' pastimes, but they were unpaid and voluntary.
>
> (Gittins, 1985, pp. 123–4)

So, much of the 'private-sphere' activity of middle-class women was located outside the home. (It is for this reason that some scholars prefer to talk about 'the domestic sphere' rather than 'the private sphere'.) Some of it constituted what would now be paid employment – for example, health visiting and social work. (The position is similar today, particularly in rural areas.) Similarly, among working-class women of the period it would have been quite normal for a portion of the 'private' time to be spent in public, for example in public houses: 'In poor neighbourhoods there was a considerable women's pub culture ... Women of all ages went out to pubs, bringing babies and children with them ... some pubs were frequented exclusively by women' (Ross, 1983, pp. 10–11). The closed and bounded nuclear family of the stereotype is a more recent invention in the working classes, and despite the advocacy of it by middle-class women it has never quite taken hold.

The oddity of the stereotyped public/private division, and its dependence on the concept of 'work' (outside the home), becomes even more apparent when we consider people at either extreme of the age spectrum.

People of over retirement age who have in fact retired from paid employment are presumably located entirely in the private sphere. There are very few social roles available for the retired man who is not in some profession which allows him to continue past retirement age (politics for example), other than that of someone waiting for death. Anything else is likely to be construed as 'a hobby', something akin to pottering round the garden. For the retired woman, on the other hand, very little changes; she still has a house and perhaps a husband to care for. Similar work may be seen differently according to the gender and class of the retired person. The retired judge or academic who serves on a commission of inquiry will generally be seen as working in the public sphere. The retired social worker (particularly if male) who works for, say, the Citizens' Advice Bureau will probably be seen as working in the public sphere. The former carpenter or plumber (male) who on retirement donates time to a voluntary service may or may not be seen as working in the public sphere. The former social worker (female) who retired from paid employment to have and rear children and now organizes the WRVS will probably have her activity considered as being located in the private sphere. The retired office-worker (female) who does a bit of knitting or cleaning for older people will almost certainly find what she does classified as 'private sphere' activity.

At the other extreme, a large segment of children's lives is of unclear status. We tend on the whole to think of children as part of the private sphere, because we think of them as located in the home, the family. Once they are aged five in this country, however, and sometimes earlier (for example, in the case of children with diagnosed special learning difficulties), they spend a quarter of their time at school for about three-quarters of the year. It is not clear whether school is to be categorized as 'public sphere' or 'private sphere'. It is certainly outside the home and, to an extent, open to public inspection. On the other hand, schools function essentially as closed institutions consisting of teachers and pupils and, even where there is a rhetoric of strong parental involvement, the reality tends to be that even parents are extraneous to the process and have difficulty penetrating it.

The welfare of children is in general a clouded area with respect to the distinction between the public and the private sphere. Children tend in our society to be seen as 'belonging' to their parents – specifically, as owned by the father but serviced by the mother – and the rhetoric of the 'family' makes what happens to children a private matter. On the other hand, education is mostly provided by the state (despite current rhetoric which makes it appear a service purchased by parents), as is health care. Beyond this, 'the nation's children' are subject to surveillance at every stage of their lives, by midwives and doctors, health visitors, teachers, sometimes educational psychologists, and by social workers and even the police if neglect or malpractice is suspected. The privacy of the family constitutes an obligation on parents, but it is on the whole a heavily policed obligation. (See Abbott and Sapsford (1988) for a discussion on how this situation has developed.) We might note also, the notion of welfare services as *challenging the existing balance of power* – defending children against parents and women against men, and defending the poor and disadvantaged against the interests of the advantaged majority.

What is at stake in the foregoing discussion is not a painstaking enquiry into what shall or not be constituted as public- or private-sphere activities, but the *range of convenience* of the construct and what that tells us about the discourse in which it is embedded. In other words, it is revealing to note what circumstances fit easily within the terminology of 'public' and 'private', and to which ones it is so difficult to apply the concept that it would appear not designed to cover them. We have no difficulty in describing paid employment outside the home and the politics of parties or trades unions as being 'in the public sphere'. We have no difficulty in describing the role of a married woman, looking after husband, children and the house, as taking place 'in the private sphere'. Anything outside these simple 'social locations' is difficult to place. We have already seen that the terms become muddied when talking about the activities of people who have retired from paid work, and when describing the lives of children. They become almost impossible to apply when considering the lives of people whose paid employment does not take them outside the home, or those who live off 'unearned' income, or voluntary workers, or those who work in a subsistence economy. The distinction does not even 'ring true' for present-day agricultural workers in this country: 'public' and 'private' often articulate themselves quite differently from the way the terms would be used in towns, about industrial or office workers. It also has difficulty with sexual relationships which are not heterosexual, unless these can be presented in terms familiar from our understanding of heterosexual relationships. Thus what we have here is a well-used and familiar set of terms which turns out to have buried within it an implicit and simplistic view of how social life is organized. Again, this leads one to suspect an ideological basis.

Politics and law are in essence public-sphere activities, and also in essence male, that is, they reflect a view of the world which favours males over females and male concerns over female concerns. Despite changes in recent years, they are also mostly staffed by males – men constitute the majority of MPs, the majority of lawyers and the majority of the police. This part of the public sphere exemplifies rather obviously what is more concealed in the structure of paid employments – the patriarchal nature of the public sphere. Ethnic differences are also very obvious in this area: very few people at policy-making level are other than white. This is not to impute some kind of conspiracy. However, structurally it is still the case that white, male, middle-class people tend to achieve the senior positions (and, indeed, many of the others) in this area, and that the system for which they are responsible tends to favour the interests of white, middle-class males. Areas of practical concern to females, to black and Asian people, to working-class people – schooling, the service provided by hospitals, the safety of the street at night, the safety of the home for those who live in it, the fairness of selections procedures for jobs and benefits – tend to be dealt with as matters of practical policing or as 'moral questions' (that is, matters whose discussion belongs properly in the private sphere). This power to 'set the agenda' as to what shall constitute a matter of public law or politics is what maintains the inequality of the system. (It also tends to maintain the 'privilege' of heterosexual relationships over homosexual ones.) The distinction shows up particularly clearly in matters of childcare: a woman is not free to 'neglect' her children, and their early life is fairly carefully policed to secure their physical health, but a man has a right to make wrong decisions about their education and upbringing without legal penalty.

Another way in which the lived concept of the private sphere functions to divide the genders and create inequalities is in the validation of 'moral orders'. Conceiving of the purpose of life as 'success' in terms of increased possessions, improved lifestyle and/or enhanced power of command – a dominant moral order of our society – and validating actions and outcomes against these criteria is a way of thinking very much associated with the public sphere of paid employment and politics. A second moral order may be posited as common in our society, however – one which bases its values on identification with the well-being of others and acceptance of responsibility for the effects of one's activities and decisions. (See Haavind, 1984; Holter, 1984; Cheal, 1988, 1989.) This order is essential for the maintenance of the concept of the private sphere: it defines the behaviour expected of women in their role as carers. Because it is relegated to the private sphere, however, the public world is protected from its effects. One edition of *Chambers' Twentieth Century Dictionary* defines 'charity begins at home' as 'generally used as an excuse for not letting it get abroad'!

Thus the 'public sphere' and the 'private sphere' are more complex than the simple stereotypes would suggest. The equation of them with 'home' and 'work' is too simple,

(a) because it does not readily hold up across the whole range of ages;

(b) because the 'private sphere' appears to reach into the lives of women even when they are carrying out paid work, and to structure the labour market within which they do so; and

(c) because some issues which are not in themselves home-related or work-related but have been relegated to one sphere or the other are hotly under contestation.

The privacy of 'the private sphere' is sometimes real – as when violent assaults on women in the home appear to be invisible to the forces of law and order – but equally one might see this privacy as having a performative element, declaring certain areas of life and certain agendas to be different in kind from what happens at work and is open to public and police inspection. (Note, however, that some of these 'moral' issues can create a kind of private sphere even in the environment of paid employment, for example in the problems of preventing sexual harassment at work; this reinforces the notion of 'the private' as process rather than place. Note also that some 'private families' are more private than others: working-class families have always been more permeable to state intervention than middle-class ones.) We have seen also that the concept of the private sphere and of women's place in it acts to marginalize a moral order which tends to be dominant in their lives – the moral order of cooperation and caring – and to exclude them from some of the powers and opportunities available to men. We should conclude at this point that the economic dependence of the private on the public, of women on men, is not the least of the power mechanisms underlying the distinction.

REFERENCES

Abbott, P. and Sapsford, R.J. (1988) 'The body politic: health, family and society', Unit 11 of D211 *Social Problems and Social Welfare*, Milton Keynes, The Open University.

Cheal, D. (1988) *The Gift Economy*, London, Routledge.

Cheal, D. (1989) 'Strategies of resource management in household economies: moral economy or political economy?', in Wilk, R. (ed.) *The Household Economy*, Boulder, CO, Westview Press.

Gittins, D. (1985) *The Family in Question*, London, Macmillan.

Haavind, H. (1984) 'Love and power in marriage' in Holter, H. (ed.).

Holter, H. (1984) 'Women's research into social theory' in Holter, H. (ed.).

Holter, H. (ed.) *Patriarchy in a Welfare Society*, Oslo, Universitetsforlaget.

Ross, E. (1983) 'Survival networks: women's neighbourhood sharing in London', *History Workshop Journal*, no. 15.

INDEX